China in World Affairs:
The Foreign Policy
of the PRC Since 1970

Also of Interest from Westview Press

China, the Soviet Union, and the West: Strategic and Political Dimensions for the 1980s, edited by Douglas T. Stuart and William T. Tow

China Among the Nations of the Pacific, edited by Harrison Brown

China: A Political History, 1917–1980, fully revised and updated, Richard C. Thornton

The Chinese Military System: An Organizational Study of the Chinese People's Liberation Army, second edition, revised and updated, Harvey W. Nelsen

China Briefing, 1981, edited by Robert B. Oxnam and Richard C. Bush

Technology, Politics, and Society in China, Rudi Volti

China's Economic Development: Growth and Structural Change, Chu-yuan Cheng

Technology, Defense, and External Relations in China, 1975–1978, Harry G. Gelber

The Chinese Communist Party in Power, 1949–1976, Jacques Guillermaz

Chinese Communist Power and Policy in Xinjiang, 1949–1977, Donald H. McMillen

Treaties of the People's Republic of China, 1949–1978: An Annotated Compilation, Grant F. Rhode and Reid E. Whitlock

From Muskets to Missiles: Politics and Professionalism in the Chinese Army, 1945–1981, Harlan W. Jencks

The Third Indochina Conflict, edited by David W. P. Elliott

The People's Republic of China: A Handbook, edited by Harold C. Hinton

China's Four Modernizations: The New Technological Revolution, edited by Richard Baum

* Available in hardcover and paperback.

About the Book and Author

China in World Affairs:
The Foreign Policy of the PRC Since 1970
G. W. Choudhury

This up-to-date textbook reviews China's foreign policy goals since the PRC's active reemergence in world affairs following the Cultural Revolution of 1966–1969. Drawing on original sources and firsthand experience, as well as on a broad academic background, Dr. Choudhury examines China's global policy, diplomatic options, and strategy in the context of the triangular relationship of Washington, Moscow, and Beijing. His discussion—offering numerous unexpected insights—covers China's quest for security, the breakthrough in China-U.S. relations, the course of Sino-Soviet rivalry (particularly in the Asia-Pacific region), the PRC's role in the United Nations since 1971, how China has championed Third World countries, and the new, dynamic elements in post-Mao Chinese foreign policy. The book is current through the summer of 1981.

G. W. Choudhury, professor of political science at North Carolina Central University, has taught at several universities, including Columbia, Johns Hopkins, Duke, Pennsylvania, and Cambridge. He has served as director general for research in the Pakistan Ministry of Foreign Affairs and as a member of the Pakistan cabinet. Author of seven previous books on Asia, Dr. Choudhury has traveled extensively in both the Soviet Union and China.

In memory of my parents,
Golam Mawla and Fatema Choudhury,
and with great affection for my wife, Dilara,
and my sons, Mabud and Sayeed

China in World Affairs:
The Foreign Policy
of the PRC Since 1970

G. W. Choudhury

Westview Press / Boulder, Colorado

Published in 1982 in the United States of America by
  Westview Press, Inc.
  5500 Central Avenue
  Boulder, Colorado 80301
  Frederick A. Praeger, President and Publisher

Library of Congress Card Number: 82-60212
ISBN 0-89158-937-6
ISBN 0-86531-329-6 (pbk.)

Printed and bound in the United States of America

Contents

Preface

The book is the result of extensive research on China begun in 1976. I have been interested in doing a work on China's foreign policy ever since 1969, when I had the unique experience of being associated with Pakistani President Yahya Khan's grand assignment, that of acting as "courier" between Beijing and Washington to help initiate the United States' new policy toward the People's Republic of China (PRC). I was involved in the top-secret negotiations for the emerging Sino-American relationship in 1969–1971, which gave me opportunities to study the Chinese perception of the world and, in particular, China's relations with the two superpowers from firsthand and original sources. Although President Nixon used other channels, Pakistani President Yahya became his principal spokesman and, in the final stages, the sole "go-between" linking Beijing and Washington. President Yahya took me into his confidence and allowed me to accompany him to China in November 1970 while the Sino-American negotiations were making good progress. Before his death in 1980, President Yahya gave me a copy of all of the correspondence channeled through him to President Nixon and Premier Zhou Enlai.

My plan to do a major work on China was, however, postponed when I became a "political refugee" as a result of the tragic happenings in the South Asian subcontinent in 1971. I eventually came to the United States and joined my alma mater, Columbia University, where I did research and taught for two years (1972–1974). I was then made a Fellow at the Research Institute on Communist Affairs (RICA), headed by Dr. Zbigniew Brzezinski, who helped me greatly in my research through his deep understanding of the Communist world. I was fortunate to continue my link with Dr. Brzezinski when he moved to the White House in 1976 as President Carter's national security adviser and, more important, the chief mover in the development of the Sino-American relationship. If President Nixon is to be credited for opening the "China door" for the United States, Dr. Brzezinski is to be credited for bringing that relationship to its fullest development in 1979. I must, however, hasten to add that the views expressed in this book should in no way be attributed to Dr. Brzezinski either directly or indirectly. I only wish to thank him for his kind gestures toward me.

I began to work on China's role in world affairs in 1976 after completing *India, Pakistan, Bangladesh, and the Major Powers,* in which I discussed China's role in Asia, in particular, in South Asia. Dr. Gaston Sigur, director of the Institute for Sino-Soviet Studies at George Washington University, made me a Fellow of his institute in 1976 before I left on my second trip to the PRC, and I am thankful to Dr. Sigur for his help in my work.

I must also express my sincere thanks and appreciation for the generous research grants I received for three successive years (1976–1978) from the Earhart Foundation, which enabled me to make three trips to the PRC. The president of the foundation, Richard A. Ware, and its secretary and program officer, Anthony T. Sullivan, were extremely helpful. For my final trip to the PRC in connection with this book, I got a grant from the Mary Duke Biddle Foundation, to which I was introduced by my esteemed friend, William L. Bondurant. I must thank him and Mrs. James H. Semans for the research grant I received in 1979.

My good friend, Dr. David Albright, of *Problems of Communism,* made some valuable suggestions and comments on my work, and I sincerely thank him for those contributions. I am also grateful to Westview Press for agreeing to publish my book and to Megan Schoeck for her excellent copyediting of the manuscript. I would be failing in my acknowledgments if I did not make reference to the cooperation and help I received from my unnamed Chinese friends, both in the PRC and at Chinese missions abroad. They gave me valuable materials and data, sparing countless hours for my lengthy discussions with them.

Last, but not least, I have no adequate words to express my feelings for the affectionate encouragement I received from my family—my wife, Dilara, and my two sons, Mabud and Sayeed. They not only endured the long period of my research and study, but also encouraged me at every stage. Dilara accompanied me to the PRC in 1976, having already bravely faced the challenges of a "new life" in our new homeland (the United States). Without her constant encouragement, this volume would not have been possible. In fact, my "new life" in the United States would not have been worth living without my family's consistent and affectionate support; this book is just one more outgrowth of that loving environment.

In conclusion, I wish to make it clear that the views expressed in this book are entirely mine and do not belong to anyone who helped me in writing the book.

G. W. Choudhury

1
Introduction

The primary aim of this book is to describe China's outward-looking foreign policy, which began at the end of Beijing's (Peking's) self-imposed isolation during the great proletariat Cultural Revolution of 1966–1969. Even in the late 1960s, while still under the leadership of Mao Zedong, who had initiated the Cultural Revolution and was thus also responsible for the country's diplomatic isolation during the upheaval caused by it, China had to pay attention to serious problems of national security and defense. The gravest threat to China's security and territorial integrity came from the country's former ideological ally, the Soviet Union, which massed nearly 1 million Russian army troops, equipped with the most sophisticated weapons, on China's northern frontiers. Mao and Premier Zhou Enlai, who was one of China's ablest statesmen, particularly in foreign affairs, had to give top priority to China's external relations as a result of the near-war situation between the two communist giants.

Communist China has been involved with the quest for security since 1949. The search for security is a universal phenomenon for all states, even superpowers, but the degree of the problem varies according to the particular circumstances of each. For the People's Republic of China (PRC), the problem was of great significance and urgency for two decades (1950–1970) because of its strained relationship with the United States and then, for a short period, because of simultaneous unfriendly relations with both of the superpowers, the United States and the USSR. Since 1969, the problem has centered on a possible confrontation with the Soviet Union. Like any country that lacks adequate military strength in comparison with its principal enemy, China has had to combine military strength with constructive diplomacy to meet its urgent problems of national security and defense.

Under Chairman Mao and Premier Zhou Enlai, China followed a foreign policy that was a mixture of ideology and pragmatism and, like any other country, practiced a policy based on both ideology and national interests. That type of policy is being continued by the post-Mao leaders. International politics are essentially power politics, and although statesmen may try to define foreign policy objectives in the light of an ideology or of broader goals, foreign policies are actually formulated and executed with regard to more immediate factors. Of course, the PRC has always stressed its ideological affinities in stating its foreign policy goals.

When Mao was confronted with the huge U.S. military presence in the Korean peninsula, South Vietnam, Japan, the Philippines, and other parts of the Asian-Pacific region, he had to look to Moscow for aid in solving China's compelling security problems. That policy was, however, backed by the Chinese theory of a world divided into two camps. In this formative phase of China's foreign policy, Mao justified his policy of a closer alliance with the other communist power, the USSR, by his theory of a world dominated by two camps—the socialist camp and the imperialist camp. In his essay, "On the People's Democratic Dictatorship" (June 30, 1949), Mao declared that externally China must "unite in a common struggle with those nations of the world which treat us as equals" and added, "internationally we belong to the side of the anti-imperialist's front headed by the Soviet Union and so we can turn only to this side for genuine and friendly help, not to the side of the imperialist front."[1] He described the latter, which was headed by the United States, as "friends with honey on their lips and murder in their hearts. Who are these people? They are imperialists."[2] So Mao decided to lean to the side of socialism and not to the side of imperialism. He dismissed any idea of a third camp, such as the nonaligned group that Asian countries' leaders like Nehru of India and Sukarno of Indonesia were trying to form, as China, during this formative phase, followed the Soviet Union in treating the newly independent countries of Asia as "stooges" of the imperialists.

But soon China began to cultivate the friendship of the new nations of Asia and Africa so the two-camp theory had to be modified. That modification process started when the five principles of coexistence (concerning Tibet) were signed by India and China on April 20, 1954, as that agreement marked one of the earliest adjustments of the two-camp theory in favor of an acceptance of a third camp, and Zhou Enlai's superb performance at the first Afro-Asian Nations Conference at Bandung in 1955 led China to accept the reality of a third camp. Mao then began to modify his earlier theory of the two camps and his total rejection of a middle path. In a speech to the Supreme Soviet in Moscow on November 6, 1957, Mao made his first comment on the concept of an intermediate zone between the two camps by referring to the American imperialist's interference in the internal affairs of all nations, "particularly in the various nations of the intermediate zones situated between the American and Socialism camps."[3] Mao's concept of an intermediate zone or zones was further developed in talks with visiting foreign delegations in China in the late 1950s. Intermediate zones were regarded as "the rear areas of imperialism," which absorbed the imperialist aggressive thrust and constituted a protective buffer.[4]

In the early 1960s, when the Sino-Soviet rift began to be manifest, China made further modifications of the two-camp theory as China no longer considered itself a part of the Soviet-led camp, nor could the Soviet Union now be regarded as genuine friend – as Mao had considered that country when he had advocated leaning "to the side of the socialist camp." In addition to the concept of an intermediate zone or zones, China now began to perceive of the world in terms of "rural" and "urban." Peng Zhen, then mayor of Beijing, explained the struggle between the "world countryside" (developing nations) and the "world cities" (industrialized nations) in a speech in Jakarta in May 1965, and the concept was also expressed by Mao's chosen successor, Lin Biao, in his 1965 essay, "Peoples' War."[5] Lin Biao's comments on the rural-urban division of the world have been referred to extensively by authors who have examined China's changing perceptions of the world. According to Mayor Peng Zhen, Asia, Africa, and Latin America are the rural areas of the world taken as a whole, and Europe and North America are its cities.[6] In order to win victory in the world revolution, the proletariat must attach great importance to the revolutions in Asia, Africa, and Latin America, that is, to the revolutions in the world's rural areas, as there is no other path.[7] As the Soviet Union belongs to the "world cities," that country was obviously excluded from the proletariat world's revolutionary movement, and the USSR was "demoted" to the group of social imperialists.

In 1974, Chairman Mao developed his theory of "three worlds," which his successor, Chairman Hua Guofeng, explained in a report to the Eleventh Congress of the Chinese Communist party on August 12, 1977. Hua said that "Chairman Mao's thesis differentiating the three worlds which he set forth in 1974 is of profound and far-reaching significance. . . . Applying the method of class analysis," Hua added, "he [Mao] studied the changes in the development of the basic contradictions in the contemporary world, the division and the realignment of the different political forces and political and economic status of each country in the international context and in consequence arrived at this scientific conclusion regarding the present-day strategic situation in the world."[8]

What is this concept of three worlds, what are their component parts, and what is the significance of the "strategic situation" in the present-day world? According to Mao's theory of three worlds, the two superpowers (the United States and the USSR) form the First World; the Second World comprises the developed states of Europe, Japan, Australia, and Canada; and the "progressive" Third World comprises the developing countries of Asia, Africa, and Latin America. The PRC considers that it belongs to the

Third World and tries to create the impression of being its champion and spokesman. China's entry into the United Nations in October 1971, after its exclusion from that world body for two decades because of strong pressure from the United States, was largely owing to the wide support the PRC got from the countries of the Third World, and since that time, the PRC has sought to identify itself with the hopes and aspirations of those countries.

Chairman Mao also developed a theory of principal enemy or primary contradictions. For instance, during the fight against Japan in the 1930s, China had considered Japan's imperialism as the principal enemy or the primary contradiction. In order to defeat the principal enemy or to fight the primary contradiction, a country, according to Chairman Mao, may enter into temporary alliances with its secondary enemies. Because of China's growing fears of a Soviet aggression against it and to counteract the Soviet policy of isolating and weakening the PRC, the post–Cultural Revolution foreign policy of the PRC seems to treat the USSR, or "the Soviet social imperialists," as the current principal enemy or primary contradiction. To meet the threats from Moscow, China has made almost revolutionary changes in its policy of alignment since 1970.

The principal aim of this book is to examine the Chinese assessment of the present-day strategic stituation in the world and to analyze how Beijing has sought to react to the changed international order. That new order is the result of the lapse of a bipolar world, which was based on the rivalry and competition between the two superpowers, and the rise of a multipolar world in which China, though strongly denying that it is a superpower, is an emerging major power if not a superpower.

Chapter 2 presents a resume of China's foreign relations from 1949 to 1969. During the early years of the PRC's external relations, Mao turned to Moscow for both security and economic reasons. Mao also made some secret attempts to normalize relations with Washington, but those attempts failed. Subsequently, Beijing's relations with Washington entered an era of confrontation, and the United States and the PRC were drawn into the Korean War in 1950. Within a year of the emergence of the PRC, therefore, hostile relations between the world's most populous nation (the PRC) and the world's most powerful nation (the United States) had begun, and that hostility continued for two decades. China's quest for security led it to develop close links with Moscow, which gave the appearance of a monolithic communist order under the control of the Kremlin at a time when the East-West cold war tensions were at their height, and during the Eisenhower-Dulles years (1952–1958), the United States initiated an active policy of isolating, weakening, and perhaps ultimately destroying the "atheistic communist regime" in China. China not only forged links with Russia, but also sought to cultivate friendly relations with its Asian neighbors. China was successful in forming close relations with a number of major Asian countries, most notably, India, but its next-door Asian neighbors in Southeast Asia were not responsive to China's gestures. They were more worried about China's support of communist insurgent movements in Southeast Asia and looked to Washington for support against those movements.

China's relations with Moscow soon began to show strains and stresses, and by the end of the 1950s, the unity between the two communist giants was being replaced by the Sino-Soviet conflict, which led to major changes in China's foreign policy. The impact of the Sino-Soviet conflict was not immediately felt because of a number of factors – such as the 1962 Sino-Indian border conflict, the Vietnam War of the 1960s, and the Cultural Revolution in China of 1966–1969 – but the Sino-Soviet rift continued to intensify until it led the two ideological allies to serious armed conflict in the spring of 1969.

By the time Richard Nixon occupied the White House in January 1969, the United States was no longer regarded as China's number-one enemy. The Soviet Union now held that status, and Soviet social imperialism constituted, according to the Chinese, the most dangerous source of a world war. That situation led to major changes in the global politics, and Chapters 3, 4, and 5 examine the profound breakthrough between Beijing and Washington that began in 1969. President Nixon realized fully the implications of the growing Sino-Soviet rift, and he sought to take advantage of it to benefit the global interests of the United States. Under Chairman Mao and Premier Zhou Enlai, Beijing responded to Nixon's gestures for a normalization of the relationship between the PRC and the United States, not out of any love for the Americans, but out of grave fears of a preemptive Soviet strike against China, and a full account is given of the top-secret negotiations between Beijing and Washington that were channeled through Pakistan. That country was an ally of the United States by virtue of its membership in the U.S.-sponsored Southeast Asia Treaty Organization (SEATO), a military pact that is partly directed against the PRC, and yet, Pakistan was also China's most friendly noncommunist ally in Asia. Although Nixon used a number of channels to find out China's reaction to his new gestures to the PRC, it was Pakistani President Yahya Khan who turned out to be Nixon's principal "courier." I was a member of the Yahya cabinet in Pakistan and was involved in the secret negotiations, and before President Yahya died in 1980, he gave me a copy of all of the unpublished correspondence between Beijing and Washington that had been channeled through Pakistan in 1969–1971 before Richard Nixon announced, to the surprise of the entire world, that he would journey to Beijing to be greeted by Mao. Twenty years of frozen and hostile relations were broken after Henry Kissinger's top-secret trip to

Beijing via Pakistan in July 1971, and a full account is given of the Sino-American relations from the 1972 Peking Summit between President Nixon and Premier Zhou Enlai to the establishment of full diplomatic relations between the two countries and ultimately to the beginning of a limited security link between Beijing and Washington. From having been an arch enemy, the PRC is now regarded by the United States as a potential "ally in arms" against the Russians.

Chapters 6 and 7 are devoted to examining the Sino-Soviet rift and the resultant triangular diplomacy between Beijing, Moscow, and Washington. The discussion on the Sino-Soviet rift is confined to developments in the 1970s and the likely trends in the 1980s, and the emphasis is on the rivalry between Beijing and Moscow in Asia, where the two communist giants are engaged in a bitter struggle for power and influence. Tokyo, New Delhi, and Hanoi have been the major targets of this competition, and there have been communist wars—the 1978 war between Vietnam and Cambodia and the 1979 war between China and Vietnam—in addition to the ever-growing cold war between Beijing and Moscow.

Since the beginning of the limited rapprochement between Beijing and Washington after the 1972 summit, the United States has seemed to play what is known as its "China card" in its dealings with Moscow, which has resulted in a triangular relationship among the two superpowers, the United States and the USSR, and the emerging power, the PRC. In this triangular diplomacy, "each country is to some degree the adversary of the other two. Simultaneously, each country is a potential ally of the remaining one against the other."[9] That triangular diplomacy is reviewed and the implications of it are examined, and the same is done for the emerging triangular relationship among Beijing, Tokyo, and Washington, which is presumably directed to contain Soviet expansionist designs in the Asian-Pacific region in light of the Soviet-backed Vietnamese aggression against Cambodia in 1978 and the Soviet invasion of Afghanistan in December 1979. The most recent tensions in the Indian Ocean and Persian Gulf areas have given rise to some common, though not identical, interests among the PRC, the United States, and Japan, backed by the Association of Southeast Asian Nations (ASEAN), ANZUS (Australia, New Zealand, and United States mutual security pact), and North Atlantic Treaty Organization (NATO) countries, against the Soviet Union's worldwide expansionism and its huge military buildup.

Chapters 8 and 9 review China's role in Asia and that country's recent vigorous moves to cultivate friendly relations with its Asian neighbors. What are the complicating factors in China's bid for closer links with its close neighbors in Asia, and how is Beijing trying to mollify the fears of its Asian neighbors without totally sacrificing its image as the leader of the national liberation movements in the Third World?

There have been great upheavals and changes in post-Mao China. Chairman Mao has already been openly criticized for his role during the Cultural Revolution and many of his socioeconomic policies have been challenged and modified. But externally, China's policy in world affairs continues to pursue the same broad objectives that shaped Mao and Zhou Enlai's foreign policy after the founding of the PRC in 1949, and China's role in world affairs is discussed in Chapter 10. China considers Asia its "national domain" in which China must have a major voice. Similarly, though China continues to deny it has attained the status of a superpower, it aspires to gain a position of military, political, and economic strength that would enable it to play a major role in world affairs. Beijing also wishes to retain its self-chosen role as the champion of national liberation movements throughout the world, especially in the Third World.

Notes

1. Mao Zedong, *Selected Works,* Vol. 4 (Beijing: Foreign Languages Press, 1969), pp. 414–415.
2. Ibid., p. 415.
3. The text of Mao's speech is printed in the 1958 *People's Handbook* (Tianjin, 1958), pp. 294–296, and is quoted in Samuel S. Kim, *China, the United Nations, and World Order* (Princeton: Princeton University Press, 1979), pp. 74–75.
4. See Kim, *China, the United Nations, and World Order,* p. 74.
5. See *Peking Review,* September 3, 1965, p. 24.
6. Based on the author's research, interviews, and discussions in London.
7. Ibid.
8. See the text of Chairman Hua's speech in *The Eleventh National Congress of The Communist Party of China (Documents)* (Beijing: Foreign Languages Press, 1977), pp. 59–61.
9. See *United States–Soviet Union–China: The Great Power Triangle: Summary of Hearings* (Washington, D.C.: Congressional Research Service, August 12, 1980), p. 3.

2
Growth of Chinese Foreign Policy, 1949–1969

The development of the foreign policy of the People's Republic of China after that government was established on October 1, 1949, has been characterized by some major shifts and changes in the country's role in world affairs. These changes were made in accordance with the domestic situation in China and in the context of changes in the international system in which the PRC found itself after its emergence in 1949. The foreign policy of any country is not formulated or executed in a vacuum, and a country has to develop its foreign policy in the light of certain basic factors such as the geopolitical realities of the region in which it is located, its quest for security, its needs and urges for economic development, and its ideological affinity. An analysis of China's foreign policy will indicate that certain basic objectives have governed it from its inception. The technique and modus operandi for attaining these objectives have varied from time to time with changing circumstances both at home and abroad, but the basic objectives have remained the same. China's quest for security, ideological background and affinity, need for economic development, and support and sympathy for the Asian peoples under colonial or semicolonial rule have always determined that country's foreign policy.

When the PRC emerged in 1949, three important factors already characterized the world situation. First, the United States and the USSR had developed their power and resources to the point where they had emerged as superpowers in a rivalry that affected the whole world. The other two factors were the decline of Western imperial rule overseas and the foundation of national states in Asia, which was to occur in Africa as well.[1] The factor that governed the international system in the late 1940s, as Arnold Toynbee pointed out, was that the victors of the Second World War failed to maintain their wartime cooperation and consequently the world was repartitioned into two hostile camps.[2] The cause of this two-superpower conflict, as Toynbee added, was not greed but fear. Because of the invention of the atom bomb, the world, which, on the economic plane, still had elbowroom for the two superpowers to live and let live, had become so small militarily that the two superpowers had been brought into confrontation with each other and led into a worldwide rivalry for power and influence—"an endeavor on the part of either power, in competition with its adversary, to bring as much as possible of the rest of the world into its own camp."[3]

The formative phase of China's role in world affairs, from 1949 to 1952, was largely determined by the world's being divided into two camps. The two-camp thesis had not been formally put forward by the communist world until the Cominform meeting in September 1947 when Andrei Zhdanov had formulated it at the opening session,[4] but the two superpowers had already begun their competitive struggle for worldwide power and influence, and China had hardly any diplomatic options in choosing between the two camps. The United States had supported Chiang Kai-shek's Nationalist forces in the Chinese civil war, and China was also aware that the United States continued to support anticommunist groups in China. It was difficult for the United States to follow the British example of trying to accept the reality of the situation in China and of coming to terms with the communist regime under Mao, so Mao had to look to Moscow for whatever help and assistance he could expect from the outside world for his country.

The Chinese were aware of the Soviet Union's lukewarm attitude to the emergence of a unified and strong China under the communist regime, yet expediency, rather than genuine ideological affinity, led Beijing to choose the socialist camp under Moscow's leadership. Mao explained his policy of alignment with the socialist camp as follows:

> You are leaning to one side. Exactly. The forty years' experience of Sun Yat-sen and the twenty-eight years' experience of the Communist party have taught us to lean to one side, and we are firmly convinced that in order to win victory and consolidate it we must lean to one side. In the light of the experiences accumulated in these forty years and these twenty-eight years, all Chinese without exception must lean either to the side of imperialism or to the side of socialism. Sitting on the fence will not do, nor is there a third road.[5]

> We oppose the Chiang Kai-shek reactionaries who lean to the side of imperialism, and we also oppose the illusions about a third road. Let readers refer to Dr. Sun Yat-sen's testament: his earnest advice was not to look for help from the imperialist countries, but to "unite with those nations of the world which treat us as equals." Dr. Sun had experience; he had suffered, he had been deceived. We should remember his words and not allow ourselves to be deceived again. Internationally, we belong to the side of the anti-imperialist front headed by the Soviet Union, and so we can turn only to this side for genuine and friendly help, not to the side of the imperialist front.[6]

Beijing's diplomacy since 1949 has mainly rotated on China's relations with the two superpowers: the United States and the Soviet Union. The strained relationships with Washington from 1949 to 1969 and, more recently, with Moscow have largely shaped China's relations with its Asian neighbors and with the outside world. China's worries over U.S. policy in the first twenty years and subsequently its growing concern about Soviet threats are vitally interrelated with the country's quest for security, always the fundamental objective of a country's foreign policy. In case of the PRC, security has always had an added importance in view of the country's strained relationships—first with Washington, then simultaneously with Washington and Moscow, and since 1969, mainly with the latter.

Before discussing China's relations with the two superpowers from 1949 to 1969, however, let us turn to China's role in Asia, particularly Beijing's support for revolutionary causes in Afro-Asian countries. From 1949 to 1969, the Asian countries had fewer worries about the threat from Red China than the European countries did with regard to communist Russia. The reasons for this difference in attitude toward Russia by noncommunist Europe and toward China by noncommunist Asia have been summed up as follows. "Europe was so small that the Russians on the Elbe and upper Danube overhung the whole continent. In Asia, on the other hand, the Chinese remained remote . . . moveover, the Russians actually stepped out far beyond their frontiers and had refused to return, whereas the Chinese with the arguable exception of Tibet, did not. The Chinese victory in 1949 was comparable with the Russian Revolution of 1917, but not with the Russian advance in Europe in 1944–45."[7] The Asians in the late 1940s and early 1950s were more concerned with their national liberation movements against the European colonial powers—such as the Netherlands in Indonesia, the French in Indochina, and the British in Malaysia—than with the so-called menace of international communism or the PRC. Nonalignment rather than alliance with the West against China was preferred by the major Asian countries, such as India, Indonesia, Ceylon (Sri Lanka), Malaysia, and Burma. India, in particular, was most vocal against any alliance with the Western camp led by the United States, and India also regarded the emergence of Communist China as the victory of an Asian awakening and an Asian spirit rather than the triumph of a Moscow-controlled communism. Indian Prime Minister Jawaharlal Nehru thought that India and the new China (the PRC) would act as a bridge between the two superpowers.

But Nehru's concept of nonalignment or of a "third force" had no appeal for Mao, just as it had no appeal for U.S. Secretary of State John Foster Dulles, who denounced Nehru's neutralism as immoral. Similarly, Mao had also denounced any idea of a third camp, and had asserted that "neutrality is a mere camouflage."[8] For both Mao and Dulles, the third force was meaningless and absurd; policy must be either "with us" or "against us."

In February 1948, the Southeast Asian Youth Conference, attended by communist and other militant students from all over Asia, had been held in Calcutta. In a message to the conference, the Communist party of China had promised the growth of armed struggle in Asia and had asserted that in this respect, the PRC had set forth on "extremely valuable experiences for the peoples of Asian countries." Liu Shaoqi had already developed the concept "the way of Mao Tse-tung" for national liberation movements in Asia: "Mao has not only applied Marxism to new conditions but has given it a new development. He has created a Chinese or Asiatic form of Marxism. China is a semi-feudal, semi-colonial country in which vast numbers of people live at the edge of starvation, tilling small bits of soil. Its economy is agricultural, backward and dispersed. . . . There are similar conditions in other lands of Southeast Asia. The courses chosen by China will influence them all."[9]

At a trade union conference of Asian countries and Australia, held in Beijing in November 1949 and attended by the communist and left-wing labor leaders from all over the region, Liu Shaoqi explained the new China's pledge to support "wars of national liberation." He predicted that there would be wars of national liberation in Vietnam, Indonesia, Malaysia, the Philippines, Japan, Korea, and also India (after two years of independence) and he made the prediction in the expectation that liberation could be achieved in most of Asia through armed struggle, following the path of the Chinese people.[10] At the conference, Communist China seemed to have attained the role of coordinator of communist movements or wars of national liberation in Asia, and Liu Shaoqi was quoted in a Cominform publication, *For a Lasting Peace, For a People's Democracy*, to the effect that Asian communists must use China as an example for the liberation movement in Asia.[11] Mao is reported to have assured the Indian Communist party of the full support of the Chinese people and to have expressed the hope that "India would soon be liberated from the oppression of Anglo-American imperialism and its Indian lackeys."[12] Liu Shaoqi claimed that the Chinese revolution was the model for the underdeveloped or semicolonial countries and that Mao had added to the treasury of Marxist-Leninist thought—a claim never made by any other communist leader or barely admitted, if at all, by the Russian leaders.[13]

Like the Kremlin leaders, the Chinese regime, whose emergence had been most enthusiastically greeted by many Asians, looked upon the new Asian governments as being controlled by bourgeois reactionaries and described their leaders as "stooges of Anglo-American imperialism."[14] It seems, however, that this distorted initial Chinese attitude toward the governments of new Asian countries and their leaders was more in deference to the Kremlin than a part of China's own thinking or wishes. China, in fact, recognized the realities and dynamics of the new countries in Asia much sooner than the USSR did, as that country's rigid and dogmatic attitude began to change only after Stalin's death in 1953.

Before we examine China's flexible attitude to the new countries of Asia, we may elaborate a little on its concept of wars of national liberation in Asian countries, which complicated its diplomatic relations with those countries from 1949 to the early 1950s. When revolution is to be organized in a nominally independent country, there are, according to Chinese ideology, more difficult and complicated problems. "The country appears to be already independent and there seems, therefore, to be no legitimate reason for national liberation."[15] The Chinese analysis of such a country was elaborated by Lin Ta-nien Wan as follows: "They [the neocolonialists] foster puppet regime and practice various subtler methods of colonial control; organize military bloc and build up military bases and plunder the wealth of countries by means of economic 'aid' and various other forms of economic exploitation."[16] The target of wars of national liberation in such cases is the neocolonial power, such as the United States and its lackeys or puppets. The first phase of the Chinese foreign policy (1949–1952) was described as a policy of uniting or joining with the revolutionaries: "The path taken by the Chinese peoples in defeating imperialism and lackeys and in founding the People's Republic of China is the path that should be taken by the peoples of various colonial and semi-colonial countries in their fight for national independence and people's democracy."[17]

Does that policy imply that Communist China aimed at achieving a hegemony in Asia? There is no evidence that China had either the ability or the ambition to establish a hegemony in Asia as the Kremlin did in Eastern Europe, but it was only natural that after establishing a strong regime and after centuries of foreign domination, China, a nation of more than 800 million people, should want to assert its voice in world affairs and particularly in Asian affairs. The doctrinaire zeal was a natural phenomenon after the victory of the Communist party in China. "The CPC [the Communist party of China], of course, realizes that Soviet satellization of Eastern Europe was made possible by a world war and at least a degree of consent from the Soviet Union's allies, circumstances that are not likely to be repeated in the CPR's [the Chinese People's Republic] case."[18]

As already stated, the emergence of a strong and united regime in China made a very favorable impression on countries like India. But

Nehru was not a communist nor a believer in any totalitarianism; nor were other Asian countries willing to lean to one side or the other. Nehru's concept of nonalignment was already making headway in other Asian countries, and neutrality or nonalignment with the politics of the big powers had a special appeal for the newly independent countries of Asia. Just as they were opposed to joining any grouping or alliance with the West, they showed no enthusiasm for joining the socialist bloc, to which China had committed itself. Having openly encouraged armed struggle for the so-called wars of national liberation, the Chinese leaders did not have much hope of success in winning the friendship and cooperation of the new countries of Asia so the policy of "join with the revolutionaries" soon had to be replaced by a policy of "union with all."

Beijing Versus Washington: Initial Phase

For a brief period in 1944–1945, Mao sought the friendship of the United States. The Communist party's official newspaper stated in a friendly editorial, "The work which we Communists are carrying on today is the very same work which was carried on earlier by Washington, Jefferson, and Lincoln,"[19] and John Paton Davis, in *Dragon by the Tail*, referred to the fact that Mao and Zhou Enlai "secretly tried to arrange a meeting in Washington with the American president" in January 1945.[20] Donald Zagoria, in his testimony on November 19, 1975, before the House Subcommittee on Future Foreign Policy Research and Development, referred to "Chinese efforts at detente with the United States," and noted, "For a summary of the evidence, as late as the spring of 1949, Mao was trying to develop closer ties with the United States in order to avoid falling completely into the Soviet orbit."[21] Zagoria also referred to a series of conversations that took place between the U.S. ambassador, J. Leighton Stuart, and Huang Hua during the spring of 1949 and added:

> Mao, for his part, is a "national Communist" who has always placed the interests of China above those of the Soviet Union and, first in 1944–46 and again in 1949, sought to balance his relationship with the United States. Mao's efforts to cultivate Washington between 1944–46 proved unsuccessful once the United States intervened on behalf of the Nationalists in 1947; similarly, Maoist initiatives as late as the spring of 1949 came to nothing when the United States adopted a policy of nonrecognition of China.[22]

When the communist victory in China was almost certain, the U.S. secretary of state, Dean Acheson, said on July 30, 1949, "We continue to believe that, however tragic may be the immediate future of China and however ruthlessly a major portion of this great people may be exploited by a party in the interest of a foreign imperialism, ultimately the profound civilization and democratic individualism of China will reassert themselves and she will throw off foreign yoke."[23] Acheson's statement reflects the U.S. failure to appreciate the depth of the profound changes that resulted from Mao's revolution in China. The Chinese communist revolution was not accomplished in the interest of a foreign power, nor were the Chinese required to throw off the foreign yoke as Mao's success in China was not due to the help or support of any foreign power. Mao articulated the Chinese people's deep-rooted sense of frustration and humiliation caused by foreign interventions in China, which had reduced the country to the status of a semicolony of the European powers, and Mao's successes were also due to the Chinese people's expectations for socioeconomic reforms under his communist program.

Even after the emergence of Mao's new regime in China, Acheson continued to express the U.S. hope that in time, the Chinese people would discover the "emptiness of communist promises."[24] In August 1949, Acheson discussed the U.S. dilemma in dealing with the new regime in China and said that U.S. policy was "now confronted with great difficulties." On the one hand, there was the Chinese communist regime, which "while in fact serving the imperialist interests of a foreign power, has, for the present, been able to persuade large numbers of Chinese that it is serving their interest." On the other hand, "the nationalist government had been unable to rally its people and had been driven out of extensive portions of the country." Acheson added, "Chinese communists, in attempting to establish a totalitarian domination over the Chinese people in the interests of a foreign power and in basing this attempt on a willfully distorted concept of world realities are committing themselves deeply on the basis of unproven assumptions as to the extent of their own strength and nature of the reactions which they are bound to provoke in China and elsewhere."[25]

That type of distorted conception of the Chinese revolution was obviously resented by the Chinese leaders. A comment by the Chinese Communist party on August 13, 1949, warned the Chinese people against "new tricks of American imperialists,"[26] and Mao, in his first major foreign policy statement, stated:

> The Communist party of China agrees with the Atlantic Charter and with the decisions of the international conferences of Moscow, Cairo, Teheran, and the Crimea, because these decisions all contribute to the defeat of the Fascist aggressors and the maintenance of world peace.
> The fundamental principle of the foreign policy advocated by the Chinese Communist party is as follows: China shall establish and

strengthen diplomatic relations with all countries and settle all questions of common concern, such as coordination of military operations in war, peace conferences, trade, and investment, on the basic conditions that the Japanese aggressors must be completely defeated and world peace maintained, that there must be mutual respect for national independence and equality, and that there must be promotion of mutual interests and friendship between states and between peoples.

The Chinese Communist party fully agrees with the proposals of the Dumbarton Oaks conference and the decisions of the Crimea conference on the establishment of an organization to safeguard international peace and security after the war. It welcomes the United Nations conference on international organization in San Francisco.[27]

The Chinese Communist party had stated in November 1948 that China wanted to have good relations with all countries, including the United States, but such countries must respect China's territorial integrity and not give aid to Chiang Kai-shek.[28] But the United States, thanks to General Chiang's friends in the U.S. Congress, continued to help the Nationalists with military aid amounting to about $2 billion and General MacArthur held the view that Taiwan was an essential link in the U.S. defense system in the Pacific. It was pointed out in a report from the Committee on Foreign Affairs of the U.S. House of Representatives on February 9, 1950, that "should Formosa [Taiwan] fall into the hands of a hostile power, history would repeat itself. Its military potential would again be fully exploited as the means to breach and neutralize our Western Pacific defense system and mount a war of conquest against free nations of the Pacific basin."[29]

It is true, however, that on January 5, 1950, President Truman announced in Washington that the United States would not provide aid or advice to the Chinese forces on Taiwan and Acheson declared that the president's declaration was proof to the world that the United States would not meddle in the internal affairs of China.[30] But the continued distorted statements about the new regime in China and expression of hopes that China would throw off its alleged "foreign domination" made the Chinese government suspicious of the U.S. policy toward the new regime in Beijing. The PRC referred to the continued hostile attitude of the United States to the PRC in its early policy statements on world issues. With regard to the U.S. recognition of the PRC, Acheson had said that to secure recognition, a regime must pass three tests: it must be in effective control of the country, it must recognize and carry out international obligations, and it must rule with the acquiescence of the ruled,[31] and according to the U.S. government, the new regime in China had not fulfilled these criteria. In reality, it was internal politics in the United States that prevented the recognition of the PRC as the "China lobby" in the U.S. Congress was still powerful enough to prevent the U.S. government from accepting the fait accompli in China.

The U.S. attitude toward the PRC was further hardened by the Chinese communist leaders' hostile remarks about the United States and their profound "solidarity" with the Russians, whom the Chinese considered, at that time, as their real friends. The arrest of the U.S. consul general in China, Angus Ward, and his four colleagues on October 24, 1949, led to a further worsening of relations between the two countries. The arrest was described as "a violation of the basic concepts of international relations."[32] Ward and his four colleagues were released and ordered to leave China on November 22, 1949, and on January 5, 1950, the State Department declared that it would be premature for the United States "to consider recognition of the Chinese Communist Government and that the question would not be decided without the fullest consultation with the Congress"[33] – where the supporters of General Chiang were still not prepared to accept the reality of the situation in China.

As the PRC grew suspicious about U.S. continued sympathy for the Nationalist government on Taiwan, it began to move closer to Moscow in its quest for security as well as to get economic and technical aid from the Soviet Union. Also, Beijing's ideological support of the national liberation movements in Indochina and other parts of Asia made Washington worry about the new regime's policy and role in Asia. So both Washington and Beijing regarded each other as a potential adversary. A U.S. National Security Council document of June 1949 expressed the U.S. "domino theory": "The extension of the Communist authority in China represents a grievous political defeat for us. . . . if Southeast Asia is also swept by communism, we shall have suffered a major political defeat the repercussions of which will be felt throughout the rest of the world, especially in the Middle East and in a then critically exposed Australia."[34] So the United States began a policy of containment of China, and Beijing began a policy of closer association with the United States' major adversary, the USSR. Commenting on the past U.S. policy toward the PRC, Senator Mike Mansfield wrote in November 1976: "In the final years of that civil war [the Chinese civil war between the communists and the Nationalists], the United States poured $2 billion of aid into a doomed cause. It was an intervention in China's civil war and it persists today through continuing U.S. recognition of the Republic of China on Taiwan, through furnishing of that government with military advice and arms . . . which are designed to preserve Taiwan as an entity separate from the Chinese mainland."[35]

Anyone who has had an opportunity to discuss and understand the depth of Chinese people's feelings over what they term the "liberation of Taiwan" will agree with Senator Mansfield that the continued U.S.

support of Taiwan as the so-called Republic of China was a flagrant provocation to the PRC and it was, and still is, futile to expect any genuinely
good relationship between Washington and Beijing as long as the former
can not keep its hands completely off the internal affairs of China. As a
self-respecting and revolutionary regime, the PRC can not be expected to
accept the existence of the so-called Republic of China, which is, in the
eyes of the mainland Chinese leaders and people, a "rebel faction,"
fostered and maintained by U.S. military support. As a senior Chinese
official asked me: "What would be the United States' reaction if China
were to recognize Hawaii as an 'independent' entity or republic outside
the United States? Could there be any friendly relations between the
Americans and any foreign country if that country were to treat an integral part of the United States as a 'separate republic'? Why doesn't the
U.S. government understand our position on Taiwan? If the United
States could accept the Russian occupation of Eastern Europe under the
1975 Helsinki agreement, why can't it accept our position on Taiwan?"
When I asked the official about a plebiscite to ascertain wishes of the
people of Taiwan, his reply was: "Did the Americans try to ascertain the
wishes of the people of Eastern Europe before signing the Helsinki agreement? Why does the U.S. government no longer insist on a plebiscite in
Kashmir before making friendship with India? Was not the United States
a party to the Indian pledge for a UN-supervised plebiscite for the people
of Kashmir? There should be a uniform practice for all peoples – whether
of Eastern Europe or of Kashmir or of Taiwan."[36]

There is, however, no universal standard or norm in international
politics or relations. The China policy of the United States in the 1950s
was dictated by a number of factors, such as China's ideological support
of communist revolutions in Asia and Beijing's leaning to the side of
Moscow in the heyday of the cold war, compounding the unfortunate era
of confrontation between Beijing and Washington that began in 1950.

Sino-Soviet Treaties

On February 15, 1950, it was announced in Moscow that a Sino-Soviet
Treaty of Friendship Alliance and Mutual Assistance, together with an
agreement for Russian long-term credits to China, had been concluded.
There were also agreements on the Chinese Changchun Railway, Port
Arthur, and Dairen. In the preamble to the friendship treaty, both parties expressed their determination to prevent the rebirth of Japanese imperialism or a repetition of aggression on the part of Japan or of any other
state that might be united with Japan. Article 4 of the friendship treaty
provided "for consultation between the signatories on all important international problems which affected their common interests."[37] The treaties

noted with satisfaction that radical changes had taken place in the Far East: Japan's defeat in the Second World War; the overthrow of the Kuomintang government; and the emergence of a strong and united government in China, which pledged a policy of friendship and cooperation with the USSR.[38]

The Sino-Soviet treaties were hailed in the communist world as a great triumph of international communism, and they caused great worry in Washington and in the Western European countries, though not to the same extent in Europe as in the United States. The Sino-Soviet negotiations, which began with Chairman Mao's visit to Moscow on December 16, 1949, and included a visit by Premier Zhou Enlai on January 20, 1950, lasted for about two months. Mao subsequently disclosed in 1960 that the two-month prolonged negotiations were due to Stalin's fear that Chinese communists, like the Yugoslav communists, would pursue an independent policy.[39] China was too big to be either blackmailed or blandished. "The ally was too big to be biddable."[40]

The United States was upset by the 1950 Sino-Soviet treaties. Acheson declared immediately that the friendship treaty would turn China into a "Soviet satellite,"[41] and the U.S. government alleged that there were some secret clauses in the friendship treaty that would do just that.[42] Earlier, on January 12, 1950, Acheson had said that communism was a subtle instrument of Soviet foreign policy and that the USSR was engaged in annexing Manchuria, Outer Mongolia, and Xinjiang (Sinkiang) Province from China, and on January 25, 1950, the State Department had released background material in support of those charges.[43] The charges had been denied in both Beijing and Moscow as absurd.[44]

Relations between the United States and the PRC got worse after the 1950 Sino-Soviet friendship treaty. On March 15, 1950, Acheson declared that the PRC had become a dependency of the Soviet political system and of the Soviet economy, and he warned that any aggressive or "subversive adventures" by the PRC beyond its borders would constitute a violation of the UN charter.[45] China reacted sharply to Acheson's speech. Zhou Enlai called the speech an attempt to dupe those people who still lacked experience of the United States' aggressive policy. The United States, Zhou added, had gotten control of Japan and South Korea and now was "attempting to control China, Southeast Asia and India."[46]

The PRC's Entry into the United Nations

On March 8, 1950, UN Secretary-General Trygve Lie implied in a memorandum to all the UN delegations that the PRC should be permitted to take China's seat at the UN. Lie pointed out that UN policy should be "to deal with whatever government exercises effective authority in a country and is habitually obeyed by the bulk of its population."[47] Acheson replied that the United States would not vote to seat the PRC at the United Nations as the United States still recognized the Nationalist government on Taiwan, but he said that the United States would not use its veto power to prevent the PRC from entering the United Nations. On June 6, 1950, Mr. Lie requested that four of the five permanent members of the UN Security Council (the United States, the United Kingdom, France, and the USSR – Nationalist China was the fifth permanent member) end the deadlock over the Chinese representation in the United Nations. Still, the seat was held by the Nationalist government on Taiwan until October 1971, thanks to U.S. opposition to the entry of the PRC to the United Nations, which was thus deprived of the representation of one-fourth of the world's population.

The Korean War and Its Impact on
Sino-American Relations

The Korean War broke out on June 25, 1950. On October 25, 1950, when the UN forces were rapidly moving toward the Chinese frontier, Chinese troops entered the war, and the intention of the United States not to meddle in the internal affairs of China, as had been announced by Acheson in January 1950, came to an end. The Sino-American relationship was no longer indifferent or unsympathetic but became hostile. The Korean War, which lasted three years and took 50,000 American lives, moved the United States from a position of neutrality or noninvolvement in Communist China's affairs to conducting an active policy of weakening and isolating China. China's problems of security and defense, therefore, became intense.

The exact origin of the Korean War is still obscure and controversial. There is evidence that indicates that the Korean War was basically Stalin's initiative and Mao a reluctant partner. Both Mao and Zhou Enlai told Pakistan's President Ayub Khan in March 1965 that the Korean War was "an unfortunate one," and both made implicit reference to "the Soviet pressures" on China at the time.[48] Zhou Enlai also made a distinction between the Korean and Vietnam wars and requested Ayub to convey to U.S. President Johnson that "the situations in 1950 and 1965" were not similar; that if the United States would not push the Chinese to a point of no return, "the Chinese would abide by international obligations and responsibilities and would not get involved in any war with the United States."[49] John Paton Davis, a China expert and former U.S. foreign service officer, told the House Subcommittee on Future Foreign Policy Research and Development that if the United States had responded to Mao's gestures toward a Sino-American relationship in 1944–1945 or in

1949, "there would not have been, perhaps, a Korean War, because the whole atmosphere in East Asia would have been different, and certainly there would not have been the Vietnam War."[50] However, those are big "ifs."

The Korean War had terrible consequences for China's relations with the United States. It led President Truman to order the defense of Taiwan and subsequently led President Eisenhower to declare, in his first State of the Union Message on February 2, 1953, that the U.S. Seventh Fleet would "no longer be employed to shield Communist China."[51] The Seventh Fleet had been present to prevent a possible Chinese attack on Taiwan and also any attempt by Chiang Kai-shek to invade mainland China, but President Eisenhower felt that after the Chinese intervention in the Korean War, the United States had no obligation to prevent Chiang from attacking mainland China. Eisenhower's new policy was interpreted in many quarters as "unleashing Chiang Kai-shek," who still had dreams of conquering mainland China.

Eisenhower's statement caused dismay in many Asian countries, such as Japan, India, Pakistan, Indonesia, Burma, and Ceylon, and even the NATO allies were worried. In the British House of Commons, British Foreign Secretary Anthony Eden described Eisenhower's new policy as having "unfortunate political repercussions without any compensating military advantage."[52] However, U.S. Secretary of State John Foster Dulles went further than Eisenhower. China, he said, was an "atheistic Communism" with which no compromise or accommodation was possible. (Emmet John Hughes, in his *Ordeal of Power,* quoted Under Secretary of State Bedell Smith as saying that Dulles was "still dreaming his fancy about reactivating the civil war in China.")[53] The U.S. ambassador in Taiwan was also of the opinion that peace in Asia was impossible until the predatory regime in Beijing was replaced by a truly Chinese government.[54] There were many Americans, however, who were greatly dismayed to see the hostilities between the United States and China grow. Professor John K. Fairbank, for instance, writes: "Only Stalin, perhaps, profited from the Sino-American war in Korea. . . . The Dullesian Cold War against Peking in the 1950s was fundamentally mistaken and unnecessary."[55]

On the Chinese side, even Premier Zhou Enlai, who was normally regarded as moderate, said in November 1951 that the Chinese intervention in Korea had not only safeguarded China itself, but had been "an encouragement to all peoples in colonial and semi-colonial regions." He bitterly attacked the U.S. policy and also reaffirmed the Chinese determination "to free Formosa from the American aggressors." However, Zhou concluded by adding that different social systems could live peacefully together and that the Chinese, who needed peace, had no desire to threaten anyone.[56] Earlier, in 1951 Chairman Mao had addressed the Chinese People's Political Consultative Conference in Beijing (on October 23) and said that Chinese assistance to the Korean people would continue until the U.S. government was willing to settle the problem peacefully. China, Mao had asserted, was opposed to aggressive action against any country, and China had intervened in Korea only because U.S. troops had invaded North Korea.[57]

The Korean War was no doubt costly to the PRC, but its intervention on behalf of a fellow Asian communist country increased its prestige and image both inside the country and in the communist world. Although South Korea could not be brought under communist control, neither could the North Korean communist regime be overthrown, and the status quo in the Korean Peninsula was maintained by China's military intervention against the most powerful nation of the world, the United States. The Chinese concept of the United States as a paper tiger could be continued, and China also assumed the status of a great power. The Soviet Union demanded a conference of the "big five" – the United States, the USSR, Britain, France, and the PRC – to settle the Korean issue, but the United States refused the proposal of a "big five" conference on the grounds that China had been declared an "aggressor" by the United Nations – but not on the grounds that China could not be treated as one of the "big five."[58] China had won respect by its own military achievements, but the war had placed heavy strains on its economy, which had already been distressed because of the civil war and foreign invasion in the preceding decade.[59] At the United Nations, the United States had been successful in branding the PRC as an aggressor, but the newly independent Asian countries, particularly India, vigorously championed China's cause in that world forum. China's image in Asia increased rather than decreased, as China had become not just another Russian satellite, but a major Asian power to be reckoned with in global affairs, particularly in Asian ones.

New Tensions in Sino-American Relations

At the opening session of the Geneva Conference, held on April 26, 1954, to discuss the Korean question, Premier Zhou Enlai blasted the U.S. policy in Asia. He called the United States an aggressor, "dreaming to impose upon the Chinese people the power of the Kuomintang remnant clique," and he added that "the countries of Asia should consult among themselves . . . seeking common measures to safeguard peace and security in Asia." Zhou demanded that the United States and the other Western powers be excluded from Far Eastern affairs.[60] Soviet Foreign Minister Molotov supported Zhou Enlai's demand by stating that "the peoples of Asia must have the full right to settle their own affairs."[61]

Zhou visited India and Burma during the intervals of the Geneva Conference and got support from Asian countries like Burma and India for the proposal that Asian affairs should be decided by the Asians themselves without outside interference, which implied the Western powers. The French war against the nationalist forces in Indochina added new impetus to this spirit of an Asian awakening which China sought to identify itself with. China began to be looked on more as an emerging Asian major power rather than as a communist power under Soviet domination, as the United States sought to depict it.

In order to contain the Chinese influence in Asia and to prevent the spread of communism in Southeast Asia, the United States began a policy of regional military pacts in the area. But although it was easy to form military alliances like NATO in Europe against threats from the Soviet Union, it was a far more difficult and complicated task for the United States to persuade the noncommunist Asian countries to join Western-sponsored military pacts against "threats" from China. The United States was successful in forming the Southeast Asia Treaty Organization (SEATO) on September 8, 1954, but only three Asian countries joined—Pakistan, the Philippines and Thailand—and Pakistan joined not out of fear of Communist China, but because of regional problems with India.[62] Upon joining SEATO, Pakistan conveyed through its ambassador in Beijing that it would not be party to any aggressive designs against China—in fact, it was because of Pakistan's insistence that Taiwan was not included as part of the territories to be covered under the defensive protection of SEATO. On the Chinese side, Zhou Enlai, though expressing disapproval of Pakistan's joining SEATO, advised Pakistan that it should develop, with U.S. assistance if necessary, its own military manufacturing capabilities rather than purchase tanks and planes. Weapons, Zhou pointed out, "become obsolete in no time and the recipient country remains always dependent on the donor country."[63]

More serious problems arose when the PRC seized a small Nationalist-held island, Yijiang, near the Tachen group and bombed the Tachen Islands in January 1955. On January 24, 1955, Premier Zhou Enlai also reiterated his country's plan to "liberate" Taiwan. These activities of the PRC created an atmosphere of war hysteria in Washington, and President Eisenhower, in a special message to the U.S. Congress, urged that body to approve the Formosa resolution, which, to quote Senator Mike Mansfield, "in effect was a blank check for the President to wage war to defend Formosa (Taiwan), the Pescadores, and other islands then in Nationalist hands."[64] Dulles told a joint session of the Senate Foreign Relations and Armed Services Committees, "We say that the island of Formosa and the Pescadores is an area which is vital to the interests of the United States," and he pointed out that the alternative to defending Taiwan by risking war with China was that "we will be driven out of this whole Asian area and will fall back to the United States. That is the choice we have got to face."[65] The resolution was passed by an overwhelming majority in the U.S. Congress in January 1955, and it continued to be in force until 1974, when the Congress revoked it because of new Sino-American ties.

Two weeks after the resolution was passed, the U.S. Senate ratified a mutual defense treaty with Nationalist China, the so-called Republic of China, in which the United States pledged to defend Taiwan and the Pescadores. Dulles, while seeking ratification of the treaty in the Senate, had said that if Taiwan were taken by Communist China, "the entire island chain will inevitably go. Japan will surely be lost, you will have a combination of power there of Russia, China and Japan, which will be a far more serious threat than anything we have ever envisaged in that part of the world."[66] But some senators, such as Wayne Morse, had said that "the treaty further increases the possibility of war in the Pacific," and Senator Estes Kefauver had said: "I can see no reason for having our nation enter into treaty obligations with the government of Chiang Kai-shek. I do not wish to give the color of sovereignty and permanency to the government of Chiang Kai-shek on Formosa."[67]

During 1954 and the early part of 1955, tensions between the PRC and the United States were acute. "Indo-China in the early months of the year and Formosa at its end both brought the world, as Mr. Dulles was to say later, to the brink of war."[68] There were risks of a general war between the PRC and the United States on Indochina, but thanks to opposition from the U.S. Congress and military circles in Washington as well as opposition from the British Commonwealth of Nations, that near-war situation was averted. The 1954 Geneva Conference could not resolve the outstanding problems of the Korean War, but it averted an armed confrontation between Beijing and Washington on the Indo-China/Taiwan Peninsula. There was an exchange of words and warnings about the situation in Taiwan.[69] Zhou Enlai declared that any foreign interference in Taiwan would "lead to grave consequences" and an occupation of Formosa by the United States would not be tolerated,[70] and President Eisenhower warned that "any communist invasion of Formosa would come up against the American Seventh Fleet."[71]

But despite those threats and counterthreats, neither Washington nor Beijing was really ready for a new armed conflict in Asia. The Chinese government seemed to be whipping up the sentiments of Asian countries against the United States by constantly referring to the U.S. "occupation" of Taiwan, and the United States was also serving notice to the noncommunist Asian neighbors of China about the militant nature of Red China. These were the days of the cold war between the East and the West, and Beijing versus Washington on the Taiwan issue was a focal point of that cold war in Asia.

In any event, the stage was set for an era of a hostile relationship between the world's most powerful nation and the world's most populous, and that relationship would last for the next one and a half decades. As a part of that hostility, the United States increased pressure to keep the PRC out of the United Nations, and the fiction that Nationalist China represented one-fourth of the world's population continued to be a sad phenomenon of world politics. After a visit to China in 1956, Pakistani Prime Minister H. S. Suhrawardy wrote a letter on December 11, 1956, to President Eisenhower pointing out how difficult it was for Pakistan to oppose the PRC's entry to the United Nations when Pakistan had recognized the regime as early as 1950. Eisenhower's reply on December 19 was rather blunt: "We shall not alter our opposition to the Chinese Communist entry to the United Nations."[72]

China's New Diplomatic Moves in Asia and Other Parts of the Third World

Following the Geneva agreements in 1954, the Chinese government began a vigorous campaign to extend its contacts in Asia and other parts of the Third World. The Chinese leaders, particularly Zhou Enlai, "discovered the potentialities of an active, positive diplomacy," and Zhou launched a vigorous drive to broaden and strengthen Communist China's influence, particularly among the nonaligned countries of South and Southeast Asia.[73] Two conferences in 1955 gave Zhou a unique opportunity to pursue his new active diplomacy. The conference of Asian countries held in New Delhi in April 1955 was attended by nonofficial representatives, mainly communist and leftist elements, and it proclaimed Asian solidarity as the central theme of the peoples' movements in Asia. That conference marked the beginning of a new campaign of peoples' diplomacy, which was to develop into a wide movement under the slogan of Asian solidarity.[74]

However, it was the Afro-Asian conference at Bandung, convened by the Colombo powers—Burma, Ceylon, India, Indonesia, and Pakistan—that gave Zhou a chance to demonstrate his diplomatic skill and statesmanship in dealing with a large number of Asian and African countries. The Bandung Conference, which met on April 18–24, 1955, and was attended by representatives from twenty-nine countries with a total population of about 1.4 billion people, was a gathering with an astonishing range and diversity of race and opinion. Nehru was the principal architect, and Zhou Enlai was comparatively a newcomer to many of the delegates, yet it was "Mr. Chou En-lai's week."[75] Zhou had been invited at the suggestion of Nehru, who wished "to create an opportunity for Indian mediation in the cold war of Asia. But in the event, it was Mr. Chou En-lai who tended to mediate between Mr. Nehru and those who challenged his conceptions."[76] Nehru was challenged by Pakistan's prime minister, Mohammed Ali, and Ceylon's (Sri Lanka) prime minister, Sir John Kotelawala. According to some reports, Nehru lost his temper in arguments with his colleagues from Pakistan and Ceylon, which created a poor impression among the delegates. Some of the Asian delegates gleefully watched the leadership of the conference passing from Nehru to Zhou, and the latter showed a surprisingly pleasant attitude to countries like Pakistan, which further irritated the Indian delegates. China's first serious contact with Pakistan was made in Bandung. Not only the Pakistani account, but also other sources, confirmed that "for Mr. Nehru, the Bandung Conference was, perhaps, to a considerable extent, a failure, but for Mr. Chou En-lai it developed into a diplomatic triumph of the first magnitude."[77]

Zhou Enlai made an extended tour of South and Southeast Asian countries from November 18, 1956, to January 1, 1957, and visited India, Pakistan, Burma, North Vietnam, and Cambodia. In India, he was welcomed by Nehru and the Dalai Lama and Panchen Lama of Tibet, who were in New Delhi at the time. There was no dearth of crowds shouting *Hindi-Chini bhai bhai* ("Indians and the Chinese are brothers"), and there were many exchanges of friendly remarks and speeches. References were made to traditional Indo-Chinese friendship and to the modern Indo-China détente in the context of the "Asian spirit," and the five principles (Pancha Shila) that had been agreed upon by China and India in 1954 were reaffirmed. These five principles were: mutual respect for each other's territorial integrity, mutual nonaggression, mutual noninterference in each other's internal affairs, equality and mutual benefit, and peaceful coexistence.[78]

However, the relationship between the two large Asian nations, China and India, was soon transformed from friendship into hostility, and there was a serious border conflict in 1962. China won a decisive military victory, again enhancing its image as a major power, but the conflict had serious adverse effects on the emerging Sino-Soviet rift. When the Soviet Union supported India against China, it demonstrated publicly the dormant tensions between Beijing and Moscow.

Beijing developed very close and friendly relations with Indonesia and Pakistan, and there was talk of a "Beijing-Jakarta-Rawalpindi axis," which caused worry in India and anger in Moscow and Washington. China cooperated with Indonesia and Pakistan and a few other Afro-Asian countries to organize a second Afro-Asian conference, but both India and the Soviet Union were opposed to another conference. The Soviet Union was unhappy with China's new role in the Afro-Asian countries since the first conference in Bandung in 1955, and India, after its 1962 conflict with China, was unhappy with China's growing influence and role in Asia—in particular, in South Asia, through Pakistan. The

Soviet Union wanted to participate in the proposed second Afro-Asian conference on the basis that it is not only a European nation, but also an Asian one, but China successfully blocked Russia's participation in the proposed conference. Beijing was supported by a majority of the Afro-Asian countries at a preparatory meeting for the conference in Jakarta on April 10–15, 1964, which caused further wrath in Moscow.

The second Afro-Asian conference was scheduled to be held in Algeria in June 1965, but the conference could not be held because of the Algerian coup against Algerian President Ben Bella on June 19. The cancellation was a big setback for Beijing's diplomatic moves in Afro-Asian countries in the 1960s. Another major setback for China's role in Asia was the change of government in Indonesia in 1965, when a communist-inspired coup failed, as the military government that emerged in Indonesia after the abortive coup adopted an anti-China policy. The Beijing-Jakarta diplomatic relationship was suspended, and it remained so in 1981.

Beijing's Role in Africa

"If Asia took first importance in Peking's assessment of the revolutionary potentialities," comments Peter Van Ness in his analysis of China's support of wars of national liberation, "Africa came in close,"[79] and the Chinese People's Liberation Army journal, *Kung-Tso t'ung hsun,* wrote in April 1961, "The center of the struggle against colonialism is in Africa; the center of the battle between East and West for the intermediate zone is in Africa; hence, Africa has become the focus of contemporary problems."[80] One of China's aims by the end of the 1950s was to secure for itself a major role in world affairs as the champion of the Afro-Asian countries by helping their national liberation movements, and an expert on Chinese foreign policy objectives in the 1960s has written, "Chinese diplomacy in the Third World during the 1960s took more than one form, but its net effect was to convey a picture of China as a revolutionary' power which supported national liberation movements with propaganda and sometimes arms."[81]

Zhou Enlai made a tour of Africa in 1964 and declared at the end of the tour, "Revolutionary prospects are excellent throughout the African continent."[82] The importance of Africa for China was conditioned by China's concept of the struggle between the world countryside (the developing nations) and the world cities (the industrialized nations), and Zhou saw a role for China in the African struggles for independence against Western colonial rule. But the Chinese revolutionary techniques proved unacceptable to a number of African countries and the Chinese suffered some setbacks.

China's interest in Africa became apparent in 1955 at the first Afro-

Asian conference in Bandung. Since the Russians did not attend the conference, the Chinese seized the chance to develop a new sphere of influence among those African nations that were moving toward independence, and they quickly established diplomatic and other relations with Ghana and Guinea, which were among the first African states to become independent. At this point the Soviet and Chinese objectives coincided, and they worked together to try to reduce Western influence.

With the outbreak of the Sino-Soviet dispute, the Chinese resuscitated the idea, put forward by Mao Zedong in 1946, of two intermediate zones of the world that are opposed both to the Soviet Union and to the United States. Mao had envisaged that these two zones – the first consisting of the underdeveloped countries of Asia, Africa, and Latin America, and the second, the countries of Western Europe, Japan, Canada, and Australia – would come together under China's leadership to form a third force.[83]

The Chinese feel that their brand of communism – with its emphasis on the leading role of the peasants as opposed to the urban proletariat – and their economic doctrines of self-reliance are of particular relevance to underdeveloped areas. They stress that they share one thing in common with African countries – poverty – and they are an economically backward, as well as a developing, country. More important, they assume that the African countries, as a result of their colonial past, share the Chinese attitude toward the world's imperialist powers. By virtue of their own experience and policies, the Chinese see themselves as the leading opponents of the hegemony and power politics practices by the one or two superpowers and the champion of the medium-sized and small countries that are fighting for the "right to settle their own affairs as independent and sovereign states and for equal status in international relations."[84] The Chinese, therefore, regard the African countries as allies of China's anti-imperialist, anticolonialist platform, which in turn forms the basis of a Chinese-led Afro-Asian–Latin American bloc. (The Russians are excluded on the grounds that they are European, white, and a superpower.) An important element in the Chinese strategy is the promise of support for liberation movements.

Zhou Enlai's 1964 tour of Africa marked the culmination of the first phase of China's relations with that continent, and it was designed to emphasize Beijing's diplomatic and economic interests. But along with this diplomatic offensive, the Chinese carried on a full-scale program of subversion against legitimate African governments. They supported the rebellion that threatened the stability of Africa's largest country, Congo/Kinshasa (now Zaire), and were expelled from Burundi for using it as a base for that purpose. They were involved in plots against Niger, Dahomey (Benin), and the Central African Republic, and in Ghana, they were found to be assisting President Kwame Nkrumah's policy of promoting subversion in other African states to further his own ends. The Chinese were expelled from all four countries.

The Chinese were particularly concerned not only with establishing their own position in Africa, but also with countering any rise in Soviet influence there. Chinese diplomatic and political activities were backed up by some economic assistance, but because China did not have the resources to compete with the Soviet Union, much less with the major aid programs of the West, its aid was highly selective, and those countries that could be offered only a little aid were urged to adopt the principle of self-reliance.

The Chinese also attempted to make their influence felt at international conferences and to win control of a number of international communist "front" organizations. When the latter policy failed, they set up rival groups, but those did not succeed in making much headway in Africa. In 1965, the Chinese suffered a major setback with the collapse of the second Afro-Asian conference, which they had hoped would mark the establishment of a major Third World group that they could dominate.

Zhou Enlai paid his second visit to Africa only a fortnight before the Algerian coup, and in Dar es Salaam, he reiterated his view that there were exceedingly favorable prospects for revolution. In Cairo, just after Ben Bella's overthrow, Zhou immediately announced China's total and unconditional support for the new regime of President Houari Boumedienne, but even so, the hoped-for Afro-Asian conference failed to materialize, for Zhou's opportunistic recognition of Boumedienne, together with his undiplomatic comments about Africa's revolutionary prospects, did not find favor with African leaders.

Following that rebuff, and with the start of the Cultural Revolution in 1966, China appears to have lost some interest in Africa and to have turned its back on its foreign policy aims in order to concentrate on internal problems. But although Chinese ambassadors serving in sub-Saharan Africa were withdrawn from their posts in 1966 to take part in the Cultural Revolution, the Chinese did not entirely neglect their African interests. For example, negotiations with Tanzania and Zambia continued on what was to become a major Chinese external aid project, the Tanzam Railway.

The reemergence of China on the world scene, and the gradual return of its ambassadors to their foreign posts after May 1969, were followed by an expansion of China's activities in Africa. Both the amount of aid offered by the Chinese to African nations and its proportion to the total Chinese aid-giving capacity were evidence of the importance of the continent to Beijing. Over the five-year period 1966–1970, almost half of all

Chinese aid went to Africa, compared with under one-tenth of overall Soviet aid, but China's worldwide aid commitments over the same period totaled only one-third of the Soviet Union's.

Trade and Aid

Following the establishment of diplomatic relations with a country, the Chinese generally enter into economic and cultural agreements with it. They are particularly interested in labor-intensive aid projects, which enable them to make a maximum impact at a minimum cost with as big a Chinese presence as possible.

China's trade with Africa, as with countries elsewhere, is based on China's need to acquire raw materials and markets for its manufactured goods. In the early 1960s, trade with African countries was small, accounting for only 14 percent of China's trade with developing countries, which, in turn, composed only 18 percent of its total trade.

Cultural Ties

China has never attempted to emulate the Soviet Union or Eastern European countries by providing educational facilities for large numbers of African students. On the other hand, China has concentrated on propaganda on a wide scale, and the penetration of the African information media is an important goal. China's propaganda effort is based mainly on printed and broadcast material, but the country also makes use of cultural agreements, which provide for exchanges of literature, radio and press material, films, artists, and athletes. Films and exhibitions project the Chinese image, and Chinese films depicting recent African history, such as the events in the Congo, have been made in an attempt to put over the Chinese revolutionary message. Tours by Chinese acrobatic or operatic troupes are frequent.

A small number of Africans received academic training in China before the Cultural Revolution, but language difficulties were particularly acute. Moreover, in the early 1960s, there were complaints from Ghanaian and Cameroonian students about racial discrimination and political indoctrination. Few African students were actually in China when all foreign students were expelled at the start of the Cultural Revolution in 1966.

"Friendship societies" in African countries provide another channel for the Chinese to promote their image and distribute propaganda. The activities of all friendship societies are controlled by a central organization—the Chinese People's Association for Friendship with Foreign Countries, an official body that sponsors cultural and social exchanges and is, in effect, an instrument of Chinese government policy. A subsidiary organization, the Chinese-African Friendship Association (CAFA), was set up in 1960 to deal specifically with Africa.

Information Media

Peking Radio can be heard clearly throughout Africa. Beijing began broadcasting to Africa late in 1959 with transmissions totaling fourteen hours weekly. By 1966, that figure had risen to seventy hours, and there were broadcasts in Hausa, Swahili, English, French, Italian, and Portuguese.

Beijing's Simultaneous Strained Relationship with Washington and Moscow in the 1960s

By the end of the 1950s, China realized that it could neither challenge the United States over Taiwan nor rely on its ideological ally, the USSR, and China's international position was weakened by simultaneous strained relationships with the two superpowers in the 1960s. After the 1955 crisis over Taiwan, there were Sino-American talks on the ambassadorial level during 1955–1977, but no significant breakthrough was achieved in the relationship between the PRC and the United States. The United States continued to refuse to recognize the PRC and successfully blocked its entry into the United Nations. Prospects for "liberating" Taiwan from "occupation" by the United States were not improved by the strong military presence of the United States in East Asia, and there was a new crisis over Taiwan in 1958. Peking Radio announced on August 29, 1958, that China was determined to liberate Taiwan, and China then started bombing Nationalist-held islands off the mainland coast. The U.S. response was strong and left no doubt that the United States would use force to protect Taiwan from Chinese attack. Beijing looked for help and support from Moscow but got only lukewarm assurances from the Soviet Union. Beijing then realized that "it could neither count on an accommodation with Washington nor trust in Soviet support as a means for breaking out of U.S. containment in Asia and attaining Chinese interests in the region."[85]

The Eisenhower-Dulles policy of containing China was continued by the Democratic administrations of Presidents Kennedy and Johnson, and any hopes for relaxation of tensions between Beijing and Washington were dashed by the Vietnam War in the 1960s. On August 1, 1960, Zhou Enlai proposed a peace pact beween China, the United States, and other Pacific powers to establish "a non-nuclear zone in Asia and Western Pacific," but the United States termed the proposal a "propaganda gesture."[86]

It was, however, new tensions with Moscow that caused the greatest worries and problems for China in the 1960s. On February 19, 1961, the *New York Herald Tribune* published an article by Edward Crankshaw that asserted that the Sino-Soviet split was wider than most Western observers had previously believed. Crankshaw said that Western leaders had come into possession of documents, obtained from the Soviet bloc and Western European sources, that indicated that China had begun to seriously suspect that Moscow "wants to isolate China and make a settlement with the U.S."[87] On June 2, 1961, while going to meet the Soviet leader, Khrushchev, in Geneva, President Kennedy said: "We desire peace and we desire to live in amity with the Chinese people . . . but it takes two to make peace and I am hopeful that the Chinese people will be persuaded that a peaceful existence with its neighbors represents the best hope for us all. We would welcome it but I do not see evidence of it today."[88]

There was as yet no sign that the growing Sino-Soviet rift would lead to any rapprochement between Beijing and Washington. On the contrary, the simultaneous U.S.-USSR military aid to India after the 1962 Sino-Indian border conflict led Chairman Mao and Premier Zhou Enlai to tell Pakistani President Ayub Khan in March 1965 that there was some "collusion between Moscow and Washington" to contain and isolate China and that India and Japan were also partners in the "grand collusion" against China.[89] The 1963 Nuclear Test-Ban Treaty was regarded by China as yet another sign of collusion between the two superpowers. The Soviet Union had already refused to help China develop its nuclear capabilities, and Soviet economic aid and thousands of Soviet technicians had already been abruptly withdrawn from China in 1960. On August 21, 1963, the Soviet news agency Tass criticized China's opposition to the Nuclear Test-Ban Treaty by accusing that "there are some people in Peking ready to sacrifice half the population of their country, half of the entire mankind in a war involving nuclear weapons." China issued a 10,000-word statement in response to the Soviet accusation on September 1, 1963.

The Chinese reply made the counteraccusation that Moscow told "lies for a living." Beijing accused the Russians of telling the Americans "secrets between China and the Soviet Union concerning nuclear weapons," and the Chinese statement then proudly asserted, "Even if we Chinese people are unable to produce an atom bomb for 100 years, we will neither crawl to the baton of the Soviet leaders nor kneel before the nuclear blackmail of the U.S. imperialists." The reply summarized Beijing's views on war:

1. China wants peace and not war.
2. It is the imperialists and not we who want to fight a war.
3. World war can be prevented.
4. Even in the eventuality that imperialism should impose a war on the people of the world and inflict tragic losses on them, it is the

imperialist system and not mankind that would perish and the future of mankind would be bright.[90]

On September 6, 1963, the *People's Daily* and the Chinese Communist party's theoretical journal, *Red Flag*, printed the first installment of a series of articles on "The Origin and Developments of Differences Between Ourselves and the Communist Party of the Soviet Union." The series gave a comprehensive account of the great schism between the two communist giants, which constituted the most dominating factor in determining China's foreign policy in the 1970s and will probably be the most important factor affecting its policy in the 1980s.

China successfully launched its first nuclear device on October 16, 1964, which enabled it to join the nuclear power club and attain the status of an emerging major power, if not a superpower. Although China had always denounced superpowers and continued to declare that it would never become one, its aim has still been to acquire the status of a major power so that it could no longer be blackmailed either by Washington or Moscow. A Chinese journal, *China Youth*, stated that "a country which has fine delivery vehicles (long-range missiles and guided missiles) and a large quantity of nuclear bombs of great variety is a superpower and only a superpower is qualified to lead the world and to control and direct those countries which do not have nuclear weapons."[91] It is only in the context of China's "confrontation with the two dominant nuclear powers" that a nuclear strike capacity was regarded as imperative by the Chinese leaders so as to warrant allocating the very substantial resources such a capacity requires.[92]

A Chinese statement on October 16, 1964, announcing the test of its first nuclear device pledged, China "will never . . . under any circumstances be the first to use nuclear weapons." Then on October 20, 1964, Premier Zhou Enlai, in a letter to the leaders of all governments, proposed an international summit meeting on nuclear disarmament, which the U.N. secretary-general considered to be very worthwhile. French President Charles de Gaulle supported Zhou Enlai's proposal, and the U.S. government said that China would have "to participate in negotiations at some stage if such agreements are to have any real meaning. . . . We never have precluded the participation of any country in disarmament negotiations."[93] But the proposed conference never took place.

China was soon plunged into one of its greatest internal political upheavals when Chairman Mao launched the much-publicized great proletariat Cultural Revolution in 1966, and China engaged in a self-imposed isolation from any role in world affairs by almost totally withdrawing from external affairs. Defense and national security were neglected, even in the face of growing tensions with Moscow and the fact that the Vietnam War was going on. China's image in the Third World also declined sharply. Most of China's ambassadors were recalled for "reeducation," and relations with its Afro-Asian neighbors were seriously strained by China's posture as a militant revolutionary power.

But a most serious development, the transformation of the Sino-Soviet cold war into a great power confrontation on China's northern frontier where both Russian and Chinese soldiers were massing, compelled Chairman Mao to discontinue the self-imposed isolation of the Cultural Revolution, though not officially end it. The situation became particularly tense when the Soviet embassy in Beijing was seized in February 1967, and Peking Radio declared on February 2 that "a plot by the Soviet revisionists" and the U.S. and Japanese imperialists to attack China through Manchuria had been smashed. All Chinese frontier troops were placed on the alert. About forty Russian divisions with the most modern weapons were massed on China's northern borders facing China's ill-equipped fifty to sixty divisions. The two countries were on the brink of war, though China could hardly afford a military confrontation with Moscow nor could it count on any help from any other major power. The situation continued, and divergent accounts, varying "180 degrees," were given by both Moscow and Beijing about alleged military incursions in March 1969 when serious armed clashes took place on the Sino-Soviet border.

China's self-imposed diplomatic isolation had to be ended, and the country had to be set in order after the serious internal upheaval caused by the Cultural Revolution. China's quest for security led it to reshape its perception of the world situation, and during a visit to Pakistan in May 1969 U.S. Secretary of State William Rogers gleefully reported to Pakistani President Yahya Khan (a friend of both the PRC and the United States) that "China now considers the USSR and not the U.S. as her enemy number one."[94] Because of a new U.S. China policy and because of China's mortal fears of a Russian preemptive attack on China's new nuclear plants in Xinjiang Province, Yahya was soon commissioned by Richard Nixon to act as a "courier" between Beijing and Washington. The ensuing events led to almost revolutionary changes in China's role in world affairs in the 1970s.

Notes

1. See Royal Institute of International Affairs, London, *Survey of International Affairs, 1947–48* (London: Oxford University Press, 1950), pp. 1–2.
2. Ibid.

3. Royal Institute of International Affairs, London, *Survey of International Affairs, 1949-50* (London: Oxford University Press, 1952), p. 1.

4. See John Gittings, *The World and China* (London: Harper & Row, 1974), p. 141.

5. Mao Zedong, *Selected Works,* Vol. 4 (Beijing: Foreign Languages Press, 1969), p. 415.

6. Ibid., p. 417.

7. Royal Institute of International Affairs, London, *Survey of International Affairs, 1953* (London: Oxford University Press, 1956), p. 3.

8. See Gittings, *World and China,* p. 158.

9. Quoted in ibid., pp. 157-158.

10. A. Doak Barnett, *Communist China and Asia: Challenge to American Policy* (New York: Harper & Brothers, 1960), p. 90.

11. See *Far Eastern Economic Review,* May 21, 1952, p. 74.

12. M. R. Masani, "The Communist Party of India," *Pacific Affairs* (March 1951), pp. 18-38.

13. C. P. Fitzgerald, *The Chinese View of Their Place in the World* (London: Oxford University Press, 1970), p. 48.

14. *Far Eastern Economic Review,* May 21, 1952, p. 74.

15. Peter Van Ness, *Revolution and Chinese Foreign Policy: Peking's Support for Wars of National Liberation* (Berkeley: University of California Press, 1971), p. 52.

16. *Peking Review,* November 5, 1965, p. 26.

17. See Liu Shaoqi's speech at the Trade Union Conference held in Beijing in November 1949, in *The International Position of Communist China,* ed. Arthur Stein, Papers for the Thirteenth Conference of the Institute of Pacific Relations (New York, 1958), p. 11.

18. Harold Hinton, *Communist China in World Politics* (London: Macmillan, 1966), p. 74.

19. See Fox Butterfield, "Mao Tse-tung: Father of the Chinese Revolution," *New York Times,* September 10, 1976.

20. U.S., Congress, House of Representatives, Committee on International Relations, *United States-Soviet Union-China: The Great Power Triangle,* Hearings before the Subcommittee on Future Foreign Policy Research and Development, 94th Cong., 1st sess. (Washington, D.C.: Government Printing Office, 1976), p. 10.

21. Ibid., pp. 62-63.

22. Ibid.

23. Quoted in Gittings, *World and China,* p. 163.

24. See Royal Institute, *Survey of International Affairs, 1949-50,* p. 37.

25. Ibid., p. 325.

26. *New York Times,* August 14, 1949.

27. Mao Zedong, *Selected Works,* Vol. 3 (Beijing: Foreign Languages Press, 1967), p. 256.

28. Reprinted in Gittings, *World and China,* p. 163.

29. R. Dennell and R. T. Turner, eds., *Documents on American Foreign Relations, 1950* (Princeton: Princeton University Press, 1951), p. 505.

30. Congressional Quarterly Service, *China and the U.S. Far East Policy, 1945-1966* (Washington, D.C., 1967), p. 48.

31. *New York Times,* October 8, 1950.

32. Department of State, *Bulletin,* November 21, 1949, pp. 759–760.

33. *New York Times,* January 6, 1950.

34. Reproduced from Pentagon papers in Gittings, *World and China,* p. 170.

35. U.S., Congress, Senate, Committee on Foreign Relations, *China Enters the Post-Mao Era,* Report by Senator Mike Mansfield, November 1976 (Washington, D.C.: Government Printing Office, 1976), p. 4.

36. Based on the author's talks with the Chinese Senior Vice Foreign Minister Han Nianlong in Beijing, July 1976.

37. For details of the Sino-Soviet treaties of 1950 see Royal Institute of International Affairs, London, *Documents on International Affairs, 1949–50* (London: Oxford University Press, 1953), pp. 541–545.

38. Ibid.

39. *The Sino-Soviet Dispute,* Keesing Research Report, no. 3 (New York: Charles Scribner's Sons, 1969), p. 3.

40. M. Conliffe, ed., *The Times History of Our Times* (London: Weidenfeld and Nicolson, 1971), p. 259.

41. *New York Times,* February 16, 1950.

42. Ibid., February 18, 1950.

43. Ibid., January 13, 1950, and January 25, 1950.

44. New China News Agency, February 7, 1950.

45. *New York Times,* March 16, 1950.

46. *Times* (London), March 20, 1950.

47. Congressional Quarterly Service, *China and the U.S. Far East Policy, 1945–1966,* p. 49.

48. Based on the author's reading of unpublished documents and papers of the government of Pakistan, 1947–1971.

49. Ibid.

50. U.S., Congress, *United States–Soviet Union–China: The Great Power Triangle,* p. 10.

51. *New York Times,* February 3, 1953.

52. Foster R. Dulles, *American Policy Toward Communist China, 1949–1969* (New York: Thomas Y. Crowell Company, 1972), p. 132.

53. Ibid., p. 133.

54. Ibid., p. 134.

55. John K. Fairbank, *China Perceived: Images and Policies in China-American Relations* (New York: Alfred A. Knopf, 1976), p. 29–30.

56. New China News Agency, November 6, 1951.

57. Ibid., October 24, 1951. For details, see Royal Institute of International Affairs, London, *Survey of International Affairs, 1951* (London: Oxford University Press, 1954), p. 365, and *Documents on International Affairs, 1951* (London: Oxford University Press, 1954), p. 573.

58. See Royal Institute of International Affairs, London, *Survey of International Affairs, 1952* (London: Oxford University Press, 1955), pp. 336–337.

59. Ibid.

60. Congressional Quarterly Service, *China and the U.S. Far East Policy, 1945–1966,* p. 68.

61. Ibid.

62. For details, see G. W. Choudhury, *Pakistan's Relations with India, 1947–66* (London: Pall Mall Press, 1968).

63. Based on the author's reading of unpublished documents and papers of the government of Pakistan, 1947–1971.

64. U.S., Congress, *China Enters the Post-Mao Era,* p. 5.

65. Reprinted in ibid., p. 5.

66. Ibid.

67. Congressional Quarterly Service, *China and the U.S. Far East Policy, 1945–1966,* p. 73.

68. For details, see Royal Institute of International Affairs, London, *Survey of International Affairs, 1954* (London: Oxford University Press, 1957), p. 1 and pp. 250–251.

69. Ibid.

70. New China News Agency, August 23, 1954.

71. *New York Times,* August 18, 1954.

72. Based on the author's reading of unpublished documents and papers of the government of Pakistan, 1947–1971.

73. Barnett, *Communist China and Asia,* p. 100.

74. Ibid., p. 103.

75. *Times* (London), April 23, 1955.

76. Royal Institute of International Affairs, London, *Survey of International Affairs, 1955–56* (London: Oxford University Press, 1960), p. 399.

77. Ibid.

78. Beatrice P. Lamb, *India: A World in Transition* (London: Pall Mall Press, 1963), p. 311–312.

79. Van Ness, *Revolution and Chinese Foreign Policy,* p. 139.

80. Ibid.

81. Gittings, *World and China,* p. 261.

82. See *Afro-Asian Solidarity Against Imperialism* (Beijing: Foreign Languages Press, 1964), p. 274.

83. Based on the author's research and discussions in London.

84. Ibid.

85. *China and Asia: An Analysis of China's Recent Policy Toward Neighboring States,* Report by the Foreign Affairs and National Defense Division, Congressional Research Service, Library of Congress (Washington, D.C.: Government Printing Office, 1979), p. 14.

86. Congressional Quarterly Services, *China and U.S. Far East Policy, 1945–1966,* p. 99.

87. Reprinted in ibid., p. 102.

88. *New York Times,* June 3, 1961.

89. Based on the author's reading of the unpublished minutes of talks between Chairman Mao, Premier Zhou Enlai, President Liu Shaoqi and the Pakistani President Ayub Khan and his foreign minister, Z. A. Bhutto, in Beijing in March 1965. The author had also exclusive interviews with Premier Zhou Enlai and President Ayub and Foreign Minister Bhutto.

90. New China News Agency, September 2, 1963; see also Congressional

Quarterly Service, *China and U.S. Far East Policy, 1945-1966,* pp. 126-127.

91. Quoted in Coral Bell, "The Foreign Policy of China," in *The Foreign Policies of the Powers,* ed. F. S. Northedge (London: Faber and Faber, 1968), p. 139.

92. Ibid.

93. Congressional Quarterly Service, *China and U.S. Far East Policy, 1945-1966,* p. 147.

94. Based on the author's reading of unpublished documents and papers of the government of Pakistan, 1947-1971.

3
Sino-American Relations: The Profound Breakthrough

Judged by any criteria, President Richard M. Nixon's announcement on July 15, 1971, that he was accepting an invitation from the People's Republic of China to go to Communist China and talk with its leaders was the result of an epoch-making diplomatic feat. Nixon's subsequent visit to China on February 21–28, 1972, followed two years of top-secret and serious negotiations channeled through friendly countries like France, Romania, and Pakistan – and toward the end, mainly through Pakistan. Nixon's visit to China was described by him as "a journey for peace, peace not just for our generation, but for future generations."[1] It was the same Richard Nixon who as late as 1960, in a television debate with John F. Kennedy, had described the threats from China with his usual rhetoric: "Now what do the Chinese communists want? They don't want just Quemoy and Matsu. They don't want just Formosa. They want the world."[2] In 1966, the U.S. House of Representatives, in a major report on U.S. policy toward Asia, had made the following conclusions about Communist China:

> Communist China is not interested in attaining peaceful accommodation with the outside world. . . . Communist China's expansionist policies pose a dual threat: on the one hand to our military security arrangements in the Western Pacific and in the Far East, and on the other hand to the continuing economic and political development, within the framework of national independence and peaceful cooperation, of the countries on the periphery of the mainland.[3]

Similarly, China and its leaders had looked upon the U.S. policy, though not the people of the United States, as being the major threat to China's security and independence. In the Chinese view, the United States had pursued an unremitting hostility toward the People's Republic of China for twenty years (1949–1969). That was how they regarded the U.S. effort to impose a trade quarantine on China for twenty years, and that was their view, too, of the sending of U.S. troops north of the 38th parallel in Korea, the positioning of the Seventh Fleet between the mainland and Taiwan, and the U.S. sponsorship of an effort at the United Nations to label China "the aggressor in Korea."[4]

When Pakistan's first military President, Ayub Khan, went to China in March 1965, Chairman Mao and Premier Zhou Enlai told him that in "the future global war, the main target will be China; in the next global war, the United States, USSR, Japan, and probably India will be fighting against China."[5] Ayub was to come to the United States following his state visits to China and the Soviet Union in 1965, and the Chinese leaders asked Ayub to tell the Americans that the United States had "committed aggression in Vietnam and it must withdraw before there could be any peace." But, significantly, the Chinese leaders requested the Pakistani president to tell President Johnson that "as long as the U.S.A. would not extend war in Vietnam, China will not enter into it." Chairman Mao also made a distinction between the different circumstances of the Korean and Vietnam wars. Ayub was specifically asked to convey the following message to President Johnson: "China will not take any provocative measure as it has proved by its attitude in Taiwan on which it had every right, but China will abide by its international obligations. . . . The United States should have no doubt about China's intentions."[6]

By the mid 1960s, both China and the United States seemed to be beginning to realize the futility and dire consequences of the era of confrontation between the world's most powerful and most populous countries, and a number of factors were responsible for the changing attitudes of the two great nations toward each other. Just as the Chinese leaders Mao and Zhou Enlai wanted to assure the Americans of their peaceful intentions, so the Americans began to have second thoughts about the risks and threats connected with Red China. Mr. Nixon, in an important article in *Foreign Affairs* in 1967, referred to the potential role of China in world affairs, particularly in the Asian-Pacific region.

> Any American policy toward Asia must come urgently to grips with the reality of China. . . . Taking the long view, we simply can not afford to leave China forever outside the family of nations, there to mature its fantasies, cherish its hates and threaten its neighbors. There is no place on this small planet for a billion of its potentially most able people to live in angry isolation.[7]

When Nixon became the U.S. president in 1969, he applied himself to the great task of breaking the China deadlock.

The bipolar world of the 1950s and 1960s, which was based on the power and strength of the two superpowers—the United States and the

USSR – was coming to an end, and it was in the process of being replaced by a multipolar world with five major powers – the United States, USSR, PRC, Japan, and Western Europe. World peace and stability required understanding and cooperation among the major powers, and if full cooperation and understanding were not attainable, it would be better if world peace were promoted through a series of balance-of-power arrangements. Communist China could no longer be ignored, nor was it considered desirable to do so. On the contrary, the alleged threats from the PRC were reviewed and reassessed, and after considerable reappraisal, the United States considered it desirable to establish links between Washington and Beijing. Toward the end of the 1960s, the global political scene was in the process of great transformations as a result of the changed perceptions of the world situation by three major powers – the United States, the USSR, and the PRC. What was happening was that "the cold war which is the struggle between political ideas fought by means short of open and general conflict" was being replaced by a "new alliance of convenience."[8] In a global triangular balance of power between Washington, Moscow, and Beijing, it seemed possible that Washington and Beijing could cooperate on a limited basis. Similarly, there could be talks of coexistence or détente between Washington and Moscow. A major realignment of the three major powers was beginning to take place.

What made the prospect of a new realignment possible? What led to the destruction of the myth of a monolithic worldwide communist movement, controlled and guided by Moscow but actively supported by Beijing? What led Washington to try to end the policy of containment of Red China, and what led the PRC to think that it might coexist and negotiate with the "imperialist United States"?

By the time Richard Nixon entered the White House in January 1969, the possibilities of a new China policy were apparent, and Nixon did not lose time in taking the great initiative to try to enact it. Also, Chairman Mao was ready to respond to Nixon's gestures.

China's Changing Attitude Toward
the United States (1969–1971)

Ideology, nationalism, and the need for economic development are important factors in determining a country's relations with any major power, but security and strategic considerations are always given priority over other factors. China is no exception to this rule of international politics. Although the PRC considers itself an ideological state, China, no less than any other country, gives the greatest attention to obtaining more security and in strengthening its strategic options in the pursuit of its foreign policy goals. So China's relations with the United States in the late 1960s and in the 1970s were governed by security and strategic considerations.

As pointed out earlier, China had had to face serious security problems since the founding of the communist regime in 1949. The initial security problems were due to China's confrontation with the most powerful nation, the United States; then from the late 1950s to 1969, China had strained relationships with both of the superpowers. Mao told Ayub in March 1965 that "the United States and the Soviet Union are now trying to have some sort of understanding so as to follow a policy of containment against China,"[9] and Mao's assessment was not without some basis. The United States, in the 1960s under Presidents Kennedy and Johnson, seemed to be hoping that it could come to a wide-ranging understanding with the Soviet Union, covering as many as possible of the issues on which they were at loggerheads with one another, so "they could both be freer to deal with what then looked like the explosive influence of a revolutionary China."[10] Johnson seemed to make that clear in October 1966 — five months after the Cultural Revolution broke out in China — when he offered the Russians the sort of settlement in Europe that later became the basis of Willy Brandt's *Ostpolitik*.[11]

At the end of the 1960s, the U.S.-USSR "understanding" showed its very limited scope, and the Sino-Soviet rift took a very serious turn.

Between March 2 and March 15, 1969, serious armed clashes took place between Soviet and Chinese frontier guards along the Ussuri River, causing considerable casualties. Conflicting accounts of the armed clashes were issued by the two sides, and both governments exchanged strongly worded notes of protest. The Soviet note demanded an immediate investigation and punishment of those people responsible for the incident, and it threatened to rebuff "reckless and provocative actions on the part of the Chinese authorities." Similarly, the Chinese note demanded punishment of the culprits and reserved the right to deliver resolute counterblows if the Soviet government continued to provoke armed conflicts.[12]

The press in both countries began a sharp exchange of polemics. Beijing's *People's Daily* described Khrushchev, Kosygin, Brezhnev, and others as "a herd of swine" and "new czars," and the *Red Star* in Moscow denounced Mao Zedong as a "traitor to the sacred cause of Communism . . . tainted with human blood" and compared him to Hitler.[13]

Western estimates of the number of Soviet troops on the Sino-Soviet border were nearly forty Soviet divisions, many of which had recently been transferred from Eastern Europe, while there were between fifty and sixty Chinese divisions, or about 600,000 men. More alarming was the report that the Kremlin leaders were planning a preemptive attack on the Chinese nuclear plants in Xinjiang Province. In his dispatches during June and July 1969, the Pakistani ambassador in Moscow reported that the Kremlin leaders had consulted with Russia's East European allies about a contingency plan to destroy China's nuclear capabilities, and Pakistan's diplomatic sources in Beijing indicated China's grave concern about such a preemptive strike by the Russians.[14] The Sino-Soviet relationship seemed to be moving toward the brink of war.

The situation in 1969 was truly alarming for the Chinese as the Soviets might have been tempted to use force against China on the pattern of the Soviet military intervention in Czechoslovakia in accordance with the so-called Brezhnev doctrine. Under that doctrine, the Soviet Union sought to justify the use of force to prevent any socialist country from straying from the Moscow brand of communism, and Soviet propaganda was already depicting China as recklessly irrational, as demonstrated by the excesses of the Cultural Revolution.[15] In a discussion with Ross Terrill in 1971, Zhou Enlai referred to John Foster Dulles's policy of an "encirclement" of China, and he added, "now Dulles has a successor in our northern neighbor."[16]

There were about 1 million Russian troops on China's northern borders in 1969, as there had been 1 million U.S. troops near the eastern and southern borders of China in 1968. But by 1969, China felt the threat from Moscow was much greater than that from Washington. Robert Scalapino described the Chinese predicament in 1969 as follows: "When confronted with what they perceived to be a grave threat from the Soviet Union, Mao and his followers found themselves without significant allies, without access to a world forum and most importantly perhaps, without the type of flexibility which relations with another major power might make possible."[17] By early 1971, more Russian troops were deployed against China than against the NATO countries in Europe. It was the largest deployment of military forces "capable of affecting the world balance of power ever to have occurred without a major war."[18]

New Soviet Moves to Contain and Isolate China in Asia

The threat of a full-scale Sino-Soviet conflict subsided in due course, but the cold war between the two communist giants continued with renewed vigor. The Kremlin's policy to contain China was evident in new Soviet diplomatic initiatives with nations on China's periphery, such as Podgorny's visit to North Korea and Mongolia and Kosygin's visit to India, Pakistan, and Afghanistan in 1969. M. S. Kapist, head of the South Asian Division of the Soviet Foreign Office, visited Burma, Laos, Cambodia, and Japan, and the Mongolian deputy foreign minister's visits to

Burma, Cambodia, Nepal, India, and Afghanistan in April 1969 were a part of the Soviet-Mongolian campaign against China.

Soon after the Sino-Soviet border clashes on the Ussuri River in March 1969, the Kremlin leaders initiated two significant plans as a part of their policy to contain China: Kosygin's proposal for regional economic cooperation and Brezhnev's plan for a collective security system in Asia.

In early 1969, Kosygin, while on a visit to Kabul, proposed a regional economic group consisting of Afghanistan, India, Iran, Pakistan, and the Soviet Union. The idea of regional cooperation among those countries was not a new one. The United States, which had resumed economic aid to Pakistan and India in 1967 after the 1965 Indo-Pakistani War, had encouraged the idea, and Pakistan had supported it as soon as it understood that regional cooperation would help its own development, as well as that of Iran and Turkey. But Kosygin's apparently innocuous plan for an economic alliance had political overtones: It was intended to consolidate the Soviet Union's position in relation to China in South Asia.

One of the ironies of the Soviet Union's feud with China is that it led the Soviets to follow the very policy, espoused by John Foster Dulles, that it had condemned for more than sixteen years – the propagation of military pacts.

The Soviets had already started to think in terms of a security arrangement for Asia early in 1969 after the fighting on the Ussuri River. Two months after that conflict, on May 29, 1969, the Soviet newspaper *Izvestia* published an article signed by V. V. Matveyev, "A Filled Vacuum," and that article gave the first, albeit rather vague, account of a collective security plan for Asia. Matveyev referred to the fact that the British were to withdraw from their bases in the Persian Gulf area, the Far East, and the Indian Ocean area by the end of 1971, and he ridiculed the concept of a vacuum: "A vacuum is an empty space . . . the use of this term in reference to our planet is altogether inappropriate today." He also referred to the "machinations of the imperialistic, expansionist forces" of the Americans, Australians, and Japanese as well as of those of the Chinese: "Mao Tse-tung and his associates have definite designs on several countries in the area while supporting the notorious 'vacuum' thesis." He then proceeded to state there would be no vacuum to fill. He concluded that India, Pakistan, Afghanistan, Burma, Cambodia, Singapore, and other Asian countries were making efforts to consolidate their sovereignty and to strengthen their economic autonomy. He also stated that the Asian nations could best resist interference from foreign powers by setting up a "foundation for collective security" in the region.

Matveyev's article was followed by a lengthy speech by Leonid Brezhnev at the International Congress of Communist and Workers' Parties on June 7, 1969. Brezhnev began his speech with an attack on imperialism: "We are in unanimous agreement that imperialism as a social system has been and remains the principal obstacle in the historically inevitable movement toward the triumph of freedom, peace, and democracy."[19] He then continued with a similar attack on Maoism. Brezhnev claimed that "the socialist orientation of a number of young African and Asian nations is an important achievement." What is the best guarantee for the young nations of Asia against those people "who would like to bind the chains of a new slavery around the young national states?" Brezhnev, who had consolidated the theory of neocolonialism in Eastern Europe after the Soviet military incursion into Czechoslovakia in 1966 with his concept of a "socialist commonwealth of nations," gave a new formula to the Asian countries to protect their independence and sovereignty: a system of collective security in Asia. After two decades of constant preaching against military pacts or blocs, Brezhnev now found virtues in this type of military alliance for the Asian countries.

Neither Brezhnev's speech nor Matveyev's article gave any definite idea as to the nature, purpose, and tasks of an Asian collective security plan. Its basic content or purpose was deliberately kept vague because, so far, the Brezhnev plan was nothing more than a trial balloon. For the next few months, the Russians contented themselves with such high-sounding phrases as "noninterference in the domestic affairs of other countries," "nonencroachment of borders," and "extensive development of economy." But it soon became apparent to the Soviet Union's southern Asian neighbors, like Pakistan (which had begun a new era of normalizing relations with Moscow in the mid 1960s), that the Soviet Union was assiduously working toward economic and military arrangements that would serve the Soviet policy of containing China and taking the place of the United States in the Asian-Pacific regions.

After the public announcement of the collective security plan for Asia in May and June 1969, the Kremlin leaders began to carry out a carrot-and-stick policy toward South and Southeast Asian countries to induce them to join the Soviet Union's economic alliance and collective security plan.

The Chinese government and press began a strong campaign against the new Soviet policy. Around the time of the third ministerial meeting of the Association of Southeast Asian Nations (ASEAN) held in Malaysia on December 16–17, 1969, Soviet propaganda revived the idea of a collective security plan for Asia. On December 14, 1969, Moscow Radio said that a new regional alliance should be formed with the assistance of and participation by the Soviet Union as that nation had territories both in Europe and in Asia. The aim seemed to be to enlist the support of as many of the Asian states as possible, including such allies of the West as Thailand and the Philippines. On December 26, 1969, Moscow Radio appealed to Japan to play an important role in Russia's collective security plan for Asia, even though Japan had already expressed its coolness toward the Soviet proposal.

Most of the South and Southeast Asian countries, as well as Japan, were unwilling to aid the Soviet Union's policy of containing China. They preferred a policy of nonalignment in the new cold war between China and Russia, the same policy they had followed in the 1950s during the cold war between the United States and the Soviet Union.

The Kremlin leaders never missed an opportunity to push their proposal for Asia's security during 1969 and 1970, although the Asian reaction was not enthusiastic. Moscow's disavowals that the plan was directed against any one state or group of states, and its efforts to play down the possible military implications, did not remove the impression in many Asian countries that the plan was primarily aimed at isolating and containing China, and Chinese diplomatic efforts were put into high gear to counter what was termed the "Soviet version of SEATO."

Following a conference of Soviet envoys in Moscow, the Soviet ambassador to Pakistan called on President Yahya and on the Pakistani foreign secretary in an attempt to sell the Brezhnev scheme. He described the proposed plan in lofty terms, stressing such features as "noninterference in internal affairs of signatory countries" and "economic, cultural, and scientific cooperation." The ambassador pointed out to the foreign secretary that the inadequacy of the economic collaboration under SEATO and the Central Treaty Organization (CENTO) was in contrast to the more worthwhile collaboration possible under the Soviet plan.[20]

However, upon being questioned about the security aspects of the plan, the Soviet ambassador was forced to reveal its main purpose, which concerned not so much economic cooperation as the containment of China. The specifics of the proposed security agreement also made plain the following: The signatories should not enter into any alliance, formal or informal, with a third country that might be hostile to any member nation, nor should they make any commitment inconsistent with the proposed security plan for Asia. The signatory nations would consult with each other in the event of any aggression by a third party. The anti-Chinese slant was also indicated by the fact that Brezhnev had announced the plan only three months after the most serious armed conflict to date on the Sino-Soviet border. Yahya wanted to know what help, if any, the Brezhnev plan would offer in the case of an aggression committed by one member country against another, such as would be the case if there were a repetition of the 1965 Indo-Pakistani War. The answer was that "the Asian security plan will put an end to such regional conflicts as those encouraged by the imperialist countries like the United States and by expansionist nations like China."[21]

China has always been convinced that it was the target of the Soviet-inspired Asian security system. When Brezhnev announced the plan in June 1969, China denounced it in unqualified terms and expressed concern to its South Asian friend, Pakistan. But the Chinese approach to Pakistan did not resemble the blunt statement of Soviet Defense Minister Marshal Andrei A. Grechko, who threatened Pakistan for "flirting with Mao." The Chinese leaders politely warned the Pakistanis, "We know the Russians better, just as you know the Indians better." Nor did the Chinese try to get any information from President Yahya, to whom the Russians gave an adequate account of their proposed security plan in June 1970. The Pakistanis gave unqualified assurances to China that Pakistan would never join any Russian-sponsored security plan that was directly or indirectly aimed against Beijing.[22]

President Yahya, as a friendly gesture to China, related to the Chinese ambassador, Zhang Dong, the substance of Yahya's talks with the Russians during his state visit to the Soviet Union in June 1970. The Chinese had other sources of information, but Yahya was perhaps one of the earliest. China's opposition to the proposal for an Asian collective security system was criticized on October 11, 1972, in a major article in *Izvestia* by V. Kudryavtsev, author of several other articles about the plan. Referring to the "correctness" of the principle of a respect for sovereignty and the inviolability of frontiers, which was clearly intended to rule out Chinese and Japanese territorial claims, Kudryavtsev said that opposition by the Chinese leaders and Japanese politicians demonstrated the truth of the saying that "an uneasy conscience betrays itself." Chinese counterattacks have frequently referred to the alleged military threat from the Soviet Union and have created the impression that Moscow has great power ambitions in Asia.

The Soviet military and diplomatic moves against China forced the Chinese to make major changes in their global policy, putting an end to their self-imposed diplomatic isolation during the Cultural Revolution in 1966–1969. During the last years of the Mao–Zhou Enlai era (1970–1976), China's foreign policy goals evidently included (1) improving relations with the United States as a counterbalance to the power of the Soviet Union and (2) normalizing relations with South, Southeast, and East Asian countries, particularly Japan. It may be added here that apart from the fear of a Soviet invasion in 1969–1970, the Chinese were also worried about the potential military and political role of Japan. The Chinese policymakers seemed to have discerned what they believed to be a U.S. or a U.S.-Japanese plan for Northeast Asia, and they thought that after the U.S. disengagement from the Asian mainland under the "Nixon doctrine" of 1969, Japan, in cooperation with the United States, would play a political and military role commensurate with its economic power.[23] They concluded that better relations with the United States would satisfy two desirable objectives: to counteract the threat from Moscow and to reduce the danger of a future Japanese remilitarization.[24]

In the meantime, great changes were also taking place in the U.S. assessment of the threats from the expansionist designs of Red China. It was realized, in the context of the many changes in the Asian-Pacific region, that despite China's ideological dogmatism or apparent militant posture, that country had shown remarkable realism and pragmatism in concrete situations.[25] The Maoist regime was, by 1970, no longer considered as a "pressing" or most dangerous phenomenon, but as a government with which the United States might usefully seek a normalization of relations. President Nixon in his first report to the U.S. Congress on foreign policy in 1970 declared that the United States should take what steps it could toward "improved practical relations" with Communist China, with the aim of establishing a "more normal and constructive relationship." He looked forward to the day when Beijing would "reenter the international community" and added that "the principles underlying our relations with Communist China are similar to those governing our policies toward the U.S.S.R."[26]

President Nixon also took some practical measures, though minor ones, such as relaxing regulations regarding travel to China by U.S. citizens and trade with the communist regime in China by U.S. subsidiaries abroad—all direct trade between the United States and China was still barred.

A U.S. table tennis team visited China in April 1971 and was greeted by Premier Zhou Enlai with the words that their visit had "opened a new page in the relations of the Chinese and American people." As early as 1960, Zhou had told the U.S. author Edgar Snow that "there is no conflict of basic interests between the peoples of China and the United States and friendship will eventually prevail."[27]

Top-Secret Negotiations Between Washington and Peking (1969-1971)

President Nixon was making friendly gestures toward and friendly comments about China in his speeches and comments at his press conferences, and his administration was taking some practical steps by easing regulations regarding travel and trade with Communist China in 1969–1971. But far more important were his top-secret negotiations with the Chinese leaders in Beijing. Those negotiations were carried on with the aid of friendly countries such as France, Romania, and Pakistan, but it was Pakistan's President Yahya Khan who turned out to be the main channel for the negotiations between Washington and Beijing during this formative phase of the new Sino-American relationship.[28] It was from

Pakistan and with Pakistan's active assistance that Henry Kissinger made his first and top-secret visit to Beijing in July 1971, and when President Nixon's own visit to China was announced on July 15, 1971, Nixon expressed his appreciation for Yahya's services in a handwritten letter dated August 7, 1971: "Through this personal note I want you to know that without your personal assistance, this profound breakthrough in relations between the United States and the PRC would never have been accomplished."[29]

During a twenty-two-hour visit to Pakistan on August 1–2, 1969, President Nixon asked Pakistan's President Yahya Kahn to act as a "courier" between Beijing and Washington and to ask the Chinese leaders what their reaction to Nixon's new initiatives to normalize relations with China might be. President Yahya was delighted to have this opportunity as it meant not only that the Sino-Pakistani relationship was approved of by the United States, but also that the U.S. president wanted to utilize it to improve U.S. ties with the PRC. It is not known why Nixon chose the Pakistani president for the role of courier. Nixon had known Ayub Khan and had seemed to have friendly relations with him, but Yahya was altogether unknown to Nixon and was also a novice in diplomacy. Of course, Pakistan had played a significant role in establishing diplomatic relations between China and a number of countries, including Canada, Iran, and Turkey, and Nixon knew that, of all the noncommunist countries, Pakistan had the most cordial and intimate relations with Beijing and, at the same time, Pakistan cherished and valued its friendship with the United States. So Nixon's choice was not unwise or inappropriate.

Yahya had an informal discussion about the Sino-American relationship with his top advisers but did not divulge his grand assignment, because Nixon had urged Yahya to carry out the assignment with "utmost secrecy." The normal diplomatic channel was to be avoided; neither the U.S. State Department nor the Pakistani Foreign Ministry would be taken into confidence. Nixon was applying "top-secret diplomacy," and I do not know how many people in Washington knew about the assignment or, particularly, the substance of the Chinese messages channeled through the Pakistani president to the White House.

Yahya began his job most secretly and also successfully even though there had been initial doubts about China's reaction. Just a few days after Nixon's visit to Pakistan, a top Pakistani Foreign Ministry official who became foreign secretary in January 1970, Sultan Khan, predicted that the Chinese would not react favorably. Sultan Khan, Pakistan's ambassador in Beijing until late 1968, told me that China maintained the view that just as the Indians did not really want to improve relations with Pakistan but were interested in talks only to demonstrate their "peaceful intentions," so the Americans wanted to talk about peripheral issues such as cultural relations, trade, etc., but not about substantial issues such as Taiwan, a Chinese seat in the United Nations, or diplomatic recognition. But Sultan Khan could not appreciate the changed attitude that had come to prevail in both Washington and Beijing.

So the messages began to carry cheerful words for Nixon, and Yahya was, of course, greatly delighted by the happy development which enabled Pakistan to consolidate its ties with both Beijing and Washington.

The Channel

The Chinese ambassador in Pakistan, Zhang Dong, carried the messages directly to Yahya rather than sending them through the Foreign Ministry, and Zhang Dong had free and unlimited access to the president's house. Yahya wanted to write down the substance of the messages himself and keep them in his own custody until he sent them, through his ambassador in Washington, Aga Hilali, in doubled-sealed envelopes (not to be opened by Hilali), to National Security Adviser Henry Kissinger and President Nixon.

The Pakistani president's role and the highest appreciation he received from Washington and Beijing are not yet fully known to the outside world. As a member of Yahya's cabinet in 1969–1971, I had full access to the messages exchanged between China and Pakistan, which led to Kissinger's and Nixon's visits to China, and Yahya took me into his confidence about his grand assignment as "courier" between Washington and Beijing.

Let us now examine the style and contents of the Sino-American negotiations conducted through Pakistani President Yahya Khan.

Contents of the Messages Exchanged
Through the Pakistani President

In October 1969, Yahya wanted Nixon to tell him the specific points the United States would like him to take up with the Chinese. The reply from the White House—Henry Kissinger sending the U.S. replies through the Pakistani ambassador in Washington, Aga Hilali—was that the United States was anxious to break the U.S.-China deadlock. Yahya could not as yet get any specific issues to take up with the Chinese premier. The chief of the Pakistani army, General Hamid, went to Beijing on October 1, 1969, and Yahya asked him to talk to the Chinese premier. Zhou wanted to know something specific, so Yahya again sought to find out what measures the Americans were prepared to take as concrete proof of the U.S. intentions to break the Sino-American deadlock. On October 10, Kissinger told Yahya to inform the Chinese that "the United States is withdrawing the two destroyers which are patrolling the Formosa straits," but no other specific points or concrete proof, such as was sought by Beijing, was as yet forthcoming from the White House. The initial messages on both sides were highly noncommittal and cautious.

By February 1970, Yahya was in a position to inform Nixon and Kissinger that "the initiatives taken by the United States in recent months have encouraged the Chinese." Yahya further added that according to "current Chinese assessment, there is no collusion between the Soviet Union and the United States against China." It might be added here that the Chinese leaders, Mao and Zhou, had told Yahya's predecessor, Ayub, in March 1965, that there was a collusion between Moscow and Washington against Beijing. Thanks to Nixon's new initiatives, China no longer had such grave fears, and that was a highly favorable factor in the emerging Sino-American ties. There was also a very significant point in Yahya's message to Washington in February 1970: the "Chinese will be very sensitive to any conclusion that their willingness for any meaningful dialogue with the United States is a reflection of any weakness on their part or any outcome of their fears about Russia." The Chinese are a proud people. The Chinese response to Nixon's gestures was the product of the near-war situation between the USSR and the PRC and Nixon and Kissinger realized that fully; yet the Chinese were highly sensitive about bargaining from a position of weakness. Yahya pointed out in his message, "The Chinese response is likely to be very measured and cautious, but China appears inclined toward a meaningful dialogue with the United States covering all matters that divide the two countries." Yahya ended with the comment, "Negotiations will be hard and difficult."

Nixon replied promptly to Yahya on February 23, 1970, assuring the Chinese that "the White House will scrupulously avoid making any such statement that the present dialogue between the United States and China is due to China's fears of Russia." At this stage, Nixon asked the Chinese, through Yahya, if Beijing would agree "to open a direct White House channel," adding that the "existence of such a channel will not be known outside the White House," but the Chinese preferred the channel through the Pakistani president. During this period, Yahya explored the possibility of Zhou Enlai's visiting Pakistan on the occasion of the inauguration of Pakistan's second ordnance factory at Dacca (then the capital of East Pakistan, now Bangladesh), but Zhou could not yet leave China, presumably because of the internal situation following the Cultural Revolution. The Chinese minister Guo Moro did visit Pakistan in the spring of 1970, and although Zhou Enlai could not go to Pakistan, he sent an important message through his cabinet colleague, Guo.

Even at this stage, the suggestion was made by the White House that the two sides should meet in Washington or in Beijing for direct talks, and a similar proposal had been discussed at the U.S.-China ambassadorial talks in Warsaw in January 1970. China's initial reply was noncommittal, and the Chinese wanted to confine the direct talks to the Taiwan issue while the United States suggested direct talks on "the broad range of issues which lie between the United States and the PRC." In reply to Nixon's suggestion for direct talks, Zhou Enlai asserted, "China has always been willing and has always tried to negotiate by peaceful means all issues dividing the two countries." But Zhou, stressing the crucial importance of the Taiwan issue, also wrote: "Taiwan and straits of Taiwan are inalienable parts of China which have been occupied by the United States for the last two decades. Negotiations and talks have been going on with no results whatsoever." Zhou then added, "In order to discuss the subject of vacation of China's territory called Taiwan, a special envoy from President Nixon will be welcome in Peking." In order to emphasize the issue, Zhou told Yahya "this reply is not from me alone, but from Chairman Mao and Vice-Chairman Lin Piao as well."

The letter was written in early 1970, when Lin Biao and his leftist group were still in power, and it could not have been easy to convince Lin Biao to accept a proposal for direct talks with the Americans. Yet this exchange was the beginning of the process that led to Kissinger's visit to Beijing in July 1971. Gradually, China began to show interest in "a Sino-American dialogue on a higher level," as was hinted in some messages from Zhou in February and March 1970. It was clear, however, that the United States would not like to confine the proposed direct negotiations to the Taiwan issue. As pointed out in another message from the White House in early 1970, if the talks were to be meaningful, they must "encompass other subjects designed to improve relations between the two countries and reduce tensions."

Throughout 1970, messages were exchanged between Washington and Beijing through the Pakistani president. Contacts were made through other sources also, and perhaps messages were also sent through other channels, but the Pakistani president was not kept informed of those contacts or of messages channeled through other sources. It is doubtful if any substantial exchanges of messages were made after late 1970 except through Yahya.

The process of the negotiations was complicated by the escalation of the fighting in Cambodia in the summer of 1970 and Prince Sihanouk's taking shelter in Beijing. In some of the messages from Beijing during this period, there was a revival of Chinese doubts about the sincerity or seriousness of the United States. Yahya was upset and did his best to assuage those doubts. The mutual need and desire for an improvement in the Sino-American ties, both in Washington and in Beijing, made it possible for the negotiations to survive such temporary setbacks.

In October–November 1970, Yahya also traveled, first to Washington and then to Beijing. Yahya went to the United States in October 1970, ostensibly to attend the twenty-fifth anniversary of the founding of the United Nations, but really for direct discussions with Nixon and Kissinger about his mission as a go-between for Washington and Beijing. On October 24, 1970, Nixon gave a grand banquet in honor of the visiting heads of state or government, including Pakistani President Yahya and Romania's President Nicolae Ceauşescu, and Yahya had an hour-long session with Nixon and Kissinger the next day. At that time, the idea of a visit to Beijing by one of Nixon's special envoys was discussed.

Yahya's next important assignment was to go to Beijing in November, and I was a member of Yahya's entourage on that trip. In Beijing, Yahya had a grand reception as thousands of Chinese greeted their "esteemed friend" from Pakistan. Yahya had meetings with both Zhou Enlai and Chairman Mao, but it was mostly Zhou who carried on discussions with Yahya at the state guest house where Yahya and his entourage were staying. The exclusive talks between Yahya and Zhou lasted for at least fifteen to eighteen hours during the Pakistani president's five-day stay in Beijing. Although it was a state visit, Yahya did not go on the usual sight-seeing tours, did no traveling outside Beijing, and, except for two state banquets—one given by Zhou and a return one given by Yahya—the usual state-visit events were avoided so the serious and businesslike discussions on the emerging Sino-American relationship could take place.

After Yahya's talks with President Nixon in Washington in October and with Chairman Mao and Premier Zhou in November, a number of important messages were exchanged between Washington and Beijing via Pakistan. In one of his letters during this period, Zhou wrote to Yahya, "We have had messages from the United States from different sources in the past," but "the United States knows that Pakistan is a great friend of China, and therefore we attach importance to messages from Pakistan." Referring to Nixon's proposal to send a special envoy to Beijing, Zhou wrote, "This is the first time that a proposal has come from a Head of State through a Head to a Head."

On December 16, 1970, Nixon sent a proposal to Zhou Enlai through Yahya expressing a willingness to send one of his special envoys to Beijing to have direct discussions with the Chinese leaders on all issues, including the question of Taiwan. The proposal from the White House also indicated a willingness for "a preliminary meeting at an early date at such a place convenient to both sides" to discuss arrangements relating to a "high-level discussion in Peking." The names of retired U.S. Ambassador Robert Murphy, Ambassador David Bruce, and former Governor

Thomas E. Dewey were suggested as the U.S. representative for such a preliminary meeting and Pakistan's interim capital, Rawalpindi, was suggested as the probable meeting place. It was stressed that if President Nixon's special envoy to Beijing were to be of such high standing as Henry Kissinger, "discussion should not be confined to Taiwan, but embrace all matters connected with the Sino-American relations and to reduce tensions." But, in view of the importance China attached to the Taiwan issue in the U.S.-China bilateral relationship, the December 16 note from the White House assured China that "it will not be difficult to comply with the Chinese request for withdrawing the U.S. military forces from Taiwan"—a step that could be taken, without much difficulty, under the Nixon doctrine of 1969.

On April 24, 1971, Zhou Enlai sent a letter through Yahya that finally set the stage for Henry Kissinger's historic visit to Beijing via Pakistan in July 1971. Zhou wrote:

> At present, contacts between the people of China and the United States are being reviewed. . . . If, however, the relations between China and the United States are to be restored *fundamentally*, the United States must withdraw all its armed forces from China's Taiwan and Taiwan's straits area. A solution to this *crucial question* can be found only through direct discussion between high-level, responsible persons of the two countries. The Chinese government therefore, reaffirms its willingness to receive *publicly* in Peking a special envoy of the President of the United States such as Dr. Henry Kissinger or the Secretary of State, Mr. William Rogers, for a direct meeting and discussion. [Italics added]

In order to not give the impression that the Chinese were overenthusiastic for such a public meeting, Zhou quickly added in the message, "If the U.S. president considers that the time is not yet ripe, the matter may be deferred to a later date." Regarding the suggestion for a preliminary meeting to discuss the details of a high-level meeting in Beijing, Zhou expressed the hope that "procedures and details of the high-level meeting can easily be made through the good offices of our esteemed friend, President Yahya Khan."

President Nixon was delighted with the contents of Zhou Enlai's message of April 24, 1971, and sent a prompt reply to him through Yahya on April 29, 1971. Nixon wrote to Yahya: "I would be grateful if you would thank Premier Chou for his message of April 24, 1971, sent through you. I appreciate its constructive, positive and forthcoming nature." This reply was just a warm acknowledgment of Zhou's constructive message; the detailed reply was sent through Yahya later.

In the meantime, Nixon asked Yahya to convey a request to Zhou as though the suggestion had come from Yahya and not from Nixon himself. The so-called request from Yahya to Zhou was, Would the Chinese government please not issue any visa to any U.S. political leader, either Republican or Democrat, until Nixon could send his reply to Zhou's message of April 24 and until the special envoy was selected by Nixon? The Chinese had no difficulty in ascertaining the source of the request and that its aim was to maintain the secrecy of the negotiations, which the Chinese fully agreed to.

Toward the Summit Meeting

By April and May of 1971, the complicated, slow, and top-secret negotiations had made so much progress that not only the visit of President Nixon's special envoy, Henry Kissinger, was guaranteed, but Nixon's own visit was also a real possibility. I had a lengthy discussion in May 1971 with the then Chinese ambassador in Pakistan, Zhang Dong, who used to personally deliver Zhou's messages to Yahya to be transmitted to Nixon, and Zhang Dong was confident not only of Kissinger's visit, but of a visit by President Nixon himself. The U.S. author Edgar Snow, in an article in *Life* magazine during this period, wrote that Chairman Mao would be willing to receive President Nixon in Beijing either as U.S. president or as a tourist. Secretary of State William Rogers, who was abroad and was not aware of Zhou's constructive message of April 24 and Nixon's appreciative acknowledgment of it on April 29, made some comments on Edgar Snow's article. When asked about it in London, Rogers replied that Mao's remarks to Edgar Snow could not be taken seriously; it was a casual remark, not a proper invitation. Nixon and Kissinger thought that Rogers's remarks in London might offend the Chinese at this crucial stage of the delicate negotiations, and Nixon sought to soften the situation at a press conference on April 29. When asked to comment about Chairman Mao's invitation to him, Nixon said, "I am not referring to any invitation, I am referring only to a hope and an expectation that at some time in my life and in some capacity, which of course, does not put any deadline on when I would do it, I hope to go to mainland China."[30] Nixon especially requested that Yahya convey Nixon's comments at the press conference, which had been made to remove any misunderstanding that might have been caused by Rogers's remarks in London. Nixon's concern showed how sensitive the negotiating process was.

Nixon's detailed reply to Zhou's message of April 24 was made on May 17, and Yahya handed over the message to the Chinese ambassador, Zhang Dong, on May 19. In his reply, Nixon said that he agreed with the premier that "direct high-level negotiations are necessary to resolve the issues dividing the United States and the PRC," and, because of the importance he attached to the normalization of the Sino-American relationship, Nixon hinted that he would accept an invitation of the Chinese government to visit Beijing for "direct conversation with the Chinese leaders. At such a meeting each side will be free to raise any issue of principal concern to it." In order to prepare for a summit meeting in Beijing and to establish contact with the Chinese leaders, Nixon proposed that Kissinger should have a preliminary secret meeting with the Chinese leaders. Kissinger would discuss the agenda of Nixon's visit and would begin a preliminary exchange of news on all subjects of mutual interest.

It was agreed by both sides that Kissinger's visit would be arranged through the good offices of Yahya, and Nixon stressed that Kissinger should have direct talks with Premier Zhou Enlai as that would serve the interests of both countries. Kissinger knew Nixon's thinking and would be able "to make a decision on the spot without having to refer back to Washington for advice or instructions."

It was agreed that to cover up his visit, Kissinger would first travel to Saigon and then visit Bangkok, New Delhi, and finally Islamabad, the capital of Pakistan. Nixon urged that Kissinger's visit to Beijing must be kept top secret. If Yahya would like to go to Beijing during Kissinger's visit, Nixon would greatly appreciate his going, but it was up to Yahya to decide if he were to go or not. Yahya, who was then in the midst of the civil war between East and West Pakistan, did not go, and neither Beijing nor Washington insisted that he do so. The Pakistani foreign secretary, Sultan Khan, wanted to accompany Kissinger, but Kissinger declined the offer.

While conveying Nixon's reply, Yahya stressed Nixon's "personal desire to develop friendly relations with the PRC," and Yahya emphasized to Zhou that Kissinger must be received by Zhou himself. Nixon sent three messages on April 29, May 17, and May 22 to Zhou Enlai through Yahya. The contents of the messages were no longer noncommittal, deliberately vague, cautious; the messages became frequent and warmer, and they began to contain concrete and important proposals or suggestions.

Zhou Enlai was equally prompt in replying to Nixon, still channeling his messages through President Yahya. In his reply of May 29, 1971, which had the "full approval of Chairman Mao," Zhou said he appreciated Nixon's suggestion of a summit meeting in Beijing and that Chairman Mao "will welcome a visit by President Nixon"—no longer a casual invitation, but a "proper" one through a head of state. Zhou also agreed with Nixon that "each side will be free to raise principle issues of concern to it," but Zhou again stressed that China considered the withdrawal of U.S. troops from Taiwan a crucial issue. Zhou assured Nixon that Kissinger would be received by him and that he was looking forward to discussing President Nixon's proposed visit to China with Kissinger. Zhou suggested June 15–20, 1971, for Kissinger's visit and agreed that Kissinger's visit should be kept top secret.

Nixon appreciated Zhou's May 29 message and Zhou's readiness to extend a warm welcome to Kissinger. Nixon again pointed out, in a message that Yahya gave to Zhang Dong on June 9, 1971, that "Kissinger will be authorized to discuss all issues of concern to both countries" prior to Nixon's own visit and also to make all arrangements for the summit meeting in Beijing. Nixon told Zhou that Kissinger's visit "will be a very positive first step in improving relations between the United States and the PRC." The date of the visit was finally fixed for July 9–11, 1971.

The Soviet Factor in the Sino-American Negotiations

The main reason the Chinese were willing to have a rapprochement with the United States was their growing fear of the Russians, particularly after the serious Sino-Soviet border clashes of 1969. There were, of course, other factors that helped make the Sino-American limited rapprochement possible in 1972. The Chinese still feared a militarization of Japan after the projected U.S. withdrawal from Asia under the Nixon doctrine, and another consideration was Beijing's concern about the prolonged Vietnam War. It now appears that the Chinese had long-standing suspicions about Vietnam's regional ambitions in Southeast Asia, in collusion with the Russians, though at that time, the Chinese, like the Russians, were "comrades in arms" with the Vietnamese. By the end of the 1960s, the Chinese were genuinely interested in ending the Vietnam War and rightly felt that an understanding between the United States and the PRC would contribute to an ending of that war. Similarly, Nixon and Kissinger knew that a breakthrough with China would give the United States favorable diplomatic options in dealing with its main rival, if not main adversary, the Soviet Union. Yet both sides refrained from making any reference to, or even any hint about, the growing Sino-Soviet tensions in the messages exchanged between Beijing and Washington in 1969–1971, and it has already been noted that at the very beginning of the secret negotiations, Yahya Khan warned Washington about making any suggestion that China was responding out of fear of Russia.

But the "Soviet factor" was present in the emerging Sino-American relationship. Nixon and Kissinger had no doubt that any move on the part of the United States toward Moscow would upset Beijing, but Nixon was simultaneously working for the SALT I agreement with the Soviet Union. The policy of a peaceful coexistence or détente with the Soviet Union was an important goal of Nixon's foreign policy, as was his desire to improve relations with the PRC.[31] However, in a message of June 29, 1971, Nixon assured Zhou that the U.S. government would not reply to the Soviet Union in regard to a "five nuclear powers' disarmament conference" until Kissinger had had an opportunity to discuss the whole issue in Beijing. That assurance was greatly appreciated by the leaders in Beijing.

Kissinger's top-secret visit to Beijing via Pakistan has been described by himself as well as by others,[32] but it must be noted here that once Kissinger's plane, provided by Pakistan Airways, left Islamabad, Yahya's role as a courier between Washington and Beijing ended. Thereafter, Washington and Beijing needed no middleman, and by July 1971, direct communications had been established at the highest level. Two decades of frozen relations had come to an end. Yahya received messages of high appreciation from Nixon, Kissinger, and Zhou Enlai, and Nixon's hand-written letter of appreciation of August 7, 1971, ended with the following words: "Those who want a more peaceful world in the generation to come will forever be in your debt."

But now that the new Sino-American relationship was out in the open, how could China, with an ultraleftist group inside the ruling elite, justify "flirting" with the Americans? The ideological motivation of China's new foreign policy was outlined in a widely publicized article that appeared on November 9, 1971, in the party's theoretical journal, *Red Flag*, as part of a press and radio campaign to explain the new cordiality toward the United States and to justify President Nixon's planned visit. Presented as an analysis of Mao's 1940 publication, *On Policy*, the article set out the advantages of a flexible foreign policy that was capable of exploiting international tensions and rivalries to advance revolution and explained the need for various forms of struggle against the counterrevolutionary policy of the enemy. Mao's 1940 precepts on forming tactical alliances with secondary enemies to defeat the primary one were said to be applicable in 1970–1971—a clear indication that the Soviet Union had been elevated to the first rank of China's enemies. The article also revealed the doctrinal basis of the attempt to assume the leadership of the Third World by cultivating closer friendships in Africa, the Middle East, and Latin America and stated that the contradiction between the industrialized and developing nations was one that China was capable of exploiting in the interests of world revolution.

Reaction to Nixon's "Great Diplomatic Leap Forward"

Kissinger's visit to Beijing on July 9–11, 1971, achieved its two immediate objectives. First, direct communications links between the United States and China were established, so the services of Pakistan, Romania, and France were no longer needed. Henceforth, direct negotiations were conducted beween Washington and Beijing, first through the French ambassadors of the two countries, then through liaison offices in Washington and Beijing, and finally, through full diplomatic establishments in the two countries.

Second, President Nixon's visit to China for the summit meeting with the Chinese leaders was finally fixed. On July 15, 1971, President Nixon announced to the great surprise of the world that he had received an invitation from the government of the PRC to visit China and that he had accepted it with pleasure. Nixon's announcement was a diplomatic coup of the greatest magnitude, and it had an earthshaking effect in various parts of the world. Nixon's actions in making the profound breakthrough received wide acclamation. He received blessings and words of appreciation from the pope; UN Secretary-General U Thant; and British, French, and other NATO allies, and most of the countries of the Third World received the news as hope for a world with reduced tensions.

India and Japan, two important Asian countries, had some initial reservations. The Indian foreign minister welcomed the announcement of the Sino-American breakthrough, but India was not happy to see that its number-one adversary (Pakistan) had helped to arrange a summit meeting between its number-two adversary (China) and the United States, particularly at a time when India was planning to wage a war with Pakistan on the issue of Bangladesh. One immediate result was the signing of an Indo-Soviet friendship treaty in August 1971. In Tokyo, the reaction was one of genuine surprise and shock – surprise because Japan could not contemplate that the United States would so suddenly move toward a détente with Beijing; shock because Tokyo had no prior knowledge of the reconciliation and certainly had not been consulted about it. Many gloomy forecasts were made about the U.S.–Japan relationship as a result of the "Nixon shock," but Tokyo adjusted to the new international reality fairly soon and in a dignified way. Relations between Japan and China, which had remained frozen because of Washington's wishes, were soon resumed. Japan's prime minister visited Beijing, established diplomatic relations, and by 1978, the two countries had even signed a treaty of friendship and peace.

North Vietnam was loud in denouncing Nixon's diplomatic initiative toward Beijing. A lengthy article in Hanoi's daily, *Nhan Dun,* on July 19, 1971, accused Nixon of "dividing the socialist countries, winning over one section and pitting against another." Nixon was also accused of making "compromises between the big powers in an attempt to make smaller countries bow to their arrangement." China tried to mollify Hanoi's fears. Zhou Enlai went to Hanoi and pledged China's continued support to Vietnam's struggle against "the American imperialists" – Beijing was continuing its anti-U.S. propaganda to prove that it had not gone soft on imperialism.

As expected, Moscow was most unhappy to see the progress of the Sino-American thaw and made predictable sneers about the insincerity of the United States and China's betrayal of its own revolutionary principles. But Russia's increasingly negative communist comment on the implications of the thaw was not echoed in Asia, where many governments stressed the advantages that could flow from a Sino-American rapprochement.

Mr. Lee Kuan Yew, prime minister of Singapore, welcomed President Nixon's gesture, which he saw as opening the way for momentous political changes, and his opposite number in Malaysia, Tun Abdul Razak, told reporters that the visit augured well for peace and stability and added that only enemies of China were disappointed by it. In the capitals of Indochina, with the exception of Hanoi, the news was received with some optimism. South Vietnam's foreign minister, Tran Van Lam, noted in Manila on July 17, 1971, that there could be no peace in Indochina without Beijing's cooperation, a point that had also been made by the Khmer minister of information the previous day when he reminded reporters that China was a signatory of the Geneva agreements, on the basis of which his government was seeking a settlement and the withdrawal of foreign troops.

International expectations that China might adopt a more conciliatory approach to the West following the announcement that President Nixon was to visit Beijing were apparently being deliberately dampened by the Beijing regime. The news was not given any prominence in the Chinese press, which continued to abuse U.S. imperialism and to ignore Washington's moves toward easing relations between the two powers. The U.S. State Department's decision to vote for the admission of the People's Republic of China into the United Nations and also to try to retain a UN seat for Taiwan was condemned as a "clumsy two Chinas trick" by the New China News Agency on August 4, 1971.

At the same time, the Chinese leaders took every opportunity to restate their foreign policy, particularly when it directly involved the United States, as if to establish their position in the wake of the announcement of Nixon's visit and before negotiations on the terms of China's admission to the United Nations began. An editorial on Army Day (August 1, 1971) concentrated to an unusual extent on foreign policy, as did the speech at the Defense Ministry's Army Day reception by the chief of staff, Huang Yongsheng.[33] The editorial's reference to Mao's "revolutionary diplomatic line"—the first use of the phrase—was clearly intended to lend the authority of Mao's name to the more outgoing policies, but Huang's remarks were generally conservative in tone, and his brief acknowledgment of China's improved foreign ties was linked with a comment that China's enemies had failed to destroy it either by isolation or encirclement. His attacks on the United States' "wild designs to dominate the world" and the USSR's "social imperialism" were standard. The call in the Army Day editorial for party, army, and people to take an interest in international affairs might have foreshadowed a trend toward normality, but for the time being, any dialogue with the West would apparently be accompanied by expressions of support for anti-imperialist struggles.

Huang's remarks on the Indochina conflict – he commended the North Vietnam National Liberation Front's seven-point peace plan and the Pathet Lao's five points for a settlement in Laos – appeared to point to Beijing's abandonment of the idea of a protracted war in Indochina. Shortly before – in an interview with the Australian Labour Party leader, Gough Whitlam – Zhou Enlai had indicated China's willingness to contemplate a political settlement there and possibly a Geneva-type conference, but, apparently in response to Hanoi's displeasure at the Sino-American rapprochement, Zhou subsequently denied any willingness to hold such a conference, and Huang also demanded a complete withdrawal of all U.S. troops from Indochina as well as from Taiwan, South Korea, Japan, the Philippines, and Thailand. A *People's Daily* "Commentator" article on August 3, 1971, rejected as "sheer fraud" any proposal to hold a new Geneva conference, demanded the total and unconditional withdrawal of U.S. and allied forces, and reaffirmed the determination of the Chinese government and people to back the war in Indochina to the end.

Beijing also showed that it would make no contribution to an easy solution of the problem of Taiwan's representation in the United Nations. Huang Yongsheng's warning that his government would "oppose any schemes of creating two Chinas, one China and one Taiwan or an independent Taiwan" (the last apparently a reference to the Taiwan Liberation Front) was an expansion of a similar statement by Zhou Enlai on July 19. Moreover, Washington's announcement that it wished to see Communist China in the UN Security Council, though not at the cost of Taiwan's expulsion from the General Assembly, was quickly followed by an unhelpful rejoinder from Beijing. A communiqué on a visit of the Algerian foreign minister to China denounced as a fallacy any supposition by the United States that the future status of Taiwan was open to negotiation.

However, Beijing was clearly genuinely interested in promoting a dialogue with the United States, not least in the hope of accelerating the eventual removal of the Americans from both Indochina and Taiwan, and behind the scenes, the Chinese leaders were apparently adopting a more realistic approach to the talks. Zhou Enlai had submitted an eight-point plan to Washington that outlined the questions on which he would welcome discussions – Taiwan, Indochina, and the alleged revival of a Japanese militarism being high on the list.[34] In general, the Chinese leaders obviously hoped that the visit would enhance China's prestige in the world at large. They no doubt also prided themselves on scoring over the Soviet Union by playing host to the U.S. president—his only other excursion into the communist world having been to Romania in 1970.

Soviet Bloc Concern

The Soviet Union's initial reaction to the news of Nixon's visit—and the prospect of new changes in the relationships among the three powers—was a ten-day silence, broken only by the comment that it was "unusual though not unexpected."[35] But on July 25, an article in the party newspaper, *Pravda*, by I. Aleksandrov (thought to be a pen name for a senior political figure) clarified the Soviet position. Its affirmation that the Soviet government favored a normalization of relations between Washington and Beijing, provided it did not develop into a political combination aimed against other states, was likely to remain the official Soviet line for the time being. But the moderate tone of Aleksandrov's article did not conceal Moscow's fear that China might steal a march on the Soviet Union by reaching agreements with Nixon—for instance, on Vietnam—and betray ideological requirements in the search for a rapprochement—a charge that Beijing had frequently leveled at the Soviet leaders.

Before the article in *Pravda*, much of which consisted of quotations from the foreign press, the weekly *Literary Gazette* had printed a Bulgarian news agency dispatch that implied that China was in secret collusion with Washington, and the Czechoslovak newspaper, *Rude Pravo*, had claimed that President Nixon's motive was to divide the anti-imperialist forces in Indochina. Other East European commentators were less ready to ascribe evil designs to China, and the Polish news agency, PAP, conceded on July 16 that the prospect of a normalization of relations between the two powers "cannot be said to be disadvantageous for the world." Two days later, Hungary's party newspaper, *Nepszabadsag*, although recognizing that difficulties might arise over Taiwan and Indochina, said that the forthcoming talks should gratify anyone who was in favor of peaceful coexistence—a theme that was echoed in the Yugoslav and Romanian press.

On the U.S. side, both Nixon and Kissinger were stressing that the intention of the proposed Peking Summit was to enable the two sides to hold wide-ranging discussions on issues of mutual concern rather than to achieve instant détente between Washington and Beijing. When Nixon's attention was drawn to Zhou Enlai's alleged hard-line interview with James Reston in the *New York Times* on August 10, 1971, his reply was "there are very great differences beween the PRC and the United States," but both Zhou and Nixon recognize that "it might serve our mutual interest to discuss these differences. . . . we have agreed to discuss the differences. That's all that has been agreed. There are no other conditions."[36]

The PRC's Entry into the United Nations

In the meantime, China got a seat in the United Nations on October 25, 1971, on its terms – i.e., by getting Taiwan expelled from the United Nations, which signaled the collapse of the policy of diplomatic isolation imposed on the PRC by the United States since 1949. China interpreted the vote at the United Nations as settling the status of Taiwan, and the New China News Agency vigorously denounced the suggestion that China's entry into the United Nations would not rule out the continued existence of an independent Taiwan. In Beijing's eyes, the UN endorsement of the PRC as the only lawful government of China made the question of how many people would continue to believe that Taiwan had any right to represent anyone outside the island of Taiwan a matter of little importance.

A leading article in *People's Daily* provided an outline of China's perception of the forces at work in international affairs and the policies the Chinese government would support at the United Nations.[37] The central plan in China's diplomatic platform would continue to be its opposition to what it regarded as the continuing collusion between Moscow and Washington to impose their will on other people – though Zhou Enlai had written in his letter of April 24, 1971, that he no longer believed that any such collusion existed. China had adopted a dual approach. One was for public consumption, both for the Chinese inside the country as well as for the outside world, and the other was for serious dialogues with Washington and, subsequently, with Tokyo and the Southeast Asian countries.

The *People's Daily* also expressed support for black Africa's fight against the colonialists' plan to utilize mercenaries and said that China would support a 200-mile territorial limit for Latin America and the nationalization of U.S. assets in South American countries. Moscow's military control over Eastern Europe was also condemned. Finally, China would act as the champion of the world's weaker nations and oppose every form of external interference in their affairs.

These declarations were a message to the outside world that in spite of China's willingness to receive President Nixon, it was not going to forsake its principles or revolutionary ideology. (Zhou Enlai could not speak as freely as his pragmatic successors in the post-Mao era have begun to speak since 1977.) Nixon and Kissinger were not surprised by China's declarations, which were made for public consumption, as it was unrealistic to expect that China could give up its revolutionary zeal or principles so soon after the Cultural Revolution. It was more difficult for Zhou to explain the rationale of détente with Washington than for Nixon to justify the new link with Beijing.

Notes

1. See President Richard Nixon's announcement of the proposed China visit on July 15, 1971, in Richard P. Stebbins and Elaine P. Adam, eds., *American Foreign Relations, 1971,* Council on Foreign Relations Book (New York: New York University Press, 1976), pp. 348–349.

2. U.S., Congress, Senate, Committee on Foreign Relations, *China Enters the Post-Mao Era,* Report by Senator Mike Mansfield, November 1976 (Washington, D.C.: Government Printing Office, 1976), pp. 3–4.

3. See U.S., Congress, House of Representatives, Committee on Foreign Affairs, *United States Policy Toward Asia,* Report of the Subcommittee on the Far East and the Pacific, May 19, 1966 (Washington, D.C.: Government Printing Office, 1966), pp. 10–11.

4. See U.S., Congress, *China Enters the Post-Mao Era,* p. 65.

5. Based on the author's reading of unpublished documents and papers of the government of Pakistan, 1947–1971.

6. Ibid.

7. See "Asia After Vietnam," *Foreign Affairs,* October 1967, pp. 111–125.

8. See "The Chinese Connection," *Economist* (London), February 19, 1972, pp. 19–20.

9. Based on the author's reading of unpublished documents and papers of the government of Pakistan, 1947–1971.

10. See *Economist* (London), February 19, 1972, p. 19.

11. Ibid.

12. The *Sino-Soviet Dispute,* Keesing Research Report, no. 3 (New York: Charles Scribner's Sons, 1969).

13. Ibid.

14. Based on the author's reading of unpublished documents and papers of the government of Pakistan, 1947–1971.

15. Lucian Pye, *China: An Introduction* (Boston: Little, Brown and Co., 1978), pp. 317–318.

16. See the statement of Ross Terrill on May 2, 1972, in U.S., Congress, House of Representatives, Committee on Foreign Affairs, *The New China Policy: Its Impact on the United States and Asia,* Report of the Subcommittee on Asian and Pacific Affairs (Washington, D.C.: Government Printing Office, 1972), pp. 20–22.

17. See Robert Scalapino's statement in U.S., Congress, *New China Policy,* p. 111.

18. Pye, *China: An Introduction,* p. 319.

19. *Pravda,* June 8, 1969.

20. Based on the author's reading of unpublished documents and papers of the government of Pakistan, 1947–1971.

21. Ibid.

22. Ibid.

23. See U.S., Congress, *New China Policy*, pp. 20–21 and 110–111.

24. For details, see A. Doak Barnett, *China and the Major Powers in East Asia* (Washington, D.C.: Brookings Institution, 1977), pp. 227–228.

25. See U.S., Congress, *United States Policy Toward Asia*, p. 42.

26. Quoted in A. Doak Barnett's statement in U.S., Congress, House of Representatives, Committee on Foreign Affairs, *United States–China Relations: A Strategy for the Future*, Hearings before the Subcommittee on Asian and Pacific Affairs, October 1970 (Washington, D.C.: Government Printing Office, 1970), pp. 2–4.

27. See Han Suyin, "In China: The American Dream," *Far Eastern Economic Review*, February 19, 1972, p. 9.

28. As indicated, Pakistan was not the only country that aided the top-secret negotiations between the United States and the PRC in 1969–1971; the reason for my elaboration of Pakistan's role is that I had full access to the correspondence channeled through that country.

29. This section is based on my access to the messages between Washington and Beijing that were sent through Pakistan from 1969 to 1971.

30. *New York Times*, April 30, 1971.

31. Stebbins and Adam, *American Foreign Relations, 1971*, p. 344.

32. See Marvin Kalb and Bernard Kalb, *Kissinger* (Boston: Little, Brown and Co., 1974), pp. 243–265.

33. Based on the author's research in London, 1971–1978.

34. Based on the author's research and interviews in Beijing, 1976–1979.

35. Based on the author's research in London, 1971–1978.

36. Stebbins and Adam, *American Foreign Relations, 1971*, p. 352.

37. Reproduced in Leo Goodstadt, "The Longest Journey," *Far Eastern Economic Review*, October 30, 1971.

4

The Peking Summit and the Beginning of the New Relations Between Beijing and Washington

President Nixon's projected visit to China was finalized when Kissinger made a second visit to Beijing on October 20-26, 1971 – at the time when the United Nations was debating the issue of the PRC's entry into that world body. Although the U.S. government's "official" policy was still to allow Taiwan to remain in the United Nations as an ordinary member while giving the "China seat" to the PRC, Kissinger's presence in Peking favored the PRC's cause and Zhou Enlai had no difficulty in understanding that fact. Just as China was continuing a dual posture toward the "imperialist United States" by harping on the hegemony of the two superpowers and yet working for a détente with Washington, Nixon and Kissinger's policy also had the dual aspects of reaffirming the "firm" commitments made to the Republic of China on Taiwan and yet seeking to obtain the friendship and cooperation of the PRC.

The date of Nixon's visit was fixed for February 21-28, 1972. Nixon reaffirmed his new China policy in his third annual foreign policy report to the Congress on February 9 – just two weeks before he undertook the journey to China, which he compared to a "journey to the moon." In his report, Nixon again stressed the importance of a process of communications between the most powerful nation in the world and the most populous nation in the world, and he also warned against undue expectations of instant solutions of the deep-seated differences that still existed between Washington and Beijing.[1]

The visit took place during an election year in the United States, and Nixon utilized the visit fully for his domestic needs. In China, the scene on the eve of the Peking Summit was one of great transformation and change. Lin Biao, Mao's designated successor, and his ultraleftist group had gone, as had Lin Biao's theory of a universal revolution against the "cities of the world." The Cultural Revolution itself seemed to have gone full circle, though officially it was not yet declared as ended. The Red

Guards had purged the Communist party; then the army had purged the Red Guards; and finally, with the exit of Lin Biao, the top men in the army had been removed, and the old and experienced party cadres had returned to their jobs. By 1972, when Nixon reached Beijing for his meetings with Mao and Zhou Enlai, the Chinese government seemed to be in the hands of practical people who had no immediate plan for a world revolution or an instant transformation of Chinese society. They also seemed to believe in the idea that "when you have two enemies, it is sometimes advisable to decide which of them presents the worst threat to you."[2]

Nixon and his entourage arrived in Beijing on February 21, 1972. Nixon got a low-profile reception at the airport: Premier Zhou Enlai was there to greet him, and a guard of honor was also present, but the usual fanfare—such as what I witnessed in November 1970 when I accompanied President Yahya to Beijing—was lacking. The Chinese explanation was that there was not yet a formal recognition between the two governments, so the "official" welcome could not be extended. But the cool reception at the Beijing airport was promptly and aptly compensated for by no less a person than Chairman Mao. According to the Chinese protocol, Mao used to receive foreign heads of state or of government just one or two days before their departure from Beijing—for instance, Yahya and his entourage were received on the fourth day of their five-day visit—but Nixon was warmly received by Mao within a few hours of his arrival. The summit meeting between Mao and Nixon, assisted by Zhou and Kissinger, began on the same day, i.e., February 21, 1972.

However, the real dialogues were, as expected, between Premier Zhou Enlai and President Nixon, assisted by Kissinger, and the secretary of state, William Rogers, had separate sessions with the Chinese foreign minister, Ji Pengfei. Nixon had fifteen hours of extensive, frank, and honest discussions with Zhou, and the talks were characterized by candor, friendliness, and courtesy.

Rarely does a diplomatic initiative promote so much speculation as that inspired by the Peking Summit in February 1972 as there were worldwide expectations, anxieties, and uncertainties about its outcome. The results of the Nixon-Mao-Zhou talks were embodied in a "joint" communiqué, but reading the communiqué or the official statements made by the leaders of the two sides can hardly give one the whole story of the epoch-making meeting. There were specific issues to be discussed, such as Taiwan, which was the key problem in Sino-American rapprochement, and the Vietnam War, whose ending was greatly cherished by the Americans. (If Nixon could make the Chinese help him to get the Americans out of that unfortunate war, it would be a great triumph for him in an election year.) But the Peking Summit was a historic one and of far greater significance than the total of any concrete progress on specific issues like Taiwan or Vietnam. The results that had real importance included subtle adjustments in both countries' perception of the world. Those results could only be hinted at in any communiqué or statement, but their fuller implications were bound to extend over a period of years.

At the final banquet in Shanghai on the evening of February 27, 1972, Nixon described his week in China with the following remark: "This was the week that changed the world."[3] That might have been one of Nixon's rhetorical expressions, but the Peking Summit in February 1972 was a great event in contemporary world affairs as it set in motion a chain of adjustments in the world order, the full significance of which is not yet fully understood. The Senate majority leader, Senator Mike Mansfield, who, with minority leader, Senator Hugh Scott, visited China soon after the Peking Summit, wrote in his report:

> the President's visit served immediately to lower the level of tension in Asia and therefore, has had a salutary effect on world opinion. It has also increased the interest of Japan and other nations of Asia in dealing a normal way with the People's Republic of China. In short, it is clear that the tree of relationships in Asia and the world was shaken for the better by the President's initiative. What cannot yet be predicted is where the leaves will fall and what will be the look of the new foliage.[4]

The Shanghai Communiqué

The Shanghai communiqué, issued just before the end of President Nixon's visit, was unique. Unlike most "joint" communiqués, it mentioned the fundamental differences that existed between the United States and the PRC on the various bilateral and world issues discussed during the Peking Summit. Nixon described the communiqué as "unique in honesty setting forth differences rather than trying to cover them with diplomatic doubletalk,"[5] and Kissinger explained the modus operandi of drafting the communiqué by saying that it had been decided that each side would state its position on issues in a section, which each would produce more or less independent of the other. It had also been decided that the communiqué would not pretend to an agreement that did not exist and would have to be interpreted away in subsequent implementations.[6] The communiqué had, therefore, three parts: the U.S. and Chinese versions and the agreed upon points. We need not discuss the Shanghai communiqué paragraph by paragraph as it has received adequate attention in academic as well as in public discussions of the new U.S.-China relationship. This analysis will be confined to an evaluation of the significance of the Peking Summit meeting on the future course of Sino-American relations and to an assessment of the summit's short-term and long-term effects on China's foreign policy and its perception of the world.

The Taiwan Issue

The Taiwan issue, to quote Zhou Enlai's words in the messages sent through Yahya in 1969–1971, was of "crucial importance" in any moves toward normalization of the Sino-American relationship. The threats from the Soviet Union were no doubt the driving force for an improvement in the relationship on the Chinese side, just as Nixon's desire for increased leverage against Moscow was, perhaps, the most important single factor in his initiatives toward Beijing—on July 1, 1970, Nixon had rather bluntly told correspondent Howard K. Smith that he wanted to improve relations with the PRC as a means of coping with the Soviet Union.[7] Yet the Taiwan issue dominated the Peking Summit more than any other single issue. As I gathered from Ambassador Zhang Dong as well as from extensive talks with Chinese foreign policy makers in Beijing during my four visits there (1976–1979), the Chinese leaders were still reluctant to admit freely to Nixon and Kissinger their fears about the Russians. But the Soviet threats figured prominently at the Peking Summit, and Nixon's strategy seems to have been to capitalize on those fears to the fullest extent; if only Nixon could convince the Chinese of the benefits of a U.S. connection in Chinese dealings with the Russians, he could expect the Chinese leaders to make major concessions on other issues.

Yet in the first dialogue in 1972, China said the Taiwan issue was their number-one priority, and it has continued to have top priority. Senator Mansfield appreciated China's sensitiveness on the Taiwan issue: "Taiwan is a point of utmost sensitivity in China's new national consciousness. Together with certain border areas along the frontier with the Soviet Union, it is the last vestige of China's humiliation at the hands of outside powers."[8] Even in August 1980, when the Republican presidential candidate, Ronald Reagan, said that if elected, he might revive "official links" with Taiwan, the Chinese reaction was one of anger, and strong protests were voiced by them to Reagan's running mate, George Bush, when he went to Beijing to explain Reagan's views. I talked about the controversy caused by Reagan's remarks with the Chinese ambassador, Chai Zemin, in Washington, and he told me rather bluntly, "If Mr. Reagan tries to revive the Taiwan issue, settled by President Carter at the time of resumption of diplomatic relations in January 1979, China might have to close its embassy in Washington."

From my extensive study of the technique of Chinese diplomacy, I can say that the Chinese do make adjustments or become flexible on what they consider to be secondary issues but they are very firm on what they consider to be basic issues or fundamental principles. The Chinese would not enter the United Nations until Taiwan was "expelled" from the world organization, and they waited seven years (1972–1979) for full diplomatic relations with the United States until the United States severed its diplomatic ties with Taiwan, abrogated its security arrangement with the island, and withdrew U.S. troops from there. Similarly, China did not sign the treaty of peace and friendship with Japan until Tokyo agreed to China's demand for an "antihegemony" clause in the proposed treaty. The Chinese take pride in adhering to their basic national interests and principles, and they will not compromise on such basic issues. They would rather wait a hundred years than make compromises on fundamental issues.

At the Peking conference in February 1972, Nixon and Kissinger found that the Chinese were firm on the Taiwan issue and that Taiwan would be the "foundation stone" of any agreement at the summit. Of course, Nixon had already realized the importance of the issue and had no illusions. Two weeks before his departure for China, Nixon had retracted some of the U.S. commitments toward the Republic of China on Taiwan, and in his report to the Congress on February 9, 1972, Nixon had stated: "With the Republic of China, we shall maintain our friendship, our diplomatic ties and our defense commitment. The ultimate relationship between Taiwan and the mainland is not a matter for the United States to decide."[9]

The Shanghai communiqué gave both the Chinese version of the issue, which reflected no change on the part of the PRC, and the U.S. version, which did indicate some significant changes in the U.S. position. It said: "The United States acknowledges that all Chinese on either side of the Taiwan strait maintain that there is but one China and that Taiwan is a part of China. The United States government does not challenge that position. It reaffirms its interests in a peaceful settlement of the Taiwan question by the Chinese themselves." Finally, the United States also added its "ultimate goal" of the withdrawal of "all U.S. forces and military installations from Taiwan."[10]

In theory, the U.S. concessions in the communiqué did not directly contradict the U.S. commitments made in the president's report on February 9, 1972, and Kissinger asserted that the Shanghai communiqué did not amount to an abandonment of the U.S. commitments to Taiwan. Yet the Shanghai communiqué was an indirect acceptance of the Chinese views that Taiwan is a part of China, that the Chinese themselves should settle the issue, and that there is no such thing as "one China, one Taiwan" or "two Chinas." Finally, the U.S. also conceded to the Chinese demand for the eventual withdrawal of U.S. troops from Taiwan. It is true that Nixon did not break diplomatic ties with Taibei—as demanded by Beijing and as finally done by President Carter in 1979—but the process of derecognition was laid down in the Shanghai communiqué. Similarly, the security pact of 1954 was not abrogated, but if it was agreed that the Taiwan issue was to be settled by the Chinese themselves without any outside help, there was no scope for a continuation of that treaty. The withdrawal of U.S. troops was justified by the U.S. policy of disengagement from Asia under the 1969 Nixon doctrine, but it was still a major concession to Beijing's demand for a total withdrawal of those troops. Finally, the United States agreed with the PRC that Taiwan is a part of China and that there is "one China."

Diplomatic and legal niceties apart, the Shanghai communiqué included a major concession to Beijing on the Taiwan issue, which the Chinese considered as the most crucial point in the bilateral relationship between Beijing and Washington. China also made some gestures. It did not refer to its often-quoted objections to the U.S. security pact with Taiwan, nor did China talk about the occupation of Taiwan by the U.S. imperialists. The position on Taiwan could not be termed a U.S. "sell-out" of Taiwan or a Chinese victory or annexation of the island. The Peking Summit sought to diffuse the Taiwan issue as the most obstructing factor in the normalization of relations between China and the United States, and what Nixon and Zhou Enlai did was to eliminate the Taiwan question as a unique and insuperable barrier to China-U.S. relations. The United States "now faces China in much the same way as Canada or Italy or any of the other countries which have recognized China in the past two years; indeed it has done further towards the Chinese position than the other recognizers who mostly took note of China's claim to Taiwan."[11] But it could not be said that the Shanghai communiqué cleared the way for a Chinese military takeover of the island. The promise of a withdrawal of U.S. troops as "tension in the area diminishes" was largely symbolic, and the real defense of Taiwan was and still is dependent on U.S. bases and aircraft carriers throughout the Pacific. Moreover, the Chinese realized that any military takeover of Taiwan would immediately destroy the U.S. goodwill and any prospects for a détente with the United States, and China was not willing to pay such a big price for the "liberation" of Taiwan.

Both sides seemed to recognize the delicate and complicated problems involved in the Taiwan question. The mutual concession and understanding implied, not so much clearly stated, in the communiqué on the Taiwan issue demonstrated both sides' desire to improve the Sino-American relationship. "In short" as pointed out by a commentator on the Peking Summit: "the Shanghai Communiqué contained a trade-off. The Chinese communists said nothing about liberating the island by force," and the United States "removed its long-standing caveat over the international status of the island."[12] Another reputable commentator, Ross Terrill, said: "On Taiwan, which is the key to United States–China relations, the Shanghai communiqué ushered in a situation in which each side holds a trump card. President Nixon's card is his choice on how quickly or slowly to implement his intention to progressively remove U.S. military presence from the island. . . . Peking leaders will no doubt tailor their responses on the normalization of relations accordingly."[13]

The Vietnam War

There was speculation as to whether a "Taiwan for Vietnam deal" could be made at the Peking Summit; whether Nixon's concessions on Taiwan could make China put pressure on Hanoi to be amenable in the peace talks that were going on in Paris between the United States and North Vietnam.[14] Nixon had given orders for the resumption of blanket B-52 bombing of Indochina before he landed in Beijing on February 21, 1972, and the massive buildup of U.S. naval and air power in the Gulf of Tonkin was President Nixon's bargaining tool at the Peking Summit. Nixon might have hoped that Hanoi's suspicions of Beijing would be increased as a result of the Chinese leaders' willingness to receive him in the midst of increased U.S. military activities in Indochina, but it was futile to expect that Beijing would put real pressure on Hanoi, or even if Beijing would have agreed to do so, that such pressure would have been truly effective.

The Chinese leaders maintained that they had no influence on Hanoi because China was not a superpower and had no desire to impose its will on a smaller power. Zhou Enlai had already declared that China was not able or could not assist the United States in settling the Vietnam War "on terms favorable to the Americans,"[15] and Zhou could not budge from that position because Hanoi could wreck the Chinese reputation for revolutionary ardor by denouncing the Peking Summit as a Chinese collusion with the imperialist camp. Hanoi was in the same position Beijing had been when President Eisenhower had met the Soviet leader Nikita Khrushchev at Camp David in 1959. In 1959, China had accused Moscow of betraying the revolutionary struggle by seeking peaceful coexistence with the United States. In the same way, Hanoi could make similar accusations against China if Zhou Enlai showed any flexibility on the Vietnam War issue. Zhou had assured the North Vietnamese in 1971 that "if anyone among us should say that we should not help the Vietnamese people in their struggle against U.S. aggression and for national salvation, that will be betrayal—betrayal of the revolution."[16]

Yet, the indications were that the Chinese leaders had been getting suspicious of Hanoi's increasingly leaning toward Moscow and of Hanoi's regional hegemony in Indochina and Southeast Asia. Chinese Vice Foreign Minister Han Nianlong told me in July 1979 that China could foresee Hanoi's regional ambitions, or hegemonic aspirations, in Southeast Asia as early as the 1950s, yet neither Mao nor Zhou could publicly support the U.S. cause in 1972. Just as the United States had to reaffirm its commitments for the defense of the Republic of China on Taiwan, so the Chinese leaders had to restate their position on the Vietnam War in the Shanghai communiqué.

A reading of the communiqué, which states the "official" stand of Beijing on the Vietnam War, does not reveal the reasoning for the changed Chinese attitude. China was no longer afraid of a U.S. military "push" to the Chinese southern flank. In March 1965, Chairman Mao had requested that Pakistani President Ayub tell President Johnson that China would not aggravate the Vietnam War if the United States would not extend the war into Chinese territory. But many things had happened since 1965, and Zhou Enlai told Ross Terrill in 1971, "the United States picked up a stone to hurl at Vietnam, but dropped it on its own feet."[17] Kissinger seems to have been successful in convincing Premier Zhou that the United States was genuinely interested in a gradual disengagement from Asian countries under the 1969 Nixon doctrine, so the Chinese seemed to be no longer terrified of U.S. bombing raids on its doorstep. The Vietnam War was a turning point in the Chinese assessment of U.S. military actions in Asia.

On the other hand, the formulation of the 1968 Brezhnev doctrine and its application in Czechoslovakia did alarm the Chinese. In fact, it seemed at the Peking Summit that the Chinese were beginning to welcome a limited U.S. presence in Southeast Asia in the face of the growth of Soviet power in Asia. Nixon and Kissinger seem to have been successful in reinforcing the Chinese concern about the growing Soviet influence and power in Asia, and if there were any deals or understandings at the Peking Summit, it was this type of subtle readjustment of China's perception of the major powers' roles in Asia—a "balance of adjustments" among Washington, Moscow, Beijing, and Tokyo. There could not be any public quid pro quo between Taiwan and Vietnam, and the critics of President Nixon's new China policy, who were anxious to find out what price Beijing had offered to the United States, were disappointed by the wording of the Shanghai communiqué. Nixon went to the Peking Summit for substantial, long-meditated diplomatic gains, and their fuller significance or implementation could not be traced in a single communiqué or a few public statements on both sides.

Other Issues

It is true that President Nixon did not get all he wanted. For instance, he did not get the permanent, quasi-diplomatic representation in Beijing that his administration had hoped for. Beijing was not yet ready for the "on-going communications belt" that Nixon talked about; instead, provision was made for visits of U.S. diplomats to Beijing from "time to time."[18] The Chinese distinguish between "state to state" and "people to people" as well as "party to party" relationships. A state to state relationship between Beijing and Washington could not be established fully because of unfinished tasks regarding the Taiwan issue; the question of a party to party relationship did not arise at all. But it was expected that people to people relations would be developed to the mutual benefit of both U.S. and Chinese peoples. The Shanghai communiqué stated: "The two sides agreed that it is desirable to broaden the understanding between the two peoples. To this end, they discussed specific areas in such fields as science, technology, culture, sports and journalism in which people to people contacts and exchanges would be mutually beneficial." Ambassador Edwin Reischauer, in his assessment of the Peking Summit, pointed out the benefits of contacts between "our one-third of the world's wealth and the Chinese one-quarter of the world's population if we as a human race are going to be able to address ourselves to the great global problems that are pressing down on us very rapidly."[19]

The Shanghai communiqué referred to a number of Third World countries, besides Taiwan and Indochina, that were of immediate concern in the bilateral relations between Beijing and Washington. On Japan, the U.S. section stated, "The United States places the highest value on its friendly relations with Japan; it will continue to develop the existing close bonds." China in the late 1960s and early 1970s was worried about what they used to call a revival of Japanese militarism. In the mid 1970s, not only were China's fears gone, but China began to support Japan's increased military budget, and Beijing also began to favor the U.S.-Japan security ties. But at the time of the 1972 Peking Summit, China still expressed concern in the communiqué about "the revival and outward expansion of Japanese militarism and firmly supports the Japanese people's desire to build an independent, democratic, peaceful and neutral Japan." Although China was worried about Japan at the time, the tone of the Chinese portion of the Shanghai communiqué is not highly polemical, one of the beneficial results of the Sino-American understanding produced by President Nixon's diplomatic initiatives.

Regarding the Korean Peninsula, the Chinese expressed their support of the North Korean plan for a peaceful unification, and the United States reaffirmed its closer ties with South Korea – the Republic of Korea. Both sides wanted to reassure their Asian allies that no secret deal was made at the Peking Summit and that neither side would give up its commitments to its old friends.

The Asian countries, both noncommunist ones, such as Japan and the ASEAN countries, and communist ones, such as North Korea and the countries of Indochina, were watching the outcome of the emerging Sino-American relations with great interest and concern. They had no doubt that whatever might be the wording of the Shanghai communiqué, the full implications of the new relationship between China and the United States would be great and the relationship's impact on the changing pattern of alignment and realignment in Asian affairs would be profound.

The Soviet Factor at the Peking Summit

The raison d'être for Chairman Mao and Premier Zhou Enlai's willingness to talk with President Nixon was their genuine fear of the growth of Soviet power and influence in Asia. Similarly, Nixon's "soft" attitude toward Beijing was motivated by his desire to increase the United States' bargaining leverage in dealing with Moscow. Ambassador Reischauer, who was a critic of the type of trip Nixon took to Beijing and referred to it as "unfortunate," also conceded: "It has always been to our great advantage to have broad and roughly equal relations with the two great communist nations. Such a dual relationship enhances our bargaining position with both. I suspect that it was the desire to increase our leverage in dealing with Moscow that loomed largest in the President's mind toward detente with Peking."[20] The Chinese calculations included, as Reischauer and many other China specialists pointed out, their serious fears of the growing Sino-Soviet conflicts and their assessment that the United States' sad experience in the Vietnam War made the Americans genuinely interested in a process of disengagement from Asia; therefore, the "paper tiger," the United States, no longer posed any serious threat to China's security. On the contrary, a rapprochement with the United States might give China some real sense of security vis-à-vis the Soviet Union.

The search for security, as already pointed out, has always been the most dominating factor in China's foreign policy goals. In the final analysis, the foreign policy of any country must be a "policy of survival," and China is no exception to this fundamental rule of international relations. French foreign policy has long been cautiously dominated by one main preoccupation, that of ensuring its security from the "threat" of Germany, and similarly, China's foreign policy since the 1969 border clashes with the Soviet Union has reflected one overriding consideration—fear of aggression by the Soviet Union. The Chinese might still refer to ideology, fighting against imperialism and so forth, but the main driving force behind China's foreign policy since 1969 has been its growing fear of the Soviet Union.

In the Shanghai communiqué, both China and the United States agreed that they would "wish to reduce the danger of international military conflict" and that "neither should seek hegemony in the Asia-Pacific region"; more significantly, "each is opposed to efforts by any other country or group of countries to establish such hegemony." Opposition to "hegemony by the Soviet revisionist social imperialist" has become a consistent and persistent theme of the Chinese policy statements. They never miss a single opportunity to denounce the hegemonic aspirations of the Soviet social imperialists, which they have begun to consider as "the most dangerous source" of the next world war. The Chinese have raised their voice against the growth of Soviet influence and power everywhere, whether in East or Southeast or South Asia, in the Middle East, or in Africa. In the Chinese press and media, one finds almost daily denouncements of any sign of the growth of Soviet power; similarly, the Soviet press and media never fail to denounce Maoism or China's chauvinistic designs.

The Nixon-Kissinger policy was to increase the U.S. bargaining position in dealing with Moscow by opening the "China door" or by using the "China card," but not to identify with the Chinese in openly denouncing the Soviet Union. Although there was common interest in containing the Soviet power and influence in Asian-Pacific region, the United States was not prepared to go along with the Chinese in their political denouncements of the Russians. There was a common, but not identical, interest in Washington and Beijing vis-à-vis Moscow. While Nixon was working for a normalization of relations with Beijing, he was equally eager to have a détente with Moscow and was engaged in negotiating SALT I with the Russians. The Peking Summit in February 1972 was followed by the Moscow Summit in May 1972.

The Vision of the New World Order

Before leaving for the Peking Summit, President Nixon had expressed his vision of a new world order.

> We must remember the only time in the history of the world that we have had any extended periods of peace is when there has been balance of power. It is when one nation becomes infinitely more powerful in relation to its potential competition that the danger of war arises. So I believe in a world in which the United States is powerful. I think it will be a safer world if we have a strong, healthy United States, Europe, Soviet Union, China, Japan, each balancing the other, not playing one against the other, an even balance.[21]

The pertinent issue was, Did Mao and Zhou share views similar to those expressed by Nixon? Did China also believe in a multipolar world in which the five great powers—the United States, USSR, PRC, Western

Europe, and Japan—could maintain world peace and stability by a new balance of power? The American sinologist Michel Oksenberg has examined this fundamental issue in the new Sino-American relationship. Oksenberg raises the questions, "Are the Chinese really responding to the world now envisioned by the U.S. administration?" "Was the last year [1971–1972] really the beginning of a meeting of minds?"[22]

There are at least two divergent assessments of Chinese foreign policy during the initial years of the post–Peking Summit era, and one recognizes China's moderation and realism in its external relations. China's performance at the United Nations, for instance, was flexible and relieved the fears of those people who had dreaded the prospect of the entry of Red China into the United Nations and its revolutionary tactics in that world forum.[23] Outside the United Nations, China diffused the Taiwan issue by taking a long-term view of the reunification of the province of Taiwan with the motherland. As a basic principle, China did not agree to denounce the use of force in the settlement of the issue as it regarded Taiwan as a domestic problem and did not feel obligated to give any commitment to any outside power on how the issue would be settled. In practice, however, China did not give any provocation or reason for any increased fears on the part of the government on Taiwan. Similarly, China welcomed the 1973 Paris peace treaty on Vietnam as China was no longer encouraging any idea of a prolonged revolutionary struggle in Indochina. China showed pragmatism and realism in its relations with the Asian countries and gave priority to state to state relations instead of people to people ones. Contrary to apprehensions, the Sino-Japanese relationship took a rapid turn toward friendlier relations, and a full diplomatic relationship was resumed on September 25, 1972. A full diplomatic relationship, which had been suspended because of the 1962 Sino-Indian border war, was also restored with India. One could continue to add examples of China's "acceptance" of a new world order in which cooperation among the five major powers should ensure peace and stability and in which there would be no room for revolutions.

But there is equally convincing evidence to prove that China did not fully subscribe to the Nixon-Kissinger policy of détente or peaceful coexistence. The Chinese leaders were lifelong revolutionists and had strong ideological convictions, and it was perhaps futile to expect any sudden, radical change in their attitude or their perception of the world. Although the Chinese government continued to open up channels of communications with foreign countries and professed wishes for increased exchanges, its ideological rigidity was still a stumbling block. Soon after the 1972 Peking Summit, China issued a number of strongly worded statements against the "U.S. imperialists' policy and actions in Indo-China,"[24] and the permanent Chinese representative at the United

Nations, Huang Hua, lodged a formal protest to UN Secretary-General Kurt Waldheim, on May 11, 1972, against the United States' increased bombing in North Vietnam and against the mining of the Vietnamese seaports.[25] Of course, China had no option but to denounce the increased bombing by the Americans in order to maintain its image in the socialist world and also to maintain its newly acquired status among the nonaligned countries of the Third World. China's principle aims remained those of winning friends among the developing countries, particularly in Africa, and of improving ties with the smaller states, which, like China, were "independent" of the two superpowers.

In a review of the 1972 UN General Assembly discussions and debates, *Peking Review* wrote against the "hegemony of the two superpowers." Though the main target was the revisionist Soviet social imperialism, the U.S. imperialists also figured in China's support of the smaller and weaker countries. Concerning the Soviet Union, it was alleged:

> Apparently the contender for hegemony and perpetration of aggression, subversion, control and interference against small and medium-sized countries, it [i.e., the Soviet Union] went out of its way to disguise itself as a peace angel. Apparently a superpower which maintains military bases and stations large number of armed forces in the territories of other countries with its air-craft warships and submarines including those carrying nuclear weapons, it made a hullabaloo about the non-use of force in international relations.[26]

The Chinese foreign minister's statement at the Twenty-seventh Session of the UN General Assembly on October 3, 1972, did not give much hope for China's acceptance of the Nixon-Kissinger vision of a cooperative world of five major powers. Mr. Jiao Guanhua said:

> A series of new victories have been achieved by the Asian, African and Latin American peoples in their struggle to win and safe-guard national independence. Countries of the third world are getting united on a wider scale to oppose the superpower policies of aggression, expansion and war.
>
> Although no new world war has occurred since World War II, local wars of various types have never ceased. Why? Because imperialism resorts to armed force in carrying out aggression and expansion. Where there is oppression there is resistance, and where there is aggression there is struggle against aggression. This is inevitable so long as imperialism exists.
>
> People condemn war and consider it a barbarous way of settling disputes among mankind. But we are soberly aware that war is inevitable so long as society is divided into classes and the exploitation of man by man still exists. There are two categories of wars, just and unjust. We support just wars and oppose unjust wars. If a socialist still wants to be a socialist, he should

not oppose all wars indiscriminately. The non-use of force in international relations can only be conditional and not unconditional. The condition is to realize peaceful co-existence through mutual respect for sovereignty and territorial integrity, mutual non-aggression, non-interference in each other's internal affairs, and equality and mutual benefit. And in order to realize this it is imperative to oppose the policies of aggression and expansion of any imperialism.[27]

In a theoretical analysis entitled "Why It Is Necessary to Study World History," a Chinese commentator wrote in May 1972, "We will more conscientiously carry out Chairman Mao's revolutionary line in foreign affairs and fulfil the duty of proletarian internationalism still better in resolutely supporting the just struggle of the oppressed people."[28]

Allowance must be made for Chinese rhetorical exaggeration, yet China's continued revolutionary zeal cannot be ignored, nor were the Chinese leaders apologetic about their support of the causes of the "oppressed" countries. Premier Zhou Enlai, in a speech at the Tenth National Congress of the Chinese Communist party, said that a major objective of Chinese foreign policy "is to oppose any attempt by the imperialist [i.e., the United States] and social-imperialist [i.e., the USSR] to subjugate China, the Third World and other nations." Zhou, however defended the policy of a normalization of relations with the United States in the spirit of the Shanghai communiqué. His main target was the Soviet Union, which he said had degenerated from a socialist country into a socialist-imperialist country under its revisionist leadership from Khrushchev to Brezhnev.[29] Zhou Enlai expressed similar thoughts in his report to National People's Congress in January 1975.

> The contention for world hegemony between the two superpowers, the United States and the Soviet Union, is becoming more and more intense. . . . their fierce contention is bound to lead to world war some day. . . . The Third World is the main force in combating colonialism, imperialism and hegemonism, China is a developing socialist country belonging to the Third World. We should enhance our unity with countries and people of Asia, Africa and Latin America . . . we support the countries and people of the Second World in their struggle against superpower control, threats and bullying.[30]

China's principle foreign policy goal in the 1970s was to acquire a major stake in world affairs, at the expense of the Soviet Union as an ideological fountainhead within the communist world, and to acquire an influence in the Third World. The attempt to assume the leadership of the Third World was based on Mao's theory of contradictions. According to Mao, contradictions and changes are permanent features of social life, and there are principal and secondary contradictions. In any given set of circumstances in world politics, the revolutionary must distinguish between the principal and secondary contradictions as well as between principal enemies, secondary enemies, and temporary allies.[31]

The policy of a limited rapprochement or limited détente with the United States was perhaps considered as a temporary alliance to meet the threats from the principal enemy, the Soviet Union, or the principal contradiction, Soviet social imperialism. By the 1970s and particularly after the 1972 Peking Summit, U.S. imperialism was considered a secondary contradiction.

There were still no clear indications of a real détente between Beijing and Washington, but Kissinger was reported to be "satisfied" that Zhou Enlai had become convinced of the desirability of a peaceful coexistence among the major powers to attain the goals of world peace and stability.[32] No other Americans had better access to Zhou Enlai's thinking in 1971–1976 than Nixon and Kissinger, so one can not dismiss their optimistic assessment of the new China policy. I do not pretend to possess any special hindsight, but I did have the unique opportunity of discussing the impact of the Peking Summit on China's perception of the world with senior Chinese Foreign Ministry officials in Beijing as well as with Ambassador Zhang Dong, who after his assignment in Pakistan in 1969–1972 was posted in Cairo where I met him for lengthy discussions for three consecutive days in July 1976. From my intensive interviews and talks with the top Chinese officials in Beijing and ambassadors abroad, I became convinced of some significant "shifts" in China's foreign policy.

It was futile to expect that China would give up its bid for leadership of the Third World or that China would cease to talk in terms of Mao's theory of contradictions or class struggle. Mao was still alive and at the helm of Chinese affairs. Zhou Enlai was the main foreign policy maker in 1972–1975 after the exit of Lin Biao—there was still the Gang of Four, who created all kinds of obstacles for Zhou, but he still had a much greater role in foreign affairs in the post–Peking Summit era—and Zhou might not have subscribed fully to the Nixon-Kissinger vision of a multipolar world. China was greatly worried about Moscow and bitterly opposed to any idea of a détente between Washington and Moscow as well as to SALT I. Similarly, it was still not certain that the Chinese were fully convinced of the peaceful intentions of the United States in Asia. Like any other initial understanding or rapprochement between two great powers, the emerging Sino-American relationship was not yet free of tensions and reservations. There was still the Taiwan issue, which had been diffused but not resolved, and the Vietnam War was not yet over. The Sino-Japanese relationship had just begun, but the East Asian triangle

of Beijing, Tokyo, and Moscow was not wholly satisfactory from the
Chinese point of view.

In its continued policy of a quest for security, China had to seek closer
ties with the countries of the Third World. Opposition to imperialism,
colonialism, etc., was still popular, and China had to pursue its national
goals in familiar terms that were readily acceptable to the countries of
the Third World, so China's continued talk of contradictions and opposition to the hegemony of the two superpowers was not surprising.

But on closer scrutiny, China's moderation and realism in its external
relations in the post–Peking Summit era were obvious. The prime cause
for changes in China's diplomatic and strategic objectives was the
emergence of a new and complex balance in the Asian-Pacific region[33] as
the geopolitical strategic maneuvering in that area was greatly influenced by the Peking Summit. The West, particularly the United States,
had referred to threats from Red China from 1949 to 1969, but in the
1970s, the United States began to appreciate the threats to China. As an
Australian commentator pointed out, "After two decades of worrying
about a Chinese threat which proved to be of little substance, Western
analysts should perhaps turn their attention to a different question: how
do the Chinese see themselves threatened and what dangers lurk in that
formulation?"[34]

Honest attempts to examine the threats to China would enable us to interpret the so-called bellicose foreign policy statements that have been
made by Chinese leaders, including the moderate Zhou Enlai. With a bitter history of subjection to the arrogance of the great powers, as Senator
Mike Mansfield seems to have realized correctly, the Chinese emphasize
that their own future is identified with the smaller or weaker nations.
They reject the status of a superpower;[35] they repeatedly assert that
China is not a superpower, nor shall it be a superpower – i.e., it should
not behave like a superpower and seek to dominate or impose its will on
others. Zhou Enlai's trusted colleague, Deng Xiaoping (subsequently the
most influential Chinese leader in the post-Mao era), declared at the
Special Session of the UN General Assembly in 1974: "China is not a
superpower nor will she ever seek to be one. What is a superpower? A
superpower is an imperialist country which everywhere subjects other
countries to its aggression, interference, control, subversion or plunder
and strives for world hegemony."[36] The Chinese insist, as Senator
Mansfield further pointed out, that their system does not permit them to
impose their views on others by force, and "on the basis of our visit, there
is no reason to conclude that the Chinese leaders mean otherwise."[37]

On the basis of my five visits to China in the 1970s, I am inclined to
share Mansfield's view about China's genuine desire for world peace and
stability. China wants, more than anything else, a prolonged period of

peace and stability so that it can devote its full attention and resources to the economic development of the country and improve the standard of living of its people. China may not endorse the Nixon-Kissinger idea of a new world based on a balance of power among the five major powers. Instead, China has its own modus operandi to safeguard its basic national interests.

Chinese foreign policy in the 1970s seemed to be based on three anti's—anti-imperialism, antihegemonism and antiequalibrism.[38] In spite of occasional outbursts of revolutionary zeal, China was basically nonimperialist and nonhegemonic in the 1970s. China did not blackmail any of its smaller neighbors (though there was a China-Vietnam war in 1979, which we shall discuss in a later chapter), and China sought to normalize relations with most of its Asian neighbors. The Chinese continued to make friendly gestures to African countries, no longer talking in terms of "exporting revolution" to the African countries, and wider diplomatic ties and growing economic involvement were two basic aspects of China's new diplomatic initiatives in the Third World. China also made known its approval of the nonaligned countries' role. Zhou Enlai sent cordial messages to the third Nonaligned Conference in Lusaka in 1970, and after that, China consistently supported the nonaligned movement and also attempted to keep the movement genuinely nonaligned, challenging the pro-Soviet leaning of some of the nonaligned countries such as Cuba and India.

Whatever interpretations might be made of China's role in world affairs in the 1970s in the wake of the new Sino-American relationship, the fact remains that China became a central power in the Asian-Pacific region, and no important issues in that area could be decided without China's participation. That fact was a source of great annoyance to Moscow, which had wanted to weaken and isolate China, but it was a diplomatic feat for President Nixon, who had wanted to build up China's influence as a counterbalance to the growth of Soviet power in Eurasia. China has not become an ally of the United States as a result of the 1972 Peking Summit, but a strong China, unfriendly to Moscow, is as vital to U.S. global interests as a stronger NATO, a stronger ANZUS, a stronger Japan, and a stronger ASEAN. One should also remember that China is not opposed to a stronger NATO, ANZUS, Japan, or ASEAN.

As a result of Nixon's and Zhou Enlai's diplomatic initiatives, there developed a number of common objectives, though not an identity of interests, between Washington and Beijing—much more so than between Moscow and Washington. In spite of all the talk about détente, the Soviet Union has not missed a single opportunity to undermine U.S. interests in the Third World—in South and Southeast Asia, the Indian Ocean and Persian Gulf areas, the Middle East, Africa, and even Latin America. As for the PRC, one perspective of the Chinese attitude regarding the U.S. role in world affairs was summed up in 1975 by Elliot Richardson, former U.S. under secretary of state.

> China's leaders want the United States to play a major role in Asia indefinitely, to head off Soviet domination of the region. I don't think the Chinese would want to see any shifts in Asia for the foreseeable future. The Chinese have an interest in the preservation of a major U.S. role toward the rest of the world, if only because Chinese security to a degree depends on a continuing American countervailing role against the Soviet Union.[39]

That was a correct analysis of the Chinese foreign policy objectives, notwithstanding occasional expressions of revolutionary themes such as hegemony of the two superpowers or opposition to domination of the world by the two superpowers.

Initial Years of the New Sino-American Relationship

The Chinese leaders attached great importance to the emerging Sino-American relationship, and Mao and Zhou Enlai were as eager for a relaxation of tension between Beijing and Washington as Nixon and Kissinger were. The favorable responses Beijing made to Nixon's gestures in 1970–1972 came only after a thorough and careful analysis of China's national interests and the global balance of power. Those responses were not merely the "brain product" of one individual, such as the late Premier Zhou Enlai, but were made under the guidance of Chairman Mao, and he took the leading members of the Chinese Communist party and generals of the People's Liberation Army into full confidence before deciding how to react.[40] It is wrong to assume that Chinese leaders take any major course of action without an adequate assessment of the internal and external factors involved, but it is futile to expect the decision-making process in a communist country to be the same as that in a Western democratic country. It may safely be presumed that China's new policy toward the United States, which began in 1971–1972, enjoyed the approval of the major groups in the country's leadership.

After Nixon's visit was announced in the Chinese press, the government conducted an extensive campaign on the grass-roots level to explain to the Chinese people the reasons for and implications of the U.S. president's visit.[41] The campaign was conducted through meetings in factories, offices, and schools and on the levels of the brigade in the countryside and the street committee in the towns. The campaign had to be conducted within the overall context of the Sino-American relationship as perceived by the average Chinese citizen. The U.S. government, not the American people, was China's enemy,[42] and the Chinese government's policy of presenting the American people in a friendly light made the task of explaining the rationale of China's new attitude toward the United States less difficult. Of course, it is always easier to project any change of policy through a controlled press in a communist country than in a free society like the United States, but the American people's perception of China was also getting changed.

Secretary of State William Rogers, commenting on the initial progress in the bilateral relations between China and the United States, expressed the view that developments since the Peking Summit had been satisfactory, and he added, "They [the Chinese] have been restrained in their comments about the United States and we, on our part I think, have been restrained in our comments."[43] The initial progress in developing Sino-American relations in 1972–1973 was a demonstration of the success of the Peking Summit.

Henry Kissinger, who was President Richard Nixon's principal executor of the new China policy, made six trips to the PRC from July 1971 to November 1973. That period was also noted for a good beginning in the normalization of relations between the PRC and the United States. Kissinger seems to have developed a profoundly good understanding with Premier Zhou Enlai, who was Chairman Mao's principal executor, if not formulator, of China's new foreign policy, and he also had cordial meetings with Chairman Mao.

Kissinger's first visit to Beijing after the historic summit meeting was in May 1972. The main purpose of that visit seems to have been to tell the Chinese leaders about President Nixon's visit to the Soviet Union in May 1972 and to assure the Chinese that no decision was made at the Moscow summit to the detriment of China.

The Soviet factor, or the Soviet-American détente, is another important and complicating factor for the future of the Sino-American relationship. There is no doubt that China is keenly watching the U.S.-USSR détente for the future pattern of relations between the two superpowers, including the problems and prospects of the SALT agreements. Like any other country, China will try to achieve a favorable balance of world power from the standpoint of its own security and basic national interests. As pointed out by George Modelski, foreign policy is the system of activities evolved by communities to change the behavior of other states and to adjust their own activities to the international environment. The fact that the behavior of one state affects other states confronts every state with the problem of minimizing adverse actions and maximizing favorable actions of foreign states.[44] Thus, foreign policy is essentially a question of states adjusting to each other, and China is no exception to this fundamental rule of the game of international politics.

China will not concede that its attitude toward the United States is dependent on Soviet-American relations, and the Chinese also seem convinced that there can be no genuine friendship or détente between Moscow and Washington. They dismiss the idea of any genuine arms agreement between Moscow and Washington, yet when SALT I was signed in Moscow on May 26, 1972, China's initial reaction was one of silence for two months. Then, in July 1972, Premier Zhou Enlai delivered the Chinese reaction. He termed the SALT I agreement a "new weapons race between the United States and the Soviet Union" and stated: "In order to contend for world hegemony, they [the United States and the Soviet Union] are engaged in an arms race not only in nuclear armaments, but also in conventional armaments, each trying to gain superiority. . . . One of the main objectives of the fraudulent U.S. imperialist–Soviet revisionist agreements on disarmament remains that of hindering the consolidation of the defense capacity of the People's Republic of China."[45]

The Chinese continue to be skeptical about the Moscow-Washington arms agreement, preferring to recall former Secretary of Defense Melvin Laird's and also James Schlesinger's warnings about the huge Soviet military buildup in spite of negotiations for SALT II.[46] The Chinese also never miss an opportunity to point out, rather gleefully, any conflict of interest, or contradictions, between Moscow and Washington. Referring to what it termed a "scramble in hegemony in the Persian Gulf and Indian Ocean," *Peking Review* has reported that "the United States and Soviet Union are locked in an intense struggle for hegemony in the Persian Gulf and the Indian Ocean."[47] *Peking Review* also reprinted extracts of an article by Joseph Alsop in the *Washington Post* (April 25, 1973), in which it was stated: "Because of the energy crisis–which is really a strategic crisis–the jugulars of the United States, Western Europe and Japan now run through the Persian Gulf. So it is deathly important news that the Soviet Union is now thoughtfully building its own naval base at the head of the Persian Gulf where all these oil jugulars can be cut."[48] The Chinese news agency Xinhua mentioned the Soviet hegemony bid in the Mediterranean Sea and said:

> In early 1967 when Soviet revisionism was still in an inferior position in the Mediterranean, Brezhnev assumed the pose of opposing the entry of foreign fleets there. He took the United States to task: "the question is" he asked, "What grounds are there, 20 years after the end of the second World War, for the U.S. Sixth Fleet to cruise in the Mediterranean?" Now it is Brezhnev's turn to answer the same question once put forward by the Soviet Union. At a time when Soviet revisionists are riding roughshod over the Mediterranean in the wake of U.S. imperialism, they speak of the "proud presence of the Soviet Fleet" in the Mediterranean as being "naturally reasonable."[49]

All of the references to the growing Soviet influence and power were made with the intention of proving the futility of the United States ever achieving détente with the Soviet Union. It would be constructive diplomacy on the part of the Chinese to wreck any progress toward détente between the two superpowers, just as the Russians made an effort to frustrate the process of a normalization of relations between the PRC and the United States.

Kissinger's next trip to Beijing on February 15–19, 1973, soon after the Paris cease-fire agreement on the Vietnam War, was highly significant for the growth of the Sino-American relationship. Kissinger had dialogues with Chairman Mao in addition to his usual lengthy sessions with Premier Zhou Enlai, and after this visit, China and the United States agreed to set up liaison offices in Beijing and Washington. The liaison offices in both the capitals were headed by senior ambassadors of the two countries. The Chinese ambassador in Paris, Huang Zhen, became chief and Ambassador Han Xu deputy chief of the liaison office in Washington, and President Nixon appointed Ambassador David Bruce as the chief of the U.S. liaison office in Beijing. Nixon called the establishment of the liaison offices in Washington and Beijing "a significant step forward in our relations with the People's Republic of China,"[50] and in announcing the decision to set up the offices, the Chinese reaffirmed the principle that a normalization of relations between the United States and the PRC would "contribute to the relaxation of tensions in Asia and the world."[51]

The significant query is, Why did China agree to set up liaison offices, which for practical purposes were quasi-embassies, before the United States severed diplomatic and security ties with Taiwan? The PRC had consistently said that it would not have any diplomatic relationship with any country as long as that country would not sever its diplomatic relations with Taiwan. From a strictly legal point of view, China could not be accused of violating that principle, because there was no exchange of ambassadors and there was no diplomatic recognition. And yet, the liaison offices were, for all practical purposes, embassies. Why did China make this major concession?

Nixon had been pressing for such an arrangement since the 1972 Peking Summit. At that time, China could not concede because of the Vietnam War—China was extremely cautious about making any concession during that conflict—but after the Paris cease-fire agreement on Vietnam, China could afford to carry the process of a normalization of relations one "big step forward." A more important factor was the sense of mutual confidence that had been created in both Beijing and Washington between February 1972 and February 1973. Nixon's gesture of sending Kissinger to Beijing immediately after his meeting with the

Kremlin leaders had made a good impression on the Chinese, who needed U.S. help to meet the growing threats from the Russians. The Americans were also pleased with China's flexibility in and realism about its role in Asian affairs, particularly in connection with Taiwan and Indochina.

According to Professor T. C. Rhee, during Kissinger's visit in February 1973 "a preliminary understanding that the United States would provide minimal, if not guaranteed, military assistance to China in the event of a Soviet military attack" was made,[52] and the decision to set up liaison offices was the result of that preliminary understanding. There is, however, no evidence to support that assertion. When I made inquiries about such an assurance on many occasions, the Chinese reply was always in the negative. When Deng Xiaoping went to the United States in early 1979, on the eve of the Chinese "punitive measures" against Vietnam, there might have been discussion of such an assurance or understanding as there were grave risks of a Soviet intervention in the ensuing China-Vietnam war in 1979, but it seems doubtful that the Americans made such an assurance to the Chinese in 1973. The Sino-American relationship had not yet reached that depth of understanding and confidence that would have made such an assurance possible.

Rhee also mentions negotiations relating to "Peking's purchase of military hardware" during Kissinger's sixth visit to Beijing in November 1973.[53] The United States and the PRC made it known in the early 1970s that there would be no direct military sales from the United States to China, and China began to negotiate to buy military equipment from the NATO countries with the United States' knowledge and approval. It was only after the Soviet invasion of Afghanistan that the idea of a U.S.-China military purchase agreement was taken up seriously. Of course, it is not unlikely that Kissinger, in his lengthy sessions with Zhou Enlai in November 1973, did discuss the issue of China's purchase of military hardware. *Newsweek,* on December 23, 1973, reported that during that visit, there was discussion on the "surprising topic" of China's buying U.S. arms including tanks, armored personnel carriers, transport helicopters and the like.

The bilateral relationship between Beijing and Washington developed fairly well, in spite of ideological and other deep differences, throughout 1972–1973, and important agreements relating to trade and cultural exchanges were signed during that period. Prior to the 1972 Peking Summit, there had been no direct trade between the two countries—on the contrary, there had been a "secondary boycott" on such trade—but the Shanghai communiqué stressed the desirability of Sino-U.S. trade. With the opening of a direct relationship between the two countries, the trade began to flow—in 1972, the volume of trade was $96 million, and U.S.

exports to China, mostly agricultural commodities, rose from $64 million in 1972 to $740 million in 1973. China was unwilling to entertain any large-scale exchange of visitors until full diplomatic relations were established, yet some 8,000 Americans, mostly of Chinese origin, visited the PRC in 1972, and a total of twenty Chinese delegations visited the United States.[54]

The main reason for the satisfactory growth of the U.S.-China relationship in 1972–1973 was the goodwill and trust created by the 1972 Peking Summit; the other important factor was the shifting balance of power in Asia following the cease-fire in Vietnam. The United States was no longer engaged in any military involvement in Asia, and that fact enabled China to promote the process of a normalization of relations with the United States. Also, the growth of the Soviet power and influence in Asia, in cooperation with friendly regional powers such as India in South Asia and Vietnam in Southeast Asia, caused worries both in Beijing and Washington. That situation, too, helped the new relationship between Beijing and Washington.

During his sixth visit to Beijing, Kissinger spoke of the "good progress" that had been made in the improvement of the new Sino-American relationship, and he assured his Chinese hosts in Beijing, "We are determined to do much more and to complete the process that we started two years ago as rapidly as possible." Kissinger also made reference of the "important common objectives" of the foreign policies of China and the United States, such as opposition to hegemony and peaceful coexistence.[55] Obviously any reference to an opposition to hegemony was pleasing to the Chinese as that topic acquired a definite meaning for the Chinese in their dispute with the Russians. Although the Chinese still continue to speak of the hegemony of the two superpowers, it was the hegemony of the Soviet Union that was the main target of attack by Beijing in the 1970s. The Chinese foreign minister, Ji Penfei, also expressed satisfaction over the progress toward a normalization of relations between the PRC and the United States. He referred to Kissinger's important dialogues with Premier Zhou Enlai and, in particular, with Chairman Mao. Then he pointed out, "It should be said that as [a] result of Dr. Kissinger's sixth visit to China, each side is better acquainted with the positions and policies of the other on a series of major issues."[56]

What made the Chinese leaders so happy about Kissinger's two important visits to Beijing in February and November 1973? Kissinger himself pointed out that the significance of the emerging Sino-American relationship could not be fully judged by a mere reading of the communiqués issued after his visits, just as the Shanghai communiqué did not reveal all of the implications of the 1972 Peking Summit. Although Nixon and Kissinger were engaged in the pursuit of détente with the Soviet Union, they seem to have realized that neither Beijing nor Moscow was an "ally" of the United States; rather, they were potential adversaries. Yet the limitations of détente with the Russians seemed to be clearer to the U.S. policymakers. The Russians were not interested, after all, in anything more than a very limited accommodation with the United States. They were happy to sign the nonproliferation of nuclear arms treaty with the United States, as the Russians, like the Americans, wanted to preserve the exclusiveness of "the nuclear club" and did not want any more countries to have nuclear weapons. The Russians were also interested, to a certain degree, in strategic arms limitation treaties with the United States. But the main aim of the Soviet Union, in spite of détente, was an erosion of U.S. power and influence in the Asian-Pacific region in the wake of the Vietnam War. They also wanted to weaken U.S. interest in the Middle East when it became evident during the 1973 Middle East war. Similarly, their expansionist designs in the Mediterranean were aimed at making Western Europe more pliable to Soviet wishes.

As already pointed out, the Chinese applied themselves vigorously in pointing out to the Americans the dangers of the Soviet expansionist designs in various parts of the globe. Once they became convinced of the implications of the 1969 Nixon doctrine, the Chinese were no longer afraid of the U.S. policy in Asia. The common concerns, if not identity of interests, about the Soviet policy, in particular about the Soviet military buildup, made Beijing and Washington closer, and that concern was the most important single factor in the emerging relationship between the two countries. The growth of Soviet power in Asia was such a worrying problem for Beijing that a détente with Washington was imperative for China. Something like a quarter of the nuclear-armed Russian army was stationed on China's northern borders, and North Vietnam's regional hegemonic aspirations were also becoming more clear by the early 1970s.

The potential and risks of a Moscow-Hanoi entente in Southeast Asia were no longer in doubt. Hanoi was not happy with Beijing's "flirting" with Washington and began to follow a "tilt toward Moscow" policy. China, therefore, was no longer very enthusiastic about a North Vietnamese victory in Indochina, though China did continue to give "full support" in its policy statements. In South Asia, the Indo-Soviet relationship had acquired a special significance after the partition of China's only faithful ally in the area, Pakistan. The 1971 Bangladesh war was a joint victory for Moscow and New Delhi just as it was a joint diplomatic setback for Beijing and Washington.[57]

After his return from Beijing in November 1973, Kissinger said at a press conference that the United States placed primary emphasis on the substance rather than the forms of communications and consultations with the PRC with the expectation that the situation in Southeast Asia "will not be exacerbated by actions of any outside country"—which presumably referred to Hanoi's Moscow-backed activities. He added, "Both sides [the United States and the PRC] had an obligation to do their utmost" to bring about "a general condition of stability and tranquility in Asia."[58]

In the context of major developments in the Asian-Pacific region in the early 1970s, China also welcomed the special ties between Japan and the United States—China was not opposed any longer to the U.S. military presence in Japan, or even in Southeast Asian countries like Thailand and the Philippines. Although the PRC had been always opposed to the stationing of foreign troops in Asian countries, the Soviet military concentrations along China's northern borders made that country accept the U.S. military presence in Northeast and Southeast Asia, except on Taiwan and also perhaps in South Korea. That acceptance was in line with Mao's analysis of primary and secondary contradictions, the Soviet military presence being the former and the U.S. military presence, the latter.

According to Moscow, quoting *Kyodo tsu shin,* Zhou Enlai had stated that China welcomed a reasonable growth of Japan's military strength as a counterweight to the USSR's aggressive designs on Asia. Zhou had also stated that China would join Japan in fighting against Moscow, "even alongside the forces of the United States."[59] Senator Mike Mansfield, however, gave a charitable interpretation of China's new strategy and foreign policy objectives: "There are no signs that China is bent on the oppression or domination of other nations. All present indications are that the People's Republic is intent on internal progress and that its military efforts are minimal in terms of its defense. Expressions of superiority are absent from its policies which appear rooted in the principle that all nations should be free of outside domination and influence."[60] These words might have represented Senator Mansfield's goodwill and friendly feelings toward the People's Republic of China, but any impartial analysis of China's foreign policy in the early 1970s would be inclined to view China as reverting to the "Bandung spirit" of the mid 1950s.

The 1970s were a period of internal consolidation after the great upheavals of the Cultural Revolution era, and China needed to restore its image in the family of nations as that image had been badly affected by the excesses of the Cultural Revolution. There seems to be some parallel between China's internal stable periods and China's moderation and flexibility in external relations. Nixon's diplomatic initiatives were made at the appropriate moment, and both internal and external factors favored Nixon's gamble to begin a new relationship with China. A period of smooth and steady improvement in the Sino-American relationship was therefore quite natural and nothing unexpected.

But soon some temporary factors, internal and external in both China and the United States, created some setbacks in the growth of a normalization of relations between Beijing and Washington, and the temporary strains and stresses in the emerging relationship between the world's most powerful and most populous nations during the period from 1974 to 1979 are examined in the next chapter.

Notes

1. Richard P. Stebbins and Elaine P. Adam, eds., *American Foreign Relations, 1972,* Council on Foreign Relations Book (New York: New York University Press, 1976), pp. 11–13.

2. See "The Chinese Connection," *Economist* (London), February 19, 1972, p. 19.

3. *New York Times,* February 28, 1972.

4. U.S., Congress, Senate, Committee on Foreign Relations, *Journey to the New China, April–May 1972,* Reports of Senators Mike Mansfield and Hugh Scott (Washington, D.C.: Government Printing Office, 1972), p. 6.

5. Stebbins and Adam, *American Foreign Relations, 1972,* p. 317.

6. Ibid., p. 312.

7. Quoted in Harold C. Hinton, *Peking-Washington: Chinese Foreign Policy and the United States,* Washington Papers, no. 36 (London and Beverly Hills, Calif.: Sage Publications, 1976), p. 35.

8. U.S., Congress, Senate, Committee on Foreign Relations, *China Enters the Post-Mao Era,* Report by Senator Mike Mansfield (Washington, D.C.: Government Printing Office, 1976), p. 8.

9. Stebbins and Adam, *American Foreign Relations, 1972,* pp. 11–13.

10. For the text of the Shanghai communiqué, see U.S., Congress, Senate, Committee on Foreign Relations, *China a Quarter Century After the Founding of the People's Republic,* Report by Senator Mike Mansfield, January 1975 (Washington, D.C.: Government Printing Office, 1975), pp. 39–40.

11. See "Taiwan Was the Price," *Economist* (London), March 6, 1972.

12. William R. Kintner, *The Impact of President Nixon's Visit to Peking on International Policy,* Research Monograph Series, no. 13 (Philadelphia: Foreign Policy Research Institute, September 1972), pp. 2–3.

13. U.S., Congress, House of Representatives, Committee on Foreign Affairs, *The New China Policy: Its Impact on the United States and Asia,* Report of the Subcommittee on Asian and Pacific Affairs (Washington, D.C.: Government Printing Office, 1972), p. 21.

14. See Hinton, *Peking-Washington,* p. 43.

15. See "Peking Summit: Fighting to the Last Vietnamese," *Far Eastern Economic Review,* February 19, 1972.

16. Ibid.

17. U.S., Congress, *New China Policy,* p. 20.

18. See "What Price Peking," *Economist* (London), March 9, 1972, and also "The Chinese Connection" and "Mahjong or a Greater Game," *Far Eastern Economic Review,* February 19, 1972.

19. U.S., Congress, *New China Policy,* p. 4.

20. Ibid., p. 11.

21. *Time,* January 3, 1972.

22. Michel Oksenberg, "How Long a March Together," *Far Eastern Economic Review,* July 1, 1972.

23. For a comprehensive study of China's role in the United Nations, see Samuel S. Kim, *China, the United Nations, and World Order* (Princeton: Princeton University Press, 1979).

24. See *Peking Review,* March 24, March 31, and April 14, 1972.

25. See the text of the Chinese protest note in *Peking Review,* May 19, 1972.

26. Ibid., December 27, 1972.

27. See speech by Jiao Guanhua at the Twenty-seventh Session of the U.N. General Assembly issued by Peking Foreign Languages Press in 1972, pp. 1, 15, and 16.

28. *Peking Review,* May 26, 1972.

29. See "Reflections on the Quarter," *Orbis* (Fall 1973), pp. 676–677. For the text of Zhou Enlai's speech, see *Peking Review,* September 7, 1973.

30. *Peking Review,* January 24, 1975.

31. See Shao-Chuan Leng, "Chinese Strategy Toward the Asian-Pacific," *Orbis* (Fall 1975), pp. 775–792.

32. Ibid.

33. See "China in World Today," *Annals of the American Academy of Political and Social Science* (July 1972).

34. Arthur Huck, "China and the Chinese Threat System," *International Affairs* (London) (October 1973), pp. 617–623.

35. U.S., Congress, *Journey to the New China,* p. 137.

36. See the text of Deng's speech on April 10, 1974, issued by the Foreign Languages Press in 1974, pp. 20–21.

37. U.S., Congress, *Journey to the New China,* p. 137.

38. Huck, "China and the Chinese Threat System," p. 621.

39. Quoted in Golam W. Choudhury, "Post-Mao Policy in Asia," *Problems of Communism* (July–August 1977), pp. 20–21.

40. Based on the author's talks and interviews in Beijing as well as on information obtained through diplomatic sources in countries friendly to China, such as Pakistan, Sri Lanka, and Tanzania.

41. See Alexander Casella, "Peking's Explanation Campaign," *Far Eastern Economic Review,* April 1, 1972.

42. Ibid.

43. U.S., Department of State, Press Release 202, August 22, 1972.

44. George Modelski, *A Theory of Foreign Policy* (New York: Praeger, 1962), p. 9.

45. See Zhou Enlai's speech in *New York Times,* July 18, 1972.

46. See New China News Analysis (Domestic Service), January 12, 1973;

translated in Foreign Broadcasting Information Service (FBIS), January 15, 1973.

47. *Peking Review,* May 4, 1973, p. 20.

48. Ibid.

49. Ibid., April 13, 1973, p. 19.

50. *Washington Post,* March 16, 1973.

51. *Peking Review,* February 23, 1973, p. 4.

52. T. C. Rhee, "Peking and Washington in a New Balance of Power," *Orbis* (Spring 1974), pp. 151–158.

53. Quoted in ibid.

54. For details, see U.S., Congress, *China a Quarter Century After the Founding of the People's Republic,* pp. 21–30.

55. *Peking Review,* November 16, 1973, pp. 6–7.

56. Ibid.

57. G. W. Choudhury, "The Emergence of Bangladesh and the South Asian Triangle," in London Institute of World Affairs, *The Year Book of World Affairs, 1973* (London: Stevens and Sons, Ltd., 1973), pp. 62–89.

58. U.S., Department of State, News Release, November 21, 1973, p. 3; also quoted in Rhee, "Peking and Washington in a New Balance of Power."

59. Rhee, "Peking and Washington in a New Balance of Power," p. 155.

60. U.S., Congress, *China a Quarter Century After the Founding of the People's Republic,* pp. 34–35.

5

Complications and Ultimate Success in the Normalization Process Between Beijing and Washington

The Chinese were happy with the improvement in Sino-American relations after the 1972 Peking Summit. From 1972 through 1973, the process of normalization, according to the Chinese, moved satisfactorily, but then came Watergate and the consequent decline of Nixon's influence and power. With the exit of President Nixon, who had been the real architect of the new Sino-American relationship in 1970–1972, a stalemate seemed to develop in the relationship. Nixon, as Chinese officials told me, had a clear perception of the Soviet threat and was, therefore, genuinely interested in a détente with Beijing. When Nixon left the White House in August 1974, U.S. foreign policy initiatives seemed to move from the U.S. president to the secretary of state—a Chinese assessment that many Americans would agree with. When Kissinger became not only executor but also initiator of U.S. foreign policy, a change in the U.S. attitude toward the PRC seems to have occurred, particularly as he gradually became, to quote the Chinese, "obsessed" about détente with Moscow.

Nixon was reported to have assured the Chinese that a full diplomatic relationship between Beijing and Washington would be established after his reelection in 1972,[1] and after that reelection, Nixon had told a delegation of Chinese journalists who visited him at the White House on May 29, 1973, that "one of my great wishes is that sometime in my second term, I would like to return to the People's Republic of China . . . to develop this relationship [i.e., the U.S.-China relationship]." He requested that the Chinese delegation carry his wishes to Chairman Mao and Premier Zhou Enlai.[2] When Nixon resigned on August 8, 1974, the interim president, Gerald Ford, received the Chinese liaison officer, Ambassador Huang Zhen, on his very first day at the White House to assure the Chinese that the new administration desired to continue the process of development of the Sino-American relationship.[3] Yet a number of factors were responsible for a stalemate in the relationship.

Kissinger was unable or unwilling "to move the U.S. relations forward an inch; if anything, they have cooled."[4] Kissinger continued to make regular visits to Beijing in 1974 and 1975, but there were changes in the content of the Sino-American dialogue during those years. In the early stages of the Sino-American talks, the main themes had been related to the Chinese doubts about the U.S. policy and role in Asia—in particular with regard to Vietnam, Taiwan, Korea, and Japan—and to an effort to assure China of U.S. support against the Russians. In a sense, the relationship between the two countries had been primarily concerned with dismantling obstacles to understanding, not with building up the new relationship.[5] In 1975 and 1976, Kissinger seemed to take pride in dealing with "grand strategy" such as the breakthrough with the PRC, détente with the Soviet Union, Middle East peace, and the SALT II negotiations. To him, normalization of relations between Washington and Beijing was a matter of "diplomatic details" that would be resolved sooner or later, preferably later. Kissinger seems to have lost interest in China once the glamour of his first mission had worn off. The Chinese, it appeared to many observers, were acutely sensitive to the low-profile position taken by Kissinger after late 1974. Of course, Kissinger would never admit any low-profile attitude toward Beijing, and he would "fly into a rage when he hears his own disparaging remarks about Chinese views of the world played back to him or reads that a Chinese official has compared him with Neville Chamberlain."[6] He would not agree with the assessment that the Chinese objected to his great interest in détente with Moscow.

For the Chinese, the normalization of relations was highly important. They interpreted the Shanghai communiqué as a U.S. commitment to normalize relations on the basis of one China, and they considered that commitment an article of faith. The Soviet Union was an important factor in the new Sino-American relationship, but the Chinese felt that no real progress toward a solid understanding, even with regard to the Soviet Union, could be made without the preliminary step of a normalization of the relationship between the PRC and the United States. Kissinger's unending enthusiasm for a détente with Moscow worried the leaders in Beijing. Before his death in 1976, Premier Zhou Enlai, the architect of the new relationship on the Chinese side, said: "There exist fundamental differences between China and the United States. Owing to the joint efforts of both sides, the relations between two countries have improved to some extent . . . [and] the relations will continue to improve so long as the principles of the Shanghai communiqué are carried out in earnest."[7] To the Chinese, the communiqué involved a definite U.S. commitment to normalize relations with the PRC by severing U.S. diplomatic and security ties with Taiwan.

By 1975, however, the United States was not willing to "abandon" Taiwan because of the communist victory in Indochina. The United States was not ready for another sign of alleged weakness in its role in Asia. There were also uncertainties about China's future after Mao and Zhou Enlai.

Kissinger's Seventh and Eighth Trips to Beijing (1974-1975)

Kissinger made his seventh trip to Beijing on November 25, 1974, on his return journey from the 1974 Vladivostok meeting between President Ford and Leonid Brezhnev. Vladivostok is only forty miles from the Chinese frontier, and there was speculation that Beijing might have been piqued by the presence of the two superpowers on China's doorstep. The Chinese were not happy with Kissinger's comments about the Vladivostok agreement—he termed it the "breakthrough with the SALT II negotiations that we have sought to achieve in recent years" and said it produced "a very strong possibility of agreement to be signed in 1975"[8]—a hope that was not realized until 1979. By visiting Beijing immediately after the Vladivostok Summit, Kissinger sought to mollify the Chinese sense of not being taken into account in the two superpowers' negotiations, though Kissinger insisted that his visit to Beijing had been arranged before the Vladivostok Summit and had not been planned to reassure the Chinese about the U.S. détente with Moscow.[9]

As Premier Zhou Enlai was in the hospital, the Chinese negotiating team was headed by Deputy Premier Deng Xiaoping. Three days of talks between Kissinger and the Chinese team headed by Deng developed the Sino-American relationship no further than the stage it had reached in 1973. Judging from the tone of the public toasts at the banquet in Beijing on November 28, 1974, and the "guarded chitchat" of the U.S. officials accompanying Kissinger, it can be presumed that no momentum in the relations between the two countries was achieved. Kissinger spent four and a half days in China during this seventh visit, and the communiqué issued at the end of the visit was rather short and vague. An indication of the displeasure of the Chinese over the stalemate in the relationship was evident by Kissinger's not having an interview with Chairman Mao, which he had had on each of his two trips in 1973. The U.S. officials, however, dismissed the speculation that Mao had "diplomatically snubbed" the U.S. secretary of state to show impatience over the lack of progress toward the establishment of full diplomatic relations between

Beijing and Washington. Yet as long as the Soviets remained a potentially dangerous adversary along China's vast northern border, China appeared determined to maintain its new relationship with the United States.

Kissinger claimed that his 1974 trip "continued the progress that has been made on each of the previous occasions,"[10] but he could give no evidence of his alleged progress. The Chinese foreign minister, Jiao Guanhua, said that the two sides had reviewed the world scene in a "cordial spirit,"[11] which in the context of Chinese diplomacy means nothing special or significant. The impatience of the Chinese over the question of diplomatic relations was confirmed by Senator Mike Mansfield, who also visited China in December 1974.[12]

In the meantime, the Chinese continued to blast SALT II in their press. A lengthy analysis of SALT II, "A Scrap of Paper: A Sheer Fraud," in *Peking Review* observed: "The ever-fierce nuclear arms race between the Soviet Union and the United States tells the people more clearly that any agreement or 'treaty' concluded between the two superpowers is an out and out fraud and is indeed, in essence, for bigger and fiercer contention. So long as imperialism and social-imperialism exist, there will be no tranquility in the world, nor lasting peace, nor peace in one generation."[13] On another issue, *Peking Review* raised the question, "Is there the slightest shadow of detente in the world today? None at all! Detente, in other words, is designed to camouflage intense rivalry for hegemony in deeds."[14]

The Chinese were terribly upset at the thought of any progress toward SALT II or détente between Washington and Moscow, and their bitter comments on SALT II reflected their concern about any genuine understanding between the two superpowers and their displeasure with Kissinger because of what they considered to be his unrealistic optimism about cooperation or an understanding with the Soviet Union. The Chinese expressed their disapproval of Kissinger's handling of the U.S. foreign policy from 1974 to 1976 in a subtle way. They felt, not without justification, that as Marxists and former allies, they knew the social imperialists in Moscow better than Kissinger did. The Chinese had told the Pakistanis in 1964–1966, when Pakistan had made serious bids to woo the Soviets: "We know the Russians in a better way, just as you know the Indians better. You warned us against the Indians and we made a mistake by not listening to you properly."[15] The Pakistanis remembered the Chinese warning in 1971, rather too late, when India, backed by the Soviets, dismembered Pakistan.

Zbigniew Brzezinski, who finally pushed the process of normalization of the Sino-American relationship in 1978, seems to have assessed the Chinese thinking better than Kissinger had. According to the Chinese, Kissinger seems to have taken China's friendship for granted, thinking that because of worries about the threat from the Soviet Union, China would accept the U.S. low-profile attitude for an indefinite period.[16] But China was not prepared to accept such bargaining tactics by the Americans, and any undue delay in normalizing the U.S.-China relationship might have resulted in a tragic ending for the great diplomatic feat the United States had begun at the 1972 Peking Summit. Any serious cooling of the Sino-American relationship would have enabled the Soviet Union to pursue even tougher policies in Europe, the Middle East, Africa, and many other parts of the Third World, as subsequent developments in world politics have demonstrated.

A Chinese performing arts troupe's visit to the United States in 1975 was canceled by the U.S. National Committee on U.S.-China Relations, and the U.S. Department of State endorsed the cancellation because of a song entitled, "People of Taiwan, Our Own Brother." The Americans demanded that the song be excluded, but the Chinese considered the demand as totally unacceptable, stating, "The liberation of Taiwan and unification of the motherland is Chinese peoples' internal affairs in which no other country has the right to interfere; for us this is a matter of principle." The Chinese also regarded the U.S. demand as being "against the spirit of the Shanghai communique in which the U.S. government has agreed that there is but one China and Taiwan is a part of China."[17] This small episode epitomizes China's super sensitiveness on the Taiwan issue, and people who thought that China would abandon its stand on the Taiwan issue, because of its fear of the Russians, were not reading the Chinese mind correctly. China is the most volatile partner in the great triangular relationship that emerged in the 1970s.[18]

Henry Kissinger made his next trip to Beijing in October 1975, mainly to make arrangements for President Ford's projected visit to China in November 1975, which had been agreed upon during the 1974 Kissinger visit. During his four-day trip, Kissinger had, as usual, wide-range discussions with the Chinese leaders, mainly with Vice-Premier Deng and Foreign Minister Jiao Guanhua. This time, Chairman Mao also received Kissinger as too much speculation had been raised by Kissinger's not being received by Mao during his previous visit in November 1974, and the Chinese wanted to dispel any undue concern about their alleged displeasure with U.S. progress toward the restoration of full diplomatic relations between the two countries. Kissinger had a very useful and cordial one-hundred-minute session with Mao, and according to a Chinese press release of October 21, 1975, the conversation was conducted "in a friendly atmosphere on a wide range of questions." The whole purpose of the Mao-Kissinger meeting was to dramatize that the Chinese, notwithstanding some strains and stresses in the Sino-American relationship, were eager to preserve, and if possible to foster, the growth of the relationship. Both sides had reservations and doubts, and yet the two countries were anxious to continue the process of normalizing relations for mutual national interests.

The October visit ended with disagreement over the U.S. policy of détente with the Soviet Union, and the Chinese foreign minister, Jiao, publicly criticized the U.S. policy toward the Soviet Union. In his speech welcoming Kissinger, Jiao warned against the dangers of détente with Moscow and urged a tit-for-tat struggle against the Soviet hegemonism. He added, "to base oneself on illusions is to mistake hopes or wishes for reality and [to] act accordingly will only abet the ambitions of expansionism and lead to grave consequences."[19] The Chinese had criticized the policy of détente in the past in many forms, and the Chinese press never missed an opportunity to expose the hollowness of the détente between the two superpowers. But the Chinese had not used any of Kissinger's previous visits to publicly warn him about the dangers of the U.S. policy toward the Soviet Union. They might have warned Kissinger privately, but previously there had not been a public denunciation of the U.S. policy in the presence of Kissinger, their guest. The Chinese persisted in their comments that the United States had been appeasing the Soviet Union and was thus risking another world war. They also attacked the U.S.-USSR talks on European security and cooperation and the SALT II negotiations. Another major topic of discussion was Korea. The Chinese repeated their position that the United States should withdraw its troops from South Korea and engage in direct talks with North Korea.[20]

In his reply, Kissinger defended his policy of détente with Moscow rather forcefully, by saying that he was alert to the dangers from Moscow but would nevertheless continue his policy of détente; he also made it clear to the Chinese that the United States would stand up to the Soviet Union if the security of a third country were involved.[21] Kissinger said, "Our two countries are too self-reliant to need reassurance and too experienced to confuse words with reality or tactics with strategy."[22] Kissinger's main theme was that just as the Sino-American relationship would not be sacrificed to satisfy Moscow, the policy of détente would continue in spite of Beijing's distrust of such policy toward Moscow. Kissinger thus kept his line of communications open in both Beijing and Moscow. He expected that the Chinese would appreciate the U.S. global policy, but it appears that the new Chinese leader, Vice-Premier Deng, did not appreciate being lectured by the former professor of Harvard University. The Chinese suspicions about Kissinger's handling of the U.S. foreign policy were further deepened by the frank and useful dialogues during Kissinger's October 1975 mission to Beijing. It was left for Brzezinski to assuage Chinese suspicions when he visited China in 1978 as President Carter's national security adviser.

There was some progress in the bilateral relations between the two countries during Kissinger's 1975 visit. Details of President Ford's forthcoming visit were worked out, though not finalized, and some progress was also made on the issue of frozen assets in the two countries – $200 million in blocked U.S. claims against China and $80 million in Chinese assets frozen in the United States. But those were secondary issues. The two real issues for the stalemate in the Sino-American relationship were the Taiwan problem and the U.S.-USSR détente, and no progress was made on either of those two vital issues. But to underline the cordiality of the meeting, the Chinese foreign minister noted that on the whole, Sino-American relations had "moved forward in the last few years," and Kissinger reaffirmed that "the United States will resist hegemony as we have already stated in the Shanghai communique."[23] The 1972 communiqué still remained the last word in the emerging relations between the two countries.

On his arrival in Tokyo from Beijing, Kissinger said that Chinese leaders' perception of the United States had changed: They regarded the United States as "less impressive in world affairs" than it was a few years ago. In China's eyes, the collapse of the U.S.-backed governments in Indochina was a sign of the weakness and incompetence of the United States. The Chinese were also unhappy to see uncertainties in the formation of U.S. policy as a result of the friction between the U.S. Congress and the administration on foreign policy.[24]

The unsatisfactory state of affairs in the Sino-American relationship was reflected by a small incident on November 3, 1975, when a White House advance team bound for Beijing to prepare for the president's visit "boarded their aircraft only to be told to debark just as the engines were warming."[25] Reliable diplomatic sources both in Beijing and in Washington indicated that it appears that the Sino-American relationship had entered into an era of uncertainty because of a number of factors in both the countries. China's internal situation, which was affected by the declining health of its two topmost leaders, Chairman Mao and Premier Zhou Enlai, was casting a shadow on the future U.S. policy toward the PRC. The communist victory in the whole of Indochina altered the balance of power in Asia; the Moscow-Hanoi entente was not yet fully developed, but its indications were already there. China's frustration over U.S. policy on the Taiwan issue was deepening. On the eve of President Ford's proposed visit to the PRC, more than a dozen resolutions, supported by over one hundred members of the U.S. House of Representatives, were filed with the International Relations and Military Affairs committees of the House in favor of Taiwan: "It is the sense of the Congress that the United States Government, while engaged in lessening tensions with the People's Republic of China, will do nothing to compromise the freedom of our friend and ally, Taiwan and its people."[26]

The White House advance party finally left for Beijing on November 17, and Ford's visit was at last finalized. The glamour of the 1972 presidential visit was not to be there; nor were there any expectations that the Sino-American relationship would be moved forward beyond the Shanghai communiqué. It was to be a minisummit, a much less significant and almost a routine one when compared with the 1972 summit.

The 1975 Minisummit

The first U.S. presidential visit to the PRC had been in February 1972; Gerald Ford gave the Chinese another opportunity to welcome the U.S. president in December 1975. During the intervening period, many changes had taken place in both countries, both internally and externally. Internally, the Chinese political scene was in a state of great suspense and uncertainty. Premier Zhou Enlai was seriously ill and died in a month's time after President Ford's visit. Chairman Mao, the eighty-one-year-old leader, was also in declining health and died in less than a year's time after Ford's visit in December 1975. President Ford's main host, Vice-Premier Deng Xiaoping was having his first "political comeback," holding important positions in the Chinese Communist party, government, and army, but he was thrown out of power less than five months later, in April 1976. In the United States, the White House occupant was an unelected and interim persident who lost the office in less than a year. He was under pressure both from his Republican party and from the U.S. Congress not to make any major concessions to the PRC at the cost of a U.S. ally and friend, Taiwan, which was the crucial issue in the Sino-American relationship.

There had been hardly any progress toward a normalization of relations between Beijing and Washington over the Taiwan issue. On the contrary, the United States had sent a new ambassador to Taiwan in late 1974, and later, in 1976, Taiwan was permitted to open two new consulates in the United States, which made a total of five new Taiwan consulates in the United States since the 1972 Shanghai communiqué. Although the United States had committed itself to the eventual withdrawal of U.S. armed forces from Taiwan in the 1972 communiqué, there were still 5,145 U.S. servicemen in Taiwan in 1975.[27] Indeed, additional U.S. air power had been sent to Taiwan in 1973, and Taiwan was allowed to coproduce U.S. F-5E fighters. The U.S. military advisory mission was still functioning on the island, and its basic purpose was "to advise, to equip and to train the Chinese on Taiwan on how best to fight the Chinese from the People's Republic."[28] Not only the Chinese, but any impartial analyst could say that the Shanghai communiqué was not being honored insofar as the Taiwan issue was concerned. Nor could President Ford do anything in December 1975 because of the ensuing U.S. election in 1976.

On the global scene, also, there had been great developments since the first U.S. presidential visit in 1972. There had been a communist victory in Indochina, and the Soviet penetration in Indochina, South Asian subcontinent, and Indian Ocean area was growing. China was worried about the decline of the power and role of the United States in the Asian-Pacific region, and China was no longer opposed to the military buildup of Japan. China was also worried about what it considered to be the United States' "soft" policy toward the Soviet Union. A dialogue between China and the United States on the summit level was mutually desired, equally so by Beijing, even though such a meeting might not produce anything tangible.

With 1 million Russian troops on China's northern frontier and the growing Soviet penetration on its southern borders—because of greater Soviet influence in Hanoi, which became a powerful regional power after the 1975 communist victory in Indochina—China had to give a high priority to its newly established ties with Washington. China was disappointed and dismayed by the slow progress of the normalization of relations in accordance with the Shanghai communiqué, and it was also worried about the prospects of détente between Moscow and Washington; about Kissinger's low-profile attitude toward the PRC as compared to China's archenemy, the Soviet Union; and about the exit of the toughest critic of détente in the Ford administration, James Schlesinger. China was still eager to review its relationship with the United States "in the frankest possible way" on the summit level.[29]

The United States was eager to demonstrate that notwithstanding its policy of détente with the Soviet Union, its China card—obtained after the profound breakthrough of 1971–1972—was still available as leverage in U.S. dealings with Moscow. The Sino-American relationship was not based on love on either side. Premier Zhou Enlai had told the Ninth Communist Party Congress in 1969 that compromise with the United States could be compared with Lenin's Brest-Litovsk treaties with the Germans in World War I, according to which, Russia gave up fighting the Germans in order to concentrate on the more serious issue of winning the revolution.[30] In 1973, the more serious issue was the threat from the Soviet social imperialists.

Kissinger pointed out in a press conference prior to the 1975 minisummit that he was keen to make clear that Beijing had nothing to fear from a détente between Washington and Moscow; that President Ford and he were no more doves than James Schlesinger; and that the United States would continue the negotiations on SALT II, but only on the basis of a balanced and sound agreement.[31] Yet the second U.S. presidential trip to Beijing, in December 1975, was a journey with a symbolic purpose rather than a substantial one. There were internal impediments in both countries to the strengthening of the Sino-American relationship, and no major breakthrough or any significant development was expected.

President Ford flew to China with his wife and daughter and, of course, Henry Kissinger on November 30, 1975. He declared at Elelson Air Force Base, Alaska, enroute to Beijing, that friendship with Beijing and Moscow would be backed by strong U.S. military power: "Let me assure you today that my administration, while striving to preserve world peace, remains aware that best insurance for peace is U.S. military power second to none."[32] The statement was perhaps meant to dispel the Chinese perception of the United States as weak and unwilling to play its role in world affairs.

Ford and his entourage were given a better airport reception than Nixon had received in 1972 – a group of forty-seven foreign diplomats were present besides the Chinese high officials and dignitaries. Then President Ford and his party were greeted by the wives of Chairman Mao and Premier Zhou Enlai at the official guest house. Ford also had a prior written assurance that he would be received by Chairman Mao himself. Because of the uncertain state of the relationship beween the two countries, Kissinger had thought it advisable to have a commitment that the U.S. president would be accorded the impressive welcome that only Chairman Mao could bestow.[33] It was a strange, almost presumptuous diplomatic procedure, but not an unexpected one in view of the unpredictable Sino-American relationship.

President Ford had three lengthy sessions with Vice-Premier Deng, who was acting for Premier Zhou Enlai though his style and manners were not the same as those of Zhou. Deng is a tough and sometimes blunt negotiator, but effective and understanding. At the first exchange of comments in public, both sides expressed, rather bluntly, their differences over the U.S. policy of détente with the Soviet Union. The Chinese were anxious to make their position known to the Americans and to the world; so also was President Ford determined to explain the rationale of his country's policy toward Moscow. Deng, in his speech at the welcoming banquet on December 1, 1975, said that "rhetoric about detente cannot cover up the stark reality of the growing war posed by the appeasement of the Soviet Union,"[34] and he labeled Moscow as the world's "most dangerous source of war." It was rather uncommon, severe public language for a summit meeting, but China's concern about Russia's hegemony was the hallmark of the 1975 Beijing Minisummit from the very beginning. However, Deng did not miss the opportunity to mention the positive aspects of the Sino-American relationship. After blasting the policy of détente, he quickly added that the Sino-American relationship had been improving since the 1972 Shanghai communiqué, and he also referred to President Ford's repeated assurances that the principles of the Shanghai communiqué will be adhered to. Deng's comments were considered as frank but not provocative.

President Ford, in his reply, preferred to stress the positive side of Deng's comments. Ford reiterated that the United States was determined to "pursue detente with caution, balancing strength, vigilance and firmness with continued exploration of new opportunities for peace without illusion." He also added a cheerful note to the occasion by saying that the United States and China "have a mutual interest in seeing that the world is not dominated by military force or pressure."[35] Having thus stated with some bluntness the extent of their differences over détente, Ford and Deng had their three sessions to discuss global issues and matters of mutual interest.

President Ford had an hour-and-fifty-minute meeting with Chairman Mao on December 2, 1975, which was described by the Chinese as "earnest and significant discussions . . . on wide-ranging issues in a friendly atmosphere."[36] The U.S. officials accompanying Ford did not challenge the Chinese interpretation of the Mao-Ford meeting, but they conceded that it did not produce anything unexpected or spectacular. Similarly, the lengthy sessions between Ford and Deng did not produce anything significant or any major breakthrough. The meeting was a "holding action."

President Ford and Vice Premier Deng were so far apart on the vital issue of détente between the two superpowers at the end of four days of lengthy talks that they were unable to agree on a joint communiqué. The talks were described as mutually beneficial and conducive to the understanding of each other's viewpoints, etc., but the 1975 minisummit did not result in any new agreements, no progress on the normalization of relations between the two countries, and not even a joint communiqué. Yet the two leaders tacitly agreed that both countries would strive to counter any Soviet adventurism in Europe, Africa, or the Asian-Pacific region, and Deng said that the Americans and the Chinese were setting a new style in negotiations.[37] It was some sort of agreement to disagree.

Both sides, while remaining split on détente, were determined to work for the improvement of bilateral relations between the PRC and the United States. Both sides, however, realized that unless the Taiwan issue were resolved and unless there were some shifts, if not significant changes, in the pursuit of détente, prospects for further improvement in the Sino-American relationship were very limited. On those two basic issues—Taiwan and détente—neither President Ford nor Secretary of State Kissinger would make any claim of progress or success. The United States was unable to proceed in the matter of full diplomatic recognition of the PRC at the cost of Taiwan in an impending election year, nor was the United States convinced by China's concern about détente with Moscow. It was not until the Soviet invasion of an independent and a nonaligned Asian country, Afghanistan, in 1979 that the United States began to have second thoughts about détente. Similarly, it took another three years of earnest and serious negotiations by another American professor, Zbigniew Brzezinski, for the Taiwan issue to be resolved and full diplomatic relations to be restored between Beijing and Washington.

So President Ford's minisummit with the Chinese leaders ended as predicted: "Sino-American relations are no better and no worse for his four days of talks with Teng Hsiao-ping and Co."[38] Deng subsequently claimed that President Ford had promised that he would restore full diplomatic relations between the PRC and the United States after his reelection in 1976.[39] Ford denied Deng's claim, but his denial was not convincing. His reply was that he had told the Chinese during his 1975 visit that "the United States might possibly sever diplomatic contacts with Taiwan to achieve normalization of relations with China." He, however, added that he had made no commitments, he had only discussed the matter as a possibility.[40]

The main result of Ford's visit was that it demonstrated to the Soviet Union that the United States was balancing détente and a developing relationship with China, Moscow's number-one enemy. It was also reassuring for the Chinese to demonstrate that Washington might not fully endorse the Chinese assessment of détente but that Beijing and Washington had a parallel, though not identical, interest in the containment of the Soviet influence and power in Europe, Africa, and Asia—that China was not alone in opposing Soviet expansionist designs in various parts of the world. For Beijing, the reassurance was not insignificant. Kissinger said, "The United States is opposed to military expansions . . . and would resist it."[41] His statement was not any guarantee of U.S. help in case of a Soviet aggression against China, but it was perhaps the nearest thing to such an assurance China could expect in view of the limited relationship between the PRC and the United States in the mid 1970s.

When I visited Beijing in July 1976, the Chinese referred to the stalemate in the Sino-American relations with anguish rather than with anger. They appreciated that it was difficult for the United States to make any decision when there was an interim president; they also realized that in an election year (1976), the U.S. government could not proceed toward a full diplomatic relationship with China – as had been promised by President Nixon and, according to the Chinese, by Ford also. But the Chinese were unable to appreciate the same U.S. government's enthusiasm for détente with Moscow or the U.S. weakness in dealing with Soviet expansionist designs in Africa, such as in Angola.

It was suggested in certain quarters that China attached greater importance to the U.S. policy of détente with Moscow than to the "liberation" of Taiwan. There might be some truth in such speculations, but they are not completely accurate. Like any other country, China wants to achieve a favorable balance of power from the standpoint of its national security and interests. There is no doubt that any good relations between Moscow and Washington would enable the Soviet Union to pursue its policy of a containment of China more vigorously, which would increase China's problems of national security. So it is constructive diplomacy on China's part to frustrate any prospects of détente between the United States and the USSR, but that fact does not imply that China has ceased to consider the Taiwan issue as being of crucial importance in China's bilateral relationship with the United States. Nor is it wise to take China's friendship for granted or to exploit its weaker diplomatic options vis-à-vis the United States because of China's rift with the Russians. In desperation, a nation, like an individual, may resort to desperate measures.

Kissinger's apparent policy of pushing China too far was full of risks. The Chinese made inquiries about Zbigniew Brzezinski and seem to have preferred his assessment of Soviet policy and strategy. According to Brzezinski, any undue delay in the normalization of Sino-American relations might have adverse effects on U.S. global interests as the Soviets would be free to pursue their expansionist designs more actively in the Third World. Even before becoming national security adviser to President Carter in 1977, Brzezinski favored a quicker process of normalizing relations between China and the United States, and he was also critical of Kissinger's undue optimism about détente with Moscow. Consequently, China approved of Brzezinski, and he subsequently played a significant role in the establishment of full diplomatic relations between Washington and Beijing in 1978.

Soviet Reaction to the Minisummit

When President Nixon took diplomatic initiatives toward the PRC in 1971–1972, the Russians were worried about a collusion between Washington and Beijing, and they were concerned about the 1972 Peking Summit. But President Ford's visit to the PRC in December 1975 caused no stir in Moscow. The Soviets seemed to have concluded that relations between China and the United States were stalled while China was unsettled internally because of Mao's poor health; they were also confident that the United States was not in a hurry to upgrade its diplomatic relations with Beijing by severing its diplomatic and security ties with Taiwan, particularly with an election year approaching. The Soviet reaction to the 1975 minisummit was one of indifference–Why make a fuss about a stalemated relationship?

Deng's warnings to President Ford about the dangers of détente with Moscow caused no worries in Moscow as the Russians knew that U.S. foreign policy could not be dictated by Beijing. They took more seriously Kissinger's warning that the Soviet-Cuban military adventures in Angola and other parts of Africa might affect détente. The Russians were so convinced of what the Chinese termed Kissinger's "one-way traffic to détente" that the Russians continued to help the causes of so-called liberation struggles in Afro-Asian countries. For the Russians, détente had a more limited meaning than it had in either Washington or Beijing. The Soviet worries about a far-reaching understanding between Washington and Beijing had subsided because of the slow progress of the process of normalizing relations between the two countries. Soviet worries increase whenever there is any warming up of the Sino-American relationship, just as prospects of détente cause worries in Beijing, and during 1974–1976, there was no reason for such Soviet concern.

The Year of Tremendous Changes in China–1976

In 1976, China lost its two great leaders, the men who had dominated Chinese affairs since the communist regime came to power in China in 1949. Zhou Enlai, the country's premier since 1949, died on January 8, 1976. He had been China's ablest administrator, particularly in external affairs, and, on the Chinese side, the architect of the new Sino-American relationship that began in 1971–1972. Then Chairman Mao, who had made the final decisions on China's vital issues, both internal and external, died on September 9, 1976. Which way China? was the obvious question after the deaths of Mao and Zhou Enlai. A country's external behavior and relations can not be understood without some knowledge of its internal situation.

Zhou Enlai died in January 1976, and four months later his successor, Deng Xiaoping, the senior vice-premier who had played the role of the host and chief negotiator during President Ford's visit to the PRC in December 1975, was unceremoniously dismissed from all his positions, inside and outside the party, on April 7, 1976, and the acting premier, Hua Guofeng, was made premier and the first vice-chairman of the Chinese Communist party. Deng's dismissal followed violent demonstrations in Tian An Men Square in Beijing on April 5, 1976, but the radical or ultraleftist group inside the Chinese Communist party had been agitating against Deng since Zhou Enlai's death in January 1976. Deng had been purged once before, in 1966 during the Cultural Revolution, but Zhou had brought him back to power in 1973, and he had virtually been Zhou's chosen successor. Deng represented the moderate and pragmatic group, and he represented Zhou's views more faithfully than anyone else in the Communist party. But, to the surprise of most China watchers, Deng was not made acting premier when Zhou died in January 1976; instead, Hua, a comparatively unknown figure, was chosen. During the period of power struggle in early 1976, Deng was the main target of the radical group, led by Mao's wife, Jiang Qing. Hua was a compromise choice as he belonged to neither the leftist nor the moderate group.[42]

After Deng's dismissal, the political instability was not yet over, and the leftist and moderate groups were getting ready for the ultimate struggle for power after the imminent death of Chairman Mao. When Mao died on September 9, 1976, there was almost a blitz between the two groups. Vice-Chairman and Premier Hua was designated chairman of the Chinese Communist party in place of Chairman Mao on October 12, 1976. Then on October 13, a senior Chinese official was reported to have said that Mao's wife, Jiang Qing, and her three principal associates—Wang Hongwen, Yao Wenyuan, and Zhang Chunqiao, henceforth known as the Gang of Four—had been arrested in Beijing by the bodyguards of Hua, whom they had put into power only six months before. They had been allegedly holding a secret conclave aimed at falsifying Mao's will and making his widow chairman of the party. Mao's widow was even accused of trying to kill Mao when "he was on his deathbed," and there were charges that she had plotted the assassination of Chairman (then Premier) Hua.[43]

The next phase of the power struggle was the rehabilitation of Deng Xiaoping on July 22, 1977; his second "political comeback" to full power and position. I was in Beijing when the Third Plenum of the Tenth Central Committee of the Chinese Communist party made the decision in favor of Deng, which marked the end of the power struggle in China caused by the deaths of Mao and Zhou Enlai. A great Chinese scholar who is also a top foreign policy adviser told me that China was now engaged in three basic movements: class struggle, production struggle, and scientific experiments. Through class struggle, China would avoid the dangers of "revisionism" as it had developed in the Soviet Union. Through production struggle, China would vigorously attempt to accelerate economic development, both agricultural and industrial. By scientific experiments, China would continue to make scientific and technological progress, which would also involve modernizing China's armed forces. The *People's Daily* summed up the new trends in China's internal policy: "If we did not learn the advanced experiences of foreign countries, then we might as well turn off the electric lights for electricity was invented by Franklin! We should also stop running trains, for the steam engine was invented by Watt."[44]

The new pragmatic leaders in post-Mao China were trained and greatly influenced by the late premier, Zhou Enlai, and the great question was, Would the new Chinese leaders continue to follow Mao and Zhou's foreign policy, particularly the policy of the post–Cultural Revolution period (1969–1976)? There were many speculations, including some pessimistic ones, that after the deaths of Chairman Mao and Premier Zhou Enlai, China would be torn by political upheavals; that political instability or even civil war might affect the country's progress and its role in world affairs. The People's Republic of China is a nation of nearly a billion people and is equipped with nuclear weapons; it is not yet a superpower but has the potential to become one. Already a major power, it is destined to play a central role in world affairs. China's international role after Mao and Zhou had, therefore, great significance. What would be the future trends in the Sino-American relationship? Would the Sino-Soviet rift, to which Mao was a major contributor, continue, or would there be a closing of differences – a development that would affect not only the two communist giants, but also the fragile triangular relationship between Washington, Moscow, and Beijing? Would there be any major change in the balance of power in the Asian-Pacific region, where the interests of all major powers interact?

The former U.S. defense secretary, James Schlesinger, made an unprecedented trip to the PRC at the time of the death of Chairman Mao in September 1976. On his return from China, Schlesinger was asked if China were headed for a period of political turmoil and did he see the danger of civil war? Schlesinger, who is held in high esteem by the Chinese because of his opposition to the U.S. policy of détente with the Soviet Union, had a unique ability to answer those vital questions after his twenty-three-day visit to the PRC. His assessment, which subsequently proved correct was: "I don't think that one should anticipate political turmoil. Chairman Mao himself provided a unifying force. The leadership fully recognizes that it is now in their common interest to avoid serious schisms."[45] Referring to the struggle between moderates and radicals in China, Schlesinger said: "It conveys a notion of two fixed groups squaring off strictly over policy. It leaves little room for the maneuverings of ins and outs. The reality is probably one of competing and overlaping [*sic*] sets of individuals with somewhat different preferences in liturgy and authority, but recognizing their common need to sustain the system."[46]

Ross Terrill of Harvard University has referred to his meeting with Premier Zhou Enlai in 1971, when Zhou reminded Terrill of the "nine great struggles within the Chinese Communist Party." Then came the purging of Defense Minister Lin Biao, and there were two purges in 1976, so Ross Terrill concludes: "In fact the pattern of purges in China does not resemble the Soviet case. . . . Hua's China will in this respect be less comparable to Stalin's Russia than to Russia under Khrushchev and Brehznev, where dramatic purges have given way to quiet demotion."[47] After my 1976 visit to the PRC, I wrote, "It is too early to predict what will be policies of new leaders in China, either internal or external, but I feel confident . . . that China will continue to pursue policies best suited to her national, regional and global interests."[48]

Henry Kissinger had stated that the leadership changes in China following the death of Chairman Mao were not expected to make fundamental changes in the country's relations with the United States. "The basic factors which brought the United States and China in contact with each other are still operating and are likely to continue" said Kissinger, evidently referring to the hostility and rivalry between China and its neighbor, the Soviet Union.[49] Kissinger did not believe that a full rapprochement between the two communist giants was likely no matter who controlled the party apparatus and government in China.[50] A similar view had been expressed earlier by the Central Intelligence Agency director, George Bush, who was also the second U.S. liaison officer in Beijing. Bush predicted that China, under the new leaders, was not likely to make any major changes in the Sino-American relationship.[51]

China's foreign policy under Mao and Zhou Enlai was a mixture of nationalism and ideology, the former getting the upper hand if there was any conflict. Since their deaths, major changes have taken place in China's internal policy, but there has not been any major change in China's foreign policy. A careful analysis of the post-Mao Chinese foreign policy would indicate that it is geared to meet China's global, regional, and national interests. Mao and Zhou tried to promote the same objectives, so it is likely that China's foreign policy goals will continue to be the same. There have been ups and downs in the Sino-American relationship, but the relationship will continue as long as it serves the national interests of China and the United States. Similarly, the Sino-Soviet rift has survived the deaths of Mao and Zhou Enlai, but one should not conclude that the great rift will continue forever. The rift may be reduced, if not wholly healed, if the Chinese and the Russians find it necessary or desirable to do so in order to promote their objectives.

After Mao and Zhou Enlai's deaths in 1976, China never reverted to any self-imposed isolation as happened during the Cultural Revolution, but it has been more engaged with internal problems and with problems of stability. China's first year without Mao and Zhou was devoted mainly to bringing about internal cohesion and stability rather than assuming an active role in the world. During my 1977 visit to the PRC, I found that the Chinese were more concerned about their internal problems than about their future role in external affairs, which was not an unexpected or abnormal situation. By the end of 1977, China's uncertainty seemed to be over, and China had begun to revive its outward-looking foreign policy with renewed vigor and with greater confidence.

Strains and Stresses in the Sino-American Relationship

The year 1976 was also an election year in the United States, and in an election year, there is always debate on U.S. foreign policy, and various issues are involved in the debate. In 1976, the normalization of relations between the United States and the PRC was discussed and debated. There had been a slowdown in the movement toward the establishment of formal diplomatic relations. The two countries had opened quasi-embassies, known as liaison offices, in 1973, but after that, no big step toward the establishment of full diplomatic relations could be taken; the reason was the same as it was at the time of the 1972 Peking Summit – the Taiwan issue, which remained the crucial issue in the bilateral relationship between the two countries. So a multiple question – whether, when, and how the United States should break with Taiwan and recognize the PRC – was debated by specialists, both inside and outside the government.

Harvard Law professor Jerome A. Cohen was a consultant on China policy to the Democratic presidential candidate, Jimmy Carter, and Cohen presented a new formula in his article, "A China Policy for the Next Administration." Cohen believed that the United States could devise a new type of guarantee for Taiwan to replace the formal 1954 security pact with Taiwan, which had to be abrogated before full diplomatic recognition to the PRC could be accorded. Cohen advocated a "solemn policy declaration by the president, conveying a national commitment, possibly strengthened by a congressional resolution, authorizing in advance any action in defense of Taiwan that might, at the discretion of the president, prove necessary." He also suggested continuing military sales to Taiwan through private auspices.[52]

Senate Majority Leader Mike Mansfield urged that the United States sever its defense treaty with Taiwan and grant prompt, full diplomatic recognition to China. Mansfield said the U.S. military pact with the Nationalist Chinese government of Taiwan was "based on a distorted view not only of America's long-range interests in the Far East, but also of the nature of the People's Republic of China." The security of the United States was not involved in the future of Taiwan, and Mansfield added:

"Treaties are not forever. They are national commitments subject to adjustment in the light of changing international realities and clearer perception of national interests." Mansfield, one of the U.S. Senate's foremost China specialists, continued: "All the world applauded [President] Nixon's trip to Peking. Whether or not it applaudes the completion of the journey he started, it is essential in this nation's interest that we move promptly in that direction."[53] Senator Mansfield made his strong pleas for full diplomatic relations with the PRC after his sixth trip to China, immediately after Chairman Mao's death in September 1976 (September 21 to October 12, 1976).

When Jimmy Carter assumed the U.S. presidency in January 1977, he was not caught up in directing a U.S. war in Asia as his three predecessors had been. His difficult decision in Asia was when and how to resume the stalled movement toward a normalization of diplomatic relations with China.[54] As already mentioned, Kissinger, in his last days as secretary of state, seemed to regard the issue of a diplomatic relationship with China as a low-priority item. The new secretary of state, Cyrus Vance, also seemed to be in no hurry to upgrade the existing relationship with the PRC. He said, "We will continue to be guided by the Shanghai communique,"[55] which set no time limit for full diplomatic relations between the PRC and the United States. President Carter's national security adviser, Zbigniew Brzezinski was more enthusiastic about China and said: "I think it is quite clear that it is enormously in the American interest to have an increasingly normal relationship with the P.R.C. . . . but I think it is also in the interest of the P.R.C. In that sense, our interest and their interests are complementary."[56] The U.S. experts began to draft and redraft a detailed China policy for the Carter administration, and the Chinese watched the process with dismay and concern.[57]

Cyrus Vance was reported to be checking to determine whether former Secretary of State Henry Kissinger had reached any "secret understanding" with the PRC concerning the abandonment of U.S. ties with Taiwan. It was revealed that although there was "no proof" that any understandings had been reached, "it now seems apparent that President Nixon and Kissinger virtually promised Peking that the U.S. would scrap the Taiwan connection in a couple of years."[58] In fact, such assurances were given while the secret Sino-American negotiations were being carried on through President Yahya in 1969–1971.[59]

Professor Allen S. Whiting, who had been a key adviser to Nixon and Kissinger in regard to opening a relationship with China in 1971–1972, said: "Full diplomatic relations with Peking are needed and can be accomplished without sacrificing Taiwan." But, he added, "It requires education of Congress and the American people by the Carter Administration and this long process has yet to begin."[60]

The Chinese leaders in the post-Mao era were prepared to give President Carter a reasonable period to take the next steps in the direction of full diplomatic relations, but they were anxiously waiting to see what President Carter's China policy would be. When China's ambassador, Huang Zhen, met with President Carter in February 1977, he reminded Carter of the U.S. promises and assurances about full diplomatic relations between the United States and China.

After an unsuccessful Vance mission to Moscow to discuss the SALT II agreement in August 1977, there were increasing signs that the Carter administration was giving more attention to China. The president's son, Chip Carter, had accompanied a congressional delegation to China in April 1977, the administration was talking about the need "to normalize relations with Peking before the end of the year,"[61] and Secretary of State Vance had planned a visit to China, which took place on August 22–25, 1977. Before Vance's visit, there was a lot of thinking and appraisal in both Washington and Beijing about the future of the Sino-American relationship. Former Senator Hugh Scott disclosed that after he had visited China in 1976, he had recommended to President Ford "that the United States sever diplomatic ties with Taiwan and normalize relations with Peking even if mainland China did not pledge to refrain from using force to take over Taiwan."[62] Views similar to Senator Scott's were expressed by Senator Edward M. Kennedy, and in a Boston speech on August 16, he presented a formula for achieving diplomatic recognition of the PRC by the United States. The "Kennedy formula" was to sever diplomatic connection with Taiwan but to maintain unofficial relations with Taiwan for its security and economic support. Kennedy advocated that since there were new leaders in Washington and Beijing, "it is now appropriate to complete the process begun in 1972 for establishing full diplomatic relations with Peking," and he added that "for its global interests the United States should accept Peking's demands for breaking official ties with Taiwan—we must end our diplomatic presence there and our defense treaty." Kennedy claimed that his formula did not mean the abandonment of Taiwan, nor did he think it "necessary or useful to extract an explicit renunciation of force [against Taiwan] from Peking." Through creative diplomacy, Kennedy pointed out, the interests of Taiwan could be preserved.[63]

Conservative senators like Barry Goldwater, however, raised their voices against what they called an abandonment of Taiwan, and the U.S. experts on China also expressed divergent opinions. Scholars such as Ross Terrill of Harvard and Donald Zagoria of Columbia advocated a quicker diplomatic recognition of the PRC, and listed the major advantages the United States would secure as a result of better relations with that country.[64] But Taiwan had also supporters in U.S. academic circles, and the Taiwan lobbyists made hectic efforts to present Taiwan's case to the Carter administration, which issued a provocative statement reaffirming its support of Taiwan on the eve of the Vance mission to Beijing. The Carter administration went out of its way to stress that "the United States will refuse to normalize ties if it means even the appearance of abandoning Taiwan"[65] — a statement that made the Vance trip to Beijing "futile diplomacy." In the words of one article, "Once again he [Vance] is travelling with an empty briefcase."[66]

The Chinese were dismayed by President Carter's low-profile attitude toward Beijing. According to Carter's foreign policy, China, they felt, had a low priority, and they did not think that Carter attached the same importance to a normalization of relations as Nixon or even Ford had. There was some sense of frustration over the Carter administration's handling of the China issue. I had lengthy sessions with the Chinese ambassadors at the UN mission in New York and also at the liaison office in Washington, and before I went to China in July 1977, I discussed in depth the Chinese attitude or, to put it more correctly, their dismay with President Carter's alleged neglect of U.S.-China relations. Between March and June 1977, I gathered the impression that China's patience on the Taiwan issue was getting overtaxed as Carter would never mention the China policy without referring to the U.S. obligations to Taiwan.

The first breakthrough was Carter's speech at the United Nations on March 17, 1977, when he said: "We will continue our efforts to develop our relationship with the People's Republic of China. We recognize our parallel strategic interests in maintaining stability in Asia and will act in the spirit of the Shanghai Communique."[67] But no tangible action followed up that speech, and the Chinese dismay was expressed by a senior Chinese Foreign Ministry official in Beijing: "We have not found any sign . . . of a decision being taken by the United States to resolve the problem [of full diplomatic relations]." He continued, "In other words there is no sign in sight at this point that the United States has made its mind to discuss normalizing relations between our two countries."[68]

I visited Beijing on July 19–31, 1977, and had the opportunity to interview top Chinese foreign affairs officials, people in the Chinese People's Institute for Foreign Affairs, and several other top officials. I also had rewarding discussions with the senior foreign diplomats posted in Beijing, particularly those from countries that have cordial and intimate relations with the PRC. From my intensive talks and interviews, I determined that the Chinese attitude toward Washington was one of bitterness and frustration. In 1976, it was anguish; in 1977, it turned to anger. When I asked about Vance's visit, a senior official told me: "Let Mr. Vance or even President Carter come; we shall extend them all courtesy and cordiality, true to our traditional hospitality. But nothing will be achieved unless they accept the fundamental reality of one China." When I asked what made the Chinese so pessimistic and how they could have such a gloomy outlook concerning the United States, the reply was: "We have been waiting since 1972; or even since 1970–1971. The Americans are not fulfilling their commitments. We appreciate their internal difficulties, but they seem to take our patience for weakness and our friendship for granted. They sometimes seem to play what they themselves call the 'China card' in their dealings with the Russians. We could have also played a 'Russian card' by pretending to respond to Moscow's post-Mao gestures; but, as you know from your experiences in Pakistan, we deal with other nations on principle and do not resort to any games."

Did the situation imply that the Sino-American relationship had really suffered a serious setback, as Chinese Vice-Premier Deng said on September 6 while commenting on Vance's visit? My assessment was that just as the U.S. policymakers were still not definite as to how to proceed with the normalization issue and just as there were divergent views in Washington, there were some leaders in Beijing who might have developed serious doubts about the future prospects of the Sino-American relations – some of those leaders had been doubtful about Mao and Zhou's responses to Nixon's gestures from the beginning. But there were also others who were inclined to share President Carter's view, expressed in his UN speech on March 17, 1977, that there are "parallel strategic interests" between Washington and Beijing. The new pragmatic leaders in China recognized that their basic security and national interests had common objectives with Washington vis-à-vis the Soviet Union. The liberation of Taiwan will never be forgotten or closed, but in addition to Taiwan, there are some vital national interests that will keep the Sino-American relationship going.

One of these common objectives is to contain Soviet influence and power in Africa. The Chinese leaders are making vigorous attacks on Soviet designs in Africa almost regularly, and whenever an African head of state or government visits Beijing, the attack against Soviet imperialism is a common theme. The United States may not speak so bluntly, but it does share China's concern about Soviet designs in Africa.[69]

Another common objective between Beijing and Washington is to limit Soviet influence in the Middle East; neither Washington nor Beijing relish Soviet influence and power in the Middle East or the Persian Gulf and Indian Ocean areas. NATO's fear of the Soviet Union's arms buildup and the consequent threat to NATO countries is another common, though not identical, concern of Beijing and of Washington. In July 1977,

Chinese leaders gave their assessment of the Soviet expansionist designs to retired Admiral Elmo R. Zumwalt, who is respected in China for his consistent opposition to détente with the Soviet Union. Zbigniew Brzezinski had asked Zumwalt to convey to the Chinese leaders the message that the Carter administration, unlike the previous administration, "is prepared to compete with the Soviet Union if necessary."[70] The Chinese leaders told Zumwalt that China and the United States "must use joint efforts in dealing with the Soviet polar bear."[71]

Apart from the negative factor—the common objective of containing the Soviet Union, though the United States does not share fully the Chinese assessment of the Soviet imperialism—there are some positive factors in the Sino-American relationship. They include China's desire to promote trade and economic ties with the United States and China's need for better weapons so it can modernize its armed forces. In 1977, China was not likely to seek arms aid from the United States, nor was the United States likely to supply arms to China. The Chinese were anxious to have indirect military cooperation with the NATO countries, especially France and West Germany, but that was not possible without at least working and having good ties with Washington. Similarly, China's foreign policy objectives in Japan and the ASEAN countries of Southeast Asia demand good relations with Washington. Japan is a top foreign policy priority with China; China has the twin objectives of wishing to develop friendly relations with Japan and wanting to weaken the Russian bid for better relations with that country. Japan is of crucial importance to the Asian policy of both Beijing and Moscow. China realizes fully that the road to Tokyo must be via Washington, and similarly, the ASEAN countries still have close ties with Washington, and any serious setbacks with Washington might jeopardize China's new active diplomacy in Southeast Asia.

All of those factors prevented the Sino-American relationship from total collapse, but the goodwill and genuine feelings generated by Nixon's gestures were damaged by the U.S. concern over Taiwan. That damage was reflected in Deng's comment about Vance's trip to Beijing in August 1977 and in Chairman Hua's comment that the United States was "a mass ally, even though this ally could be temporary, vacillating, unstable and conditional."[72]

Toward a Normalization of Relations

The relationship between Washington and Beijing, which had begun with Nixon's visit to China in 1972, was in danger of collapsing as a result of China's frustration with Washington and growing rift with Moscow. It was the bold and imaginative initiatives of President Carter's national security adviser, Zbigniew Brzezinski, that saved the relationship. The Chinese have always had great admiration for Brzezinski, since they know that he has a profound knowledge of Soviet strategies and policies. Although he is not opposed to a détente between the two superpowers, Brzezinski also knows that China's friendship is important for Washington in dealing with Moscow. This Chinese friendship is sometimes referred to as "the China card" in certain circles in Washington. Whatever it may be called, a good and stable relationship between Washington and Beijing is vitally important in the current global balance of power.

Brzezinski's visit to China in May 1978 was highly significant and may be compared to Nixon's first visit to China in February 1972. Brzezinski had frank and wide-ranging discussions with the top Chinese leaders, including Chairman Hua, Vice-Premier Deng, and Foreign Minister Huang. No other U.S. visitor since the heyday of the Nixon era in 1972–1973 had impressed the Chinese so favorably as Brzezinski did, and diplomatic analysts were particularly struck by the length of time Brzezinski spent conferring with Chinese leaders. The Chinese called his visit highly beneficial, and when I visited Beijing in July 1978, they were full of praise for Brzezinski. His trip ushered in a new era of Sino-American understanding and helped China know where the United States stood on the Soviet Union, China, and Japan. At his farewell dinner on May 22, 1978, Brzezinski told his Chinese guests that "our commitment to friendship with China is based on shared concerns and is derived from a long-term strategic view. We recognize and share China's resolve to resist the efforts of any nation which seeks to establish global or regional hegemony" – nothing could please the Chinese more than the reference to hegemony, which the Chinese interpret as Soviet expansionism. Brzezinski went further by saying, "neither of us dispatches international marauders who masquerade as non-aligned to advance big-power ambitions in Africa" – a reference to the Cuban-Soviet military adventures in Africa, which Beijing and Washington were bitterly opposed to.[73]

Brzezinski and his aides gave the Chinese officials an unprecedented, detailed briefing on the status of the Soviet-American strategic arms talks and explained at length the contents of some secret White House memorandums on U.S. security. In an exclusive interview with the *New York Times* published on May 27, 1978, Brzezinski said, "The basic significance of the trip was to underline the long-term strategic nature of the United States relationship to China."

As a result of Brzezinski's visit, both the United States and China recognized that there were certain common global and strategic areas, such as Africa, East and Southeast Asia, Iran, the Persian Gulf, and the

Middle East. That recognition led to a warming up of the Sino-American relationship, which eventually led to full diplomatic relations. Brzezinski stopped over in Seoul and Tokyo on his return journey from Beijing, and he was reported to have advised the Japanese leaders to conclude their peace treaty with China.

Even the Taiwan issue was resolved. In a major shift of tactics prior to the establishment of full relations, the Chinese leaders told a group of U.S. congressmen led by Lester Wolff that China was willing to negotiate with Taiwan, and Vice-Premier Deng was reported to be most conciliatory on the Taiwan issue.

The new trends in China's foreign policy, particularly its active policy of containment of the Soviet influence in many parts of the Third World and its penetration into Eastern Europe, made the United States look at the normalization of relations with Beijing not only in terms of the Sino-American relationship, but in the broader context of the U.S.-USSR-Beijing triangular relationship. The Chinese were staking out positions parallel to those of the United States on global issues, which was a great help to the United States and put a different light on the prospects for the future—that was the assessment of a top U.S. foreign policy expert.[74] Washington was pleased to see Chairman Hua joining Yugoslavia in pressing for a genuine nonalignment rather than "tilting toward Moscow" through the leadership of countries like Cuba. Another example of the common global activities was China's support of the slogan, Africa for Africans, which was aimed against the Cuban-Soviet military activities in Africa.

President Carter lifted the ban on the sale of airborne scanning equipment to Beijing, and that decision opened the door for a policy move of global proportions. It was also reported that the United States would now encourage its European allies to sell defensive weapons to China.[75] A Chinese military delegation visited a number of NATO countries in early 1978 to look at Western weapons, and Beijing subsequently negotiated an agreement for French antitank missiles. The Chinese have also expressed interest in British transport planes and other weapons, and Beijing has made contact with West Germany for the purchase of Leopard tanks as well as various Western satellite systems. There was no sign as yet that the United States was willing to supply arms to Beijing, but the indications were that China could acquire, with U.S. consent, if not encouragement, Western military equipment and technology from NATO countries.

The Carter administration imposed a moratorium on most high-level official trips to Moscow because of trials of dissidents and other Soviet actions for a period of time in 1978. But at the same time, the Carter administration approved new official delegations to China. In a move to strengthen ties with China, President Carter announced on June 27, 1978, that a high-level delegation of government scientists would go to Beijing, and the science mission, led by Carter's science adviser, Frank Press, made its official visit to China in July 1978. That occasion marked the first government-to-government talks on science and technology between China and the United States, and the science mission had four basic purposes: (1) to establish official contacts in science and technology, (2) to explain the U.S. government's science policy, (3) to assess the present state of science and technology in China, and (4) to suggest ways of expanding such exchanges between the United States and China. The mission's trip was regarded as highly successful in both Washington and Beijing, and it may be added that a proposed subsequent trip by Frank Press to go to the Soviet Union was canceled as a sign of Washington's displeasure with Soviet actions.

President Carter, in a press conference in June 1978, said: "We have some very important relationships with the Chinese that need to be pursued. These are world-wide common hopes that we share with the Chinese. We have bilateral relations that need to expand – trade, exchange of science and technology, etc. At the same time, we want to have peace with the Chinese – almost a billion people."[76] In another of its rapid moves to improve ties with China, the Carter administration scrapped a plan to sell F-4 fighter bombers to Taiwan, and that decision was a part of the U.S. policy to strengthen relations with the PRC.

On its part, China demonstrated its willingness to cooperate with the Western nations against Soviet and Cuban influence in Africa, which became evident during Chinese Foreign Minister Huang's trip to Zaire in June 1978. Another Chinese gesture was the visit of Chinese reporters to the U.S. nuclear aircraft carrier *Enterprise* in Hong Kong in June 1978, which could be interpreted as approval of the U.S. military muscle in the Asian-Pacific region. China also agreed to a student exchange program with the United States before full diplomatic relations were established.

China's trade with the United States more than doubled in the first half of 1978: U.S. exports to China totaled $211.1 million in the first half of 1978 compared with $62 million in the same period of 1977 – a 240 percent increase – and U.S. businessmen and economists expected that the U.S. trade with China would accelerate. The pragmatic post-Mao Chinese leaders were considering a number of financing and development plans that would have previously violated the doctrine of self-reliance. These plans included the use of cheap Chinese labor to produce U.S. products under U.S.-China joint venture projects in Hong Kong and a U.S. exploration of Chinese natural resources. It was, however, too early to predict the future pattern of the Sino-American economic cooperation except to say it would expand.

Washington and Beijing: The Final Breakthrough

One of the great, if not the greatest, foreign policy achievements of the post-Mao leadership of Deng and Hua has been the establishment of full diplomatic relations between the most powerful and most populous nations of the world – the United States and China. Both President Carter and Chairman Hua stunned the world by announcing from Washington and Beijing on December 15, 1978, that the United States and the PRC would establish a full diplomatic relationship on January 1, 1979. That announcement was the final outcome of the Shanghai communiqué signed by President Nixon and Premier Zhou Enlai on February 27, 1972. It had taken seven years to achieve the goal set out in the communiqué.

The most complicating factor had been the U.S. commitment to Taiwan, and China had set three conditions for full diplomatic relationship: U.S. withdrawal of recognition from the so-called Republic of China, i.e., Taiwan; abrogation of the 1954 U.S. defense treaty with Taiwan; and withdrawal of all U.S. troops from Taiwan. President Carter's announcement on December 15 fulfilled all three conditions by the Chinese, but the pragmatic Chinese leaders, particularly Deng Xiaoping, made a big concession on the U.S. sale of arms to Taiwan. The United States will continue to sell defensive weapons to Taiwan, even after the termination of the 1954 mutual defense pact, and the pact was not even terminated on January 1, 1979, when the two countries established full diplomatic relations. The 1954 treaty was abrogated in accordance with the provision of the treaty that there should be a one-year formal notice of termination, so the United States had full diplomatic relations with the PRC as well as a defense pact with Taiwan for one full year – 1979. The United States, following the "Japanese formula," will also maintain cultural, commercial, and other nonpolitical ties with Taiwan. Basically, the United States met China's preconditions, and the Japanese formula was also acceptable to Beijing. The major concession was Beijing's "agreement to disagree" over the U.S. arms sales to Taiwan.

On the Chinese side, the key role was played by Deng, who visited the United States in January 1979. On the U.S. side, the main driving force was Brzezinski. Former President Nixon will be regarded in history as the U.S. president who opened the China door after two decades of frozen Sino-American relations, and Brzezinski will be credited with establishing full diplomatic relations between the two countries. Nixon's initiative led to a global triangular relationship between Washington, Moscow, and Beijing, and Brzezinski's dynamic role may usher in a new global triangular relationship – Washington, Tokyo, and Beijing – which may dramatically change international politics. In any case, the existing great triangular relationship between Washington, Moscow, and Beijing gained new significance when diplomatic relations were established between Washington and Beijing.

The U.S. decision was welcomed by its allies and friends in both Europe and Asia. President Carter, unlike Nixon, gave the news to the Japanese prime minister prior to the formal announcement in order to avoid any "1972 Nixon shock," and Prime Minister Masayoshi Ohira expressed the hope that the U.S. move "will contribute to the peace and stability of Asia."[77] The NATO allies all welcomed the move, as did the ASEAN countries of Southeast Asia. Most of the Southeast Asian countries are now far more worried about Soviet-backed Vietnam than about China. The *Bangkok Post* termed the establishment of diplomatic relations "a good move. It returns the U.S. to the arena in this region."[78]

Notes

1. See *New York Times*, April 11, 1977.

2. *Peking Review*, June 8, 1973, p. 17.

3. Ibid., August 16, 1974, p. 13.

4. See David Bonavia, "The Wizard That Was," *Far Eastern Economic Review*, July 2, 1976, p. 36.

5. See *Times* (London), October 5, 1974.

6. See Bonavia, "The Wizard That Was."

7. See excerpts from Zhou Enlai's address at the National People's Congress of China on January 13, 1975, *New York Times*, January 21, 1975.

8. See news conference of Secretary of State Kissinger at Vladivostok on November 24, 1974, in R. P. Stebbins and Elaine P. Adam, eds., *American Foreign Relations, 1974*, Council on Foreign Relations Book (New York: New York University Press, 1977), pp. 509–510.

9. *New York Times*, November 27, 1974.

10. *Washington Post*, November 29, 1974.

11. Ibid.

12. *New York Times*, December 19, 1974.

13. *Peking Review*, June 7, 1974, pp. 23–24.

14. Ibid., January 20, 1975, pp. 6–8.

15. Based on the author's reading of unpublished documents and papers of the government of Pakistan, 1947–1971.

16. Based on the author's talks and discussion with Chinese foreign ministry officials in Beijing, July 1976.

17. *Peking Review*, April 11, 1975, pp. 10 and 21.

18. See Chapter 7 in this book.

19. See *New York Times*, October 20, 1975, and *Peking Review*, October 25, 1975, pp. 8–9.

20. *New York Times,* October 23, 1975.

21. Ibid.

22. Ibid.

23. Ibid.

24. Ibid., October 24, 1974.

25. Ibid., November 5, 1975.

26. Quoted in Stephen Barber, "The Taiwan Ties That Bind," *Far Eastern Economic Review,* November 28, 1975.

27. See U.S., Congress, Senate, Committee on Foreign Relations, *China a Quarter Century After the Founding of the People's Republic,* Report by Senator Mike Mansfield (Washington, D.C.: Government Printing Office, 1975), pp. 21–23.

28. Ibid.

29. See Leo Goodstadt, "The Ford Trip: Peking's Anxiety," *Far Eastern Economic Review,* November 21, 1975, p. 28.

30. See *Washington Post,* November 30, 1975.

31. See Stephen Barber, "Kissinger Smoothes the Way," *Far Eastern Economic Review,* November 21, 1975.

32. *Washington Post,* November 30, 1975.

33. See *Newsweek,* December 8, 1975.

34. See *New York Times,* December 2–5, 1975; *Washington Post,* December 2–5, 1975; *Newsweek,* December 15, 1978. For full texts of Vice-Premier Deng's and President Ford's speeches, see *Peking Review,* December 5, 1975, pp. 8–9, and December 12, 1975, pp. 6–7.

35. Ibid.

36. *New York Times,* December 31, 1975.

37. See *New York Times,* December 2–5, 1975; *Washington Post,* December 2–5, 1975; *Newsweek,* December 15, 1978. For full texts of Vice-Premier Deng's and President Ford's speeches, see *Peking Review,* December 5, 1975, pp. 8–9, and December 12, 1975, pp. 6–7.

38. See Stephen Barber, "It's As You Were After Ford," *Far Eastern Economic Review,* December 19, 1975, p. 29.

39. *Washington Post,* September 7, 1977.

40. Ibid., September 8, 1977.

41. Quoted in Barber, "It's As You Were After Ford."

42. See *Washington Post* and *New York Times,* April 8, 1976, and *Far Eastern Economic Review,* April 16, 1976, pp. 8–11.

43. See David Bonavia, "Total War on Shanghai Four," *Far Eastern Economic Review,* October 29, 1976.

44. *People's Daily,* July 3, 1977.

45. "Inside China Now," Report on a twenty-three-day visit by James Schlesinger, *U.S. News and World Report,* October 18, 1976.

46. Ibid.

47. Ross Terrill, "In China Losing Out Isn't Fatal," *Washington Post,* May 15, 1977.

48. G. W. Choudhury, "Post-Mao China and the World," *Pacific Community* (Tokyo), (January 1977), p. 258.

49. *Washington Post,* October 16, 1976.

50. Ibid.

51. Ibid., April 8, 1976.

52. See Jerome A. Cohen, "A China Policy for the Next Administration," *Foreign Affairs* (October 1976), pp. 20–37; also see Peter Grose, "Carter's China Advisor Outlines New Policy on Peking Regime," *New York Times,* December 17, 1976.

53. See *Washington Post,* November 22, 1976.

54. See Fox Butterfield, "Challenges Ahead in Asia for Carter Administration," *New York Times,* December 20, 1976.

55. See Stephen Barber, "Following Ford on China," *Far Eastern Economic Review,* January 21, 1977.

56. Ibid.

57. See G. W. Choudhury, *Chinese Perception of the World* (Washington, D.C.: University Press of America, 1977), pp. 82–90.

58. *Washington Post,* February 28, 1977.

59. See Choudhury, *Chinese Perception of the World,* pp. 39–43.

60. *Washington Post,* June 9, 1977.

61. *New York Times,* April 12, 1977.

62. Ibid., August 18, 1977.

63. *Washington Post,* August 16, 1977.

64. See "Case for Normalization of Relations," Chapters 1 and 2 in G. W. Choudhury, ed., *Sino-American Relations in Post-Mao Era* (Washington, D.C.: University Press of America, 1977).

65. *New York Times,* August 20, 1977.

66. Marquis Childs, "Futile Diplomacy," *Washington Post,* August 23, 1977.

67. See the text of President Carter's address at the United Nations on March 17, 1977, in *New York Times,* March 18, 1977.

68. *Washington Post,* April 29, 1977.

69. See Walter F. Hahn and Alvin J. Cottrell, *Soviet Shadow over Africa,* Monographs in International Affairs, Center for Advanced International Studies (Miami: University of Miami, 1976).

70. *Washington Post,* August 23, 1977.

71. Ibid.

72. See "Political Report" by Chairman Hua Guofeng to the Eleventh National Congress of the Communist Party of China, August 12, 1977, in *Eleventh National Congress of the Communist Party of China (Documents)* (Beijing: Foreign Languages Press, 1977), p. 61.

73. New China News Analysis (Peking), May 20–22, 1978.

74. Based on author's personal interviews in the United States, 1978–1979.

75. See G. W. Choudhury, "China's Dynamic Foreign Policy," *Asia-Pacific Community* (Winter 1978–1979), p. 57.

76. *New York Times,* June 8, 1978.

77. Choudhury, "China's Dynamic Foreign Policy," p. 62.

78. Ibid.

6

The Sino-Soviet Conflict

The Sino-Soviet rift constitutes one of the great schisms of contemporary international relations, and it is fraught with great strategic and diplomatic implications that have a considerable impact on the external policies of both China and the Soviet Union. It has already been pointed out that the prime reason for China's favorable response to President Nixon's new China policy in 1970–1971 was that country's fear of the Soviet Union, and reference has also been made to the Soviet policy of containing China by both diplomatic and military means. The cold war between the two communist giants has proceeded into its third decade, and there is a mass of literature on the Sino-Soviet conflict. This discussion of the conflict will concentrate on China's role in world affairs since the 1970s and especially on the growing contest between Beijing and Moscow for greater influence and power in Afro-Asian countries.

An Asian diplomat posted in Moscow told a U.S. journalist in 1978: "The big story of the past thirty years has been East-West conflict but the big story of the next twenty years is going to be the East-East conflict between Russia and China. That will affect everything from now on."[1] With due allowance for rhetorical expression, there seems to be considerable truth in that prediction. The two communist giants "are circling and being circled by each other like two heavyweight wrestlers, trying hammerlocks, footholds and feints."[2] This geopolitical grappling has become more acute and tense in Asia since U.S. disengagement from the region under the 1969 Nixon doctrine and especially since the 1975 communist victory in Indochina. Since the end of the Vietnam War, the struggle for influence has intensified. China has accused the Soviet Union of working overtime to fill up the vacuum caused by the U.S. withdrawal, and the Soviet Union has charged China with being the chief warmonger and with creating tensions in collusion with the United States and Japan.

The cold war between the two major communist countries has exposed the myth of an international communism. The rift is now most conspicuous in the triangular conflict in Indochina involving China, Cambodia, and Soviet-backed Vietnam, and the rivals have even gone so far as to solicit support from countries they used to denounce as imperialist (the United States), militarist (Japan), or stooges of imperialism (such as the ASEAN countries in Southeast Asia or Iran and Pakistan in Southwest Asia). But, except for a few countries such as Afghanistan or Vietnam, the Asian countries generally are as wary of any direct involvement in the new cold war between Moscow and Beijing as they were of being involved in the cold war between Moscow and Washington in the 1950s and 1960s. Tokyo, Hanoi, and New Delhi, as well as smaller powers like Bangladesh and Burma, are the targets of the Sino-Soviet competition for spheres of influence, and the ASEAN countries are also courted by Beijing and Moscow. Although China sees Asia as its cultural and natural sphere of influence, the Soviet Union claims to be not only a European power, but also an Asian one.

The Sino-Soviet dispute, which, as Ross Terrill points out, has been perhaps the most potent factor in international politics for more than one and a half decades,[3] is a struggle for (1) leadership in the worldwide communist movement, (2) territory claimed by each of the two countries, and (3) leadership in Third World. The conflict has grave military implications, but it is also multidimensional and involves economic, ideological, and social factors. The first point of conflict concerns a vying for control of the communist and other left-wing movements, and the third has locked the two countries in a bitter struggle over spheres of influence in Asia and Africa.[4] The second source of the conflict – territorial claims – led the two countries into a near-war situation in 1969, and it is dramatized by the heavy concentration of troops of both sides along the Xinjiang frontier.

Although China and Russia are both communist countries, their traditions, histories, and cultures are different. The Russian Communist party was first based on the industrial working classes of Moscow and Saint Petersburg, and the Chinese Communist party grew out of a peasant resistance movement. Khrushchev is reported to have told Zhou Enlai, "You and I are Prime Ministers of our respective countries; otherwise we have nothing in common."[5] China under Mao Zedong was secretly opposed to Russia. The Russians did not agree with Mao that the communist revolution should be a revolution of the agricultural people, the peasants, and Mao made a statement during the Chinese communist revolution that he was not "promoting the independence of China so as to bring them under the leadership of Moscow."[6]

The Chinese communist leaders challenged Moscow's supremacy and raised the question of authority and discipline in the communist movement; they wanted to share in the decision-making process for the overall strategy tactics of the communist movement as a whole.[7] Although Hungary, Poland, and Czechoslovakia could be made parts of Brezhnev's "commonwealth of socialist countries," the PRC was too large to be either blackmailed or coaxed into submission. Doctrinal issues were the initial factors in the Chinese challenge to Soviet leadership in the communist world, but soon the rift turned into a major conflict between the two neighboring large countries with thousands of miles of common boundaries and divergent social, cultural, and economic backgrounds. The prospect of nearly 1 billion Chinese equipped with nuclear weapons on the Soviet border represents an obvious threat to the Russians, and vice versa.

In detailing the background of the Sino-Soviet rift, Zhou Enlai told the British author Neville Maxwell: "This [the rift] was mainly because their revisionism had developed and had become a reactionary train of thought in the international communist movement. . . . India has inherited the mantle of the British Empire and Soviet revisionism has inherited the mantle of the Tsars. One carried out subversion against us in 1959 and the other in 1962. What the Soviet Union did in 1959 led to the Sino-Indian border conflict in 1962."[8] Zhou Enlai also told Pakistani President Ayub Khan that "the Soviet Union encouraged the movement of Indian troops in the Sino-Indian border war of 1962."[9] The fact that both the United States and the USSR sent military supplies to India after the 1962 Sino-Indian war convinced Chinese leaders such as Chairman Mao and Premier Zhou that there was some collusion between the two superpowers for a policy of containment of China in the 1960s.

The War Scene Among the Chinese

Since the serious border clashes near the Ussuri River in the spring of 1969, China appears to have been caught up in a war scare. The most serious aspect of the Sino-Soviet rift is the presence of forty-five to fifty-five armed divisions on each side of the border. According to the 1973 survey of the International Institute for Strategic Studies (London), the Soviet Union and China each built up their forces to a record number of forty-five divisions in the border areas. A great deal of the Soviet effort has been devoted to the construction of barracks, roads, rail links, and permanent training areas near the border, and the Soviet forces include surface-to-surface missiles and missiles with a range of five hundred miles. "With the powerful Pacific Fleet and its land-based naval arm base, these Soviet theatre forces in the Sino-Soviet border area provide a balanced, hard-hitting and effective force which is trained and equipped for nuclear and for non-nuclear operations."[10]

It was the quest for security that led the Chinese to respond to Nixon's new China policy in 1971–1972, but China also began to develop an effective defensive force. The Chinese communes acted quickly after Mao's appeal to "dig tunnels deep, store grain everywhere and accept no hegemony."[11] On the day of my arrival in Beijing on July 22, 1976, I was taken to see an underground shelter in the center of the Works Compound. The director of the Civil Defense Committee told me that such shelters had been built in all major cities, and when I asked, "Why this huge preparation for underground shelters; from which country does China apprehend aggression?" the reply was clear and unambiguous; "The Soviet social imperialists constitute the main danger." There was no hint of any other external threat, such as from the United States. Everywhere I went—factories, communes, educational institutions—I was repeatedly told about the danger from the Soviet social imperialists.

China has also built a deterrent nuclear force to protect itself from Soviet aggression. The nuclear test explosion announced on September 26, 1976, was in response to the Chinese Communist party's call to turn grief over Mao's death into strength,[12] and it was China's nineteenth blast in nearly twelve years (1964–1976). China has shown restraint as a nuclear power. As Jonathan Pollack of Harvard University has pointed out: "Chinese leaders have not been prone to reckless actions nor have they used atomic blackmailings against non-nuclear states. Peking has not transferred nuclear technology or fissionable materials to other countries," and the Chinese officials have always insisted that their country's "development of nuclear power is solely for the purpose of self-defense." The principle objective is to assure that China acquires an unspecified but survivable retaliatory capability, particularly against the Soviet Union.[13] According to a report by Central Intelligence Agency experts on China, "Peking has been cutting back substantially in the last three years [1972–1975] on her expenditures for military equipment."[14] China has not yet truly developed intercontinental ballistic missiles (ICBMs), which many experts thought China would be able to produce by the mid 1970s, nor has China yet deployed any sea-launched ballistic missiles.

What does China's nuclear program indicate? China is not interested in an expensive arms race with the two superpowers, nor does China have any hegemonic aspirations, particularly against the global and security interests of the United States or of its allies in the Asian-Pacific area. China is basically interested in self-defense against any potential Soviet aggression; like any other nation, it wants to enjoy freedom from fear. In my extensive talks with Chinese foreign policy makers, experts, party officials, and others, it became apparent that the Soviet Union can no longer launch a preemptive attack on China without major Russian cities, including Moscow, being destroyed by China's nuclear retaliatory capability.

"Today war with China, a bloody war, involving colossal loss of life, but a victorious war is the most pressing and principle foreign policy aim of the Soviet government"—those words appear in a document of nearly

3,000 words that was delivered to the emigré-Russian Possev publishing house in Frankfurt and was published in the September 1973 issue of *Possev.*[15] The main theme of the document is that the Kremlin was contemplating a preemptive nuclear attack against China's atomic bases, and China's rapid progress in the development of nuclear weapons was considered to be the major reason for the preemptive attack. Two other factors mentioned were the murder of Mao's heir apparent, Lin Biao, which had put an end to any hope that post-Mao leaders would come to terms with Moscow, and second, that the 1972 Peking Summit had raised the threat of a Sino-American collusion against the Russians.

Chinese policy in the 1970s was focused on efforts to foster "an Asian and international environment antagonistic to Soviet 'expansion' while avoiding direct Chinese military confrontation with the vastly superior Soviet forces along the contested Sino-Soviet border."[16] China stepped up its diplomatic and political offensives against the hegemony of the Soviet social imperialists by cultivating better relations with its Asian neighbors, particularly Japan, and also with the other superpower, the United States. But China also maintained correct, but not cordial, state to state relations with the Soviet Union. The border negotiations begun on October 20, 1969, have been continued with many ups and downs. They have not yet produced any significant results, but they have kept the cold war between the two communist countries from turning into a hot war, as it threatened to do in 1969. The Chinese are fully aware of their military weakness vis-à-vis the Russians. The present balance of power is not in their favor, but time may be, so the Chinese strategy in the bilateral relationship with the Russians has been noted for its caution in avoiding any direct confrontation. The conflict has been confined to sharp exchanges of words rather than any exchange of guns.

Diplomatic Confrontation and Battle of Words

Both China and the Soviet Union have carried on a vigorous campaign against the other. Neither of them misses any opportunity to expose the other, and there is hardly a week when there is no sharp, polemical exchange of words between Beijing and Moscow. Since China's entry into the United Nations in 1971, the Chinese delegates have used almost every opportunity to expose Soviet expansionist or hegemonic designs. Similarly, the Russians have also sharply attacked Maoism and China. The Central Committee of the Communist party of the Soviet Union (CPSU) denounced China in strong terms at a plenary meeting in April 1973, calling "Maoism an enemy of revolutionary forces in the whole world." It also declared that "the P.R.C. leadership's stubborn struggle against the cohesion of Socialist countries and the world communist movement, against the efforts of peace-loving states and peoples striving for an easing of international tensions and Peking's anti-Soviet course, damage the cause of peace and international Socialism."[17] It further stated that Beijing's main aim is to secure its hegemonic ambitions by means of various maneuvers to turn China into the leader of the Third World by sowing seeds of anti-Sovietism and hostility to world socialism.[18]

In a 15,000-word analysis, "China Today," the Soviet Communist party Central Committee's bimonthly journal, *Kommunist,* delivered one of its strongest attacks on the policies of Mao Zedong and called on "true communists" to smash Maoism. It also declared that anyone who remained neutral to Mao's theories was serving China's antisocialist aims. Maoism was called a danger to all states, communist and capitalist alike. The article, published on August 23, 1975, was the climax of an increasingly virulent campaign in the official Soviet press against every aspect of China's policy, from its role in Southeast Asia to its civil defense. "The ideological, theoretical and practical activity of Marxist-Leninist in the conditions of today is aimed at smashing Maoism in its theory and its politics as an anti-Marxist and anti-Leninist movement hostile to the entire contemporary revolutionary movement."[19]

The condemnation of neutralism to Maoism was a veiled threat to Yugoslavia and Romania, as those countries refused to join the "Soviet thunder" against China. The significant aspect of the sharp attack on China was that it came in the wake of the U.S. defeat in Indochina in 1975, which seems to have provided new impetus to the Sino-Soviet rift. Moscow's growing links with Hanoi and Beijing's increasing concern about Hanoi were some of the reasons for the renewed Soviet attack on China; another was Moscow's diplomatic triumph at Helsinki, where the Soviet Union negotiated its coveted European security agreement.[20]

At the 1975 Helsinki Summit, which drafted that agreement, the Russians achieved a major goal: the tacit acknowledgment of their territorial conquests in northern, central, and Eastern Europe during World War II—referred to by Aleksandr Solzhenitsyn as "the moral sellout of those countries and people under Kremlin rule."[21] Shortly after the conclusion of the European security conference held in August 1975, the Russians revived their plan for collective security in Asia.[22] The Soviet commentator, Vladimir Kudryavtsev, wrote in *Izvestia* that the principles adopted at Helsinki were universally applicable to Asia and to all countries striving to ensure security and development for peaceful purposes."[23]

China has always been convinced that the Soviet-inspired Asian security system was aimed at the PRC and Chinese counterattacks frequently refer to the alleged military threat from the Soviet Union and create the impression that Moscow has great power ambitions in Asia. During a visit to Britain and France in June 1973, Chinese Foreign Minister Ji Pengfei said that détente in Europe carried the threat of increased Soviet activity in Asia,[24] and the Chinese regard Western Europe's policy of détente as "appeasement of the unappeasable."[25] Ji's subsequent journey to the Soviet Union's southern neighbors, Iran and Pakistan, was devoted to exposing the Soviet Union's expansionist designs in Asia. In a speech in Tehran on June 14, 1973, he declared that "certain big powers have not abandoned their aggressive, expansionist policy";[26] obviously, he was referring to the Soviet Union. China gave full support to Sri Lanka's proposal for a zone of peace in the Indian Ocean as a means of containing the growing Soviet naval presence there, and Beijing even welcomed the U.S. presence in the Indian Ocean because of China's anxiety about the increased Soviet presence in the Indian Ocean–Persian Gulf areas. Similarly, on March 28, 1973, Jiao told a New Zealand ministerial delegation to Beijing that the Pacific "has become an arena of rivalry between the superpowers."[27] He assured New Zealand that China would work with the Pacific countries to preserve peace there – again in the context of Chinese opposition to the expansion of Soviet influence in the Asian-Pacific region.

The entry of the PRC into the United Nations in 1971 has enabled that country to voice its opposition to the Soviet policies and role and to seek the support of the countries of the Third World at the world forum. As the self-appointed spokesman of the Third World, China regularly attacks both of the two superpowers, but China's activity at the United Nations in the 1970s was primarily aimed against the Soviet Union. The leader of the Chinese delegation made it a special point to expose Soviet social imperialism at UN General Assembly sessions in 1971–1975, and the Chinese foreign minister, Jiao Guanhua, spoke against the Soviet Union in a speech at the Twenty-eighth Session of the UN General Assembly. First he made his routine attack against the two superpowers, but then he focused on the Soviet Union. "The Soviet leaders noisily proclaim that as a socialist state, the Soviet Union is 'the natural and surest ally' of the developing countries, . . . but what the Soviet Union practiced was not internationalism but great power chauvinism, national egoism and territorial expansionism."[28] In his speech at the Twenty-ninth Session of the UN General Assembly, the Chinese foreign minister repeated the same performance: first an attack against the two superpowers and then the real blast against Soviet social imperialism. "No wonder the superpower with the label of 'socialism' has, of late, arrogantly boasted that it is 'on a historic offensive along the entire front of the global confrontation' and that the pace of its advance is 'rapid.' "[29] China's strongman, Vice-Premier Deng Xiaoping, made a similar speech at the 1974 Special Session of the UN General Assembly. Again, he began with the customary criticism of both of the superpowers but reserved his strongest remarks for the Soviet Union. "The superpower which styles itself as a socialist country is by no means less proficient at neo-colonialist economic plunder under the name of so-called economic cooperation . . . it uses high-handed measures to extract superprofits in its 'family.' In profiting at other's expense it has gone to lengths rarely seen in the case of other imperialist countries."[30]

The world body was appalled by the intensity of the bitterness between the delegates of the two communist giants, which shattered completely the image of unity of the world communist movement. The Sino-Soviet rift has divided the communist world into two main camps. "One of these camps with its center in Moscow has its roots in European civilization. Its following is derived from within the more advanced industrialized countries. The other camp is centered in Peking. It looks for its main support among the developing countries of Asia, Africa and Latin America and seeks to appeal to the racial differences of the people involved."[31]

Moscow challenges the Chinese theory that a people's war led by the rural community is the most suitable form of revolution for the predominantly agricultural populations of Africa, Asia, and Latin America. As an industrialized country, the Soviet Union is hostile to the Chinese view that revolutionary war involves the "encirclement" of the cities of the world (represented by the countries of North America and Europe, including Russia) by its rural areas (represented by the countries of Asia, Africa, and Latin America). The Soviet author A. Iskenderov brusquely dismisses the division of the world into a "rich north" and a "poor south" and the contention that revolutionary fervor has passed from the proletariat to the liberation movement. He argues that capitalism can be finally destroyed only by the worldwide action of the working classes, led by the Soviet Communist party.[32] The main objectives of the Soviet approaches to the Third World are to discredit China's views on the national liberation movement and to advance the Soviet Union's claim to revolutionary leadership in the world.[33] The Soviets seize every chance to denigrate the "adventurist," Beijing-inspired revolutionary movements in Asia. For example, the Soviet news agency Tass made an attack on the Chinese theory of inevitable revolution on March 28, 1970, and blamed China for the abortive communist coup in Indonesia in 1965.

The Chinese attacks on the Soviet Union's policy and role are equally sharp. In a book entitled *Ugly Features of Soviet Social Imperialism,* the Chinese made an all-out campaign against "the superpower label for Soviet revisionism"; "the Brezhnev clique is following in Hitler's footsteps"; "Soviet Union: superpower and superexploiter"; the "sinister programme of neocolonialism"; "honey on lips, murder in heart"; "repulse wolf at front gate, guard against tiger at back door"; and so forth.[34]

The sharp exchange of words reflects the intensity of the Sino-Soviet rift, and reading such inflammatory words may lead to the conclusion that the two communist partners are rapidly heading toward a war. But despite the growing tension, China has been extremely careful to not precipitate any armed confrontation with the Russians. This sense of realism in Beijing is responsible for negotiations with Moscow, and trade and diplomatic relations have not been discontinued.

The Sino-Soviet Border Negotiations

Soon after the serious Sino-Soviet armed clashes in the spring of 1969, the two countries agreed to hold negotiations on the border problems. Soviet Premier Kosygin made a short visit to Beijing on September 11, 1969, when he went to Hanoi to attend the funeral of the Vietnamese leader Ho Chi Minh. The brief communiqué on the four-hour meeting between Zhou Enlai and Kosygin described the meeting as useful and frank but gave little hope for any real improvement in the relations between the two countries. Yet that meeting – the first high-level contact in four years – diffused a highly explosive situation that had been created by the 1969 armed clashes along the Ussuri River and inspired by leaks about the possibility of a Soviet preemptive strike on the Chinese nuclear installations in Xinjiang Province. The border negotiations began in Beijing on October 20, 1969, on the deputy-foreign-minister level. In order to create a favorable atmosphere for the border talks, the Chinese proposed that the two countries withdraw their forces from all the disputed areas along the border and that both sides should maintain the status quo and avoid armed conflicts so the negotiations could be held free from any threats. China also made a significant concession by dropping the precondition that Moscow should acknowledge the inequality of the old treaties made under the czars.

The basic issue in the Sino-Soviet border dispute is not territory but whether the czarist treaties are valid or not. China's stand is that the present Sino-Soviet boundary is based on unequal treaties imposed on a weakened China by czarist Russia at a time "when power was in the hands of neither the Chinese nor the Russian people."[35] The Chinese position is that although Beijing wants to wipe out past humiliations by replacing the unequal treaties with an equal one, China gives emphatic and unequivocal assurance that it does not demand the return of the vast territories annexed by the unequal treaties. So the Russian charge that Beijing claims 1,500,000 square kilometers of land that rightly belong to the Soviet Union is not correct; in fact, the Chinese have made it clear that a new treaty would virtually confirm the frontiers established in the nineteenth century by the treaties of Aigun, Tientsin, and Peking. What China seeks to redress are the subsequent infringements of those treaties allegedly committed by the Russians. A Chinese statement of October 8, 1959, demanded that any territory occupied in violation of the treaties by either side should be returned unconditionally, though necessary adjustments might have to be made.[36]

The Chinese statement is noted for its flexibility and spirit of compromise when compared with Soviet letters of September 18, 1969.[37] But the Chinese statement also angrily rejected Moscow's insinuations that China intended to launch a nuclear war against the Soviet Union, and China also asserted it would never be intimidated by war threats: "Should a handful of war maniacs dare to raid China's strategic sites . . . that will be war, that will be aggression, and the 700 million Chinese people will rise up in resistance and use revolutionary war to eliminate the war of aggression."[38]

Moscow's first comment on the border negotiations with Beijing came on October 27, 1969, in a speech by Brezhnev in which he expressed hopes for a reduction in Sino-Soviet tensions. Moscow also made efforts to demonstrate to the outside world Russia's moderation and reasonableness toward Beijing. The Russians sought to prove that the initiative for the Kosygin–Zhou Enlai meeting on September 11, 1969, had come from Moscow and that the meeting was responsible for the beginning of the border negotiations.

From the outset, however, it was clear that the talks had very limited prospects; they could not bring about any real rapprochement between the two countries or even a permanent solution to the frontier issue. The most that might be achieved was an agreement to retreat from the brink of war, as had been threatened in the spring of 1969, and to find a modus vivendi based on practical measures.

There was a brief interval in which the direct propaganda attacks against each side subsided, but in early 1970, they were revived. China complained in January 1970 that Russia had not complied with the preliminary condition for any meaningful dialogue – the withdrawal of Soviet forces, numbering about 1 million, from the disputed areas along the border.[39] The Soviet Union renewed its complaints against China, and the top Soviet leaders made attacks against China in June 1970. Kosygin, for instance, alleged on June 10, 1970, that the Chinese were following a line that was not conducive to any appreciable progress in the bilateral talks.[40] On June 30, 1970, Moscow withdrew its chief negotiator, Foreign Minister Vassili Kuznetsov, ostensibly because of illness. In the meantime, there was a step forward when the two countries agreed to resume the exchange of ambassadors, which was done in October and November 1970. The new Soviet chief negotiator, Deputy Foreign Minister L. F. Ilichev, also had gone to Beijing for a resumption of the border talks. In November 1970, the two countries signed a new trade agreement, the first since 1967, and in early 1971, Zhou Enlai made a conciliatory gesture by personally receiving the Soviet chief negotiator and Soviet ambassador on March 21.

Then came Nixon's dramatic announcement of July 1971 about the great breakthrough in the Sino-American relationship. The Soviet Union seemed to adopt a policy of "wait and see" about the emerging relations between Beijing and Washington, or what the Russians seemed to regard as the collusion between the PRC and the United States against the USSR. The obvious casualty was the Sino-Soviet border talks, and during 1971–1972, Moscow accused China of "going slowly" in the negotiations. It was also during that period that the Sino-Soviet tensions increased because of the partition of China's South Asian ally, Pakistan, as a result of the 1971 Indo-Pakistani War over Bangladesh. There was a bitter exchange of words between the Chinese and the Soviet delegates at the United Nations when the 1971 Indo-Pakistani War was discussed by that world body. China accused the Soviet Union of dismembering an Asian country, Pakistan, and the Soviet Union countered by accusing the Chinese of opposing a national liberation movement in Bangladesh.

In December 1972, Brezhnev made a strong attack on the Chinese policies and accused Beijing of laying claim to Soviet territory, sabotaging efforts toward an East-West détente, and attempting to split the communist world.[41] China was also said to have failed to respond positively to a Soviet offer in March 1973 to apply international law rather than the 1860 Treaty of Peking to the northeastern river boundary—a step that would have moved the frontier in some places from the Chinese bank to midstream and therefore would have conceded several hundred small islands to China. The Soviet chief negotiator, Ilichev, left Beijing on July 19, 1973, and did not return to China for almost a year. In the meantime, the Russians made a proposal for a nonaggression pact between Moscow and Beijing, but China ridiculed the idea of such a pact when there were 1 million Russian troups on China's border. The Chinese told their Pakistani friends that the Soviet proposal was comparable to India's "no-war" offer to Pakistan when India had continued to occupy the disputed state of Kashmir and had concentrated troops along the Pakistani border in the 1950s and 1960s.

For the next three years, 1974–1976, the Sino-Soviet talks were suspended because of Moscow's uncertainty about China's future after Mao and also because of Moscow's concern about the progress of the Sino-American relationship. China, as already noted, missed no opportunity during this period to expose the Soviet social imperialist, both inside and outside the United Nations. Like many other international issues, China's border negotiations with the Soviet Union also waited for Mao's impending death, which occurred in September 1976.

Sino-Soviet Conflict in the Post-Mao Era

There were speculations that after the death of Mao, a prime actor in the Sino-Soviet rift, the Sino-Soviet relationship might be improved, and there was talk that there might be limited rapprochement or better relations on the government to government level. But the post-Mao China has not smiled toward the Russian bear. The Chinese have seemed to be less worried about any imminent threats from the Soviet Union than they were before, but the vigilance and preparedness to meet any threats from the Soviet Union have remained the same.

Chairman Hua, in his political report to the Eleventh National Congress of the Communist party of China, spoke against Soviet social imperialism. "In the last few years it [the Soviet Union] has further betrayed its aggressive and expansionist features by sabotaging the wars of Arab countries and the Palestinian people against Israeli aggression, employing mercenary troops to intervene in Angola and invade Zaire, plotting to subvert the government of Sudan, interfering in internal affairs of many countries, sowing dissension among Third-World countries and undermining their unity."[42] Hua also pointed out that the Soviet Union "suffered one telling blow after another" and added, "The Soviet social imperialism is on the offensive and U.S. imperialism on the defensive."[43]

The Chinese Academy of Social Science published an article in *Hungchi (Hongqi)* in 1977 that elaborates on the Soviet Union's strategic offensive by pointing out:

> One of the salient features of the contemporary international situation is the visible growth of the factor for war, and Soviet social imperialism is now the most dangerous source of world war. While singing paens of "peace" at the top of its voice, it harbors sinister ambitions and reaches out for advantages everywhere. Its expansionist activities are gathering ever greater momentum. Brezhnev has publicly declared: "We now have to reckon, in one way or another, with the state of affairs in virtually every spot in the globe." This arrogant and ambitious craving for the world [is] like a wild beast running amok; and wherever it goes, it leaves a trail of turmoil and unrest.[44]

Then the article refers to the Soviet designs in the NATO countries.[45] A stronger NATO and a more united European Economic Community (EEC) are now among China's important foreign policy goals; so is a stronger Japan. China no longer talks about a revival of militarism in Japan; on the contrary, China seems to be pleased with Japan's growing role in Asian affairs. Concerning Japan, China's main concern is Moscow's attempts to gain influence there; China has no objection to the United States' having a special relationship with Japan, particularly if such a relationship acts as a countermeasure to the Soviet designs. Any country of the Third World or the Second World that has a setback in its relations with Moscow is assured of a red-carpet reception in Beijing because China must follow the basic rules of international politics: those of minimizing the influence and power of its principal adversary and of welcoming any setbacks to its adversary's policies. The Soviet Union has been actively engaged in isolating and weakening China in world affairs since 1969, and China's present reactions and external behavior are the direct products of the Soviet hostility toward the PRC.

There was some speculation that the purging of the Gang of Four might have resulted in some prospects for an improvement in the relations between China and the Soviet Union. But a Chinese Foreign Ministry official declared on March 18, 1977, "I do not see any prospect of improvement of relations between the two countries," and he rejected the suggestion that the Gang of Four was more anti-Soviet than the current Chinese leadership.[46] When I asked about the suggestion during my stay in Beijing in July 1977, I got the same reply. One of the top foreign policy advisers even told me that since the Gang of Four was associated with Lin Biao, who had tried to run away to Moscow after his unsuccessful attempt to assassinate Mao in 1971, its members were pro-Moscow, not anti-Moscow.[47]

Currently, a usual occurrence at Chinese diplomatic receptions in Beijing honoring African or Arab visitors is that the Soviet and East European countries' diplomats walk out because of the Chinese hosts' attack on the "superpower that styles itself a natural ally of the Third World, but uses all ways and means to carry out aggression and expansion everywhere and interferes in internal affairs."[48] The Sino-Soviet rift has continued, and the Soviet Union has made some attempts to test the new Chinese leaders. The Russians might have been successful in healing the rift with China, at least partially, but due to crude Soviet diplomacy, the "friendly" Soviet gestures had not been successful. Moscow has only intensified the Chinese fears, and the Sino-Soviet rift has been further widened.

The Soviet Union was naturally unhappy about the warming up of the Sino-American relationship and those two countries' diplomatic ties in 1977–1979. China and the Soviet Union are locked into a bitter, irreconcilable struggle; each wants to see the other weak and isolated. China wants U.S. support against Soviet efforts to gain military domination over China, the rest of Asia, the Middle East, and Western Europe, and the Soviet Union is engaged in power politics in Africa.

The Soviet leaders appear to be alarmed by what they see in the improved Sino-American relationship and consider it an extremely grave challenge to their global interests. The real source of alarm is the possibility of Sino-American cooperation, or even tacit understandings, which the Kremlin leaders feel might mean a "significant switch in the strategic balance at Moscow's expense."[49] The Russians frequently refer to the "yellow peril," and the Soviet press has mounted a propaganda campaign against China that is unmatched in its bitterness since the days of the Sino-Soviet border clashes in 1969. Underlying the Soviet concern about Beijing's new diplomacy is a deep suspicion that the United States will move closer to Beijing, which would increase the level of the danger on Russia's eastern flank. President Leonid Brezhnev charged on June 25, 1978, that President Carter was pursuing a "short-sighted and dangerous policy of trying to play the 'Chinese card' against the Soviet Union." The policy's architects, Brezhnev warned, "may bitterly regret it." Brezhnev also strongly criticized the policy of NATO countries' selling arms to China, which he considered a threat to the East-West understanding.[50]

On September 19, 1978, the *People's Daily* wrote about the "new developments in Kremlin's global strategy." It reminded the NATO countries that Europe "remains the key area for Soviet aggression," and added, the "Russians are now devoting their military attention in the Red Sea and the Persian Gulf areas as well as the Southern flank of Europe while Africa in particular, has become a hot spot." The *Daily Express* wrote on September 18, 1978, that the extent of the Chinese fear of Soviet aggression is not fully grasped by the NATO countries and said that China understands the threat more accurately than any NATO country, as the Chinese understand far better and have a greater knowledge of Soviet strategy and plans. The article advocated stronger Anglo-Chinese military cooperation, and similar views had been expressed by the British chief of staff during a visit to Beijing in early 1978.

There have been ups and downs in the bilateral talks and relationship between Beijing and Moscow, and neither side wants to take the blame for a total breakdown of negotiations, though no real progress has been made. After eight years of talks, the two sides reached a limited agreement on the rules of navigation on the Ussuri River, but the river accord did not solve the bitter dispute over large sections of the border itself. Both sides made it clear that the agreement related to only technical navigation problems and nothing else.[51]

In the meantime, Beijing gave notice for the termination of the thirty-year Sino-Soviet treaty of friendship and alliance signed in the heyday of friendly Sino-Soviet relations in 1950. The treaty was due to expire in the spring of 1980, and in July 1979, the Soviet Union proposed a nonaggression pact between the two countries to replace the 1950 treaty. Beijing turned down the proposal as China considered it a "fraud" since there were about 1 million Russian troops on China's border.[52]

The Soviet Union and China, however, did sign a trade agreement on August 6, 1979,[53] which was a sign of a little improvement in the relationship between the two countries. The agreement reflected the dual patterns of the Sino-Soviet relationship in the 1970s—a correct, but not cordial relationship; a polemical exchange of notes and diplomatic battle, but efforts to avoid a total breakdown or an armed conflict.

In the fall of 1980, there was another minor clash on the Sino-Soviet border, which resulted in the killing of two Chinese soldiers. The Chinese Foreign Ministry lodged a strong protest with Soviet embassy in Beijing on October 6, 1980, and described the border clash as "armed provocations and an encroachment of China's territorial sovereignty."[54]

The Chinese also protested to the Soviets in September 1980 about the alleged harassment of two Chinese diplomats by Soviet agents in Moscow. The relations between Moscow and Beijing continued to be full of strains and stresses, and the new Chinese premier, Zhao Ziyang, reaffirmed that China will stage a tit-for-tat fight against Soviet hegemonism in the world.[55] So the post-Mao leaders have continued the same relationship with Moscow that Mao and Zhou Enlai established in the 1970s.

The Sino-Soviet Rivalry in Asia

The most recent phase of the Sino-Soviet rift is greatly focused in Asia, where the two communist rivals seem to be engaged in all-out efforts to gain power and influence at each other's cost. "The no-quarter conflict between the Soviet Union and China for power and influence is turning the huge continent of Asia into a potential battlefield."[56] Already, there have been wars between communist countries in Asia—Vietnam's invasion of Cambodia and China's military intervention against Vietnam in favor of Cambodia (see Chapter 8, section on "China and Indochina")—but there has also been a Sino-Soviet cold war for power and influence in Asia in recent years.

Asia seems to be a natural geographical area for both Beijing and Moscow to pay special attention to—theirs is a competition along the long "arc of neighboring countries from North Korea to Afghanistan."[57] But though China and the Soviet Union are direct antagonists, other major powers—the United States and Japan—are also indirectly involved in the struggle for Asia, and the stakes are high in terms of population, resources, and strategic position. Moscow's aim is to establish a strategic foothold in Southeast Asia and Indochina in order to outflank China. The

Kremlin leaders are worried about China's recent diplomatic offensive among ASEAN countries, Japan, Australia, and New Zealand, and the Russians are particularly worried about China's improved relations with Washington and Tokyo. The Russians seem to be "haunted by the nightmare of a hostile China, the world's most populous nation, allied with the world's two most powerful industrial nations, the United States and Japan."[58] So the Russians have taken up the late John Foster Dulles's unfinished task of keeping China poor, weak, and isolated and have chosen Indochina as the testing ground for the confrontation with its archrival in Asia, the PRC. (For a full account of the Sino-Soviet conflict in Indochina, including the "communist wars" in the area, see Chapter 8.)

Sino-Soviet Rivalry in Southeast Asia

In addition to Indochina, the noncommunist Southeast Asian countries are a major arena for the Sino-Soviet competition for influence, and the intense competition between the Soviet Union and China in Southeast Asia underlines the strategic importance of the area to both countries and the extent to which the U.S. withdrawal has provided new openings for external influence. China, apparently fearing encirclement from the south, has denounced the Soviet Union's attempts to propagate its collective security scheme and also its large number of spies in Southeast Asian countries. Peking Radio, on August 11, 1976, warned against "letting the [Soviet] tiger in at the back door while driving the [United States] wolf out at the front." The Soviet Union, on the other hand, is concerned that China is developing relations with its neighbors and has accused China of having designs on their territories and of supporting insurgency.[59]

Since May 1974, the political leaders of Malaysia, Thailand, the Philippines, Burma, and Singapore have paid official visits to Beijing, and China has established diplomatic relations with the first three. (China has long had ties with Burma, those with Indonesia have been suspended, and Singapore is reluctant to move ahead of Indonesia.) The Soviet Union has made it clear that it is annoyed with China's diplomatic successes and its attempts to commit Southeast Asian leaders to anti-Soviet positions. The Russians were especially displeased that the Chinese were able to establish diplomatic relations with the Philippines in June 1975, a year before the Russians succeeded in doing so themselves—though the Soviet Union now has diplomatic ties with all the noncommunist Southeast Asian countries. Moscow's Radio Peace and Progress said on June 12, 1976, that despite Beijing's move, "the Chinese leaders have no intention whatsoever of ending their influence in that country's internal affairs. On the contrary . . . they envisage increased possibilities of interfering." The visit by President Ne Win of

Burma to Beijing caused Moscow Radio to comment on January 17, 1976, that "some Burmese papers have been trying to create the impression that Mao Tse-tung has changed his attitude towards Burma and decided not to interfere in Burmese internal affairs. But this idea has no foundations."

The Sino-Soviet rivalry is pursued on various levels, and there is often direct competition in offers of trade and aid, trade fairs, exhibitions, sporting and cultural events, and exchanges of official visits. The rivalry occasionally degenerates into petty squabbling involving the host country.[60] When a Thai dance troupe visited the Soviet Union early in 1976, Chinese and certain Bangkok newspapers reported that the troupe had received insulting treatment. The allegation was denied by the Soviet embassy in Bangkok, which in turn attacked the press for carrying the story. On May 20, the Bangkok *Nation* protested that "the growing acrimony between the Soviet Union and China should not be brought into Thailand." (According to the *Far Eastern Economic Review* of September 26, 1975, the Russians had insisted that the troupe visit the USSR when they discovered that it had been invited to China.)

Political considerations underlie the efforts of both sides to extend their economic relations in Southeast Asia. One method favored by the Soviet Union has been the establishment of joint shipping companies (for example, with Singapore, Thailand, and the Philippines) that offer lower freight rates on Soviet vessels than those established by the Far East Freight Conference.[61]

Charges of economic imperialism figure prominently in the exchanges between Moscow and Beijing. China is "determined to dominate the Southeast Asian market," Radio Peace and Progress claimed on October 10, 1974, and China was said to be using oil as an instrument of foreign policy, particularly in Thailand and the Philippines, by exploiting the dependence of those countries on oil and hoping to become their main source. Chinese sales of cheap oil to Thailand and Japan are said to have seriously damaged Indonesian oil exports. According to the Chinese, however, the USSR "has joined the desperate oil-rush by sending oil specialist groups and engaging in oil exploration to exploit greedily the oil resources of the region" (Peking Radio, December 9, 1975).

The Soviet and Chinese missions in Southeast Asian countries are bases for covert competition between the two countries.[62] New China News Agency (NCNA) said on June 10, 1976, that the Soviet Union was competing with the other superpower (the United States) for hegemony in Southeast Asia by a policy of "insidious expansion" under the cover of economic penetration, cultural exchanges, etc. When the Singapore prime minister, Lee Kuan Yew, visited Beijing in May 1976, his Chinese counterpart, Hua Guofeng, told him that the USSR was "trying to take the chance to squeeze in, to carry out infiltration and expansion . . . but it has been strongly condemned by the peoples of the South-East Asian countries for its scheming activities in the area. We are pleased to note that more and more countries in South-East Asia have clearly stated their opposition to the practice of hegemony" (NCNA, May 11, 1976). Radio Peace and Progress replied the following day: "The Chinese premier evidently thinks Lee Kuan Yew arrived in Peking straight from the moon or some even more distant cosmic body, that he does not know that anti-government rebels in Southeast Asian countries are armed with Chinese and not Soviet weapons, that he does not know what government owns the radio stations broadcasting subversive propaganda to Southeast Asian countries from the southern provinces of China."

Moscow has been critical of any moves to establish a neutral Southeast Asia or a zone of peace there, as such a plan would destroy Russia's hopes for its collective security plan. However, China has welcomed such proposals, as such a system would check the Soviet Union's expansionist designs, and Tun Razak of Malaysia reported that Zhou Enlai reacted favorably to proposals for a neutral Southeast Asia.[63]

Since the communist victory in Indochina, the ASEAN countries have become increasingly concerned about the military adventures of Moscow and Hanoi. The Soviet-backed invasion of Cambodia by Vietnamese forces in December 1978 had a profound impact on the ASEAN countries, and they condemned the military action in unqualified terms both at the United Nations and at other international forums. Beijing took full advantage of the anti-Soviet feelings in Southeast Asia and intensified its diplomatic offensive among the ASEAN countries. Beijing has strongly supported ASEAN moves against the Moscow-Hanoi joint ventures, and as a result, China has gained a better image in Southeast Asia. A useful survey of the Soviet image in Southeast Asia noted:

> The Soviet Union poses the greatest single threat to Asia today. It is the superpower most likely to drag the region into a Third World War through direct conflicts with China (and possibly Japan) or as a result of the support it is giving to the policies of its ally, Vietnam. It is the only actively expansionist superpower and is obviously preparing to use the toe-hold it has acquired in Indo-China to spread its power and influence in the region.[64]

It is certain that Beijing would endorse such an assessment wholeheartedly.

From Phnom to Kabul, a short book produced by Singapore's Ministry of Foreign Affairs, denounces the Soviet-backed Vietnamese occupation of Cambodia and the Soviet occupation of Afghanistan in such sharp and strong terms that it may easily be mistaken as a publication of the Chinese Ministry of Foreign Affairs. It pours scorn and derision on the professions of goodwill and peaceful intent by the Vietnamese and Soviet leaders and warns of an alarming new twist in Moscow's earlier "devotion" to the principle of noninterference: "The fear of nations is the rise of a new imperialism born in the name of proletarian salvation."[65]

Such reactions among the countries of Asia are highly advantageous for Beijing's diplomatic offensive against Moscow in the current struggle for power in the region. The policy of containment pursued by Moscow and Beijing against each other is more comprehensive than the U.S. policy of containment against the menace of international communism in Asia in the 1950s, when SEATO was born. The Sino-Soviet rivalry in Asia has produced uncertainties and fears and is fraught with the danger of armed conflict, as has already occurred in Indochina and in Southwest Asia.

South Asia Between Moscow and Beijing

Like other parts of Asia, South Asia has not been unaffected by the growing Sino-Soviet rift. In fact, the Soviet stand on the Sino-Indian border dispute, which culminated in a war between those two large Asian countries in 1962, offered early evidence of the rift between the PRC and the USSR in that area. That conflict marked the first time the Soviet Union supported a noncommunist country, India, against a communist one, the PRC. Another peculiar phenomenon resulted as well: Pakistan, which was still a member of both SEATO and CENTO, became China's most friendly noncommunist neighbor in Asia. Following the ancient maxim, "the enemy's enemy is a friend," China and Pakistan became close friends, and India became Russia's partner in its policy of isolating and weakening China. That Indo-Soviet alliance culminated in 1971 when the two countries signed a treaty of friendship–a treaty that enabled the Indian army to dismember Pakistan. After the 1971 Indo-Pakistani War, which created a new sovereign country, Bangladesh, the Soviet Union gained leverage in the balance of power in South Asia while China and the United States suffered a setback.

During 1975–1977, Beijing had an opportunity to regain some lost ground. The pro-Moscow, pro-India regime in Bangladesh was overthrown by a military coup, and elections were held in both India and Pakistan. In India, Indira Gandhi, who had strengthened the Indo-Soviet friendship, suffered a defeat, and Morarji Desai, who was attacked in the Soviet press as reactionary, became India's prime minister. Soon after taking office, Desai repudiated Gandhi's tilt toward Moscow and declared that he would follow a genuine nonalignment policy. The Chinese press welcomed Desai's statement and expressed satisfaction over Mrs. Gandhi's defeat as a sign of a setback for Moscow in South Asia. But in spite of all that and the fact that the Desai government tried to reduce India's dependence on Russia, particularly for military supplies, there has been little change in India's policy toward either Moscow or Beijing.

The Sino-Pakistani friendship has survived changes of governments in both China and Pakistan. The relationship between the two countries has actually deepened as it is founded on such mutually advantageous factors that internal changes in either country do not affect the growing alliance. China had no diplomatic relations with the new South Asian nation, Bangladesh, from 1972–1975. A full diplomatic relationship was established in 1975, however, and since then, the two countries have made steady progress in improving their relationship. Bangladesh, overshadowed by "big-brother" India, welcomes the opportunity to widen its diplomatic options by maintaining close ties with China. Similarly, as China is happy to welcome another South Asian ally, there seems to be a solid basis for the Sino-Bangladesh friendship.

Let us now examine the South Asian international scene in the context of the competition between the USSR and the PRC to increase influence and power in Asia. The South Asian subcontinent is not as strategically important as East Asia, Indochina, or the Indian Ocean–Persian Gulf areas, but it has always been politically important. It contains more than one-sixth of the world's population within an area of 1,627,000 square miles, and it has been the focus of Third World politics since the Nehru era. The interrelation of the global interests of the major powers—the United States, the USSR, and the PRC—and of the regional tensions and conflicts—such as the Indo-Pakistani wars, Indo-Bangladesh disputes, India's nuclear explosion, Pakistan's potential nuclear explosion—have been of great significance to the Asian international system. Currently, South Asia may not be as explosive an area as Indochina or Korea, where the PRC and the USSR sometimes reach near-war situations, but the Sino-Soviet rivalry in Asia has affected South Asia, and internal instability in all three South Asian countries has rendered the region more vulnerable to external pressures and influences.

The PRC, USSR, and India. New Delhi, like Hanoi and Tokyo, receives special attention from both Moscow and Beijing because of their current struggle in Asia. Obviously, the Chinese benefited from the election of Desai, and the Indian foreign minister, Atal Vajpayee, disclosed in December 1977 that the Chinese had expressed a general desire to have better relations with India. (The message was conveyed through the U.S. secretary of state, Cyrus Vance, and President Tito when they visited China in late 1977.) India endorsed China's hopes, and Vajpayee was congratulated for taking the initiative in repairing the Sino-Indian relationship, which had been fractured by the 1962 border war between the two countries. The Chinese regard any dent in the Indo-Soviet friendship as a major diplomatic feat in Asia, and they even welcomed the improvement in the U.S.-India relationship that resulted from President Carter's visit to India and the Indian prime minister's return visit to the United States. China expected that the improved U.S.-India relationship would reduce India's dependence on the Soviet Union.

Nevertheless, in spite of the hopes and efforts on the part of India and China, the situation has not altered. Moscow redoubled its efforts in India after Mrs. Gandhi's defeat, and India is still heavily dependent on Soviet military and economic aid. Furthermore, among the noncommunist countries, India has been one of the largest beneficiaries of Soviet assistance. Thus, neither Beijing nor Washington could easily dent the Moscow–New Delhi entente. Desai, during his short tenure as prime minister (1977–1979), received the same red-carpet treatment from Moscow as his three predecessors had. When Desai suggested to the Russians, during his first visit to Moscow in 1977, that the special relationship of Mrs. Gandhi's era might be replaced by a pragmatic relationship based on mutual national interests, the Russians offered no challenge—they were bidding for time. The Soviet strategy in 1977 was to prevent any rapprochement between India and China. Moreover, Desai assured the Russians that an improvement in Sino-Indian relations would not injure India's long-standing and more stable relations with the Soviet Union.

Before visiting Beijing, Vajpayee went to Moscow in 1978 to reassure the Kremlin leaders about India's attempts to improve relations with China. The Soviet foreign minister severely denounced China during Vajpayee's visit, and when Vajpayee finally visited Beijing in early 1979, during the China-Vietnam war, he actually cut short his visit to protest China's aggression against Vietnam. This action accorded with the pro-Soviet lobby inside the ruling Janata party in India, which had vigorously protested China's military action against Vietnam. The Indian government was one of the few Asian countries to raise its voice on behalf of Vietnam during the 1979 China-Vietnam war.

Immediately after the failure of Vajpayee's goodwill visit to Beijing, Russia's Prime Minister Kosygin visited India and used the occasion to criticize China for its aggression against Vietnam and for its role in Asia. Kosygin also pushed, unsuccessfully, for India's recognition of Cambodia's new regime. Within twelve weeks of Kosygin's visit to India, Desai made his second trip to Moscow, on June 12, 1979, and a number of economic cooperation accords were signed as well as an agreement for a joint venture for Soviet-Indian space satellites.

On the situation in the "arc of instability"—Afghanistan, Iran, and Pakistan—India concurred with Soviet views: support the pro-Soviet regime in Afghanistan and be apprehensive about the Pakistani and

Iranian support to the Muslim rebel groups that opposed the pro-Soviet regime in Kabul. India's demonstration of support of the Soviet Union's global interests occurred at the 1979 session of the UN General Assembly when the Indian delegate tried to oust the Pol Pot regime from the United Nations by proposing the "Havana formula," which would have excluded both regimes as Castro had done at the nonaligned conference in Havana on September 3–7, 1979. Thus, it is clear that India's basic policy of friendship with the Soviet Union has not altered, nor has its posture toward Beijing. With Mrs. Gandhi's return to power, it can be expected that there will be a strengthening of ties to Moscow; she is not expected to forget or forgive China's celebration of her defeat in the 1977 elections.

The Sino-Pakistan and Soviet-Pakistan Relationship. Turning to Pakistan, the trend is the same: a continued friendship with Beijing and correct, but not cordial, relations with Moscow. The Russians, however, work continuously to gain Pakistan's goodwill by capitalizing on that country's frustration over the United States' Pakistani policy. The United States has stopped all economic aid to Pakistan because of Pakistan's alleged attempts to acquire a nuclear bomb. Pakistan claims the U.S. policy is discriminatory in light of the fact that the United States continues to support the Indian nuclear projects despite India's nuclear explosion in 1974, and Pakistan says it is seriously considering altering its relationship with Moscow because of the U.S. policy as well as the situations in Afghanistan and Iran.

China, on the other hand, continues to try to lead Pakistan away from Moscow. China urges Pakistan not to listen to sweet words from Moscow, while it pressures the United States to change its policy toward Pakistan in view of the volatile situation in the "arc of instability."[66]

Bangladesh. The new South Asian country of Bangladesh seeks Chinese friendship and cooperation. Although helped by India in 1971, Bangladesh fears domination by that much larger and more powerful neighbor, and like Nepal, Burma, and other smaller countries of the region, Bangladesh looks toward China as an alternate source of diplomatic, political, and even military assistance. China profited by the change of government in Bangladesh in 1975. The new president, Zia-Ur Rahman, made one state visit to China and two other stopover visits while en route to Japan and North Korea. Nevertheless, Bangladesh is wary of offending Moscow, and to a certain degree, Bangladesh follows a policy of genuine nonalignment between Moscow and Beijing.

East Asian Triangle: Beijing, Moscow, and Tokyo

In their competition for power and influence in Asia, both Moscow and Beijing have paid special attention to Tokyo because of Japan's growing economic and political influence in Asian affairs. Until it signed the friendship treaty with China in August 1978, Japan tried to maintain an equal distance between Moscow and Beijing and, like most other Asian countries, wanted to follow a policy of genuine nonalignment in the new cold war between the PRC and the USSR. Since the 1978 friendship treaty, Japan's foreign policy has been tilted toward Beijing, but it would be naive to say that Japan has become an ally of the PRC to the degree that Vietnam has become an ally, if not a "satellite," of Moscow.

Japan still attaches importance to its relationship with the Soviet Union, particularly in the economic sphere. Between 1965 and 1975, Moscow and Tokyo signed twenty-seven bilateral treaties and agreements, mainly economic ones. The Soviets would prefer closer ties to Japan, especially for the development of the Siberian region, but Japan's recent tilt toward Beijing and its fears, along with those of the ASEAN countries, about Soviet expansionism in Southeast Asia have adversely affected even the economic relationship between Japan and Russia.

The recent Soviet naval buildup in the Pacific has also seriously affected the Soviet-Japanese relationship. The Russians have boasted about a 12 percent increase in the overall capacity of their Vladivostok-based Far Eastern Fleet, and defense officials in Tokyo, Beijing, and Washington have expressed concern over the fact that the Soviet Union has grown from a third-rate naval power to a first-rate one.

The Russians, however, out of economic necessity as well as because of apprehension concerning any Sino-Japanese accord, continue to court Japan, but Japan still remains fearful of the Soviet-Vietnamese military adventures in Southeast Asia. Ironically, a stable and strong ASEAN has emerged as a priority in the foreign policies of Tokyo, Beijing, and Washington, and it is just such a Washington-Tokyo-Beijing alliance that the Soviets fear most.

Although Japan shares ASEAN's concerns about the Soviet-backed military actions in Indochina, it wants to avoid playing the role of a "big brother" in any major conflict in Asia arising from the Sino-Soviet rift. That rift, more than any other issue in recent years, has perplexed the foreign policy makers in Tokyo. Since the establishment of Sino-Japanese diplomatic relations in 1972 by Prime Minister Kakuei Tanaka, every Japanese government has tried to maintain an equidistant or omnidirectional policy vis-à-vis the Sino-Soviet situation.

One of the best illustrations of Japan's efforts not to offend either of its communist neighbors was its lengthy, cautious, and complicated negotiations with Beijing for a treaty of friendship. It took six years (1972–1978) for the elusive peace and friendship treaty between Japan and China to be concluded. Tokyo wanted to avoid Moscow's displeasure over the treaty and was uncomfortable with China's insistence on placing an antihegemony clause in the treaty. Opposition to any form of hegemony had become an important feature of China's post–Cultural Revolution foreign policy, being stated in the 1972 Shanghai communiqué, in the 1972 Sino-Japanese joint communiqué after Tanaka's visit to Beijing, and in most of the joint communiqués issued after the visits of Asian leaders to the PRC. The Chinese foreign policy makers defined the word for me during my visits to Beijing in 1976, 1977, and 1978, and they gave it a clear and unambiguous meaning, adding that they were opposed not only to the hegemony of the Russians, but to that of any power, including Chinese hegemony. Japan on the other hand wanted to exclude the word hegemony in the proposed treaty in order to avoid Russian wrath.

Nevertheless, the new international patterns in Asia offer little hope for any remarkable improvement in the Soviet-Japanese relationship. A White Paper published by the Japanese defense planners speaks "in unusually plain language in assessing possible Soviet threats." It points out that although the two superpowers are trying to avoid a nuclear confrontation through a rough strategic balance, "there has been no change in basic undercurrents which still pit East (Moscow) against West (Washington)."[67] These undercurrents increase Japanese concern about the Soviet military buildup of land and sea forces in East Asia. Moreover, the White Paper stresses the fact that Soviet military forces and their readiness have been improved qualitatively as well as quantitatively. Since the summer of 1978, Moscow has deployed a considerable number of ground forces in the Japanese-claimed "northern islands," which have been occupied by the Soviet Union since World War II, and the Soviet Pacific Fleet is also perceived as a real threat by Japan. Needless to say, the 1979 Japanese White Paper on Defense calls for action to upgrade Japan's self-defense forces.

In summary, the current East Asian triangle – Moscow, Beijing, and Tokyo – offers little hope of better relations between Moscow and Tokyo; rather, it suggests closer cooperation between Tokyo and Beijing with the blessing of Washington.

The Sino-Soviet Rivalry and the Nonaligned Movement

The nonaligned movement was founded in 1961 by Nehru of India, Nasser of Egypt, and Tito of Yugoslavia. The objective of the movement was to create an alternative to the military alliances of the two superpowers – the United States and the USSR – and two outstanding facts dominated the movement. One was the continued existence of European colonial rule in Africa and elsewhere; the other was a recognition of the tension between the United States and the USSR, which threatened the world with a new world war in the age of nuclear weapons. Since 1961, the thrust of the movement has changed considerably because forty-three former colonies have become sovereign states and European colonial rule has become a matter of the past. Moreover, the newly independent countries of the Third World are now a dominating force in the United Nations.

New challenges face the nonaligned movement. Regional conflicts among the member states are now prominent issues, as was reflected at the Sixth Summit Conference in Havana in September 1979. Furthermore, a group of the Third World countries, such as Cuba, are, for all practical purposes, allied to the Soviet Union, though they may still feign non-alignment. The Soviet-Cuban military adventures in Africa and the Soviet-Vietnamese expansionism in Southeast Asia pose more serious threats to the movement than the European colonial rule or the East-West cold war ever did. Similarly, though the tension persists between the United States and the USSR, there is more talk of détente than of cold war, and many people have been lulled into believing that the "balance of terror" among the nuclear powers has made the world safer. Now regional, rather than global, wars worry the world more. More significantly, a cold war is now developing between the PRC and the USSR, particularly in Asia, and that phenomenon profoundly affects the nonaligned movement.

Although the Soviet Union, following the Leninist dogma that Russia was the predestined leader of all ex-colonial people, did not initially favor the movement, the Kremlin soon cultivated alliances with certain of the nonaligned countries. Nehru and Nasser inclined toward Moscow, but Tito feared the Soviet threat more than Western domination. China was excluded from the nonaligned movement because of its treaty with Moscow. At one stage, China encouraged a Bandung-type Afro-Asian conference, but after the abortive second Afro-Asian conference, the idea of any grouping other than the nonaligned one faded away. So China also attempted to cultivate alliances with the nonaligned countries and has recently made good headway.

The 1979 Sixth Summit Conference in Havana threatened the original objective of the nonaligned movement as Fidel Castro, host of the conference and chairman of the movement for the next three years, tried to shift the movement from being genuinely nonaligned to being pro-Soviet. In the draft resolution presented by Cuba, the Soviet Union and its bloc were designated as the natural allies of the nonaligned movement, and Castro urged the members of the movement to conclude agreements with the Soviet Union and its bloc as they held the same interests as and shared the aims of the members of the movement. Yugoslavia and other older members of the movement, such as India, Egypt, and Indonesia, would not permit Castro's subtle tactics and strategy to prevail. Led by Tito and strongly supported by the ASEAN countries, members of the movement challenged Castro's policy and proposed so many amendments to the draft resolution that the pro-Soviet tone was dropped in the final communiqué. However, since Castro is chairman until 1982, the nonaligned movement risks being turned into a forum that acts against both the United States and China. That possibility became clear when the movement began to sponsor certain colonial causes, to resist the racial policy in South Africa, and to support the Arabs in the Middle East, and the Soviet Union "proved" by its gestures that it was a better friend of the nonaligned countries than the United States or its NATO allies. Thus, at this point, the Soviet Union maintains an edge in its relations with the nonaligned countries.

In the context of the ever-growing Sino-Soviet rift in Asia and elsewhere, the Soviet Union faces more new and more effective challenges from the PRC than it does from the West working through the agency of the nonaligned countries. Asian countries friendly to China, such as Pakistan (which is now a full member of the nonaligned movement) and the ASEAN countries, fear Soviet hegemony and expansionism rather than the old colonialism of the West or China's exporting subversion to its Asian neighbors. On the eve of Fidel Castro's speech to the UN General Assembly on October 12, 1979, ambassadors from the nonaligned countries in the United Nations as the spokesman of those countries, met in New York and watered down the Cuban draft of a document that was sharply critical of China as well as of the United States. This action by a large group of the nonaligned countries demonstrates that Castro's attempt to turn the nonaligned movement toward Moscow and against the PRC will not be easy nor is it likely to be successful.

The Soviet Invasion of Afghanistan and Its Impact on Sino-Soviet Diplomacy in Asia

The Soviet Union's 1979 Christmas blitzkrieg against its weaker South Asian neighbor, Afghanistan, plunged the whole world into a new era of uncertainty and danger. The clockwork operation that took some 40,000 to 50,000 Soviet troops into Afghanistan was timed to coincide with the doze that descends on the Western world during the holiday season and with the snows that would immobilize the Afghan insurgents in the hills.[68] Soviet troop carriers began landing at Kabul airport on Christmas eve; on December 27, 1979, the Russians moved against the three-month-old regime of Afghan President Hafizullah Amin, killing him and his followers. By the new year, the tens of thousands of Soviet reinforcements that continued to arrive by air and by land across the Oxus River frontier were fanning out across the country to garrison the main towns, and one force positioned itself at the Afghan end of the Khyber Pass to Pakistan.

The Soviet invasion of Afghanistan showed, for the first time since World War II, that the Soviet leaders are ready to undertake direct military adventures outside of Eastern Europe. To many observers, the Soviet direct military intervention against its South Asian neighbor means that Russia has a strategic plan for global domination. As a sphere of influence, Afghanistan ranks quite high on Moscow's priority list. Although landlocked, Afghanistan provides the Soviets with a base of operations for a cluster of pressure points that extend from the tip of Indochina, across central Asia, down through the Arabian Peninsula, and to the Horn of Africa. Today, Soviet forces or their surrogates, the Cubans and the Vietnamese, operate over a huge arc of territory known as the "crescent of crisis" – Vietnam, Laos and Cambodia, Afghanistan, Southern Yemen, and Ethiopia are all arc countries that have been placed under the Kremlin's umbrella since 1975.[69] Afghanistan adjoins Iran and Pakistan and is only 400 kilometers from the Indian Ocean. From Afghanistan, Soviet military aircraft are within striking distance of the strategic Strait of Hormuz at the entrance to the Persian Gulf, which is the world's chief oil-producing center. Military analysts think that the Russians are trying to stretch a net across the Strait of Malacca in the Indian Ocean, the Strait of Hormuz in the Persian Gulf, and the Gulf of Aden, which guards the entrance to the Red Sea and the Suez Canal. It will be difficult now to check the Soviet juggernaut in Asia.

The reactions against the Soviet invasion of Afghanistan were severe and almost worldwide. The Security Council passed a resolution calling for the immediate and unconditional withdrawal of all foreign troops from Afghanistan, but the resolution was vetoed by the Soviet Union. Then the General Assembly adopted a similar resolution, and the fact that it was supported by more than 100 member countries, including the majority of the nonaligned and Muslim countries, was a shock to the Soviet Union, which usually gets support from the Third World and nonaligned countries. The Islamic countries' foreign ministers met in a special session in Pakistan and passed another strongly worded resolution demanding the withdrawal of the Soviet troops. Those troops have met with unexpected and almost unbelievable resistance from the Afghan people. It is now more than two years since the Soviet troops entered Afghanistan, and they now number nearly 100,000, but the Soviet Union has failed to pacify the heroic Afghan people, who are making unique efforts to oppose the Soviet occupation of their homeland.

The Chinese government naturally came out with the strongest condemnation of what they called the "naked aggression" of the Soviet hegemonists. The Chinese government called the Soviet invasion a "great threat to peace and security in Asia and the whole world" and a "wanton violation of all norms of international relations."[70] Obviously, the Chinese were pleased by the worldwide condemnation of the Soviet actions and policy.

Impact of the Afghan Crisis on Japan

The Soviet invasion of Afghanistan has added substantial momentum to the already growing campaign for a greater Japanese military budget – government and political leaders sensitive to shifts in public sentiment say the "trend is toward support for more military spending."[71] There are several factors that are responsible for the change in Japanese public opinion in favor of larger military expenditures. One is the fear that the United States would reduce its presence in Asia after the Vietnam War and leave Japan vulnerable to Soviet pressures. Another is the fact that China now endorses Japanese rearmament after once fiercely opposing it. A third is the growing Soviet military presence in the Kuril Islands, coupled with Moscow's deployment of SS-20 missiles and Backfire bombers in the Far East.

"The impact of Afghanistan on Japanese public opinion has been quite substantial," said Michita Sakata, chairman of a newly formed security committee, and the inauguration of that committee in March 1980 was itself a reflection of the changed attitude toward military spending. Outside the Soviet sphere, Afghanistan is considered an independent Third World country, he said, and the invasion makes the Japanese think about what might occur in their own country.[72]

Defense officials in the United States have urged Japan to increase its military spending and expand protection for its ships at sea in the light of some Soviet military moves. The U.S. defense secretary, Harold Brown, visited Japan in January 1980, after an eight-day visit to China where he had explored Sino-American military cooperation, not alliance, in the wake of the Afghan crisis. Brown advised the Japanese leaders that because of Soviet moves – he cited the Soviet invasion of Afghanistan and the buildup of Soviet forces on the Kuril Islands north of Japan – Japan should reassess and increase its defense spending over a period of time. Brown, to the delight of Japan's defense agency, wanted an acceleration of that agency's intermediate-range plan, which envisions reaching defense spending equal to 1 percent of Japan's gross national product by

1985. Brown also reported that China, because of its own anxiety about the Soviet moves, would welcome Japan's military strength. The U.S. pressure for Japan's increased military spending was unusually direct after the Afghan crisis, and maybe that crisis will lead to the emergence of an effective cooperation among Washington, Beijing, and Tokyo.[73]

Impact of the Afghan Crisis on South and Southeast Asia

In South Asia, Pakistan was seriously upset by the Soviet invasion of its closest neighbor, Afghanistan, and took a leading part in condemning the Soviet action both at the United Nations and at the Islamic countries' conference. The Chinese foreign minister visited Pakistan almost immediately after the Soviet action in Afghanistan, and Pakistan's president, Zia-ul Haq, also visited China and held important defense and security talks with the Chinese leaders. China has assured Pakistan of its full support in the case of a Soviet attack against Pakistan. The threats from the Soviet Union have put Pakistan into a real crisis situation, and its hopes for getting adequate military help and a guarantee of assistance from the other superpower, the United States, have not been realized. A high-powered U.S. delegation led by Zbigniew Brzezinski visited Pakistan in February 1980, but the talks concerning a U.S.-Pakistan military cooperation failed. So Pakistan, though terrified by the presence of Soviet troops on its borders, has become extremely cautious toward Moscow. Pakistan is trying to follow a nonalignment policy toward Moscow and is most anxious not to offend the Russian bear, as Pakistan fully realizes that China's help would not be adequate in a conflict with the Soviet Union. So Pakistan, contrary to its earlier position, has become rather "soft" toward Moscow; not out of love, but out of fear.

Bangladesh joined the majority of the Third World countries in condemning the Soviet military intervention in Afghanistan, but without offending Moscow unduly. Bangladesh's President Zia also visited China in July 1980. India, under Indira Gandhi, has followed a cautious policy in dealing with the Afghan crisis. Unlike other Afro-Asian countries, India did not "loudly" oppose the Soviet action; nor is India very happy to see such a large Soviet army so close to its borders. So the Indian reaction to the Soviet military action in Afghanistan is governed by two factors: India's special relationship with the Soviet Union and India's concern about a serious crisis so close to its border. In the explosive situation, Mrs. Gandhi has not closed off all options concerning China, and the good relations between the two largest Asian countries have continued, though Mrs. Gandhi's tilt toward Moscow is evident, particularly since Moscow has offered to send huge military supplies to India. But China is also making a serious bid to normalize relations with India, again in the context of the growing Sino-Soviet rift in Asia.

The ASEAN countries' reaction to the Afghan crisis is definitely anti-Soviet. They are watching the Soviet expansionist designs with grave concern, first those in Indochina and now in Southwest Asia. China's image has gained in Southwest Asia because the threats from Russia increased after that country's military intervention in another Asian country.

Before concluding this discussion of the Sino-Soviet conflicts in Asia, it should be noted that in spite of the growing struggle in Asia, Moscow and Beijing occasionally conduct serious discussions on a state to state level to improve their bilateral relations. Although China worries about the situation in Indochina, Moscow has experienced serious problems in Afghanistan. The possibility, albeit a slim one, exists that the two rivals might agree to a mutual relaxation of tensions on their "next-door neighbors." China could be relieved on its southern border by Russian leverage on Vietnam just as Russia could be relieved on its southern border by China's goodwill with Pakistan, which constitutes the focal point of the opposition to the pro-Soviet regime in Afghanistan.

Thus, in spite of severe differences and conflicts, and in spite of the fact that the Sino-Soviet rift in Asia has proved occasionally volatile, it is important to take note of the periodic Sino-Soviet efforts for some agreement.

Mongolia Between the Two Giants

Mongolian charges of Chinese border violations and interference, made on September 3, 1973, only ten days after the Chinese prime minister had told the Tenth Party Congress in Beijing that Russia could show its desire to relax world tension by withdrawing its troops from Mongolia, were clearly part of the cold war between Moscow and Beijing and clearly had particular reference to their own border dispute. Although Mongolian policy is dominated by the Soviet Union, the Chinese government formally abandoned its traditional suzerainty over Mongolia in 1950, and the Sino-Mongolian frontier, unlike the Sino-Soviet border, was settled in 1962.

The Mongolian accusations, first made in the journal *Utga dzohiol urlag* [Literature and art] in September 1973 and since repeated widely by both local and Soviet propaganda organs and by Mongolian spokesmen at international conferences, were apparently intended to refute Beijing's claims to be a genuine friend of the small and medium-sized countries and a defender of their vital interests and to expose China's ambitions to secure the leadership of the Third World as a means to world hegemony.

These aims served the Soviet interest because they made the Chinese appear as bullies of their small neighbors and preempted any Chinese attempt to make friends with the Mongolians. Concern about such an attempt was reflected in the journal's admission that Beijing's policy toward Mongolia had recently changed from pressure to gentler methods.

Beijing's alleged readiness to give "selfless assistance" to other countries was challenged in a section of the article quoted by Moscow Radio, in Chinese, on September 7, 1973. It said that the Chinese had tried to undermine Mongolia's economy by reneging on their obligations concerning construction projects during 1962–1964 and by inciting Chinese workers to strike and to avoid work by feigning sickness. Chinese laborers had been withdrawn by 1964, largely because Mongolia had sided with Moscow in the Sino-Soviet dispute, though the Chinese claimed that the withdrawal had been requested and the Mongolians said that the contracts had expired. Relations had deteriorated further in 1967, when a Mongolian diplomat in Beijing was manhandled by Cultural Revolution mobs, and ambassadors had been withdrawn until 1971, when the atmosphere improved slightly. Although trade protocols have since been signed, economic relations seemed to have developed little. In March 1973, the Chinese agreed to hand over seven unfinished aid projects, which, under the terms of the original agreement, remained China's property until completed. Mongolia's participation in the newly intensified Sino-Soviet propaganda war underlines the inability or unwillingness of the ruling Mongolian People's Revolutionary Party (MPRP) to emulate the North Korean balancing act between the two major communist powers.

Renewed charges of Chinese border violations, made by Mongolia in a Soviet magazine,[74] seemed to be partly a counter to Beijing's proposal to Moscow in November 1974 for a nonaggression pact. The unexpected offer left the Russians temporarily at a propaganda disadvantage and was at first ignored by them, but in a speech in Ulan Bator on November 26, 1974, where he was attending the fiftieth-anniversary celebrations of the Mongolian People's Republic, Brezhnev described the Chinese approach as absolutely unacceptable, despite its appearance, at first glance, of seeking to normalize relations with the Soviet Union. Beijing again seized the initiative in January 1975 when Zhou Enlai reiterated his country's case at the National People's Congress.

Mongolia accused China of wanting to seize "neighboring Asian countries and also vast territories of the Soviet Far East," and of making "anti-Sovietism" the central theme of its international activities.[75] The accusation was also made that the Chinese opposed the creation of an Asian collective security system – the Soviet proposal – which had as one of its basic principles the inviolability of frontiers and therefore ruled out Chinese territorial claims.

The Chinese message of November 6, 1974, had called for an agreement "on maintaining the *status quo* on the border, on averting armed conflicts and on the departure of the armed forces of both sides from disputed areas," and the agreement was to be followed by talks.[76] The Russians might well have been caught off balance by this proposal, as they had suggested a nonaggression pact on several occasions since armed conflict broke out over an island in the Ussuri River in 1969 but had failed to gain Chinese support for the idea. China seems to have been trying to correct any impression that the Soviet Union was being more reasonable than China, and similar motives appear to have inspired the return to Beijing of the chief Soviet negotiator at the border talks. The Chinese initiative came shortly before President Ford's meeting with Brezhnev at Vladivostok.

Moscow withheld the full text of the Chinese message from the Russian people, and a summary in the Soviet party newspaper, *Pravda*, on November 9, 1974, omitted all reference to the nonaggression pact. Six days later, the Soviet party secretary and Politburo member, Kirilenko, again without mentioning the proposal, said in Turkmenistan that the Soviet policy toward China remained one of resistance to "anti-Soviet slanders and hostile intrigues" and of "constant readiness to hold businesslike talks."[77] Meanwhile, according to East European correspondents in Moscow, official circles there thought that the Chinese were merely repeating the stand that had deadlocked the border talks since 1969. The Chinese proposal for the withdrawal of forces was said by the Hungarian newspaper *Nepszabadsag* (November 13, 1974) to involve 1.5 million square kilometres of Soviet territory, and the same newspaper denied the claim made in the Beijing message that the Soviet and Chinese prime ministers had reached an understanding along those lines in September 1969.

Replying formally to the Chinese message on November 26, 1974, the Soviet Union recalled its own proposals and dismissed Beijing's overture, with its "presentation of all kinds of preliminary conditions," as failing to furnish "foundations for an understanding." In Ulan Bator, Brezhnev accused Beijing of demanding the withdrawal of the Soviet frontier guard from "a series of areas to which the Chinese leaders have now decided to lay claim."[78]

Zhou Enlai, in his report on January 13, 1975, to the Fourth Chinese National People's Congress in Beijing, made it clear that despite his desire for fresh negotiations, he still had serious doubts about Soviet intentions. He complained that the Soviet leadership had conducted subversive activities and had even provoked armed conflicts on the border. In violation of the "understanding" reached between him and the Soviet prime minister in 1969, the Soviet side still refused to sign an agreement along the lines of the Chinese message. He added that "they even refuse to do anything about such matters as the disengagement of the armed forces of the two sides in the disputed areas on the border and the prevention of armed conflicts; instead they talk profusely about empty treaties on the non-use of force against each other and mutual non-aggression." He deduced that the Russians were trying "to deceive the Soviet people and world public opinion" and advised them to negotiate honestly.[79]

China's treatment of the Mongols has been a prominent feature of Ulan Bator's propaganda. Beijing has retaliated — notably during Brezhnev's visit to Mongolia in November 1974 — by claiming that Mongolia has become a Soviet colony and is being ruthlessly exploited for mineral resources and animal products. Every now and then, Mongolia continues its anti-China propaganda in order to please the Russians. Mongolian President Yuinjaagiyn has talked about Maoist subversion, Mongolia expelled a Chinese diplomat on June 4, 1980,[80] and the president of the Mongolian Academy of Sciences has accused China of having territorial designs on Mongolia. As the Soviet invasion of Afghanistan drew severe condemnation from the countries of the Third World, Mongolia, as a Soviet client-state, stepped up its anti-China propaganda. In an address to Mongolian People's Army in September 1980, President Yuinjaagiyn asked for more Soviet arms and military help for what he described as Chinese threats to his country, and he disclosed that Soviet arms supplies continued to pour into his country. His aim was to pinpoint China as the main enemy of Mongolia and to thus divert the world's attention from Soviet aggressive policy in Indochina and Afghanistan.[81]

Sino-Soviet Rivalry in Africa

The evolution of the Soviet and Chinese attitudes toward Africa in the 1970s has been conditioned by their own estrangement as well as by the need to modify ideological positions as African concepts of socialism have become more clearly defined and established. Soviet thinking about Africa has undergone continuous reappraisal since the first guidelines were laid down by Professor Potekhin, head of Moscow's Africa Institute until his death in 1964, and Chinese policy has changed even more markedly since a famous remark by Zhou Enlai in 1974 that the continent was ripe for revolution. Now both countries, after fluctuating fortunes in Africa, seem to have accepted the necessity of working through normal diplomatic and trade channels to extend their influence there—often with the aim of rivaling each other. At the same time, both repeat the traditional anti-imperialist slogans; the Russians appeal to all "progressive" Africans to unite and turn to the USSR rather than to the West for advice and contacts, and the Chinese urge self-reliance or Afro-Asian solidarity against the superpowers, including the Soviet Union.[82]

The Soviet ideological output about Africa, with the theorists continuing wherever possible to make African developments fit the Marxist-Leninist framework, shows that the Soviet leaders have not lost sight of their long-term objectives there. The Chinese, on the other hand, while no longer preaching violent revolution, claim that their own example is valid for the African states. Beijing's interest in Africa in China's new era of open diplomacy is clear from the volume of Chinese exchanges with the African states and the growth of aid to the continent.[83]

With the return to more active diplomacy following China's self-imposed isolation during the Cultural Revolution, the 1970s brought Chinese efforts for worldwide recognition, and by mid-1972, a majority of the African states had diplomatic relations with Beijing rather than with Taiwan. By that time, also, the Chinese were offering proof of their interest in developing exchanges with the African nations by inviting their leaders to Beijing and extending aid on easy terms.

The eagerness of the Soviet and Chinese leaders to make friends in Africa whenever the opportunity arises is particularly apparent from the wide range of African nations they have dealings with. Somalia, which proclaimed its adherence to scientific socialism, enjoyed considerable interest on the part of both Moscow and Beijing—no doubt partly because of its strategic position. One reason for the communist countries' keenness to maintain a presence in such states as Congo/Brazzaville, Tanzania, Zambia, and Guinea—almost regardless of the regime in power—is their interest in infiltrating, training, and, if possible, controlling the African liberation groups,[84] and the Sino-Soviet rivalry has been particularly bitter in this respect. During China's preoccupation with its own Cultural Revolution, the Russians were able to gain a predominant influence among the principal liberation movements, but the Chinese have returned to the fray, basing their appeal on the claim of a similar background in the form of economic backwardness and a history of struggle against imperialists.

Both the Soviet Union and China have lined themselves up in support of nationalist movements in South Africa, Rhodesia (Zimbabwe), and South-West Africa. Since the second half of 1971, there have been signs that the Chinese are reviving their assistance to such movements and in some cases extending it to groups formerly linked mainly to Moscow. But in general, they appear to have become wary of spreading their aid too thinly, and therefore ineffectively, and are cautious about helping dissidents and militant opposition elements in such countries as Ethiopia, with which they have developed good relations.[85]

Soviet propaganda, however, continues to try to discredit Beijing by accusing China of adventurism in Africa, of urging armed struggle regardless of circumstances, and of mainly supporting those groups that are influenced by "anti-Sovietism." On February 11, 1973, a Moscow Radio broadcast for Africa said that the Chinese leadership was playing a "highly indecorous" role in the liberation movement in Portuguese Africa, despite its verbal support. The broadcast complained that Beijing was isolating the liberation groups from the Soviet bloc–the "decisive force of the world revolution process"–and labeling them as movements of Africans against whites, thus ignoring the "class nature" of the struggle.

In Moscow's view, the correct class approach for national leaders and liberation groups in Africa still seems mainly to comprise siding with the Soviet Union and its allies against the West and resisting the capitalist path of development. The time is apparently not yet ripe for the internal class battles that, according to orthodox communist theory, should eventually produce the emergence of a genuine proletariat and a vanguard Communist party.[86]

Notes

1. Don Oberdorfer, "East-East Conflict," *Washington Post*, November 1, 1978.
2. Ibid.
3. Ross Terrill, "Bear-Dragon Flirtation," *Washington Post*, December 19, 1976.
4. See *United States–Soviet Union–China: The Great Power Triangle: Summary of Hearings* (Washington, D.C.: Congressional Research Service, August 12, 1980), p. 17.
5. See *Sunday Telegraph* (London), April 3, 1977.
6. See statement of James S. Duncan, former Canadian deputy minister of defense for air, in U.S., Congress, House of Representatives, Committee on Foreign Affairs, *United States Policy Toward Asia*, Report of the Subcommittee on the Far East and the Pacific, May 19, 1966 (Washington, D.C.: Government Printing Office, 1966), pp. 394–395.
7. U.S., Congress, House of Representatives, Committee on Foreign Affairs, *Sino-Soviet Conflict*, Report on Sino-Soviet conflict and its implications by the Subcommittee on the Far East and the Pacific, H. Res. 84 (Washington, D.C.: Government Printing Office, 1965), pp. 3R–5R.
8. See Neville Maxwell's exclusive interview with Premier Zhou Enlai, *Sunday Times* (London), December 19, 1971.
9. Based on the author's reading of unpublished documents and papers of the government of Pakistan, 1947–1971.
10. *Times* (London), May 16, 1974.

11. *Guardian* (London), May 17, 1974.

12. *Washington Post,* September 26, 1976.

13. *New York Times,* April 12, 1976.

14. Ibid., July 6, 1975.

15. *Daily Telegraph* (London), August 10, 1973.

16. *China and Asia: An Analysis of China's Recent Policy Toward Neighboring States,* Report by the Foreign Affairs and National Defense Division, Congressional Research Service, Library of Congress (Washington, D.C.: Government Printing Office, 1979), p. 27.

17. *Reprints from the Soviet Press,* Vol. 19, no. 5, September 15, 1974, from *Politic cheskoye samoobrasovaniye* (New York: Campus Publications, 1974), pp. 45–60.

18. Ibid.

19. See the summary of the article in the *Washington Post,* August 24, 1975, and "Editorial Comment: 'Thunder from Moscow,'" *New York Times,* September 1, 1975.

20. Ibid.

21. *Impact International* (London), September 12–25, 1975, pp. 30–31.

22. See Chapter 3 in this book.

23. See Golam W. Choudhury, *Brezhnev's Collective Security Plan for Asia* (Washington, D.C.: Center for Strategic and International Studies, Georgetown University, 1976), p. 1.

24. Ibid., p. 39.

25. *Sunday Telegraph,* April 3, 1977.

26. *Dawn* (Karachi), June 15, 1973.

27. *People's Daily* (Beijing), March 29, 1973.

28. See speech by Jiao Guanhua at the Twenty-eighth Session of the UN General Assembly issued by Foreign Languages Press, 1973, p. 7.

29. See speech by Jiao Guanhua at the Twenty-ninth Session of the UN General Assembly isued by Foreign Languages Press, 1974, p. 4.

30. See speech by Deng Xiaoping at a 1974 Special Session of the UN General Assembly issued by Foreign Languages Press, 1974, p. 11.

31. U.S., Congress, *Sino-Soviet Conflict,* p. 5R.

32. Y. Zhukov, A. Iskenderov, and others, *The Third World: Problems and Prospects* (Moscow: Progress Publishers, 1970), Chapter 1.

33. Ibid.

34. See *Ugly Features of Soviet Social Imperialism* (Beijing: Foreign Languages Press, 1976).

35. Based on the author's research and interviews at the Royal Institute of International Affairs, London, and the Research Institute on Community Affairs, Columbia University.

36. Ibid.

37. Ibid.

38. Ibid.

39. *China and Asia: An Analysis of China's Recent Policy Toward Neighboring States,* pp. 27–28.

40. Ibid., p. 28.

41. Ibid.

42. *Peking Review,* August 25, 1977.

43. Ibid.

44. Ibid., July 15, 1977, or *Hungchi (Hongqi),* no. 7 (1977).

45. *Peking Review,* July 15, 1977.

46. *Washington Post,* March 25, 1977.

47. Based on the author's interviews and talks in Beijing, July 1977.

48. See Chinese Deputy Prime Minister Li Xiannian's welcoming speech to the head of the state of Niger on September 19, 1977, in *People's Daily* (Beijing), September 20, 1977. That was the fifth time in 1977 such a walkout took place.

49. *Washington Post,* August 24, 1978.

50. *New York Times,* June 26, 1978.

51. Ibid., October 8, 1977.

52. *Pakistan Times* (Rawalpindi), July 28, 1979.

53. *Financial Times* (London), August 7, 1979.

54. New China News Agency, October 6, 1980.

55. *Washington Post,* October 7, 1980.

56. See "Russia vs. China: Struggle for Asia," *U.S. News and World Report,* February 5, 1979.

57. Ibid.

58. See "The Battle of Red Giants in Asia," *U.S. News and World Report,* November 27, 1978.

59. Based on the author's research and interviews in London.

60. Ibid.

61. Ibid.

62. Ibid.

63. Golam Choudhury, "Sino-Soviet Rivalry in Asia," *Spectrum* (Bangkok), (January–March 1976), pp. 9–16.

64. Derek Davies, "Shadow of Kremlin," *Far Eastern Economic Review,* August 24, 1979.

65. See the summary of *From Phnom to Kabul* in *Far Eastern Economic Review,* October 5, 1980.

66. Based on the author's talks and interviews with Chinese and Pakistani leaders in the summer of 1979.

67. See "Japan: A Hard Look at the Real World," *Far Eastern Economic Review,* August 3, 1979, and "Japanese Foreign Policy in the Seventies," *Dawn* (Karachi), June 30, 1979.

68. *Economist* (London), January 8, 1980.

69. *New York Times,* January 10, 1980.

70. *Peking Review,* January 5, 1980.

71. *Washington Post,* April 20, 1980.

72. Ibid.

73. Ibid., January 15, 1980.

74. *Problems of the Far East,* no. 4 (1974).

75. Based on the author's research in London, 1971–1978.

76. Ibid.

77. Ibid.

78. Ibid.

79. *Documents of the First Session of the Fourth National People's Congress* (Beijing: Foreign Languages Press, 1975), p. 59.

80. Alan Sanders, "Mongolia: A Diplomatic Lesson for China," *Far Eastern Economic Review,* July 11, 1980.

81. Alan Sanders, "Mongolia: More Help from the Kremlin," *Far Eastern Economic Review,* October 31, 1980.

82. Based on the author's research, interviews, and discussion in London.

83. Ibid.

84. Ibid.

85. Ibid.

86. Ibid.

7
The Great Triangular Relationship: Beijing-Moscow-Washington

In the wake of the 1972 Shanghai communiqué, a fragile triangular relationship developed among the United States, the USSR, and the PRC. There are two major triangular relationships in contemporary world politics: Washington-Moscow-Beijing and the United States–European Economic Community–Japan. The first one, the two superpowers and the emerging superpower, the PRC, is characterized by a lack of mutual trust, ideological affinity, or common interests in global security or economic interests. The U.S.-EEC-Japan relationship, on the other hand, is based on common trust, security, economic interests, and ideological factors and on cultural affinities between the United States and the EEC countries.

The Washington-Moscow-Beijing relationship has the greater importance and significance for global peace and for the avoidance of any nuclear war. The triangular balance of power emerged as a result of President Nixon's opening a relationship with China in 1971–1972 and his subsequent trip to Moscow in May 1972, when Nixon and Brezhnev signed a document asserting the basic principles of mutual relations between the United States and the Union of Soviet Socialist Republics, which may be described as a counterbalance to the 1972 Shanghai communiqué. The great powers triangle is a product of two major factors—the Sino-Soviet rift and the limited Sino-American rapprochement begun in 1971–1972—and it has transferred world politics from a bipolar emphasis to a multipolar one. The relationship in the triangular diplomacy among Washington, Moscow, and Beijing, as one expert describes it, is that "each country is to some degree, the adversary of each of the other two. Simultaneously, each country is a potential ally of the remaining one against the other."[1]

China's foreign policy and its role in world affairs have been greatly concentrated on its relations with the two superpowers, the United States and the USSR, and we shall analyze how the triangular relationship has influenced China's global policy. The triangular relationship has a great impact on China's policy toward its neighbors in East, Southeast, South, and Southwest Asia as well as in many other parts of the Third World. The Soviet Union's policy toward Beijing and Washington has been greatly affected by the triangular relationship, as has China's policy toward Washington and Moscow.

The United States seems to be in favorable position in the great powers triangular relationship as both Moscow and Beijing seek U.S. friendship, not out of love for the Americans, but out of their growing mutual distrust and fear. In 1971–1972, Beijing and Washington were disquieted by the Brezhnev doctrine, and each recognized the potential leverage that the other offered. Soviet military intervention in Czechoslovakia in 1968 under the Brezhnev doctrine had alarmed China, and the fear of a preemptive attack on its emerging nuclear plants was the main reason China responded to President Nixon's friendly gestures. The United States was engaged in negotiations with the Soviet Union over SALT I, European security talks, and mutual reductions of armed forces in Europe, and Nixon recognized that a link with Beijing would serve as a useful lever against Moscow. The Kremlin leaders were no longer in a position to take the U.S.-China hostility for granted; on the contrary, they were worried about a U.S.-China collusion against Moscow. Nixon rightly termed that worry as "fanciful," but Soviet anxiety about the emerging Sino-American relationship was beneficial to both the United States and China: to Washington, as it made Moscow more amenable in negotiations like SALT I; to Beijing, because China felt that it would not be alone if there were a Soviet military action of the 1968 Czecho-slovakian type under the Brezhnev doctrine. So the great powers triangu-lar relationship was a stabilizing factor in world politics in the 1970s.

Although the new great powers relationship is described as "tri-angular," there have not yet been any triangular meetings or discus-sions, merely U.S.-USSR or U.S.-PRC talks. But the absentee third party has been of crucial importance in Washington's negotiations with both the Soviet and the Chinese leaders. China never misses an opportunity to tell the Americans and the world about the "danger" of Soviet social im-perialism. The Kremlin leaders, for their part, never tire of designating Maoist China as the potentially greatest threat to world peace and stability.

Nixon and Kissinger gave the world hope for peace in our generation. The U.S. image in the world, which was adversely affected by the Viet-nam War, was greatly enhanced by the new triangular relationship. U.S. troops could be withdrawn peacefully from Vietnam; Nixon was given the red-carpet treatment in Moscow at a time when he ordered a renewal of the bombing in North Vietnam and a blockade of its ports; and the SALT I agreement could be signed with the Soviet Union much more readily because China was a major factor in the Soviet Union's foreign policy. Nixon said bluntly: "We want to improve relations with the P.R.C. as a means of coping with the Soviet Union."[2]

The U.S.-China limited rapprochement reduced tensions in the Asian-Pacific region, where threats from Communist China had been a source of worry for the United States and its Asian allies. Japan and Southeast Asian countries, such as the Philippines, Thailand, Malaysia, Indonesia, and Singapore, began to have a better diplomatic situation because of the improved Sino-American relationship and because of the growing Sino-Soviet rift. Japan and two Asian members of SEATO, the Philippines and Thailand, established diplomatic links with the PRC; Pakistan, the other Asian member of SEATO, already had very close and friendly relations with Beijing. Australia and New Zealand, the U.S. partners in ANZUS, had also established full diplomatic relations with the PRC. The 1975 communist victory in Indochina did not cause any alarm among the non-communist Asian countries, and the domino theory was disproved.

How did the reduced tension affect U.S.-USSR relations? The Soviet Union had to show flexibility toward Washington in the pursuit of Russia's major foreign policy objective: the prevention of any closer ties between the United States and the PRC. In 1972-1974, the world was no doubt safer from a third world war than it had been earlier, so the Nixon-Kissinger triangular diplomacy with Moscow and Beijing served both U.S. global interests and world peace and security. True, there were regional wars and tensions—as in South Asia (1971), the Middle East (1973), and Africa (1975)—but the chances of global crises such as the Cuban missile crisis of 1962 and the earlier Berlin crises, which threatened direct confrontation between the two superpowers, were considerably lessened. Similarly, basic U.S. interests in the Asian-Pacific region were not threatened; only Taiwan and South Korea continued to feel insecure.

In many parts of the Third World, such as southern Africa and the Middle East, the two superpowers continue to use diplomacy in an effort to gain influence and power. Similarly, Moscow and Beijing have intensified their diplomatic efforts to acquire greater influence and power in the Third World, particularly in East, South, and Southeast Asia. Although the United States plays a stabilizing role in areas of tension in the Third World, the Soviet Union has continued its expansionist designs. China, on the contrary, wants the U.S. presence and a more active U.S. role in areas of regional tension, not out of love of the United States, but out of a desire to pursue a policy of containment of Soviet influence and power in the Third World. The Chinese leaders have expressed these views to U.S. policymakers as well as to leaders of Asian countries.

The Kremlin leaders were upset by the prospect of closer Sino-American ties, but as they began to perceive that the Sino-American relationship had to overcome a major hurdle on the Taiwan issue, they began to act on their expansionist designs, at some cost to the United States and China. Dimitri K. Simes has judged that the Soviet Union regards détente as an "activist offensive strategy." Simes added that "the USSR did not forgo any opportunity to improve its international standing at the expense of Washington and Peking but on the other hand it dared not rock the boat hard" and concluded, "Despite detente, the Soviet Union felt free to work against the vital interests of the United States."[3]

Moscow was emboldened by the slow progress of the normalization of relations between Beijing and Washington in 1975–1977. The Sino-American ties did not develop as the 1972 Nixon visit had led many people to believe they would, and the deaths of Premier Zhou Enlai and Chairman Mao and the subsequent Chinese internal power struggle placed some strains and stresses on the Sino-American relationship. Some U.S. policymakers seemed to prefer to adopt a policy of "wait and see" toward China; others were of the opinion that any undue closer Sino-American ties might destroy the détente between Washington and Moscow, which was considered more important than a limited détente between Beijing and Washington. "For the next generation, at least," the *New York Times* stated in an editorial comment, "the highest American interest must be the preservation of the nuclear balance with the Soviet Union, through arms control as well as arms development. Only Russian missiles threaten our survival or that of our allies, for the time being, and China's condemnation of the arms talks and refusal to participate must not alter our priority."[4] On a previous occasion the *New York Times* had stated:

> The Soviet Union undoubtedly is more of a potential threat to the United States than is China. . . . Washington should continue to reject Chinese arguments that the United States must have bad relations with Moscow if it is to improve relations with Peking . . . there is no reason to delay efforts at attaining a second Strategic Arms Limitation Treaty (SALT II) with Moscow. The best policy for the United States at this point is to continue its efforts to improve American relations with both China and Russia . . . this calls for an astute American diplomacy to make the triangular relationship a key factor in the preservation of peace.[5]

The Chinese were obviously concerned about the U.S. policy of giving priority to détente with Moscow over the normalization of relations between China and the United States, and they began to express their concern about U.S.-USSR relations, particularly SALT II. During my 1977 and 1978 trips to China, I had the opportunity to listen to the Chinese express concern about the détente between Moscow and Washington, though they felt convinced that no genuine understanding was possible between the two superpowers because of "interest contradictions" between imperialists and social imperialists. The Chinese also claimed that they did not create any problems for the United States in the Asian-Pacific region, the Middle East, or Africa. In fact, the Chinese referred to common, though not identical, interests with the United States on many issues of contemporary world politics.

The Chinese also referred to views expressed by the U.S. army generals and military experts on the huge Soviet military buildup in the 1970s. A top Chinese foreign policy maker showed me the comments made by Major General George J. Keegan, the retired U.S. Air Force chief of intelligence, who gave a grim picture of the Soviet military buildup: "By every criterion used to measure strategic balance—that is damage expectancy, throw-weight, equivalent megatonnage or technology—I am unaware of a single important category in which the Soviets have not established a significant lead over the United States."[6] It was this type of Soviet military buildup and the consequent Soviet military adventures, such as in the Horn of Africa, that according to the Chinese, constituted the real threat to the great powers triangular relationship and not the "expected" normalization of relations between the PRC and the United States.

The fact is that both China and Russia are locked into a bitter and growing struggle for domination of the communist world as well as for leadership in the Third World, and both try to play "the American card." Beijing's constructive diplomacy lies in enlisting U.S. support against any Soviet military threat to its borders, such as those in the spring of 1969 and during the 1979 China-Vietnam war. China therefore welcomes a strengthening of the U.S. role in the Asian-Pacific region, the Middle East, Africa, and the Indian Ocean–Persian Gulf area. Similarly, China welcomes closer links with Western Europe and with Eastern European countries such as Romania and Yugoslavia. Soviet diplomacy demands increased tension with the United States up to a point, but not to the extent of driving the United States into any alliance with Beijing or any new triangular relationship between Washington, Tokyo, and Beijing, supported by NATO and ANZUS countries.

The great powers triangular relationship was highly favorable to U.S. global interests as both of the communist giants were forced to seek good relations with Washington. The triangular relationship put constraints on the role of both the Soviet Union and the PRC vis-à-vis the United States. Whenever Nixon or Kissinger went to Beijing in the early 1970s, Kremlin leaders would be fearful of a collusion between the United States and the PRC. Similarly, the Chinese were worried about the prospect of a détente between the two superpowers. Leonid Brezhnev was reported to have advised the United States, Britain, and France that the Soviet Union was in no sense worried about "present" Chinese hostility, but added ominously that by the century's end, China would be formidable. He proposed "a more cooperative Soviet-Western relationship to block the danger that Peking, backed by the Third World, might threaten both Russia and the West in another generation."[7]

For their part, the Chinese leaders pleaded with the United States to guard against the Soviet social imperialists, who, according to the Chinese, constituted the most dangerous source of war. The Chinese perception of Soviet social imperialism was summed up as follows:

> Engaged in unbridled aggression and expansion abroad in contending for world hegemony, the Soviet Union inevitably will go to war. Above all, this is determined by its social system. Once a socialist state, the Soviet Union has degenerated into a social-imperialist state ever since the renegade Khrushchev-Brezhnev clique usurped Party and state power and began pursuing a revisionist line, restored capitalism. Having placed itself in the ranks of the imperialist states, the Soviet Union inevitably comes under the basic law of imperialism and is enmeshed in a multitude of inherent imperialist contradictions. Social-imperialism is, therefore, entirely the same as the capitalist-imperialist system, made however, even more rapacious and more truculent in its aggression and expansion abroad.[8]

One may ask, Why should the United States worry about the Chinese reaction to the Soviet-American relationship? However, in the present triangular relationship of the great powers, China is as entitled to express concern about the détente between Moscow and Washington as the Americans are to express interest in, if not worry about, any prospect of a Sino-Soviet thaw, or what has been termed "the bear-dragon flirtation."[9] The Americans realize that in the absence of Chinese hostility, the Soviet Union would become an uncontrollable "bear" in many parts of the world, including Japan, the NATO countries, the Middle East, and Africa. Similarly, the Chinese realize that if the two superpowers were to reach a genuine understanding, the Soviet Union's menacing threats to China would be extremely serious. So it is in the interest of China to prevent any meaningful understanding between Moscow and Washington, just as Moscow considers it constructive diplomacy if they can frustrate the emerging Sino-American relationship. The Soviet Union has also expressed its concern whenever there is any move toward an improvement in the Sino-American relationship. When Secretary of State Vance went to China, the Soviet Union declared on August 26, 1977, that the "new Chinese attempts to improve relations with the West are a threat to world peace," and a political commentary by Tass said that Beijing was trying "to provoke a deterioration in United States–Soviet relations and encouraging a step-up in the arms race." The warning was carried in a major analysis of China in the Soviet monthly *Kommunist,* which said, "The new Chinese leaders were going even farther with Maoist policies than Mao Tse-tung had" and that those policies were leading them to "an even greater striving for rapprochement with the imperialists." It also said that Beijing was "pushing the world to a new war."[10]

Triangular Relationship in the Post-Mao Era (1976–1977)

Brezhnev is reported to have warned the West in 1975 that if it failed to reach a meaningful agreement with the USSR soon, Moscow would have only one obvious alternative: to restore the old alliance with China after Mao died.[11] The Chinese also tried to create the impression in 1976–1977 that if there were undue delay in the normalization of relations with the United States, or if the United States were only using the China card as leverage in its bargaining position with Moscow, they might try to normalize their relations with the Russians. During my 1977 visit to China, I got that impression from my discussions with the Chinese foreign policy makers, but it might be added that there was a group within the Chinese ruling elite that seemed to be disinclined to "flirt with Washington." Their line of argument immediately after the deaths of Mao and Zhou Enlai seems to have been as follows: "We have tried with the Americans; why not now do the same with the Russians? None of them are our friends. But we waited for five years [1972–1977] with the Americans, why not pause a little and look to Moscow for a better deal?"[12] But that faction and that line of argument were insignificant. The chances of any genuine rapprochement between Beijing and Moscow, even in the initial first two years of the post-Mao era, were very limited. On the contrary, even during the power struggle in 1976–1977, the Chinese leaders did not cease to speak strongly against the Russians.

On the eve of Mao's death, Foreign Minister Jiao Guanhua welcomed the former U.S. defense secretary, James Schlesinger, on September 8, 1976, and said: "The Imperialist power that styles itself 'socialist' uses the rhetoric of 'detente' most vociferously while most energetically expanding its armaments and preparing for war." As Schlesinger has rightly pointed out, Russia "talks peace, but it practices war."

> Confronted with the expansionist ambitions of this superpower, some people try appeasement and concession, or even sacrifice others in an attempt to protect themselves. This is, of course, wishful thinking. The lesson of Munich in the thirties proves that to do so can only mean rearing a tiger cub

and bringing ultimate disaster upon oneself. In our opinion the correct policy should be to face reality, mobilize and rely on the people and unite with all the forces that can be united with to wage a tit-for-tat struggle against it.[13]

In China's first major foreign policy statement after Mao's death, the Chinese foreign minister told the 1976 UN General Assembly: "The Soviet Union is trying to expand its influence in the world and it ultimately will wind up in a war with the United States." In addition to the usual Chinese denunciation of Soviet social imperialism and expansionist activities, Jiao declared that European and developing countries should shake off any fear of the Kremlin because its outward appearance of strength was undermined by internal dissension: "There is now a strange phenomenon in the world. Some people are terrified at the mention of the Soviet Union, thinking that it cannot be touched. . . . This is superstition. Soviet social imperialism is nothing to be afraid of. It is outwardly strong, but inwardly weak."[14] The reference to Soviet internal problems, coupled with specific denunciations of Soviet activities in Eastern and Western Europe, Africa, the Mideast, and Asia, signaled a new militance among the post-Mao leaders toward the Kremlin.

But the pertinent and the vital issue is, Should the United States and its allies take the Sino-Soviet rift as permanent and should they also take the Chinese friendship for granted? Either would be a fatal mistake. One must not forget that in international politics, there are no eternal friends or eternal enemies; there are only eternal interests. The United States needs a good relationship with Beijing as a counterbalance to the Soviet Union, which poses a real threat not only to the United States, but to its NATO allies, Japan, and friendly countries in Southeast Asia, ASEAN, and many parts of the Third World.

The China Card in the Triangular Diplomacy

A regular phenomenon of the triangular diplomacy that emerged after the Peking Summit in 1972 is that any cooling off in the U.S.-USSR relationship, or any stalemate over SALT I or II, would warm up the Sino-American relationship; any delay or complications in the process of normalizing relations between Beijing and Washington would be welcomed in Moscow; any warming up of the Sino-American relationship would cause worries in Moscow; and any progress toward détente or SALT II would make the Chinese leaders unhappy and worried. Ever since the opening of relations with China in 1971–1972, the U.S. government has held what has come to be called "the China card," which the United States uses to try to take advantage of the growing Sino-Soviet rift and to build up China, the weaker party, as a counterweight to the Soviet Union, the stronger one. This tactic is in accordance with the classic rule of "balance of power" in world politics. There is no doubt that Washington gains from the Sino-Soviet cold war, as long as it does not turn into a hot war, and the U.S. policy is not unusual or particularly novel in world politics. On the contrary, the United States has maintained a correct and pragmatic stand on the Sino-Soviet rift, and it has not given encouragement to either party to increase tension. It has only fashioned its global strategy in accordance with its vital national interests.

Robert Sutter of the U.S. Congressional Research Service has identified three schools of thought with respect to the China card: the manipulative school, the low-impact school, and the nonmanipulative school.[15] Manipulative policy is designed "to exploit the differences between China and the Soviet Union" and to focus special effort on using the improved relations with China "to gain greater leverage in America's continuing competition with its major adversary, the USSR."[16] This school has urged that the United States "play the Chinese card"—i.e., build closer U.S. political, economic, military, and technological ties with the PRC—for the purpose of gaining more leverage against the Soviet Union. This school believes that the growing Sino-Soviet rift has been of great advantage to Washington in the great powers triangular relationship and that the United States should take initiatives—including sales of arms and transfer of advanced technology to the PRC—to strengthen the weaker side in the Sino-Soviet rift and thereby ensure the continued benefits of the rift to Washington. President Nixon, the initiator of the new U.S. China policy in 1970–1971; President Carter's national security adviser, Zbigniew Brzezinski, who was largely responsible for the establishment of full diplomatic relations between China and the United States in 1978–1979; and former Defense Secretary James Schlesinger may be regarded as belonging to this school. The Chinese themselves seem to be unhappy when the U.S. use of the China card is referred to; they seem to resent the idea that the new Sino-American relationship is given such a manipulative meaning.

The low-impact school is of the opinion that "the U.S. relations with China have had and are likely to have little direct impact on the USSR."[17] Professor Hans Morgenthau says that "if playing 'the China card' becomes, at very least implicitly, the official policy of the United States, one must subject its assumptions, advantages and risks to critical scrutiny."[18] He adds that

> playing the Chinese card assumes that China represents a power factor of
> such magnitude that by joining one side or the other it will, at best, change
> the balance of power decisively and at worst, give the side it joins a

considerable advantage. . . . the Soviet Union cannot be unaware of the fact and we ought not to be either that China is only potentially a great power . . . in terms of American interests, playing the Chinese card, prematurely at present, would achieve the exact opposite of what it is intended to do. It would provoke, rather than frighten the Russians and eliminate the Chinese for the time being from the great power game.[19]

That seems to be an extreme view in the opposite direction as the China card no doubt has great advantages for the United States in the current global balance of power. Former Secretary of State Cyrus Vance and his adviser on the Soviet Union, Marshall Shuman, seemed to subscribe to the low-impact theory.

Proponents of the third school, the nonmanipulative school, believe that the United States "should anticipate and adjust for the impact on the Soviet Union of its policies toward China, but should not try to manipulate or exploit its China policy . . . vis-à-vis the Soviet Union."[20] This school would like to see an evenhanded U.S. policy toward Moscow and Beijing. The *New York Times,* in an editorial on June 30, 1978, made some significant comments about the China card.:

> American Presidents [since 1971] have held in their diplomatic hands what has come to be called the "Chinese card." That is the possibility of exploiting the deep-seated Sino-Soviet hostility by building up China as a counterweight. And whenever Soviet-American relations turn sour, Presidents are tempted to play it. It is a temptation that they are wise to resist. . . . The "China card" is likely only to complicate the continuing game with Moscow and to do so in ways that do not enhance American interests. Washington should continue trying to strengthen ties to Peking. But the purpose should be clear: to draw China further into the international system and to help resolve the vexing problems of Taiwan and a divided Korea, not to bait the Russian bear.

The Chinese reactions to these lines of arguments relating to the Sino-American relationship also differ, but it is not as easy to assess the different schools of thought in China as it is those in the United States. Yet one may make some general comments about the Chinese reactions. As already stated, they do not like the idea of the United States' using the China card to increase U.S. leverage against the Soviet Union, yet they realize that that school of thought represents the best hope for them. They are more resentful of those schools that hold that China is an insignificant factor in the great powers triangular relationship or that Washington should treat Moscow and Beijing equally. If the Chinese had to make a choice between the three schools of thought concerning the China card, they would perhaps prefer the manipulative one rather than the low-impact or nonmanipulative ones. The Chinese prefer to deal with the so-called hard-liners, like Richard Nixon, General Alexander Haig, or the conservative party leaders in England, rather than with the so-called liberals or socialists who advocate détente or SALT I or SALT II with the Soviet Union.

Soviet Reactions to the China Card

The Kremlin leaders were worried about the prospect of a warming up of the Sino-American relationship in 1978–1979 and about the simultaneous worsening of the U.S.-USSR relationship. Those two situations were regarded as possibly leading to a significant switch in the strategic balance at Moscow's expense.[21] The Soviet concerns about Beijing's success in the triangular diplomacy are so deep-rooted and widespread that the Russians often refer to what they call "the yellow peril." Just as the Chinese warn the Americans about the dangers of the Soviet expansionist designs, so the Russians never tire of telling the Americans that they should not be taken in by the current Chinese anti-Soviet policies and that ultimately, Europe and North America will have to contain Chinese expansionism. The Russians argue that China's warmth toward the West is a tactical maneuver with the aim of damaging Soviet-American détente and then provoking a confrontation between the two superpowers should Washington be tempted to play the China card. The Russians argue that the Soviet Union would be weakened temporarily but greater long-term damage would be inflicted on the United States as a result of profound changes in the global balance of power.[22] A commentary in *Literaturnava gazeta* on August 23, 1978, depicted the Chinese in unfavorable terms.

> Their lack of political principles, their duplicity and cynicism are known to the whole world. A rapprochement or alliance with them represents risks for everyone. Their reliability is deceitful. Perfidious stabs in the back are their way of operating. It is a short-sighted view if one believes that they could be pacified. Their covert objective is to provoke a military conflict between the United States and the Soviet Union and this is a permanent part of the basic Maoist doctrine aiming to establish world hegemony. The final play of the Chinese card (would permit) Peking to turn it into a catastrophe for the entire humanity.[23]

Russian experts on the U.S.-China relationship began to be increasingly concerned that the Carter administration, particularly Brzezinski, had decided to shelve détente in favor of building closer ties with Moscow's ideological enemy and neighbor, China. By the latter part of 1978, the Russians had begun to suspect that there was a "growing web linking Washington and Peking, a development in which Americans are described as 'playing the Chinese card' in an effort to weaken Moscow."[24]

By 1978, the Russians seem to have become reconciled to the idea of full diplomatic relations between Washington and Beijing, but they were concerned about the prospects of political cooperation or U.S. or Western European sale of arms or transfer of U.S. technology to China. Such cooperation would constitute a "grave threat to Russia's long-term interests."[25] The Soviet press and propaganda media have spoken out not only against China, but equally against the United States' China card. According to the Soviet analysis, a Soviet-American confrontation – or, still better, war – is the "cherished dream of Peking."[26] The Russians alleged that some officials of the Carter administration, such as Brzezinski, were so obsessed with anti-Russian feelings that they ignored the fact that alignment with China on an anti-Soviet basis would destroy SALT II and thereby increase the risks of a global nuclear war.

When I referred to the Soviet concern about the China card in my interviews with Chinese foreign policy makers in Beijing in July 1979 their opinion was clear: They do not believe in any China card, Russian card, or American card. They do, however, fully appreciate the implications and meaning of the triangular diplomacy between Washington, Moscow, and Beijing, and they attribute Soviet outbursts against any improvement in Sino-American relations to the Soviet policy of isolating and weakening China by any means. Their interpretation of the cooling off, if any, in the U.S.-USSR relationship was that U.S. policymakers, such as Brzezinski, had realized the danger of the Soviet expansionist designs and the implications of the huge Soviet arms buildup. China, they stressed, had nothing to do with worsening the ties between Moscow and Washington, and the Russians were to be blamed for increased tensions, such as in Indochina, the Middle East, or even Europe. Without conceding any idea of a collusion between Beijing and Washington, they would, however, admit freely the desirability of a grand coalition of Washington, Beijing, Tokyo, NATO countries, ASEAN countries, and ANZUS countries against the Soviet hegemonic designs.[27]

President Carter, however, dismissed both the Russian and Chinese interpretations of the China card. He said at a news conference in June 1978, "We are not trying nor will we ever try to play the Soviets against the PRC, nor vice versa," but, he added, "There are world-wide common hopes that we share with China."[28] These common hopes cause worry in Moscow just as any prospect of SALT II or détente causes worry in Beijing. Basically, the China card gives the Soviet Union a new incentive to avoid creating new tensions and thus driving Washington closer to Beijing.[29] In a message to Soviet President Brezhnev in June 1978, French President Giscard d'Estaing pointed out that the Soviet-Cuban military adventures were the main factors for a cooling off in the East-West détente and for increased tensions in world politics,[30] and similar views have been expressed by the Chinese.

What seemed to worry or annoy the Kremlin leaders was their belief that the Carter administration had decided to shelve U.S.-Soviet détente in favor of building closer ties with Moscow's arch enemy. The Kremlin leaders seemed to have concluded that President Carter, under Brzezinski's influence, would no longer honor the pledges of more trade and technological exchanges or the relationship that Henry Kissinger had held out to Moscow after Nixon's resignation. But that was not a correct assessment. The cooling off in the Soviet-U.S. relationship in 1978–1979 was the result of Soviet actions and policy, such as their expansionist designs in Africa and Asia. Washington could not afford to be a passive spectator of the Kremlin's moves and Brzezinski correctly charged the Soviet Union with breaking the fundamental rules of détente. Washington's attitude toward Moscow and Beijing in 1978–1979 was based on Russia's unfriendly actions and China's friendly gestures toward Washington. Also, China never misses a single opportunity to warn the United States and Western Europe about Soviet war aims.

Soviet Reaction to the U.S.-China Diplomatic Relations (1978)

President Carter received a formal letter from President Brezhnev in December 1978, which was described as "positive in tone" and conveyed the Soviet leader's alleged "understanding of the U.S. decision to normalize relations with China."[31] It was, however, nothing but diplomatic courtesy in response to Carter's gesture of informing the Russians, through the Soviet ambassador in Washington, of the decision to normalize those relations several hours prior to the announcement on December 15, 1978.

But the Soviet wrath and concern were expressed in the Soviet press. On November 3, 1978, Brezhnev, "in a pugnacious proud toast" to the Soviet-Vietnamese friendship treaty, had made the following comment aimed at Beijing: "The pact is a political reality and whether they want it or not, they will have to reckon with this reality."[32] On December 15, the Chinese could make similar comments to the Kremlin leaders. The tie with the United States, coming soon after the Japanese treaty, was a spectacular asset for Beijing's bid to challenge the Soviets on a global basis. The Soviet armed forces newspaper, *Krasnaya zvezda,* published an article on December 19, 1978, entitled "NATO for Asia?" and it raised the specter of "American gamblers" constructing a "Chinese-Japanese-American axis in Asia" aimed against Soviet interests. Although President Carter tried to stress that the U.S. move was not aimed against Moscow, the Kremlin leaders could not feel happy when Carter joined the Chinese in condemning hegemony in his declaration of December 15, 1978, just as Moscow was furious at Japan's approval of the antihegemony clause in the Sino-Japan peace treaty of August 1978. The Soviet press commented that the U.S. move might create "new obstacles in the path of detente that will cause joy in Peking."[33] Secretary Vance's final round of talks in December 1978 on a SALT II agreement failed, though both sides expressed a desire to continue the dialogue. Carter's expectations were that he would be able to greet both Brezhnev and Deng in Washington in January 1979, but Vance's failure to resolve the remaining issues of SALT II ended that hope.

The new Sino-American relationship is a very significant factor in contemporary world politics, and its full implications may be revealed by the Kremlin's next moves in relation to Washington and the many trouble spots in world politics such as Indochina, Iran, Pakistan, Africa, the Middle East, and both Eastern and Western Europe. It is too early to predict the exact move or type of Kremlin action and its impact on Washington, Beijing, and Tokyo and on Western Europe. We can join with the late Japanese Prime Minister Masayoshi Ohira in hoping that the new U.S. move will contribute to peace and stability, though that hope may appear, at the moment, to be wishful thinking. In the global triangular relationship between Washington, Moscow, and Beijing, China made considerable gains by promoting better relations with Washington and as a result of the worsening of the Soviet-American relationship in 1979–1980.

Worsening of the U.S.-USSR Relations and Reaction in Beijing (1979–1980)

Soon after his inauguration, President Carter, in his first major foreign policy speech at Notre Dame University in May 1977, said: "We are now free of that inordinate fear of communism which once led us to embrace any dictator who joined us in that fear. We fought fire with fire, never thinking that fire is better fought with water."[34] Carter expressed the hope that both the Soviet Union and the United States would stay out of local conflicts in the Third World, but he soon realized that the Russians did not share his pious wish. Cuban troops—proxies for the Soviet Union—poured into Ethiopia, and other Cuban troops supported the invasion of Zaire's southern province of Shaba.

In another major speech on March 17, 1978, President Carter modified his optimism, saying, "The Soviet Union apparently sees military power and military assistance as the best means of expanding their influence abroad,"[35] but Brzezinski had no illusions about the Soviet Union's aggressive designs. On "Meet the Press" on May 28, 1978, Brzezinski said:

> I am troubled by the fact that the Soviet Union has been engaged in a sustained and massive effort to build up its conventional forces in Europe, to

strengthen the concentration of its forces on the frontiers of China, to maintain a vitriolic worldwide propaganda campaign against the United States, to encircle and penetrate the Middle East, to stir up racial difficulties in Africa and to make more difficult a moderate solution of these difficulties, perhaps now to seek more direct access to the Indian Ocean.[36]

According to Brzezinski, that pattern of behavior was not compatible with what was once called the code of détente. Brzezinski's views were greatly appreciated in Beijing, and also in the United States after the Soviet invasion of Afghanistan in December 1979, but bitterly attacked in the Soviet press. The Russians called Carter's speech of March 17, 1978, "strange."[37]

From June 1979 to June 1980, there were great developments in the triangular relationship. There were several ups and downs in U.S.-USSR relations, and Sino-American relations showed a steady improvement during the same period. When Nixon initiated the triangular diplomacy, Washington could use the China card to extract concessions from Moscow, but the situation is now changed. Sino-American cooperation now makes the Kremlin leaders furious, and that cooperation threatens to spoil the good relations between the two superpowers.

A great turning point in the relationship between the two superpowers was the signing of the SALT II agreement by the Presidents Carter and Brezhnev in June 1979. After seven arduous years of bargaining between the two governments, the SALT II agreement was "sealed with a kiss." President Carter said, "Good relations between the United States and the Soviet Union would preserve peace for the entire world," and President Brezhnev replied, "God will not forgive us if we fail." Carter was greatly touched by Brezhnev's mention of God.[38] Yet the enthusiasm and high hopes surrounding the signing of SALT I were lacking. In five plenary sessions and one ninety-minute private session, the two presidents agreed to disagree on practically everything else: the Soviet Union's adventuring by proxy in Africa and Asia, U.S. support for a separate Egyptian-Israeli peace, the problem of reducing conventional forces in Europe. "'There is no Spirit of Vienna,' said one U.S. source," and U.S. Senator Henry Jackson compared Carter's Soviet policy to Neville Chamberlain's handling of Hitler. Senator Jackson used the word "appeasement" repeatedly.[39]

The Chinese expressed skepticism about the SALT II agreement during Vice-President Walter Mondale's visit to China in August 1979, which was made because the United States was anxious to keep its good relations with China despite the Carter-Brezhnev summit meeting. The Chinese denounced SALT II as useless and dangerous, and the Chinese leaders told Mondale that it was useless to sign an agreement with a country set on global domination. Mondale pleased the Chinese by declaring, "Any nation which seeks to weaken or isolate you [China] in world affairs assumes a stance counter to American interests."[40] The only country that may try "to weaken or isolate" China is the Soviet Union, so Mondale's warning was obviously meant for the Russians, who were already annoyed with the warming up of Sino-American relations. Singapore's foreign minister, Sinnathamby Rajaratnam, said, "The nightmare that haunts Moscow today is that the Western powers and Japan might use the Chinese card against them as the Soviets used it against the West in the past few decades."[41]

Chairman Hua had already accepted an invitation to visit the United States, and a countersummit was being planned. But before any Sino-American summit could be held, the U.S.-USSR relationship received a serious setback when President Carter announced, in a grim television speech to the American people on September 9, 1979, that there was a "Soviet combat brigade" in Cuba. He added, "The purpose of this combat unit is not yet clear,"[42] but Secretary of State Vance, on behalf of President Carter, declared, "The presence of a Soviet combat brigade in Cuba is a very serious matter and . . . is not acceptable."[43] Carter's and Vance's statements about the Soviet troops in Cuba created a crisis atmosphere that was comparable to that during the 1962 Cuban missile crisis, though not of the same magnitude. Senator Frank Church, chairman of the Senate Foreign Relations Committee, announced the postponement of the discussions on SALT II—the first serious blow to that agreement. According to a public poll, Americans demanded, by a 3 to 1 margin, that the Senate should not consider SALT II until the Soviet troops were removed.

The Carter administration's handling of the issue of Soviet troops in Cuba was disappointing and betrayed weakness in dealing with the Soviet Union. After declaring that the presence of the Soviet combat troops in Cuba was "unacceptable," Mr. Carter was forced to back away when it became clear that Moscow would not remove them. Many harsh comments were made: "The acquiescence in Cuban status quo declared only ten days ago to be unacceptable is wholly in keeping with the animating spirit of an administration which describes the US-Soviet relationship as one of 'cooperation and competition,' but cannot tell the difference between them."[44] Having been rebuffed by Moscow, President Carter sought to save face by telling Americans that the brigade issue was certainly no reason for a return to cold war. He appealed to the Congress to ratify SALT II, but the damage to détente and SALT II was already done.

Turning to the Sino-American relationship, many Americans, including Brzezinski and Defense Secretary Harold Brown, seemed to be convinced that the United States and the PRC had a common interest in countering the spread of Soviet influence in many parts of the world, but staying on good terms with two such bitter enemies as China and Russia is no easy task for the United States. The good relations between Washington and Beijing began to develop after the normalization of relations between the two countries at a time of growing U.S. distrust of Soviet aims in Africa, Europe, the Middle East, and Asia, and China hopes the West will help to contain the Russian thrust. The Sino-Soviet rivalry has reached a dangerous pitch. The Russians deployed another 250,000 troops against China in 1977–1978, which brought the number posted near the Sino-Soviet border to an estimated 650,000. It is not likely that Russia will attempt to conquer all of China – the cost would be too high, both in blood and money – but a limited Sino-Soviet war in the next two or three years, before China becomes a full-fledged nuclear power, cannot be ruled out. China has also drawn closer to Japan, which has been encouraged to rearm by the United States and which has its own serious misgivings about the Russians. The Russians are already worried about an emerging relationship between Washington, Beijing, and Tokyo, backed by the NATO allies and ASEAN countries, which are worried about Moscow and Hanoi's joint military adventures in Southeast Asia.

In early November 1979, Iranian militant students occupied the U.S. embassy in Tehran and held fifty U.S. diplomats as hostages. Although the Soviet Union supported the Security Council's resolution and the International Court of Justice's pleas to release the hostages, the overall Soviet attitude toward and role during the U.S.predicament cast deep scars on détente and the Soviet-American relationship. The United States received disturbing evidence that the Soviet Union developed direct links with the Iranian radicals who held the Americans hostage,[45] and, certainly, Moscow exploited the hostage crisis to the disadvantage of the United States. According to some sources, the Soviet Union carried on a consistent campaign to undercut every settlement effort made by Iranian President Bani-Sadr and other moderates. The Kremlin seemed to have its own agents inside the U.S. embassy, and they were determined to keep the hostage pot boiling "as part of overall Soviet policy to gain eventual control of the Persian Gulf and its oil."[46]

The year 1979 saw the beginning of a number of changes in the global balance of power among Washington, Moscow, and Beijing and the far-reaching impacts of that triangular relationship on Tokyo and the NATO countries, but the Soviet invasion of Afghanistan on December 27, 1979, had an earthshaking effect on the global scene; it altered the whole process of détente and coexistence and killed the hope of peace in our generation. But before discussing the impact of the Soviet invasion of Afghanistan on the great powers relationship, we shall discuss China's quest for arms from the Western countries, including the United States, and its diplomatic bids in Eastern Europe and the reactions in Moscow.

China's Quest for Western Arms and Technology and the Soviet Reaction

China does not and will not for many years have the means to bid for military parity with the Soviet Union as the Chinese economic superstructure is not strong enough to produce the quality or quantity of essential weaponry.[47] The odds against the People's Liberation Army of China in any confrontation with the Soviet Union are formidable, and the post-Mao Chinese leaders have expressed their determination to modernize the army because of what they perceive to be serious Soviet threats on China's northern frontier. The 1979 China-Vietnam war reinforced the Chinese desire to modernize the army, but, because of limiting factors, modernization of the Chinese army is likely to be painfully slow. A number of conferences were held in Beijing in 1977 and 1978 to discuss the problems of modernizing the Chinese army, but there was no intention, or rather no resources, to match Soviet equipment levels. Yet serious discussions have taken place to address the problem of deficiencies in the weaponry. As the Chinese economy is in disorder—thanks to the policies of the Gang of Four after the 1966 Cultural Revolution—even a modest reequipment program must be tackled piecemeal[48]—so, Why not buy abroad? The shopping list is, however, long and requires huge amounts of foreign exchange. By any criteria, the Chinese army is deficient in everything from missiles to sonar. The Chinese have nuclear weapons, for instance, but their delivery systems lag behind those of the Soviet Union and the United States, or even those of Britain and France. The Chinese need the technology for computers and control and command equipment as well as prototypes of modern fighter/bombers, such as the British–West German–Italian multipurpose Tornado.[49] Western analysts report that Beijing is not willing to buy obsolete equipment or to pay excessive prices, nor is China willing to allow Western advisers in China "to have access to military secrets."[50]

China's main problem concerning arms purchases is one of national priorities: how to allot its limited resources for economic development and for defense. Mao was in favor of spending not more than 20 percent of the budget on defense; the post-Mao leaders, such as Chairman Hua, are reported to be in favor of spending more for defense, but the strong man of post-Mao China, Deng, is not inclined to sacrifice his ambitious economic programs. At the same time, threats from Russia on the northern border and from Soviet-backed Hanoi on the southern frontier cannot be ignored, so China has to give some top priority to defense.

There were reports in the Chinese press during the first years of the post-Mao era that China was interested in buying 300 Jump-jet Harriers from Britain, 200 Mirage fighters from France, helicopters from Germany, and other weapons from Italy and Sweden.[51] There were also reports that China was eager to buy French wire-guided antitank missiles and French surface-to-air missiles, and China indicated its interest in improving the fighting capabilities of its tank force.

The Institute of Strategic Studies, London, pointed out in a 1980 report that China was working on missiles that could hit any city in the Soviet Union. China does not need many ICBMs to deter the Soviet Union from "thoughts of a preemptive strike or widening of a border conflict to nuclear destruction of industries and centers of population,"[52] and the thornier questions relate to the relative importance of tactical nuclear weapons, antitank and antiaircraft systems, and the effectiveness of submarines.

China has no option but to buy, at tremendous cost, entire weapons systems and, if possible, the technology to manufacture them.[53] China's military planners are aware that they do not have the means to resist a major Soviet military thrust through Mongolia or in the northwest, and Mao's strategy of guerrilla fighting would not be suitable in a major confrontation with the Soviet Union. China has no option but to give top priority to a rapid development of the capabilities of its defense, though such a move will mean big sacrifices in its much needed economic development projects.

China's need for arms purchases from Western countries, including the United States, is now a major goal of its foreign policy objectives. In the triangular relationship between Washington, Moscow, and Beijing, China's plans to acquire modern advanced weapons from the West have become a major issue. Nothing upsets the Russians more than the prospect of arms sales by the Western countries to the PRC, as the Russians regard such sales as the beginning of a possible alliance between Beijing and the West. Any improvement in China's military capability is regarded as a serious threat by the Russians. China, on the other hand, is so preoccupied with its fear of a Soviet aggression that Beijing now welcomes a stronger Europe, and China's press and radio have taken a close interest in European defense matters. Without openly endorsing the Western alliance, the Chinese leaders have told visiting European politicians that they approve of NATO's existence and of the role it can play as a counter to aggressive Soviet designs. The Chinese give favorable attention to moves to strengthen the Western armed forces and are generally critical of NATO countries' defense cuts. Similarly, China does not look with favor on conferences such as the Conference on Security and Cooperation in Europe (CSCE) or on talks in Vienna about mutual balanced force reduction (MBFR). They consider such conferences futile and worthless in light of what they consider to be a Soviet military buildup and aggressive designs in Europe, and they treat CSCE and MBFR in the same way as they do détente or the SALT II agreement between Washington and Moscow. China sees any search for peace through compromise as tantamount to an appeasement of the Soviet expansionist ambitions. China's approach to a militarily stronger Western Europe is influenced by its robustness in standing up to Soviet pressures.[54]

Moscow's Wrath About Western Arms Sales to Beijing

In a leading commentary on August 5, 1978, *Pravda* blasted China's policy of seeking arms from the Western countries. Beijing, according to *Pravda*, "is in alliance with the most aggressive forces of imperialism and reaction . . . they [the Chinese] have been gripped in a veritable military hysteria, preaching hatred and hostility among peoples, building up a military psychosis and incitement toward a new war. This is the essence of the Peking leaders' current foreign policy."[55]

The chief of the Soviet secret police (KGB), Yuri Andropov, said: "Those politicians in the West, trying to play the 'Chinese card' against the Soviets, are making a serious miscalculation. Only short-sighted people can expect that the sphere of common interest of the United States and China can be developed on such a basis."[56] Andropov also attacked Beijing for allegedly supporting NATO and for trying to set Japan against the Soviet Union. Another senior Soviet official, Georgi A. Arbatov said, "It is not our policy to try to spoil our relations with countries that improve their relations with China,"[57]—a statement that can hardly be accepted in view of the fact that the Soviet Union brings pressure against any Third World country that seeks friendly relations with Beijing. Then Arbatov added, "But if it is done on an anti-Soviet basis, it can affect our relations." He particularly referred to the possibility of China's becoming "some sort of military ally to the West even an informal ally. Then the whole situation would look different to us. We would have to reanalyze our relationship with the West." Then he continued, "For instance, what sense would it make for us to agree to reduce armaments in Europe . . . if armaments are simply to be channeled by the West to the Eastern front?" Referring to the contemplated sale of British Harrier jets to China, Arbatov said that "such sales would be comparable to our selling rockets to Northern Ireland.'[58] (One may ask, Do the Russians consider China a part of its territory as Northern Ireland is a part of the United Kingdom?)

The Soviet reaction to arms sales to China for defensive purposes is a clear illustration of the Soviet policy of isolating and weakening China. Any observer of the global balance of military power will agree that even with China's contemplated purchases of arms from the Western countries, there cannot be any parity of military strength between the PRC and the Soviet Union, and the Russians know full well that Beijing's attempt to modernize China's military equipment is modest, and that China's military equipment lags, at best, twenty years behind that of the Soviet Union. The most the Chinese can hope for is to modestly improve their ability to defend themselves against a Soviet attack, but China's military capability cannot constitute any real threat to Soviet security in the foreseeable future, which is why countries such as England and France are inclined to look favorably upon some sales of arms like anti-tank and antiaircraft missiles, to China.[59] Both Britain and France have announced that they would consider supplying arms to China "on a case by case basis,"[60] but the Western European countries can hardly supply enough weapons to China to make a real difference in the global military balance of power. So Moscow's rage against the idea of the West's selling defensive weapons to China is merely a reflection of the Kremlin's desire to keep China militarily weak so the Soviet Union can pursue its expansionist designs in the Asian-Pacific region and keep China under constant threat.

A warning issued by the Politburo, the Soviet Union's supreme policymaking body, on August 26, 1978, against arms sales to Beijing indicates how the issue is of deep concern to the Kremlin leadership. The warning linked arms sales to Beijing with SALT II and stated, "In the present situation, it is especially necessary to resolutely counter any step that could undermine the process of detente and remove the international development back to the cold war." Then it added, "Trying to gain access to NATO's military arsenals, the rulers of China in various ways are advertising their hostility toward the Soviet Union."[61]

China's Diplomatic Ventures in Eastern Europe

The Soviet Union's leaders were annoyed when China's Communist party chairman, Hua, made visits to Romania, Yugoslavia, and Iran as part of the post-Mao Chinese leaders' dynamic efforts to win friends in Europe, including Eastern European countries. The Chinese leader launched a thinly veiled attack on Russia in the capital of one of the member countries of the Warsaw Pact—Romania—which showed a new confidence in China and a willingness to get into the diplomatic arena in places that are in the Soviet sphere of influence, or Brezhnev's "commonwealth of socialist states." Hua's visit to two of the communist countries of Eastern Europe, including one that is a member of the Warsaw Pact, was regarded by the Russians as a provocative encroachment on their sphere of influence. For the Chinese, Hua's visit to Romania and Yugoslavia in August 1978 underscored Beijing's new and dynamic involvement in world affairs. It was an unprecedented display of Chinese interest in a region that is regarded as vital by the Russians; it also demonstrated China's support to two Eastern European communist countries that have been subjected to Soviet pressures. Hua's visit to Eastern Europe dramatically illustrated the opening of "a new, more outward-looking era in China's foreign policy."[62]

In Romania, Hua delivered a warning to the Russians when he said they would be "crushed to dust by the iron blows of the people" if they tried to "set up a world empire,"[63] and Western diplomats in Bucharest said that Hua's trip was bound to provoke Moscow.[64] In Belgrade, Hua blasted the Soviet Union for its alleged attempt to turn the nonaligned movement into a pro-Moscow movement, with the help of allies such as Cuba. He said, "They [the Russians] are trying at all costs to disrupt the unity of the nonaligned movement, to divert it and subordinate it to their own hegemonistic objectives."[65] No wonder *Pravda* accused Hua of using his trip "for crude attacks on our country and its policies."[66]

The main objective of Hua's trip seemed to be to outmaneuver the Soviet Union in Eastern Europe. By his very presence in Romania and Yugoslavia on the tenth anniversary of the Soviet-led invasion of Czechoslovakia, Hua succeeded in putting on record in Eastern Europe the Chinese view that Soviet aggressive policies abroad, such as in Africa and subsequently in Indochina and Southwest Asia, pose a threat to world peace.[67] The trip also strengthened the antimonolithic group within the world communist movement as the Chinese have endorsed the Yugoslav, Romanian, and Western European Communist parties' views that there can be many very different roads to socialism.[68]

China's policy of developing closer links with Western European countries, including its attempts to buy weapons from the West European NATO countries and its unprecedented ventures to make inroads into Eastern Europe, had a great impact on the triangular diplomacy: It enhanced Beijing's diplomatic options and its image; it pleased Washington at no cost to the United States; and it annoyed Moscow, giving a further impetus to the Sino-Soviet rift.

Sino-American Military Cooperation?

Since the new Sino-American relationship began, as a result of the 1972 Peking Summit, U.S. newspapers and magazines have occasionally referred to China's interest in purchasing U.S. arms and intelligence equipment, but such reports in the 1970s were not confirmed either by Beijing or by Washington. During Kissinger's 1973 visit to Beijing, there was speculation that Kissinger and Premier Zhou Enlai, in their lengthy dialogues so soon after the 1973 Middle East war, talked about possible U.S.-China military ties, but again there was no confirmation of any definite proposals. In December 1973, a Singapore newspaper carried a story about China's interest in the purchase of U.S. military equipment, and similar stories appeared through the Japanese Kyodo news agency. Relying on these stories, Moscow reported that "reliable sources had disclosed the details of a Chinese request for U.S. military equipment."[69] Immediately Moscow Radio warned: "Reports of Peking's interest in American supplies of arms reflect the desire of the most reactionary militaristic circles in the United States to support the aggressive hegemonic aspirations of the Mao group. These circles would like to cash in on the openly hostile attitude of the Chinese leadership toward the Soviet Union and the Socialist community as a whole."[70]

In the early 1970s, Beijing was not likely to show any interest in the purchase of U.S. arms for several reasons. First, the process of normalizing relations between the PRC and the United States had just started, and the two sides could not yet think in terms of military cooperation. Second, the Taiwan issue and the U.S. security pact with that island were still factors, and finally, Mao and Zhou Enlai could not openly advocate military ties with the United States so soon. However, those reasons do not mean that during the lengthy dialogues that Kissinger had with Zhou and also occasionally with Mao, the idea of a U.S.-China military tie was never discussed.

The first official confirmation of such talks was given by former Defense Secretary James Schlesinger in April 1976. He disclosed that U.S. officials had discussed "in recent years" the possibility of giving military assistance to the PRC, but, he added, "There was never a formal addressing of the issue "while he was in the U.S. government" (until 1975). In giving his own views on the subject, Schlesinger said, "I would not reject it out of hand." He argued that the United States supplied technological and economic aid to "a major foe," the Soviet Union, while denying the same to China, which he called a "quasi ally."[71] After Schlesinger's statement, a high State Department official confirmed that military assistance to China had been "discussed as we looked at future options," but he emphasized that "aid had not been considered specifically." He added, "I am not saying it will never be done," but he hinted that "any reversal of the past U.S. policy would begin with sales of advanced technological equipment not directly related to military items, rather than with a military assistance program. The United States is essentially even-handed in approving such sales to Soviet and Chinese buyers."[72]

After his twenty-three-day visit to China at the time of Mao's death in September 1976, Schlesinger discussed the Chinese attitude toward any idea of military ties with the United States. When asked if the Chinese had expressed a desire for sophisticated antitank weapons or masses of antiaircraft weapons, which the United States might provide, he said, "I suspect that there is some interest there – particularly in the military establishment – but it is well hidden for diplomatic reasons." He added that China might turn to the United States for weapons, but "we should not anticipate the Chinese initiating any requests. I have suggested in the past that we should not reject out of hand the notion of supplying them with weapons. But I don't think that we should press any such deliveries on them."[73]

There were dissenting voices against any sale of U.S. arms to China on the grounds that it would have severe adverse reactions on U.S.-USSR relations and on SALT II. Paul C. Warnke, the U.S. chief SALT II negotiator, spoke strongly against any military ties with Peking,[74] and a major policy review in June 1977 concluded that the sale of U.S. military technology to China would lead to a fundamental reassessment of Soviet policies toward the United States and an increase of tension between Moscow and Washington.[75] Some key figures in the Carter administration, such as Brzezinski, were reported to be in disagreement with the conclusions of the report. That group would have liked to accelerate diplomatic and military links to China in order to use China to offset Soviet power and to gain some leverage over Moscow in the SALT II negotiations.[76]

Although both Beijing and Washington were reluctant to discuss publicly the possibilities of cooperation on military matters, the two countries had discussed the subject in quiet diplomatic dialogues. There is no doubt that China was seeking some form of military relationship with the West, first with Western European countries and then directly with the United States. Until full diplomatic relations were established with the United States in 1979, however, the Chinese would not agree to any idea of military ties with that country, particularly as long as the U.S. security pact with Taiwan was not abrogated. I raised the issue during my visits to Beijing in 1977 and 1978 and in my frequent discussions with Chinese ambassadors abroad, but I failed to get any definite answer. Still, I had no doubt about China's growing interest in the subject in view of China's increasing worries about the Soviet military buildup on the northern border and about Hanoi's Soviet-backed anti-China policy.

The Soviet Union continued to warn against any sale of Western arms to China. During former Secretary of State Cyrus Vance's visit to Moscow in October 1978, senior Soviet officials complained about West European arms sales to China and voiced their suspicion that the United States was fostering such arms deals with China to build up military pressure on the Soviet Union's eastern border. Vance is reported to have denied any alleged U.S. encouragement for arms deals between the West European countries and China, particularly in order to put any pressure on the Soviets,[77] and Vance was genuinely opposed to any such use of the China card against Moscow. The Russians compared the West European arms sales, and contemplated U.S. arms sales, to China to European arms deals with Hitler before Germany launched World War II. The Soviet Union contended that military equipment sold to China would be used not only against the Soviet Union and other socialist countries, but ultimately against the seller countries.[78]

Impact of the Soviet Invasion of Afghanistan on the Triangular Relationship

The Soviet invasion of an independent Asian country had serious effects on the détente between Washington and Moscow, and it also favorably influenced U.S. policy toward the PRC and gave impetus to a limited military cooperation between Beijing and Washington. China watched gleefully the setbacks to détente and SALT II that occurred as a result of the Afghan crisis. The United States' and the Western countries' severe condemnation of the Soviet military adventures in Afghanistan made the Chinese happy, because their assessment of the Soviet Union's aggressive designs seemed to have been vindicated by the Soviet invasion of a weaker neighboring country. The Chinese foreign minister, Huang Hua, exposed the Soviet military intervention in Afghanistan to the fullest extent in his speech to the Thirty-fifth Session of the UN General Assembly on September 24, 1980.

Prior to the Afghan incident, the Soviet Union had normally carried out its military invasion or subversion of third world countries through its agents. But this time in Afghanistan, it dropped its mask and sent its troops to fight. Moscow even advanced a theory to justify its aggression stating that, to the Soviet Union, "a hostile Afghanistan is unacceptable, because there is a common border 2,200 kilometres long." This "doctrine" of allowing no hostile neighbors means that all the neighbors of the Soviet Union must show complete obedience. It is even more peremptory and aggressive in nature than the notorious doctrine of "limited sovereignty." Huang Hua pointed out: "In spreading these fallacies, the Soviet Union is trying both to defend its present aggressions and to create theoretical justifications for similar acts in the future. Whether in theory or in practice, the Afghan incident marks a new stage of development in the external expansion of the hegemonists."

Huang Hua went on to say: "The sending of troops to Afghanistan and supporting the Vietnamese invasion of Kampuchea are important steps taken by the hegemonists in their policy of a southward drive. Their drive south towards the Indian Ocean and into the Pacific Ocean in coordination with their activities of expansion in the Red Sea and in the Horn of Africa is aimed at seizing strategic sites in the vast area of crucial importance – from the Red Sea and the Arabian Peninsula in the west, through the Strait of Malacca in the middle and to the South China Sea in the east – encircle the oilfields in the Gulf and control key international sea lanes. In other words, while further threatening the whole Asian/Pacific region, the Soviet Union intends to outflank Western Europe and to hasten the completion of its global strategic deployment for world domination."[79]

The U.S. Reaction

President Carter said that the Soviet invasion of Afghanistan "has made a more dramatic change in my opinion of what the Soviets' ultimate goals are than anything they have done in the previous time I have been in office."[80] Carter's faith in the basic decency of the Soviets had already been undermined by their cavalier attitude toward the suffering of the Cambodians and the refusal of the Soviet Union's Vietnamese allies to facilitate international relief efforts in Cambodia, and Carter's disillusionment was completed by Brezhnev's response to Carter's protest, over the Washington-Moscow "hot line," about the massive military movement of the Soviet troops in Afghanistan in December 1979 before the actual Soviet invasion on December 27. Carter publicly termed Brezhnev's response a "lie."

Carter's punitive measures against the Soviet Union included asking the U.S. Senate to postpone ratification of SALT II, which was, of course, already deadlocked by the presence of Soviet combat troops in Cuba and by the Iranian crisis. His further punitive measures were an embargo on grain sales to the Soviet Union, a halt to exports of high-technology items, and moves to block Western credits to the Soviet Union. Carter also campaigned for an official boycott of the Moscow Olympics. Then in his State of the Union Message to the Congress on January 23, 1980, President Carter formulated the Persian Gulf doctrine and warned the Soviet Union that the United States would use armed force to repel a Soviet thrust into the Persian Gulf. His message contained the following measures.

1. The Soviet Union must pay a concrete price for its aggression.
2. The Soviet Union must realize that its decision to use military force in Afghanistan will be costly to every political and economic relationship it values.
3. The United States will increase and strengthen its naval presence in the Indian Ocean.

4. The United States will seek naval and air facilities in the countries of northern Africa and the Persian Gulf.

5. NATO allies are urged to deploy modernized intermediate-range nuclear forces to meet the increasing threat from nuclear weapons of the Soviet Union.

Carter also referred to the "good relations" with China, which, he felt, "will preserve peace and stability in Asia and Western Pacific," and he offered military assistance to the United States' old, but neglected, ally, Pakistan (Pakistan, however, declined the U.S. arms offer). President Carter ended by saying: "The situation demands careful thought, steady nerves, and resolute action. It demands collective efforts to meet this new threat to security in the Persian Gulf and Southwest Asia."[81] President Carter urged the NATO allies and Japan to join the United States in imposing economic sanctions against the Soviet Union and also urged Japan to increase its military budget.

Sino-American Limited Military Cooperation

One of the significant developments resulting from the Afghan crisis has been the emergence of some form of military tie between Beijing and Washington. The U.S. defense secretary, Harold Brown, paid a highly significant eight-day visit to China soon after the Soviet invasion of Afghanistan (January 5–13, 1980). Although Brown's visit had been scheduled months earlier, it acquired, to quote Brown's words, "added significance," and Pentagon spokesman Thomas Ross said, "Afghanistan undoubtedly will be a topic of discussion." Brown's visit was supposed to increase Sino-American security relations from "passive to more active forms." Referring to the U.S. policy of evenhandedness in dealing with Beijing and Moscow, a senior U.S. military official accompanying Secretary Brown said rather bluntly, "It would be foolish for us not to behave differently toward the Chinese and Soviets since they behave so differently toward us."[82]

Brown had extensive talks with the Chinese leaders, including Premier Hua, Vice-Premier Deng, and Defense Minister Xu Xiangqian. At the welcoming banquet in Beijing on January 6, Secretary Brown said that he wanted "to exchange views" on how the United States and China might facilitate wider cooperation on security matters. Such cooperation, he added, "should remind others that if they threaten the shared interests of the United States and of China, we can respond with complementary actions."[83] Vice-Premier Deng told Brown, "The United States and China should coordinate their policies in the face of the threat from the Soviet Union."[84]

Brown's visit to China and the U.S. defense team's having the opportunity to inspect the Chinese war machinery, including touring a Chinese submarine, had a strong symbolic value, which was "to emphasize and explore different kinds of security collaboration. . . . The Kremlin's aggression against Afghanistan sharpened the focus, making more urgent the need for tightening Sino-American security links."[85]

The Soviet wrath against any potential Sino-American security relationship was given expression by Brezhnev. In an interview with a former French prime minister, Jacques Chaban-Delmas, Brezhnev, pounding his desk again and again, shouted, "Believe me, after the destruction of Chinese nuclear sites by our missiles, there won't be much time for the Americans to choose between the defense of their Chinese allies and peaceful co-existence."[86] The Russians also warned Japan and the NATO countries against any measure of collaboration with the United States.

There is no doubt that Brown's visit to China and the return visit of Vice-Premier Geng Biao were meant to stress the growing security cooperation between Washington and Beijing in the face of Soviet expansionism. Brown's visit, as the U.S. officials explained, should not be judged by any concrete agreements or treaties. (The only agreement announced during Brown's visit was the United States' decision to permit China to buy a ground station for a Landsat earth resources satellite, which has some military significance.) The visit should be measured by its psychological impact; for the first time since 1949, the United States and China showed an overlapping security relationship.

Soon after Brown's trip to China, the United States, in a major policy shift related to the Afghan crisis, announced on January 25, 1980, that it was willing to sell military equipment to China. The equipment, however, will not include "weapons." Although the U.S. Defense Department said that the military sales to China would be limited first to such basic support equipment as trucks, communications gear, and early-warning radar, the decision to help the Soviet Union's major communist adversary with military equipment was meant to convey a warning to the Russians of further collaboration with China.

China and the United States each signed a memorandum of understanding on January 24, 1980, to build an earth station, which will enable China to receive data from a U.S. satellite. Another significant step in the growing Sino-American relationship was the United States' granting "most-favored nation" status to China again on January 24, 1980. The approval of the U.S. Congress for a favored trade status for China means that the trade agreement between the two countries signed on July 7, 1979, will go into effect. U.S. tariffs on Chinese goods will be reduced from 20 percent to about 10 percent, and U.S. business activities in China will be facilitated. Granting a most-favored nation status to China without giving it to the Soviet Union was also a departure from the U.S. policy of evenhandedness toward the two communist giants; it was also a by-product of the U.S. policy of protest against the Soviet invasion of Afghanistan. In the meantime, China launched its first intercontinental ballistic missile, which signaled a major step toward its status as a nuclear power.

The Chinese deputy prime minister, Geng Biao, led a military delegation to the United States in late May 1980 — it was the return visit by the Chinese defense officials to Secretary Brown's visit to China in January 1980. The Carter administration formalized the arms sale policy to China as announced on January 24 by offering the visiting Chinese military delegation the list of military equipment China is allowed to purchase from the United States. The list included air-defense radar, helicopters, transport planes, computer equipment, trucks, navigation equipment, and underwater search gear. As already noted, the Pentagon officials had insisted that no weapons be sold to China, but China will benefit greatly from the high-technology equipment on the list.

While making the announcement of the military sales to China on May 29, 1980, Defense Secretary Brown declared, "The United States looks forward to continued step by step strengthening of ties between our two defense establishments as an integral part of our effort to normalize all facets of our relationship." In his reply, Vice-Premier Geng blasted the Soviet Union and its ally, Vietnam, and said, "Since they represent a strategic challenge, they call for a strategic response." Asked if China would like to buy weapons from the United States, Geng replied: "I do not think there is such a possibility at present. But I believe there might be such a possibility in the future."[87]

As pointed out by the U.S. Department of State, the real significance of the deal is "that a China that feels secure within its frontiers is going to be more of a source of stability than a source of instability in Asia and elsewhere in the world."[88] From a position of an "implacable enemy" in the 1950s, China was raised to the status of a potential "brother in arms" in 1980. The Soviet Union's contribution to that transformation was great.

Emerging Triangular Relationship: Washington-Beijing-Tokyo

Beijing's rapid establishment of simultaneous good relations with Washington and Tokyo in diplomatic, political, economic, and, most recently, security matters has given the appearance of a new triangular relationship between Washington, Beijing, and Tokyo. Defense Secretary Brown's visit to China and Japan in January 1980, soon after the

Soviet invasion of Afghanistan, and then Vice-Premier Geng's visit to the United States and Premier Hua Guofeng's visit to Japan seem to have given further impetus to the emerging relationship. All three countries share a common concern about the Soviet military buildup and the Soviet moves in Asia, Africa, and elsewhere.

During a six-day visit to Japan (May 27–June 2, 1980), Premier Hua did not miss any opportunity to speak against the hegemonic Soviet Union. Although the United States and Japan share China's worry about the Soviet moves, neither Washington nor Tokyo will fully endorse Beijing's opinion of Moscow. So Hua's anti-Soviet speeches were listened to carefully during his visit, but not responded to fully as Japan does not want to give undue provocation to Moscow. But the three countries are now reacting almost in concert to the Soviet aggression in Afghanistan. Former Japanese Prime Minister Tanaka told Hua that the new relationship is "an equilateral triangle" and an important factor in contributing to peace in Asia—an assessment Hua readily agreed to.[89] Apart from a common concern about the Soviet Union's designs, weighty economic factors bind the three countries. The United States and Japan want to capture the vast Chinese market, and China wants technological help and assistance from Washington and Tokyo for its "four modernization plans."

Hua's visit to Japan, which was considered "the first official visit" by a Chinese head of government in the 2,000-year history of the Sino-Japanese relationship, was a continuation of the warm relationship that has develped between Beijing and Tokyo in recent years, particularly since 1978. Hua stressed the need for Japan, China, and other countries to close ranks to guard themselves against the Soviet threat, and he made strong pleas for sustained efforts by Japan, the United States, China, and Western European countries to preserve peace and stability in the Asian-Pacific region. During his visit to Japan, the Chinese premier is reported to have discussed the situation in the Korean Peninsula and to have given assurances to Japan that China would use its good offices to preserve peace on that peninsula[90]—China has nothing to gain from any new war in Korea but much to lose. Hua also expressed his government's appreciation for Japan's refusal to recognize Hanoi's puppet regime in Cambodia, and Hua favored Japan's remilitarization. Finally, the Chinese leader utilized his visit to explore the possibility of further economic collaboration between Japan and China. In the joint communiqué issued after his visit, both countries reaffirmed that economic cooperation should be further expanded on a long-term basis. Hua's visit strengthened the existing bonds between Tokyo and Beijing, and those bonds are now also backed by Washington.

The emerging ties between Washington, Tokyo, and Beijing got further impetus when President Carter and Premier Hua met in Tokyo on July 10, 1980, both having gone to Tokyo to attend the memorial service for the late Japanese Prime Minister Ohira. They were reported to be in "full agreement that Soviet invasion of Afghanistan and Vietnam's military presence in Kampuchea posed threats to the peace and stability in Asia."[91] It was, however, stated by President Carter's press secretary, Jody Powell, that unlike China, the United States did not want its growing ties with Tokyo and Beijing to "form a block against the Soviet Union." But Mr. Powell added, "There is essential agreement between the U.S.A. and the P.R.C. with regard to strategic perspectives."[92]

A Soviet official in Tokyo asserted that the Carter-Hua meeting was set up deliberately on Japanese soil to embarrass the Soviet Union, and the Soviet paper *Izvestia* wrote on July 10, 1980, that the Carter-Hua meeting in Tokyo "gave fresh cause for concern for the international situation in Asia," and added, "There is no doubt that discussions dealt with a joint strategy of actions by the imperialist forces in alliance with Peking in a vast region from Iran and Afghanistan in the West to the Korean peninsula and Australia in the East."[93] The Russians have accused the Japanese of ganging up with the Chinese against Russia for the past several years, particularly since the peace treaty between the two countries in 1979, and the Russians have begun to make similar accusations against the United States, especially since Defense Secretary Brown's visit to China in January 1980, soon after the Soviet invasion of Afghanistan. They have begun to show concern about a Washington-Tokyo-Beijing collusion directed against Moscow.

Implications of Sino-American Military Links

U.S. officials and experts debated the implications of Sino-American military cooperation, and one senior State Department official has said, "Like Yugoslavia, China is our ideological adversary, but a strategic partner."[94] Former Secretary of State Cyrus Vance expressed his concern about the possibility of Sino-American military cooperation, which was made more likely by the Soviet invasion of Afghanistan. One scholar, Banning Garrett, told the House of Representatives Subcommittee on Asian and Pacific Affairs that the United States was sliding into far-reaching military ties with China. He had interviewed about one hundred Pentagon, CIA, State Department, and National Security Council officials, and he referred to two Pentagon-sponsored studies on military cooperation with China. According to Garrett, the idea of a Sino-American military link had been discussed as early as 1973, and in a 1979 secret study, the "possibility of stationing U.S. war planes, naval vessels or even ground forces in China during a crisis" had been examined.[95] State Department officials denied any such far-reaching military cooperation between the United States and the PRC, and neither China nor the United States is ready for such far-reaching military ties.

One possibility for Sino-American military cooperation was for both countries to help strengthen Pakistan's defense capabilities after the Afghan crisis. Foreign Minister Huang Hua visited Pakistan in January 1980, and Brzezinski led a high-powered U.S. delegation to Pakistan in February 1980. I discussed the matter with Pakistan's President Zia and Foreign Minister Aga Shahi, but they denied any joint Sino-American military plan for Pakistan. Similarly, the Chinese diplomats dismissed the idea categorically, but the Russians continued to talk about joint U.S.-China-Pakistan military operations against the Soviet-backed Afghan regime in Kabul.

Recent Developments in the Washington-Moscow-Beijing-Tokyo Relationship

The year 1980 was a presidential election year in the United States, and the Republican candidate, Ronald Reagan, accused the Carter administration of "letting down" allies like Iran, Pakistan, South Korea, and above all, Taiwan. Mr. Reagan gave assurances that on his being elected, he would "upgrade" the U.S.-Taiwan relationship and hinted that he might even restore some kind of official relationship with Taiwan. Reagan's election campaign speeches relating to Taiwan posed a serious threat to the Sino-American relationship. The depth of the Chinese feelings about the Taiwan issue is not always fully appreciated in the United States. There are two basic factors in the current Sino-American relationship: the Taiwan issue and "the Soviet Factor," i.e., the Chinese fear of a Soviet armed attack against their country, or if not a full armed invasion, at least the Soviet policy of weakening and isolating the PRC. Some U.S. policymakers, including some reputable sinologists, seem to have concluded that the Chinese would cooperate with the United States as long as Washington continues the policy of containment of the Soviet expansionist designs, no matter what Washington does with regard to Taiwan. That conclusion is, however, a serious miscalculation of the Chinese attitude on the Taiwan issue.

I had full access to the top-secret Sino-American negotiations in 1969–1971, and from the very beginning, the Chinese made it abundantly clear that Taiwan was the most crucial factor in the Sino-American relationship. The Chinese waited for seven years (1972–1979) for full diplomatic relations with the United States until the fulfillment of their three conditions: withdrawal of the U.S. troops from Taiwan, withdrawal of recognition of Taiwan, and the abrogation of the 1954 U.S.

security pact with the island. They would not make any basic compromise with regard to the Taiwan issue. Whether the policy is wise or unwise, whether it is called rigid or something else, I am convinced, after extensive research and talks with the top Chinese leaders, that the Chinese would not cooperate with the United States in a common objective of containment of the Soviet Union if the Americans were to revive any form of official relationship with Taiwan. No Chinese leader can afford to accept any basic compromise on the issue of Taiwan.

The strong Chinese views on the Taiwan issue were correctly perceived by former President Carter, who after his visit to the PRC in August–September 1981, said: "differences over Taiwan now constitute the main obstacle in improving Chinese-American relations. The Chinese leadership gave me a clear message: now Taiwan will determine future ties with the United States." Mr. Carter added: "I was surprised and impressed at the vehemence with which they put the issue to me. All of the Chinese leaders with whom I met at the national level went out of their way, I thought, to impress on me the importance of this issue, not as a threat, but as a firm statement that this issue is of profound importance to the Chinese people."[96] Whether one considers Sino-American military cooperation desirable or not is a separate issue, but one thing is certain: There cannot be any meaningful cooperation between the United States and the PRC if official links with Taiwan are revived in any form.

So Ronald Reagan's pro-Taiwan remarks during the election campaign were a potential threat to the Sino-American relationship as a whole at a time when Sino-American military ties were in the formative stage. In spite of this complicating factor, military cooperation between the two countries has continued to grow and develop. There is always a big difference between a presidential candidate and an elected president occupying the White House, and Ronald Reagan is no exception. He soon began to realize that China is of great importance for his policy of containment of the Soviet Union and that if he were going to get China's full cooperation, he would have to keep his pro-Taiwan sympathy in cold storage.

A period of uncertainty and "wait and see" followed Reagan's election as the U.S. president in November 1980, but the whole atmosphere, including Sino-American military cooperation, got new impetus and new potential when Reagan's secretary of state, Alexander Haig, went to China in June 1981. Secretary Haig, unlike his Democratic predecessor, Cyrus Vance, is liked by the Chinese because of his strong views on what the Chinese call the Soviet Union's "hegemonic aspirations" and because of his policy of containment of the Soviet expansionist designs in the Third World.

Secretary Haig's Visit to China

The Chinese began to express their willingness to hold high-level talks with the Reagan administration in view of President Reagan's election campaign statement about favoring closer ties to Taiwan, but since President Reagan took office in January 1981, the new administration—particularly Secretary of State Haig—has affirmed its intention to abide by the 1979 accord that established full diplomatic relationship between the United States and the PRC and which severed diplomatic ties with Taiwan, though unofficial trade and other contacts have continued. More important was the new administration's strong attitude toward the Soviet Union's expansionist designs in the Third World and the threats to the world peace as a result of the huge Soviet arms buildup. Both President Reagan and Secretary Haig have made strong statements condemning the Soviet Union's policies and actions, such as its continued military occupation of Afghanistan and its backing of Vietnam's military presence in Cambodia.

China's current view of the world situation may be compared to the late John Foster Dulles's belief that the whole world must unite to defeat a common foe that threatens the rest of the world. The Chinese seem to be convinced that the Soviet Union's backing of Vietnam's conquest of Cambodia and its direct aggression of Afghanistan are parts of a Soviet global strategy to dominate Asia and the rest of the world, and the Chinese have urged the noncommunist Asian countries, the United States, Japan, and NATO and ANZUS countries to unite "to contain the Soviet presence in Afghanistan and Cambodia and not allow it to advance further."[97] The Reagan administration's tough policy toward the Soviet Union and the Chinese desire to contain the Soviet Union's expansionist designs have provided new impetus to an improvement in Sino-American relations, including military ties between Washington and Beijing.

Because of the two countries' common, though not identical, views about the Soviet Union's global policy and designs, it was announced on May 13, 1981, that Haig would visit China in June as a part of a grand Asian tour. It was stated by the U.S. Department of State that Haig's talks with the Chinese would cover the two countries' views of the world, "in particular their concerns about the Soviet Union." Specific topics would be the future security ties between the two countries, U.S. military sales to Taiwan, and possible support for anti-Vietnamese Cambodians.[98]

On the eve of Haig's trip to China, the Reagan administration was moving toward decisions that would give more of a "military cast" to Sino-American relations. The U.S. National Security Council met on June 4, 1981, to consider removing "China from the list of communist countries subject to special export controls,"[99] which would allow for the transfer of military technology, such as engine and electrical equipment from the new F-16 fighter plane, and for the sale of TOW antitank missiles. The issue before the Reagan administration was whether China would be treated in the same category as the Soviet Union, meaning restrictions on the export of materials with potential military applications; whether the PRC would be put in the same special category as Yugoslavia, in which exemptions can be made for items of a military use; or whether it would be placed in the same general category as Britain and India, with virtually no restrictions.

There is almost total agreement in the administration that China should not be treated the same way as the Soviet Union. A statement from the State Department said, "It is nonsense to treat China like an unfriendly State like Russia and be prepared, in principle, to sell anything to a State like India, which buys arms from and has a friendship treaty with Moscow."[100] There seems to be a consensus among many people in the Reagan administration that the United States should try to find ways of strengthening a common anti-Soviet front in cooperation with the PRC, and China has indicated that it wants the same kind of security relations with the United States that Egypt has recently developed. Under the late Chairman Mao Zedong, China was adverse to a security relationship with any country, but the pragmatic post-Mao Chinese leaders have changed Mao's concept of self-help. The China-Vietnam war of 1979, which has been described as a "Chinese lesson" for Vietnam, proved to also be a lesson for the Chinese leaders in regard to China's military capabilities. They came to realize that the Chinese military machinery needs a far-reaching overhaul if China is to engage in any direct or indirect military confrontation with the Soviet Union, so the issue of military ties with the West—including, of course, with the United States—acquired added urgency and significance. Similarly, some people in the Reagan administration, including Defense Secretary Caspar Weinberger and Secretary of State Haig, seemed to have concluded that military links with the PRC could have great significance for the United States' new, tough policy toward the Soviet Union. So Haig's visit to the PRC occurred under highly favorable circumstances.

Before his arrival in Beijing on June 14, Haig made the significant statement that he intended to tell the Chinese leaders that because of a growing Soviet military threat to both countries (the United States and the PRC), there was a "strategic imperative" for the United States and China to establish even closer political, security, and economic ties.[101] Press reporters accompanying the secretary of state were told that the need for strategic collaboration with China had risen since the early 1970s because of the increased Soviet military expansionism in Asia and the rest of the world. The reporters were also briefed about the Soviet Union's use of the old U.S. base at Cam Ranh Bay in Vietnam and its transformation into an elaborate intelligence-gathering station.[102]

The U.S. Decision to Sell Arms to the PRC

Secretary Haig announced on June 16, 1981, after three days of wide-ranging talks with the top Chinese leaders—including China's strongman, Deng Xiaoping, and the Chinese premier, Zhao Ziyang—that the United States had agreed, for the first time, to supply arms to the PRC.[103] Haig said that a decision had been made in Washington by President Reagan to remove munitions control restrictions preventing any sale of lethal weapons to the PRC which, in the 1950s and 1960s, was considered as the United States' most implacable foe. Haig added that once the restrictions were lifted, Chinese arms requests would be considered on a "case by case basis" after consultation with the U.S. Congress and U.S. allies.[104]

The U.S. arms sale decision, considered in the context of what Chinese and U.S. officials described as "growing coordination and cooperation against the Soviet Union," was bound to provoke a strong reaction in Moscow. Georgi Arbatov, director of the Soviet Institute for the Study of U.S.A. and Canada, told *Time* magazine's diplomatic correspondent in Moscow that Haig's trip to China was "all part of a campaign of blackmail against the Soviet Union."[105]

There was no doubt that Haig's main objective seemed to be to strike a "strategic consensus" with the Chinese in order "to limit the Soviet Union's opportunities for exploiting its military power."[106] A notable feature of Haig's visit to China was the U.S. decision to adopt the Chinese use of the word *hegemonism* to denounce the Soviet Union's policies and actions. Haig said that the strategic realities governing the Sino-American cooperation were "more pressing than ever," and he also said that China and the United States saw "eye to eye" on the need to expel foreign occupation forces from Cambodia and Afghanistan. The two countries also agreed to help Pakistan in its defense against any potential threats from the Soviet Union.

Haig seemed to be inclined to downplay the arms sale announcement by pointing out that no specific request for arms had been received from the Chinese,[107] and it is likely that the Chinese shopping list for U.S. arms might not be long in view of the fact that China has placed a rather low priority on the modernization of its military forces. There are reports that China's strongman, Deng Xiaoping, and the Chinese army generals do not see eye to eye on many of Deng's reform measures, and the Chinese People's Liberation Army also seems to be unhappy with Deng's attempts to denounce the late Chairman Mao, so Deng may not be inclined to buy expensive military items for the Chinese army, at least not in the near future.[108] The significance of the arms sale decision was not so much military as it was a political demonstration that now, a decade after the historic 1972 Nixon visit, China is treated as a friendly country, though not an ally, and it is free of the discrimination applied against the Soviet Union and its allies.[109]

It was further disclosed on June 17, 1981, one day after Haig's announcement of the U.S. decision to sell arms to the PRC, that the United States and China had been jointly operating an electronic intelligence-gathering station in China to monitor Soviet missile tests.[110] The station was opened in 1980 in a remote region of the Xinjiang Uygur Autonomous Region in western China near the Soviet border, and its existence involved a far deeper level of military cooperation between the United States and the PRC than either government had previously acknowledged. The station had filled a critical vacuum when similar stations in Iran were abandoned after the fall of the shah in 1979. The equipment for the station was provided by the United States, but it is run by the Chinese technicians, and the intelligence collected is shared by the United States and China. The Russians claimed that it was an "open secret" that the intelligence services of the United States, Britain, China, and Pakistan were engaged in an exercise called "Karakoram-80," the goal of which was to find sites in the Karakoram Mountains along the China-India border for posts to monitor activities in the Soviet Union, Afghanistan, and India. Moscow called China a "voluntary agent of imperialist intelligence services."[111]

Haig's announcement on June 16, 1981, and the disclosure of a joint electronic listening post in China only confirmed that the United States had been slowly moving toward a closer military relationship with China since former Defense Secretary Harold Brown's visit to the PRC in January 1980, shortly after the Soviet Union's invasion of Afghanistan in December 1979.

Impacts on Noncommunist Asian Countries

The implications of the emerging Sino-American military cooperation go beyond eventual arms sales by the United States to the PRC as the cooperation has profound political and symbolic significance not only for the Soviet Union and Vietnam, the communist enemies of China, but also for China's noncommunist Asian neighbors.[112] The list of concerned nations includes Japan and South Korea in Northeast Asia; the ASEAN countries in Southeast Asia; India, Pakistan, and other smaller countries in South Asia; and last but not least, Taiwan.

After his China visit, Secretary of State Alexander Haig went to Manila on June 19 where the foreign ministers of the ASEAN countries and

Japan were gathered for the annual meeting of ASEAN. He reassured the noncommunist Asian neighbors of China by pledging that no weapons would be sold to the PRC without full-scale consultations with the United States' "allies." Haig also portrayed the U.S. arms sale decision as a limited move, describing it as "an internal decision in the U.S. bureaucracy" that merely involved moving China from one category to another in regard to arms sales.[113] He also reassured the Asian countries about the United States' firm pledge to maintain and strengthen its own military capability in Asia and in the Pacific as a contribution to the security of the area against external threats – external threats, according to the U.S. assessment, meaning threats from the Soviet Union and its proxy in Southeast Asia, Vietnam. There is a general consensus about the U.S. assessment among the ASEAN countries and Japan, and it is shared by the ANZUS countries. They all agree with the Sino-American assessment that the current threats to Asia and the Pacific area have resulted from the huge Soviet military buildup and the Soviet Union's expansionist designs as demonstrated by military interventions in Cambodia and Afghanistan as well as by potential threats to countries like Thailand and Pakistan – where Soviet proxies like Vietnam and Afghanistan, equipped with Soviet weapons, have already resorted to armed clashes on the borders of those countries.

In recent years, both inside and outside the United Nations, Japan and the ASEAN and ANZUS nations have supported China's denunciation of Soviet military adventures and policies in Asia. Moscow and not Beijing is now considered as the main threat to Asia and the Pacific region. Therefore, it is not surprising that the U.S. decision to treat China as a friend, though not an ally, met with "total unanimity, total support and total enthusiasm" when Secretary Haig discussed the Reagan administration's arms sale decision in his private talks with the foreign ministers of the ASEAN countries and Japan in Manila while attending the annual meeting of ASEAN of June 17–20, 1981. The noncommunist Asian countries were also pleased with the United States' firm policy toward Vietnam and its total opposition to the continued presence of the Vietnamese occupation forces in Cambodia. It was pointed out that the Reagan administration's Asian policy is based on a "fundamental strategic perspective" and is not merely related to selling arms;[114] it is basically the result of the United States' renewed determination to maintain the status quo and peace in the Asian-Pacific region. Japan, the ASEAN countries, South Korea, and even Taiwan could not take any exception to the new U.S. policy toward Asia and the Pacific, and it seemed to mark an end to the traumatic climate that had resulted from the communist victory in Indochina in 1975.

Yet the U.S. decision to sell arms, including lethal weapons, to the PRC was received with mixed reactions in some of the ASEAN countries, such as Indonesia and Malaysia, and negatively in Taiwan. Taiwan expressed its strong disapproval of arming the PRC with U.S. modern military equipment, and Haig diminished Taiwan's hopes of getting U.S. advanced military equipment when he said that there was "no urgency" to the possible sale of advanced U.S. jet fighters to that country. However, Haig also said that he had told the Chinese that the United States would honor its commitments to sell "defensive weapons" on a limited scale to Taiwan—as had been made known to the Chinese at the time of normalization of relations with the PRC in 1979.[115] It was expected that Taiwan would express its disapproval of the U.S. decision to sell arms to the PRC, but the pertinent question is, Does that decision really constitute a new threat to Taiwan? As long as the PRC feels threatened by the Soviet Union and as long as Beijing cares to maintain the goodwill of the United States—not merely for U.S. arms or advanced technology—it can not afford to take military steps to "liberate" Taiwan. The Chinese leaders will continue to tell the Chinese people about the "liberation" of Taiwan, but that appears to be only an internal policy in the PRC. I am convinced, after repeated and lengthy discussions with the Chinese leaders and foreign policy makers, that the PRC has no military plan concerning Taiwan—at least, not for the near future.

Similarly, the Chinese are loud in demanding the withdrawal of U.S. troops from South Korea. They will not recognize the Seoul government, and they talk of a peaceful "unification" of the country, but again, the Chinese are genuinely interested in maintaining the status quo on the Korean Peninsula. They were not happy when President Carter wanted to withdraw the U.S. troops from South Korea because after their bitter experiences with Vietnam, the Chinese are not eager to see another so-called communist victory as if it takes place, it would be to the advantage of Moscow, not Beijing.[116]

The Japanese leaders are happy to see the growing relationship between the United States and the PRC because Japan's relationship with China is increasingly cordial and close and Japan is no longer afraid of any threats from Red China—particularly as long as Beijing has closer ties with Washington. In fact, Japan welcomed the U.S. decision to sell arms to China in the expectation that a stronger China might reduce instability in Asia and thus also indirectly reduce U.S. pressure on Japan to increase its defense budget. There is nothing for Tokyo to lose from there being closer and even security ties between its main ally, the United States, and its new friend, if not ally, the PRC.

The ASEAN countries were not happy that the United States had not consulted them prior to making such a big decision about its relationship with a major Asian country like the PRC. Some of them agreed with

Indonesian Foreign Minister Mochtar when he expressed dismay that the ASEAN countries had not even been "informed beforehand," let alone consulted. He called the U.S. decision a "jolt" to ASEAN and added that the U.S. decision could bring "Vietnam and other Indochina states deeper into the Moscow camp."[117] Indonesia—particularly its military generals, who have not yet forgotten the allegedly Chinese-inspired attempted coup in their country in 1965—still appears to maintain the traditional concerns of some of the Asian countries about China and has not yet resumed its diplomatic ties with the PRC.

Singapore and Malaysia also seem to have some reservations about the arming of China by the United States, though unlike the Indonesian foreign minister, their leaders did not make any adverse comment about U.S.-China military cooperation because of ASEAN's current policy on the Cambodian crisis, which is in general agreement with that of the PRC. An Asian diplomat in Manila summed up the ASEAN attitude to the Sino-American military cooperation by saying, "The attitude would depend in large degree on the nature of arms being sold; rifles are okay, but not F15s."[118] Thailand and the Philippines, like Japan, seem to be relieved by the growing ties between the PRC and the United States.

In South Asia, India, the traditional friend of Moscow, was not happy to see a further development of the Sino-American relationship, especially the military ties. The new U.S. policy was particularly unwelcome in New Delhi as the United States, with the full support and cooperation of the PRC, also decided to arm India's traditional foe and rival, Pakistan.

Thanks to the persistent tense Indo-Pakistani relationship, any news that is bad in New Delhi is welcomed in Islamabad and vice versa. So, the news of the U.S. arms sales to the PRC was greeted favorably in Pakistan. The smaller countries of South Asia, such as Bangladesh and Sri Lanka, are also happy to see a stronger China as they are traditionally fearful of their "big brother," India. They feel that a strong China will keep India busy so that they will have fewer worries because of New Delhi.[119]

Notes

1. *United States–Soviet Union–China: The Great Power Triangle: Summary of Hearings* (Washington, D.C.: Congressional Research Service, August 12, 1980), p. 3. See also U.S., Congress, House of Representatives, Committee on International Relations, *United States–Soviet Union–China: The Great Power Triangle,* Hearings before the Subcommittee on Future Foreign Policy Research and Development, 94th Cong., 1st sess. (Washington, D.C.: Government Printing Office, 1976).

2. Quoted in G. W. Choudhury, "Great Powers Triangle," *Worldview* (May 1978), pp. 46–49.

3. Dimitri K. Simes, *Detente and Conflict: Soviet Foreign Policy, 1972–1977,* Washington Papers, no. 44 (Washington, D.C.: Center for Strategic and International Studies, Georgetown University, 1977), p. 22.

4. "Troubled Triangle," editorial comment in *New York Times,* May 18, 1977.

5. "The Giants' Triangle," editorial comment in *New York Times,* November 30, 1976.

6. See Choudhury, "Great Powers Triangle," p. 48.

7. C. L. Sulzberger, "Brezhnev's Cruise to China," *New York Times,* July 5, 1975.

8. *Peking Review,* January 30, 1974.

9. Ross Terrill, "Bear-Dragon Flirtation," *Washington Post,* December 19, 1976.

10. Cited in *New York Times,* August 26, 1977.

11. Sulzberger, "Brezhnev's Cruise to China."

12. Based on the author's talks and interviews in Beijing, July 1977.

13. Press release of the PRC mission to the United Nations, New York, September 8, 1976.

14. See the speech by Jiao Guanhua, chairman of the delegation of the PRC at the Plenary Meeting of the Thirty-first Session of the UN General Assembly. October 5, 1976, issued by Foreign Languages Press, 1976, p. 9.

15. *Playing the China Card: Implications for the United States–Soviet-Chinese Relations,* Report prepared for the Subcommittee on Asian and Pacific Affairs of the Committee on Foreign Affairs, U.S. House of Representatives, by Foreign Affairs and National Defense Division, Congressional Research Service, Library of Congress (Washington, D.C.: Government Printing Office, October 1979), pp. v and 1–2.

16. Ibid.

17. Ibid.

18. Hans J. Morgenthau, "Gambling on China," *New York Times,* July 25, 1978.

19. Ibid.

20. *Playing the China Card,* p. v.

21. See "Kremlin Showing Alarm as Sino-U.S. Ties Grow," *Washington Post,* August 24, 1978.

22. Ibid.

23. Reprinted in *Washington Post,* August 24, 1978.

24. "U.S. 'China Card' Worries Kremlin," *Washington Post,* September 5, 1978.

25. Ibid.

26. Soviet statement, "U.S. Course 'Fraught with Serious Danger,' " *Washington Post,* July 18, 1978.

27. Based on the author's research, interviews, and discussion in Beijing, July 1979; see also G. W. Choudhury, "Triangular Diplomacy," *Asia-Pacific Community* (Tokyo), (Summer 1980), pp. 50–62.

28. *New York Times,* June 27, 1978.

29. See "Detente by Soviet Rules?" *U.S. News and World Report,* July 24, 1978.

30. *New York Times,* June 15, 1978.

31. *Washington Post,* December 20, 1978.

32. Ibid., November 5, 1978.

33. *New York Times,* December 16, 1978.

34. Ibid., May 23, 1977.

35. Ibid., March 18, 1978.

36. Elaine P. Adam and R. P. Stebbins, eds., *American Foreign Relations, 1978,* Council on Foreign Relations Book (New York: New York University Press, 1979), p. 19.

37. *New York Times,* March 19, 1978.

38. *Newsweek,* June 25 and July 2, 1979; and *Washington Post* and *New York Times,* June 23–July 2, 1979.

39. *Newsweek,* July 2, 1979, and June 25, 1979.

40. *New York Times,* August 28, 1979.

41. See Derek Davies, "Shadow of the Kremlin," *Far Eastern Economic Review,* August 24, 1979, p. 27.

42. *New York Times,* September 10, 1979.

43. Ibid.

44. Richard Perle, "An Arms Control Treaty Built on American Illusions," *Washington Post,* October 7, 1979.

45. *Washington Post,* April 9, 1980.

46. Ibid.

47. For China's defense requirements and problems, see Russel Spurr's articles on China's defense in *Far Eastern Economic Review,* January 27, 1977, and October 7, 1977 ("Men Against Machines" and "PLA Modernization Has to Be Painfully Slow"); see also Roger Kelly, "Shopping in EEC," *Far Eastern Economic Review,* October 6, 1978.

48. Russel Spurr, "China's Defence: Men Against Machines," *Far Eastern Economic Review,* January 27, 1977, pp. 24–25.

49. Drew Middleton, "China Looking to Western Europe for Arms Supplies," *New York Times,* April 14, 1978.

50. Ibid.

51. Victor Zorza, "Peking Debates Its European Option," *Washington Post,* December 21, 1977.

52. See "Defense: China '80 Gambling on a Quick Missile Deterrent," *Far Eastern Economic Review,* September 26, 1980, pp 55–56.

53. Ibid.

54. Based on the author's research, interviews, and talks in London.

55. Reprinted in *Washington Post,* August 6, 1978.

56. Ibid.

57. See *New York Times,* November 13, 1978.

58. Ibid.

59. See "On Selling Arms to China," editorial comment in *New York Times,* December 1, 1978.

60. *Financial Times,* November 22, 1978.

61. Reproduced in *Washington Post,* August 27, 1978.

62. *Washington Post,* August 30, 1978.

63. *International Herald Tribune,* August 19–20, 1978.

64. Ibid.

65. *Washington Post,* August 22, 1978.

66. Reprinted in *Washington Post,* August 28, 1978.

67. See Michael Dobbs, "First Trip West Transforms Hua into a Dapper in World Politico," *Washington Post,* August 30, 1978.

68. Ibid.

69. Michael Pillsbury, "U.S.-China Military Ties?" *Foreign Policy* (Fall 1975), pp. 50–64.

70. Ibid.

71. *Washington Post,* August 12, 1976.

72. Ibid.

73. "Inside China Now," Report on a twenty-three-day visit by James Schlesinger, *U.S. News and World Report,* October 18, 1976.

74. See Paul C. Warnke, "We Don't Need a Devil (to Make or Keep Our Friends)," *Foreign Policy* (Winter 1976–77), pp. 78–87.

75. See the summary of "Policy Review Memo No. 24" in *New York Times,* June 24, 1977.

76. Ibid.

77. Don Oberdorfer, "Soviets Warn Not to Sell Peking Arms," *Washington Post,* October 27, 1978.

78. Ibid.

79. *Beijing Review,* October 6, 1980, p. 12.

80. See Stephen Barber, "Carter's Rude Awakening," *Far Eastern Economic Review,* January 18, 1980, pp. 10–11.

81. *New York Times,* January 24, 1980.

82. *Washington Post,* January 6, 1980.

83. Ibid., January 7, 1980.

84. Ibid., January 9, 1980.

85. Ibid., January 12, 1980.

86. *Pravda,* March 9, 1980; reprinted in *Washington Post,* March 10, 1980.

87. *New York Times,* May 30, 1980.

88. Ibid., June 2, 1980.

89. See John Lewis, "Come and Join Us," *Far Eastern Economic Review,* June 6, 1980.

90. Ibid.

91. *Times* (London), July 11, 1980, and *Far Eastern Economic Review,* July 10–17, 1980, p. 6.

92. *Times* (London), July 11, 1980.

93. *Izvestia,* July 10, 1980; reprinted in *Times* (London), July 11, 1980.

94. Nayan Chanda, "This Far but No Further," *Far Eastern Economic Review,* October 3, 1980, p. 15.

95. Ibid.

96. *New York Times,* September 4, 1981.

97. Ibid., April 21, 1981.

98. Ibid., May 14, 1981.

99. Ibid., June 5, 1981.

100. Ibid.

101. *Durham Morning Herald* (Durham, N.C.), June 14, 1981.

102. Ibid.

103. For details of the U.S. arms sale decision, see *Washington Post* and *New York Times,* June 17–18, 1981.

104. Ibid.

105. *Time,* June 29, 1981, pp. 28–30.
106. Ibid.
107. David Bonavia, "Haig Opens up a Candy Store," *Far Eastern Economic Review,* June 19, 1981, pp. 12–13.
108. Based on the author's interviews and research in Beijing, August 1981.
109. See Bernard Gwerltzman, "Haig in China: Gain for U.S.," *New York Times,* June 18, 1981.
110. *New York Times,* June 18, 1981.
111. Ibid., June 19, 1981.
112. See Don Oberdorfer, "Implications of Sino-U.S. Accord Go Beyond Eventual Arms Sales," *Washington Post,* June 18, 1981.
113. *Washington Post,* June 21, 1981.
114. For details, see *New York Times* and *Washington Post,* June 18–22, 1981.
115. Ibid.
116. The author had lengthy talks with the Chinese Senior Vice Foreign Minister, Han Nianlong, during trips to China in 1976–1981.
117. See *Far Eastern Economic Review,* June 26, 1981, pp. 10–11.
118. *Washington Post,* June 20, 1981.
119. *Far Eastern Economic Review,* August 28, 1981, pp. 20–22.

8

China and Its Asian Neighbors: Japan, Korea, and Indochina

The emergence of a Communist China under Mao, in declared alliance with the Soviet Union, caused anxiety in Washington, particularly in the 1950s when the East-West cold war tensions were at their height. In Asia, however, and especially in India in the early years, the rise of a strong China was welcomed. A particularly friendly tie developed between India and China, and following Nehru's vigorous support of China during the Korean War, the two countries signed a treaty of five principles of coexistence in 1954. China also made an active effort to win the friendship of the newly independent Afro-Asian countries. China's next-door neighbors—such as Thailand, the Philippines, and Japan—did not respond to China's friendly gestures, but many other Afro-Asian countries were favorably impressed by China at the first Afro-Asian conference in Bandung in 1955.

Many Asians looked upon the emergence of a new and powerful China as a great feat for the spirit of Asian nationalism, not as a triumph of international communism controlled and directed by the Kremlin.[1] Nehru, for one, believed that China and India could form a third force in the world to act as a bridge between Moscow and Washington, but that proved to be an immature assessment as Mao at that time did not believe in any friendship or alliance with a bourgeois Asian regime like the Nehru government in India.[2]

In the initial years of Chinese nationalism (1949–1952), foreign policy was dominated by doctrinaire and ideological considerations, and the focal point of China's foreign policy was its alliance with Moscow. This was the period of the concept of a "world of two camps" and a period of ideological intransigence and revolutionary militancy for the communist world. As China was then under Soviet influence and desperately needed Soviet assistance, both for security and for economic development, Mao seemed to follow the Soviet policy of treating the newly independent Asian countries, such as India and Pakistan, as "stooges of Anglo-American imperialism." This initial, distorted attitude of China toward the governments of the new Asian countries was more in deference to the Kremlin than the result of China's own thinking or wishes. China, in fact, recognized the realities and dynamics of the new countries in Asia much sooner than the Soviet Union did, as the latter's rigid and indifferent attitude began to change only after Stalin's death in 1953. China's friendship with India during the Korean War is an illustration of China's policy of "uniting with revolutionaries" being transformed into a policy of "union with all." Although China has long been a magnet for its Asian neighbors, it has no desire or ability to seek hegemony in Asia. No doubt, the Chinese think of Asia as their natural cultural domain and as an area in which China must eventually play a crucial role in the search for stability there.

China's attitude toward its Asian neighbors cannot adequately be explained without reference to its relations with the two superpowers—the United States and the USSR. During the twenty years of frozen relations with the United States when China considered, not without justification, the United States as its main enemy, Beijing's relations with those Asian countries that were U.S. allies or friendly to Washington were hostile or unfriendly. Japan in East Asia; Thailand, the Philippines, and Malaysia, in Southeast Asia; and Pakistan in South Asia were regarded as unfriendly as many of them joined the United States in military alliances or pacts directed against Beijing. Since the Sino-Soviet rift began in 1969, Asian countries, such as Vietnam, India, and Afghanistan, that are tied to Moscow by so-called treaties of friendship have been regarded by Beijing as unfriendly, if not hostile.

Of course, other factors have also influenced China's relations with its Asian neighbors, such as trade and economic relations. China's needs in terms of its industrial development plans to raise the standard of living of its citizens and other ambitious plans under the four-modernization schemes of post-Mao China influence China's relations with Asian countries such as Japan and the ASEAN countries. Ideological factors and China's bid for leadership of the antihegemony struggle also influence its relations with Asian countries. The twentieth anniversary of the outbreak of the Korean War on June 25, 1970, was observed in China with lavish celebrations, and the occasion was fully utilized to enhance China's bid for the leadership of an Asian anti-imperialist front. Prince Norodom Sihanouk, the exiled leader of Cambodia was then in Beijing, and he described the unity of North Korea, China, and the three Indochina states (Vietnam, Cambodia, and Laos) as a formidable nucleus of the Asian anti-imperialist front,[3] and a joint editorial in China's newspapers—*People's Daily, Red Flag, Liberation Army Daily*—on the same occasion was directed against Soviet social imperialism. The Soviet Union had recognized the Lon Nol regime in Cambodia, and the editorial said that the proposed front was opposed to "certain powers which were maintaining dirty relations with Lon Nol."[4]

China's entry into the United Nations in 1971 was actively supported by many of its Asian neighbors as China's entry into that world body was regarded as an important step toward the recognition of Asian realities, as Singapore's Prime Minister Lee Kuan said on the occasion of China's entry into the United Nations in October 1971. China's respect for the principles of "mutual observance of sovereignty and territorial integrity, reciprocal non-aggression and non-interference in internal affairs of her neighbors" were regarded as arguments for the PRC's admission to the United Nations.[5] However, many Asian governments, including those of Burma, India, and Malaysia, which voted to seat China at the United Nations, had cause to be skeptical about China's observance of those principles in view of the Chinese-inspired insurgency problems in their countries.

China's Asian policy in the post–Cultural Revolution period offered hope of a relaxation of tensions, for although Beijing's encouragement to communist guerrillas did not cease, China began to actively cultivate government to government relationships with its Asian neighbors. China began the process of rapprochement with its Asian neighbors after the diplomatic setbacks caused by upheavals during the Cultural Revolution, and the number of delegations sent to China's neighbors increased in 1970 after the self-imposed seclusion of the Cultural Revolution period was over. Chinese Prime Minister Zhou Enlai went to North Korea, and the Chinese minister, Guo Moro, visited Pakistan and Nepal. Zhou Enlai wrote to Pakistani President Yahya that Pakistan would be among the first few countries he would visit in 1970; Zhou's visit to Pakistan did not take place, but the Pakistani president went to China in November 1970.

China also established diplomatic links with Pakistan's two closest Muslim neighbors, Iran and Turkey, in 1970–1971, and a $6.5-million loan agreement was signed with Ceylon (Sri Lanka) on October 8, 1970. During the 1971 political upheavals in Sri Lanka, China cooperated with the government in Colombo rather than supporting the insurgents, and similarly, China supported the Pakistani government during the civil war concerning Bangladesh in 1971. There were also signs of improved relations with India. During the Pakistani president's visit to China in November 1970, Zhou Enlai told his Pakistani guest that full diplomatic relations between China and India, which had been suspended because of the 1962 Sino-Indian border conflict, might be restored "soon."

Despite China's earlier emphasis on economic self-sufficiency, China was interested in importing steel, fertilizer, and manufactured products from Japan by 1970, even before a diplomatic relationship was established between Beijing and Tokyo. Chinese leaders hinted at the 1970 spring trade fair in Canton, which opened on April 15, that China was interested in trading with governments of almost any political inclination, and they emphasized that trade should be conducted on the basis of domestic needs. That interest was an indication of China's forward-looking foreign policy of the post–Cultural Revolution era, which culminated under China's strong man, Deng, after Mao's death in 1976.

The New China News Agency greeted the year 1971 with a special report on the progress of revolution and the anti-imperialist struggle in Africa, Latin America, and Oceania, but with regard to Asia, it noted only the communist guerrilla operations in the Philippines during 1970.[6] China's diplomatic offensive in 1970–1971, after the Cultural Revolution, helped to enhance its image of reasonableness among its Asian neighbors, which had been disturbed by China's internal upheavals during the Cultural Revolution in 1966–1969. The trends toward normality in China's foreign relations and that country's tentative moves to end its self-imposed isolation were manifested by an exchange of delegations with its neighbors and by the return of Chinese ambassadors to some of the Asian countries, such as Afghanistan, Pakistan, Nepal, and Mongolia as well as North Korea and Cambodia.

While Beijing was engaged in secret negotiations to normalize China's relations with Washington in 1971–1972, and while Beijing's relations with Moscow were taking a serious turn after the 1969 border clashes with the Soviet Union, China began a new policy toward its Asian neighbors. Several Asian countries – India, Burma, Malaysia, Japan, the Philippines, and Thailand – simultaneously indicated their desire to normalize relations with China, but Beijing was cautious and slow in responding to such signals. Beijing seemed to give priority to the more distant Third World countries in Africa and Latin America, and China still seemed to be indecisive about its support of so-called liberation movements in some of the Asian countries such as Burma, Thailand, and India. However, the growing Sino-Soviet rivalry in Asia meant that China had to give priority to a government to government relationship with its Asian neighbors.

Soon after the profound breakthrough between Beijing and Washington in 1971–1972, China's diplomatic initiatives with its Asian neighbors intensified, and a new era of diplomatic relations and an exchange of high-level delegations between China and its Asian neighbors began after the 1972 Peking Summit. The most notable diplomatic venture was between Beijing and Tokyo as the Sino-Japanese relationship was transformed from a state-of-war relationship to a friendly one in a period of seven years (1972–1979), and the two countries signed a peace treaty that was of great significance not only for the two countries, but also for the new international patterns in Asia.

The 1970s witnessed major changes in the international political system in all of Asia, and by and large, those changes stemmed from a decreased emphasis on purely ideological concerns and a corresponding preoccupation with concrete national interests and aspirations on the part of the Chinese leaders after the Cultural Revolution. In the post-Mao era, those changes were made in the context of China's decision to push for a rapid modernization of the country and in the context of China's security problems vis-à-vis the Soviet Union and Soviet-backed Vietnam.

Beijing and Tokyo

Although the Chinese had entered into extensive trade contacts with Japan in the early 1950s, their attitude toward Tokyo fluctuated greatly in the years prior to 1970, and hostility reached high levels in 1958–1960 and 1966–1969. The signing of the Nixon-Sato communiqué in 1969, which returned Okinawa to Japan, provoked anti-Japanese outbursts in China, because China feared that Japan, with the blessing of the United States, would begin remilitarization. The 1969 Nixon doctrine envisaged the disengagement of the U.S. military presence in Asia, and China was afraid that the United States would encourage Japan to fill up the resulting power vacuum. Chinese suspicions of the Japanese policy during this period were reflected in the Chinese press: "Japan will go nuclear," "Japan under U.S. influence is inciting Asians to fight Asians," "Japan's militarism supports the bandit Chiang Kai-shek's slogan 'reconquest of the mainland.'"[7]

The whole atmosphere changed dramatically when the new Sino-American relationship began in 1971–1972. China no longer worried about the alleged Japanese remilitarization; on the contrary, a strong Japan backed by the United States became a major factor in China's foreign policy. Beijing's diplomacy policy regarding Japan in the 1970s aimed at strengthening closer cooperation between Japan and China, particularly in economic matters; strengthening Japanese-American military ties as a counterbalance to the Soviet power in the Asian-Pacific region; and preventing Moscow's bids for friendly relations with Tokyo. China ceased publicly attacking Japan's militarism almost overnight.

There were strong reasons why China and Japan should develop closer relations. For the Japanese, China's proximity and size, its growing diplomatic stature, and its changing relationship with the United States as well as traditional cultural ties were some of the compelling reasons for a rapprochement with China. Japanese businessmen also anticipated major economic benefits from being able to reach the vast Chinese potential market.

For the Chinese, Japan was already China's largest trading partner, and China also realized fully that Japan's position as the world's third-largest economy and its reemergence as a major political power would give Japan a key role in the changing balance of power in Asia. As one analyst pointed out, "The American connection with China [has] a serious impact on Russia only if the United States also maintains a close rapport with Japan."[8]

All of those considerations led the two countries closer to the establishment of formal diplomatic links between Beijing and Tokyo, and Zhou Enlai listed three conditions that Japan had to fulfill before a full diplomatic relationship between China and Japan could be established:

1. Recognition of the PRC as the sole legitimate government of China
2. Acceptance of Taiwan as an integral part of China
3. Abrogation of the Japan-Taiwan peace treaty, which China had always considered to be illegal

Japan decided to accept those three preconditions, because Nixon's acceptance of an invitation to visit China without first consulting Tokyo had made the Japanese feel isolated and humiliated. Japan's anti-China policy in the 1950s and 1960s had been dictated by Washington, so when Tokyo learned that the United States had approached China without Japan's knowledge, not to speak of approval or consultation, why shouldn't Japan move one step further? That was perhaps the main reason why the Japanese leaders decided to accept China's three preconditions.

Prime Minister Tanaka went to Beijing in September 1972, and a full diplomatic relationship was established between the two major Asian countries after twenty-two years of cold war confrontation. In the joint communiqué that established that relationship on September 29, 1972, Japan recognized the PRC as the sole legal government of China and expressed a full understanding of China's stand on Taiwan as "an inalienable part of the territory of the People's Republic of China." The Japanese government also deeply reproached itself for Japan's aggression against China, and the Japanese treaty with Taiwan was declared invalid. The Chinese renounced demands for reparations, and both sides proclaimed that the abnormal state of affairs – the undeclared war – between the two countries was terminated.[9]

The two countries' agreement to establish diplomatic relations and to end the abnormal state of affairs between them marked the beginning of their new relationship. Trade was developing rapidly, and by 1971, Japan had already become China's largest trading partner. China had begun to import Japanese steel on a long-term basis, and in the first ten months of 1972, Japan's exports to China ($477.7 million) had exceeded those to the Soviet Union ($430.2 million). Now, however, a rapid rise in Chinese exports to Japan nearly brought the Sino-Japanese trade into balance in 1973 after years of deficit on the Chinese side.

China and Japan began to negotiate agreements on civil aviation, navigation, and fisheries. Although the extravagant hopes in some Japanese quarters, which were raised by the normalization of relations with China, proved to be unrealistic, one major stumbling block – the lack of official trade channels and agreements – had been removed by the establishment of diplomatic relations in 1972, and the Japanese trading companies now had a formal framework for their operations. A full government agreement negotiated in the second half of 1973 and signed by Japanese Foreign Minister Ohira during a visit to Beijing in January 1974 provided for most-favored-nation treatment in tariff and payment arrangements, the establishment of joint companies on the official level, the holding of trade fairs, and an extension of technical exchanges. Thus the new relationship between Beijing and Tokyo in the 1970s gave China an opportunity "to open the doors wide to Japanese business concerns, accept interest-bearing loans from Tokyo, send many students to Japanese universities and carry out the terms of a multibillion dollar 20-year trade treaty."[10]

Although economics loomed large in the newly established Sino-Japanese relationship, political considerations also brought Beijing and Tokyo closer together. Following the 1975 communist victory in Indochina, there was uncertainty about the future of defensive alliances in Asia, particularly in view of China's active diplomacy – Beijing had already established diplomatic links with Australia and New Zealand. The Soviet Union began to revitalize its plan for collective security in Asia, and Japan was a prime target because of Moscow's concern about the growing Sino-Japanese links. Both China and Japan had frontier disputes with the Soviet Union, and Chinese and Japanese "irrendentists" were both criticized by Soviet commentators for opposing Brezhnev's plan for a collective security system in Asia, one of the basic principles of which is "the inviolability of frontiers."[11] But apart from the frontier problems, Japan was not responsive to the Soviet Union's collective security plan because it was aimed at China and in view of their new relationship, Tokyo would not join in any anti-China military grouping in Asia. The New China News Agency pointed out on January 16, 1976, that the Soviet proposal was an attempt to tie Japan to Russia as a means of undermining U.S. influence in Asia (which China no longer considered a threat to its security) and of "condemning the U.S. for world hegemony."[12] A 1975 study of Japan's defense issues by the Japanese minister of state for defense includes the following comment on Brezhnev's Asian collective security plan:

> There is a probability that the Soviet Union, its self-confidence buttressed by the Pan-European Security and Cooperation Conference, will strongly advocate the idea of an "Asian Collective Security System" in the near

future. This idea has already been proposed by Soviet Communist Party
General Secretary Leonid Brezhnev.

In general, Asian countries have so far remained cool to this idea,
primarily due to the many divided nations in this part of the world. Now
that Vietnam has been virtually reunified, however, Soviet drives to sell
this idea may intensify.

However events develop in Asia's future, though, the basic Soviet aim is
to lure Japan away from China, and increasingly alienate China on the international scene. China, on the other hand is expected to counter Soviet
moves by maneuvering for an advantageous position through friendly relations with the U.S. and Japan.[13]

The Russians, on the other hand, believed there was a danger of closer
Beijing-Tokyo-Washington links as a result of the Pacific doctrine enunciated by President Ford in Hawaii in December 1975.

In the meantime, a major obstacle to the Sino-Japanese relationship
was overcome in 1974 when Japan signed a civil aviation agreement with
China. Japan had to declare that it no longer regarded the Taiwan airline
as a "national carrier," and Taiwan subsequently cut off Japanese flights
to the island (but it was agreed in 1975 that they should be resumed).
Sino-Japanese trade and maritime agreements were also concluded in
1974. China's supplying aid to Japan was mutually beneficial to both
countries, particularly after the 1973 Arab oil boycott. There was some
deadlock on that oil supply, and the matter was discussed during
Japanese Foreign Minister Ohira's visit to Beijing in January 1974, but
nothing was said about future Chinese oil supplies to Japan. The
Japanese were hoping for anything up to 10 million tons annually, and
there was further discussion in March 1974 about the oil supply to Japan
when Nagano, head of Japan's Chamber of Commerce, visited Beijing.
The Chinese government assured him it would "study Japan's request for
more oil positively."[14] China objected strongly to a Japanese–South
Korean agreement in 1974 for joint exploration and development of oil in
the adjoining offshore area, ownership of which was still in dispute. An
agreement between China and Japan was signed in Beijing on December
6, 1979, for exploration for oil in the Bo Hai Gulf Area on China's northeast coast, and that signing marked the first time that the Chinese had
agreed to foreign participation in the development of one of its oil
fields.[15] Although trade and technical delegations dominated the growing
exchanges between Beijing and Tokyo until the mid 1970s, there were
occasional sports and "friendly" delegations, such as the large Chinese
contingent that participated in the second Asian table tennis championships held in Japan on April 2, 1974.

So, although economics figured prominently in the new relationship
between China and Japan, security and political problems also provided

reasons for closer cooperation and closer links between the two countries. The test of the new relationship between Tokyo and Beijing focused prominently on the peace treaty negotiations between the two countries, which continued intermittently from November 1974 to August 1978. The major obstacle was the inclusion of a hegemony clause in the proposed treaty, which has already been mentioned in the discussion of the Sino-Soviet rivalry in Asia.[16]

The Complicated Treaty Negotiations Between Beijing and Tokyo (1974–1978)

From the moment they established diplomatic relations in 1972, China and Japan pursued "an elusive 'peace and friendship treaty'—suffering through embarrassing silences, conflicting interests, deliberate snubs and one mini-invasion of some disputed islands."[17] The rocky negotiations on the treaty extended over a period of nearly four years (1974–1978), and the Sino-Japanese relationship was further complicated by outside factors: The Soviet Union threatened Tokyo concerning the treaty, and the United States encouraged Japan to go ahead with it. Japan wanted to follow a policy of genuine nonalignment in the new cold war between Moscow and Beijing, but the complicated international scene in East Asia did not allow the Japanese leaders to follow their preferred path, and the Soviet threats and protest notes seemed to be counterproductive. In July 1976, I talked extensively with the foreign policy makers in both Tokyo and Beijing about deadlock over the much-debated hegemony clause in the proposed treaty, and I found that Japan's reluctance to include an antihegemony clause was based on mainly three factors. First, *hegemony* had acquired a definite meaning and significance in the Sino-Soviet conflict, and Japan wanted to remain neutral in that conflict. Second, China's 1975 constitution spoke against the "hegemony of the two superpowers," and Japan was not willing to join China in accusing the United States of hegemony or more accurately, in condemning the U.S. presence in Asia, which is vital to Japan's security. Third, if Japan were to sign the treaty with an antihegemony clause in it, Moscow would be so offended that Japan's hopes of getting back four northern islands that Russia had seized after Japan was defeated in World War II would be lost for good.

The Chinese replies to the Japanese objections were conveyed to me in my discussions in Beijing. First, the Russians never return any territory once they occupy it, so even if Japan were to refuse flatly to sign a treaty with China, it would still be futile for Japan to expect the return of the four northern islands. Second, concerning the Japanese objection to the antihegemony clause, the Chinese replied that the word *hegemony* has a clear and unambiguous meaning. China is opposed to any form of hegemony, not just the hegemony of the Soviet Union, and China itself does not aspire to any hegemony. Third, as to the hegemony of the two superpowers, the Chinese appreciated Japan's special security and other ties with the United States, but felt that Japan, as a self-respecting Asian nation, could not support hegemony of the United States. Friendship, special relationships, security pacts, etc., are different from hegemony. The Chinese felt convinced that Japan was opposed to any form of hegemony, and had so committed itself to that principle when it had signed the joint communiqué with China in September 1972 when the diplomatic relationship between the two countries was established.

The Soviet Union continued to issue protests and warnings against the treaty. A "statement to the government of Japan" issued through the Soviet Tass agency on June 17, 1975, said "that it was in the common interest of both countries [USSR and Japan] to rebuff attempts by 'third states' to create obstacles to the improvement of Soviet-Japanese relations." On November 26, 1975, *Pravda* warned that the Soviet Union would regard inclusion of a hegemony clause in the treaty as an unfriendly step by the Japanese government. Japanese Prime Minister Takeo Miki made a statement in January 1976 in which he said that Japan would conclude a peace treaty with China; the statement was made just four hours after the Soviet foreign minister, Andrei Gromyko, had ended a five-day visit to Tokyo, during which he had expressed strong Soviet disapproval of the treaty.[18] The Chinese commented in the following way on the Soviet Union's designs in Japan.

> The Soviet *Tass* News Agency issued on June 18, 1975 a "Statement to the Government of Japan," crudely exerting pressure on the Japanese Government against including the anti-hegemony clause in the proposed Japan-China treaty of peace and friendship. Thus the Soviet authorities have revealed their hegemonic features.
>
> The *Tass* statement attacked China for allegedly "striving to impose by all possible means the inclusion into the treaty of peace and friendship, whose conclusion is being negotiated at the present time, a provision which . . . is aimed, first and foremost, against the Soviet Union."
>
> However, the wordy statement failed to make clear what provision "is aimed, first and foremost, against the Soviet Union." The Brezhnev clique taboos all mention of "anti-hegemonism" because it is pursuing a policy of hegemonism. Any mention of "opposition to hegemony" throws it into a fit.
>
> The statement also slanderously accused China of wanting "to involve Japan . . . in the orbit of their policy." Who after all wants to involve Japan in the orbit of his foreign policy? That the Japanese and Chinese governments are negotiating for a Japan-China peace and friendship treaty in accordance with the spirit of the Japan-China statement is a matter concerning only Japan and China. But the Brezhnev clique is so full of rancor against this that it is trying hard to obstruct and undermine the negotiations.[19]

Japan formally informed China on June 23, 1978, that it would go ahead in finalizing the negotiations on the peace treaty—the talks were scheduled to begin in July 1978. The Soviet Union had issued yet another stern warning on June 19, 1978, telling the Japanese that the treaty might result in "a reversal of the present relationship between Japan and the Soviet Union." The Soviet statement had also made a violent attack on China: The "Chinese have stepped up their policy of undermining progress in detente, fanning the menace of war and plotting conflicts between nations."[20] Japanese Prime Minister Takeo Fukuda gave the correct reply to the crude Soviet blackmail attempt by telling Moscow that "Japanese-Chinese relations are one thing and Japanese-Soviet relations another."[21]

When the final negotiations began in Beijing in July 1978, I had a three-hour exclusive talk with the head of the Chinese negotiating team, the senior vice foreign minister, Han Nianlong, whom I have known for a long time. The press reports about the progress of the negotiations were rather pessimistic, but after my discussions with Han, I had no doubt about the successful conclusion of the long and complicated negotiations on the treaty. Both sides were determined to conclude the treaty, and both sides showed mutual understanding and expressed the need for friendly and closer relations between the two countries in light of the changing patterns of the international system in Asia.

The conclusion of the Sino-Japanese treaty constitutes Beijing's greatest diplomatic triumph in Asia after the deaths of Mao and Zhou Enlai in 1976. China and Japan signed the treaty on August 12, 1978, when the two countries' foreign ministers put their signatures on a five-article document. The antihegemony clause was the most important one, and it was almost identical to the wording used in the 1972 China-Japan joint communiqué. A clause was added to the effect that the treaty would not affect the position of either contracting party in regard to its relations with third countries, and Japan hoped that the clause would mollify Moscow. The treaty was hailed in Tokyo, Beijing, Washington, and most of the Asian and Western European countries as a major stabilizing factor in the Asian-Pacific region. Only Moscow and its satellites blasted the treaty. It put an end to the abnormal Sino-Japanese relationship, which had lasted forty-one years and six days since the Sino-Japanese War started in the 1930s.

The treaty was formally ratified on October 23, 1978, when Chinese Vice-Premier Deng went to Tokyo to launch a new era of diplomatic relations and economic cooperation. Political ties and trade are important, but the fact that the treaty represents a return to a centuries-old relationship is more significant.[22] In Tokyo, Deng behaved like a seasoned diplomat, like his political mentor, the late Premier Zhou Enlai. In an unprecedented audience with Emperor Hirohito, the emperor told Deng that "there were unfortunate events in the long history of Sino-Japanese relations," to which Deng replied that China would endeavor to build peaceful relations with Japan by "letting bygones be bygones."[23] The Japanese people looked upon the treaty as a reaffirmation of millennia-long cultural ties with their ancient Asian neighbor. The Japanese businessmen looked upon it as an opportunity to pursue the enticing prospect of promising export deals for the costly capital goods the Chinese needed to help them reach the goals of their prodigious in-dustrialization drive. Deng told the Japanese business community that the $20-billion eight-year trade agreement between the two countries, signed in February 1978, should be "doubled and doubled again."

The treaty was welcomed by anyone who wished peace and stability in Asia, particularly in East Asia. There were some worries in North Korea, but the years of good relations with China and the recent Soviet gestures to South Korea will leave the China–North Korea relations unaffected by the treaty. Only the Kremlin leaders were unhappy. The Russian Peace and Progress Radio, commenting on Deng's visit to Tokyo, said: "It should be clear that Peking is trying to involve Japan in the intrigues that undermine peace in the Far East and throughout Asia. It is also well to remember that Peking has lately given open endorsement to Japan's security treaty with the United States and has urged speedier militariza-tion of Japan."[24] The treaty will have a profound effect on the changing patterns of alignment in Asia, and it will also have a great impact on the global balance of power. At the moment, it appears that Washington, Tokyo, and Beijing have developed a "soft" alliance against the Soviet ex-pansionist designs.

$20-Billion Trade Agreement

Before the conclusion of the much-publicized treaty of peace and friendship, China and Japan signed a $20-billion trade pact on February 16, 1978, and that agreement set the scene for a marked improvement in their growing relationship. The trade agreement was highly beneficial to Beijing's ambitious economic programs under the four-modernization plans and a welcome economic plan for Japan. For the Chinese, the trade pact promises a source of foreign exchange and assures supplies of steel and modern equipment, plants, and advanced industrial technology as China attempts to increase its own economic development.[25] For Japan, it means "a handsome headstart into vast Chinese market for Japanese manufacturers."[26] In addition to that trade pact, another Sino-Japanese agreement for a major low-cost loan was signed on December 6, 1979, during Prime Minister Ohira's visit to Beijing.[27]

The Chinese leaders expressed a desire to learn from the Japanese peo-ple the secrets of the high-growth Japanese economy, and a Japanese diplomat said that the Chinese "are interested in understanding how we adapted what we found in the West so quickly."[28] During Prime Minister Ohira's visit to China in December 1979, Japan offered the major low-cost loan for several Chinese modernization projects and the agreement for joint Sino-Japanese drilling in the potentially oil-rich Bo Hai Gulf was also concluded. Ohira, endorsing China's four-modernization programs, said that good relations between Japan, Asia's richest nation, and China, its largest, would contribute to the stability of Asia and of the world.[29]

The Sino-Japanese relationship, established soon after the 1972 Peking Summit between President Nixon and Premier Zhou Enlai, became a major factor in the Asian international system in the 1970s and is likely to develop further in the 1980s. Such development would mutually benefit the two major Asian countries, which have been hostile to each other in the past but have now been transformed into allies. That alliance is beneficial for peace and stability in the Asian-Pacific region in particular and for world peace generally. Notwithstanding some ups and downs in China-Japan relations, the diplomatic ties between the two countries have developed both in depth and scope and have been markedly beneficial to both.

China and the Korean Peninsula

The PRC is committed to the concept of one Korea, and the Chinese consider the division of Korea into South and North a result of the power policies of the two superpowers. The division of the country, according to the Chinese interpretation, is artificial and does not reflect the wishes of the people of Korea, either South or North. Recalling China's direct participation in the Korean War of 1950–1953, the Chinese do not recognize the government of South Korea, nor is it expected that they will do so.

Does the situation imply that the PRC will encourage North Korea to unify the country by force? After extensive talks with Chinese foreign policy makers—including the present foreign minister, Huang Hua—and with senior Chinese diplomats in the United States, I feel convinced that the PRC will not encourage any outbreak of war in Korea and thereby cause instability in Northeast Asia, which might enable the Soviet Union to gain more influence at China's expense. China's experiences in the Indochina wars of 1978 and 1979 made the Chinese realize that since the Soviet Union currently has far better military capabilities, any military conflict in East or Northeast Asia will further Soviet expansionist designs. So, as far as I could gather from interviews and research during my visits to Beijing from 1976 to 1979, the Chinese are not likely to give any encouragement to North Korea to resort to force in order to unify the country.

President Kim Il-Sung's sudden visit to Beijing in April 1975, just before the fall of Saigon, was interpreted in some quarters as evidence that following the communist success in Indochina, the North Koreans were seeking support for a military venture of their own. If a revolution were to occur in South Korea, President Kim Il-Sung said in Beijing on April 18, 1975, "we as one and the same nation will not just look at it with folded arms, but will strongly support the South Korean people."[30]

But Kim Il-Sung received little encouragement from the Chinese, who made it clear in a joint communiqué that although backing Kim Il-Sung's policy toward South Korea in general terms, they favored a peaceful unification. The North Koreans have probably noted with concern that the Chinese are not as bitterly opposed as they used to be to the presence of U.S. troops in Asia, although it is true that the Chinese press and the Chinese representatives at the United Nations demand the withdrawal of U.S. forces in Korea. *People's Daily,* for instance, in an editorial on July 4, 1975, strongly demanded the withdrawal of U.S. forces from South Korea, and similar views have been expressed by the Chinese diplomats at the United Nations on many occasions. But when one discusses the Korean problem with the Chinese, one gets the clear impression that China does not want another war in Korea. I had a lengthy discussion with Chinese diplomats in August 1975 after two U.S. soldiers had been killed by the North Koreans because of a "tree-cutting incident," and I was fully satisfied that the Chinese were genuinely anxious to avoid any military confrontation. However, they made it clear that if the United States were to resort to force against North Korea, they would give full support to North Korea against the U.S. aggression, because if a communist ally becomes the victim of foreign aggression, the Chinese, true to their ideological commitments, must come to the aid of that ally. It is my conclusion that the Chinese are committed to the concept of one Korea, but they favor a peaceful reunification; unless North Korea becomes a victim of aggression, they are not expected to support any plan for resorting to arms in order to achieve the goal of reunification.

The Chinese also criticize the Soviet Union for failing to endorse North Korea's desire for an independent and peaceful reunification and for encouraging the continued existence of two Koreas by developing contacts with Seoul.[31] China has also opposed the South Korean proposal that both North and South Korea be admitted to the United Nations as an attempt to perpetuate two Koreas. Kissinger's proposal, made on September 22, 1975, for a conference at which the United States, China, and both Koreas would discuss ways to preserve the armistice agreement and other measures to reduce tension was rejected by China on the grounds that the Korean question should be solved by the Korean people themselves without foreign interference.

In the new balance of power in the Asian-Pacific region, China seems to have adopted a new line about the U.S. military presence in Asia. Rather than oppose it, except on Taiwan, they have decided to regard it as a necessary evil to counterbalance the Soviet Union's expansionist designs in the area. It was not even clear whether President Carter's policy of withdrawing U.S. troops from South Korea had been received with unqualified approval in Beijing. China is more worried about Soviet social imperialism than about U.S. imperialism and is genuinely interested in peace and stability in Asia. Any military confrontation, whether in Korea or in South or Southeast Asia, is not welcome in Beijing.[32]

Post-Mao China is expected to follow Mao and Zhou's policy of working for a unification of Korea without provoking or encouraging any armed conflict between the two Koreas or any increase of tension between them, and Admirals Elmo Zumwalt and Worth H. Bagley agreed with that expectation in their analysis of the strategic situation in the region.[33] One should not conclude, however, that China's policy toward South and North Korea has changed in any significant way. Beijing's opposition to the Japanese prime minister's conclusion of the Tokyo-Seoul agreement on the joint development of the continental shelf is an illustration of Beijing's continued policy toward South Korea. Beijing is not likely to welcome any violent change in the status quo in the Korean Peninsula unless one of the Koreas causes a radical shift in the Sino-Soviet rift. There was a report that South Korea is the only Asian country other than Mongolia to support the Brezhnev Asian collective security plan,[34] but neither Moscow nor Beijing commented on that report, which indicates its lack of authenticity or seriousness of purpose.

The Sino-Japanese treaty of peace and friendship, signed in August 1978, caused some worry in North Korea, but the Chinese leaders assured their friends in Pyongyang of China's continued support of the Democratic People's Republic of Korea (DPRK), which China regards as the sole government of Korea. Post-Mao China's strong man, Deng Xiaoping, made a visit to Pyongyang in August 1978 as the leader of the Chinese delegation to the thirtieth anniversary of the founding of DPRK, and during his stay, Deng reaffirmed China's policy toward the unification of Korea and sought to mollify the DPRK's reservations about the Sino-Japanese peace treaty and about China's growing ties with Japan and the United States.

China's current policy toward the Korean Peninsula was reaffirmed by Chinese Vice Foreign Minister Han during a visit to Tokyo in March 1980 when Han is reported to have assured the Japanese government that Beijing considered the division of the peninsula and the presence of U.S. troops in South Korea as "acceptable" – heightened tensions in the peninsula would cause China unwanted problems in its improving relations with Japan and the United States.[35] A similar hint was conveyed to Pyongyang when Chinese Vice-Chairman Li Xiannian went there to attend the Korean Workers' Party (KWP) Congress held on October 10–14, 1980, as Li's message was that China would not support destabilization of the peninsula.[36]

China and Indochina

Hanoi has turned out to be an important regional power in Southeast Asia, and Beijing was not happy about the Moscow-Hanoi entente after the 1975 communist victory in Indochina, to which the PRC had also contributed. According to the International Institute for Strategic Studies (London), North Vietnam had, at the end of the Vietnam War, 700,000 men under arms, 900 Soviet medium tanks, and 60 light tanks. It had also captured a large quantity of U.S. arms and equipment, including one squadron of F-5 fighters.[37] There had been a 500,000-man South Vietnam army, many of whom must have been "reeducated" and absorbed into the united Vietnam armed forces. Hanoi's biggest problem is economic reconstruction after a decade of war and destruction, and the only solid source of economic assistance has been the Soviet Union and its satellite Eastern European countries. China does not have the capacity to undertake any major economic assistance to Vietnam, and subsequent developments have made Vietnam's chances of getting any assistance from the United States, which was talked about after the 1973 cease-fire, bleak. So Hanoi has had to rely on Moscow for Vietnam's urgent need for economic reconstruction, just as China itself turned toward Moscow in the 1950s as the only external source of economic assistance.

But, as I could gather from my talks in Beijing in 1976, the Chinese seem to be confident that time and geography are in their favor. Hanoi, they noted, "is not likely to be a satellite of Moscow or of any other power, including China. The Vietnamese have made such sacrifices for more than a decade that they will not be a satellite of any big power."[38] China, like the United States, was worried that the Soviet Union might get a base at Cam Ranh Bay, but there is no evidence as yet that the Soviet Union will get such facilities. "It would be a major shift," as Philip C. Habib pointed out, "in terms of deployment in the area if Cam Ranh Bay could be a substantial Soviet naval installation."[39] The Soviet presence in the area, through fleet movements and through Moscow's relations with Hanoi, caused concern in both Beijing and Washington, but the Chinese still took the "long-term view" and seemed to be hopeful that Moscow's bids in Hanoi cannot be successful.

In 1975–1977, there was a triangular diplomacy between Moscow, Hanoi, and Beijing; its future course was still uncertain, but its potential impact on the emerging balance of power in Southeast Asia following the 1975 communist victory in Indochina was bound to be great. Beijing did not seem to be unhappy at the talks between Washington and Hanoi in the post–Vietnam War period, and China would probably welcome a limited rapprochement between the United States and Vietnam, which might reduce Hanoi's dependence on Moscow for economic and technical assistance.

Tensions in Indochina

When Chairman Mao died, the top leadership of the Vietnamese Politburo showed up at the Chinese embassy in Hanoi to mourn the death of an "esteemed and beloved friend."[40] There were several visits by Vietnamese top leaders to Beijing in the post-Mao era, including visits by party boss Le Duan, Defense Minister Vo Nguyen Giap, and others, but the dormant tensions between Beijing and "Moscow-oriented" Hanoi already existed. The growing tensions between Cambodia, China's special ally in Indochina, and Vietnam caused worries in Beijing, and China tried to get Cambodia and Vietnam to settle the situation along their borders, but without success.

The Third Indochina War

By 1978, the cold war between China and the Soviet Union was reaching the edge of a precipice. The tensions in Indochina have had a long history, and they stem from regional and cultural differences between Vietnam, Cambodia, and Laos. Those tensions remained dormant during the first Indochina War against France and then during the war with the United States, but when Hanoi ousted the United States in 1975, the old dream of an Indochina federation, consisting of Vietnam, Cambodia, and Laos, was revived. Because of its size and military strength, Vietnam would be a dominating power in such a federation. The foreign minister of the Pol Pot regime, Ieng Sary, told an Asian ambassador posted in Beijing in 1978 that Vietnam, with Soviet backing and support, sought to exercise a sphere of influence in Southeast Asia and to establish a so-called Indochinese federation, in which smaller units such as Cambodia and Laos "will forever be bound to one another" in defense, foreign affairs, and all important matters. The Cambodians also interpreted Hanoi's publication of a 1954 French map showing the 1939 Brevie line as the border between Vietnam and Cambodia to be an effort to put pressure on them to accept the Indochina federation scheme and hence, from their point of view, "annexation by Vietnam."[41]

The Chinese, who had contributed $10 billion to Vietnam's success against the United States, watched the growing tensions in Indochina with increasing concern. Although the Chinese tried to play down the developments from 1975 to 1977, it was clear by the beginning of 1978 that Vietnam had become, to quote the words of Chinese Vice Foreign Minister Han to me during my visit to Beijing in the summer of 1978, the "agent" of Soviet "world hegemony" in Southeast Asia. Vietnam had developed its own regional hegemonic aspirations as well as becoming an "Asian Cuba" for Russian expansionism.

By mid 1978, it had become evident that the Sino-Soviet global struggle would erupt into open war in Indochina. In its initial stages, the war was to be fought, not directly by the Soviet Union and China, but by their client-states, Vietnam and Cambodia. In January 1978, President Carter's national security adviser, Zbigniew Brzezinski, predicted that "the Soviet Union and China may be engaged in a new Indo-China conflict by proxy."[42] Although Brzezinski was challenged by the Soviet news agency Tass, a U.S. intelligence report in 1978 revealed "overwhelming evidence" that Vietnam, with strong Soviet support, was preparing to attack Cambodia, China's only ally in Indochina. Hanoi's aim, according to the report, was to "reassert a historical claim to dominance over all Indo-China."[43]

Both the Soviet Union and China viewed the new war in Indochina as a crucial test of their struggle in Asia. Moscow seemed determined to humiliate China after Beijing's diplomatic victory in Tokyo in August 1978 and a similar success in Washington in December 1978. China was equally determined to preserve the independence of Cambodia "to demonstrate that Russia cannot call the turn in Asian conflicts."[44]

U.S. sources made the assessment that neither Beijing nor Moscow was thinking in terms of a direct Sino-Soviet war in Indochina but that the indirect conflict could lead to a nightmare scenario in which Russia and China would be inexorably drawn deeper into a war. Neither China nor Russia could afford to see its client-state in Indochina lose the war because of the wider implications such a loss would have in the global struggle.

Hence, the new wars in Indochina in 1978 and 1979 added impetus to the growing Sino-Soviet conflict. Moscow sought to establish a strategic foothold in Southeast Asia, with the aim of outflanking China. The Kremlim leaders feared the impact of China's diplomatic offensive among the ASEAN countries, Australia, and New Zealand, and particularly China's successes in strengthening ties with Japan and the United States. The upshot was Vietnam's aggression against Cambodia in December 1978 and the subsequent Chinese military actions against Vietnam in February 1979.

Vietnam's Invasion of Cambodia

The Vietnam-Cambodia armed clashes began in early 1978. Simultaneously, tension arose on the Sino-Vietnamese border, and the

Vietnamese government began to harass its 1.5 million ethnic Chinese minorities. When China, in retaliation, put a total ban on its aid to Vietnam, Moscow gave all-out support to that country. In June 1978, Vietnam became the tenth full member of the Council for Mutual Economic Assistance (COMECON), the communist economic grouping of Eastern Europe under Moscow's leadership. Ultimately, the Soviet Union and Vietnam signed a treaty of friendship on November 3, 1978, modeled on the treaty of friendship Moscow had signed with India on the eve of the third Indo-Pakistani War in 1971. The Kremlin leaders seem to have given the go ahead signal for Vietnam's military operations against Cambodia, as they had in 1971 for India to attack Pakistan, China's special ally in South Asia. Once again, Moscow was encouraging a powerful regional power to attack its weaker neighbor to further Soviet global influence at the expense of China.

Vietnam commenced military operations against Cambodia on December 25, 1978. In a two-week blitz, the Vietnamese reached Cambodia's capital city, Phnom Penh, and ousted the China-supported Pol Pot regime of Cambodia. The defeat signified a military/diplomatic victory for the Soviet Union and a humiliation and setback for China, which had only a month earlier (December 15, 1978) established full diplomatic relations with the United States.

The noncommunist countries of Asia, particularly Japan and the ASEAN countries, were alarmed by the combined Soviet-Vietnamese military action against a smaller neighbor. Vietnam had advocated a zone of peace in Southeast Asia, but its aggression in collusion with a superpower destroyed that idea. Another consequence of Vietnam's aggression was the suspension of talks about the normalization of relations between Hanoi and Washington. Although the Pol Pot regime had been universally condemned for its gross violations of human rights, both in the United Nations and elsewhere, Vietnam's aggression against Cambodia produced worldwide disapproval and shock. In the United Nations, the United States and China joined the Asian countries in condemning Vietnam's incursion into Cambodia and demanded the withdrawal of foreign troops from that country. The UN resolution was, of course, vetoed by Vietnam's ally, the Soviet Union.

The Chinese Reaction

China now faced a challenge and a dilemma. It could not afford to remain a passive spectator of the overthrow of its ally in Indochina, but any military action against Vietnam, now linked with the Soviet Union by a friendship treaty, could lead to a direct confrontation with Moscow. China found itself faced with two unacceptable alternatives: to lose its prestige in Asia and be labeled a "paper dragon" or to chance a direct and disastrous confrontation with Moscow.

The strong man of post-Mao China, Deng Xiaoping, visited the United States in January and early February of 1979. In his various speeches, and particularly in his exclusive talks with President Carter, Deng made it clear by indirection that China would have to take some military measure against Vietnam. The U.S. government expressed concern about the proposed action, which Beijing called a "punitive measure," against Hanoi, because Washington feared a direct Sino-Soviet armed conflict with all its grave consequences. Deng also stopped in Tokyo and presumably informed the Japanese leaders of the Chinese decision to act against Vietnam. The world probably came closer to a war involving the major powers than at any time since World War II because the chain of actions and reactions in the Asian-Pacific region, as a result of a direct Sino-Soviet armed conflict, could have had many ramifications.

As many as 150,000 to 170,000 Chinese troops, according to a U.S. intelligence source, massed along the Sino-Vietnamese border.[45] China charged that Vietnam had violated its borders, thereby endangering the peace of China; Vietnam then countered with a complaint of naked aggression by a big power.[46] Finally, the Chinese military action began on February 17, 1979, and continued for seventeen days until China announced the withdrawal of its troops on March 5, 1979. China had expected a quick victory, such as in the 1962 Sino-Indian War. The military victory was neither so easy nor so successful, however, in 1979 as it had been in 1962, but it did save China's image as a major power in Asia.

The Aftermath of New Wars in Indochina

Indochina has been the scene of fighting for more than three decades. First there was the war against colonial French rule in the 1950s and then the U.S. Vietnam War in the 1960s. Next there was "the Sino-Soviet war by proxy" and, finally, the open wars between Vietnam and Cambodia and Vietnam and China in 1978–1979.

When Vietnam, backed by a friendship treaty with Moscow, invaded and defeated China's ally, Cambodia, a *pax Sovietica* seemed to be in the process of being established not only in Indochina, but in the whole of Southeast Asia. ASEAN countries seemed to be worried about future joint Soviet-Vietnam military adventures, and China was running the risk of proving it was a "paper dragon." China, it was alleged, could not stop the Soviet-backed Indian invasion of its ally, Pakistan, in 1971, which had led to greater Soviet influence in South Asia. In fact, China had never condoned Pakistan's military actions in Bangladesh, nor had China ever given Pakistan any assurance of military intervention against India in the 1971 war; yet that 1971 South Asian crisis had adversely affected Beijing's image.

China's punitive action against Vietnam, with its grave risk of Soviet intervention, was a major national issue for the PRC, and the following results seem now to be emerging as a result of China's military action against Vietnam in 1979.

Negative Aspects

1. Vietnam's hostility toward China is likely to continue, and Soviet influence in Indochina will dominate, at least temporarily.
2. China's objective of overthrowing the pro-Hanoi regime in Cambodia has not yet been achieved, and Cambodia, Laos, and Vietnam are, at least for the time being, united against the PRC.
3. China failed to elicit any direct international support for its military intervention in Vietnam.
4. China's military performance was not impressive during the invasion itself, and a previously concealed weakness was therefore revealed to China's potential adveraries.

Positive Aspects

1. China gave Vietnam a real military jolt and thus demonstrated that any country signing a friendship treaty with Moscow is not immune from countermilitary action by any other major power. That demonstration should have a stabilizing effect, not only in Southeast Asia, but also for countries such as Afghanistan, Iraq, and South Yemen as well as African and Latin American countries. The myth of a Soviet "automatic military backing" is at least tarnished.
2. ASEAN countries are now less worried about any joint Hanoi-Moscow military adventures in Southeast Asia.
3. Senior Chinese diplomats in both the United States and Asia told me that they were confident that national uprisings in Indochina against the Hanoi-dominated regimes in Cambodia and Laos would grow stronger, just as anti-Indian feelings arose in Bangladesh soon after 1971. According to this Chinese diplomatic assessment, Vietnam's regional hegemony received a big setback, as did its dream of an Indochina federation. In particular, China feels confident that a national hero like Prince Norodom Sihanouk will soon emerge in Cambodia and that China will support that person fully to contain the Soviet influence.
4. Although the ASEAN countries will continue to follow a policy of nonalignment in the Sino-Soviet rift, they have seemed, with the possible exception of Indonesia, more amicably inclined toward China than toward the Soviet Union.

After more than a year and a half, the mighty Vietnamese military machine has failed to stamp out the guerrilla army of the Pol Pot regime in Kampuchea and thus consolidate its position as the unchallenged ruler of Indochina. It also looks as though the 25,000 Khmer Rouge troops, with overt assistance from China and with covert Thai help, will continue to oppose the Vietnamese occupation of their country. This is an encouraging development for the ASEAN countries because they still recognize, though reluctantly, the Pol Pot regime. The ASEAN countries have never condoned the atrocities of the Pol Pot regime, but they realize that it is the only effective obstacle to Hanoi and Moscow's joint military and political adventures, not only in Indochina, but also in Thailand and other areas of Southeast Asia. In the spring of 1980, there were, however, indications that the ASEAN countries were getting weary of the unending confict in Kampuchea.

The United States has also called for a political settlement of Indochina's problems. The U.S. assistant secretary of state for Far East Asia and Pacific affairs, Richard Holbrooke, was reported to be suggesting that the ASEAN countries seek some accommodation with Hanoi in order to prevent a further strengthening of the Soviet position in Indochina. On April 2, 1980, Holbrooke said: "The Vietnamese are truly at a crossroads. They can be peaceful participants in the region, establishing good relations with ASEAN and seeking to reduce their tensions with China or they can become, whether they intend it or not, a Soviet stalking house in Southeast Asia."[47] These new developments have caused serious concern in China, and the senior Chinese vice foreign minister, Han Nianlong, has warned against "the dangers of moves for a compromise and settlement" with what Beijing sees as "the global hegemonist the Soviet Union and its regional partner, Vietnam."[48]

But Vietnam's armed incursion into Thailand on June 23, 1980, changed the situation dramatically in favor of China's position with the ASEAN countries and reduced any chances of a compromise between Hanoi and the ASEAN countries. Vietnam's armed attack was the result of Thailand's three-week-old program of repatriating refugees to Kampuchea, and there was also a minisummit of Soviet, Vietnamese, and Kampuchean leaders in Moscow. Hanoi considered the repatriation of the Kampuchean refugees from Thai border camps as a thinly disguised cover for the infiltration of Khmer Rouge guerrillas, and that led to the Vietnamese armed intervention in Thailand. The reaction to the Vietnamese military action against one member of ASEAN was simply disastrous for Hanoi. Thailand's and Singapore's attitudes toward the Moscow-Hanoi bids in Southeast Asia were hardened, and even Indonesia and Malaysia, which were less favorably inclined toward China's policy in Indochina, had to give up their hopes of coexistence with Hanoi.

China was pleased with the outcome of the Vietnam-Thailand border conflict in June 1980. The Thai foreign minister went to Beijing in July 1980 and there denounced the Hanoi-Moscow joint ventures in Southeast Asia, which must have been most pleasing to the Chinese in view of China's ever-growing rivalry with Moscow in Asia. The Chinese assured Thailand that "if Vietnam continues to create incidents on the Thai-Kampuchean border and provoke Thailand, China would not stand idly by. . . . The Vietnamese know exactly what we mean by that."[49]

Indochinese Refugees

The legacies of the communist wars in Indochina in 1978–1979 have given the PRC new ammunition for its active diplomacy in Asia. Those legacies are the Indochinese refugee problems and the Cambodian representation issue, both in the United Nations and in other international forums.

One of the greatest tragedies of the contemporary period, comparable to Hitler's persecution of the Jews or Stalin's suppression of dissident groups in the central Asian republics, resulted from the 1978–1979 Indochina wars. Hanoi began by expelling hundreds of thousands of ethnic Chinese from Cambodia and Vietnam. That action caused destabilization in the ASEAN countries and in Hong Kong, and grave military, economic, and social problems arose for the whole of Asia, particularly Southeast Asia.

According to the Chinese interpretation, Vietnam began to "export" the refugees for three reasons: to extract money from the refugees, to create social and economic problems in Southeast Asia, and to infiltrate Russian/Vietnam agents into ASEAN countries. China's net political gain as a result of the recent Indochina wars has been augmented by the terrible image Vietnam has created for itself in its brutal treatment of its subjects. The ASEAN countries' leaders think that Hanoi and Moscow have sinister designs in forcing the exodus of the Indochinese refugees.

Most of the "boat people" (refugees) are ethnic Chinese, and Hanoi seems to intend to expel most or all of the 1.1 million Chinese citizens of Cambodia. The international impact of the refugee problem was discused at the Big Seven Nation Summit Conference in Tokyo on July 2, 1979; then at a meeting of ASEAN countries' foreign ministers in Bali later in July 1979; and finally in the old League of Nations Hall in Geneva, where delegates of sixty-five nations gathered to discuss the plight of the refugees, also in July 1979.

However, unless there is a political settlement of Indochina's problems and unless the Vietnam-Cambodia and Sino-Vietnamese tensions, which are ultimately linked with the global Sino-Soviet rift, are resolved, the agony of the refugees is not likely to be alleviated. Vietnam is afraid of, or at least pretends to be afraid of, a second and larger military action by

China, and China fears that Vietnam, backed by the Soviet Union, is preparing to wipe out the "patriotic" elements in Cambodia that are resisting Vietnam's occupation of their homeland. As long as these fears and tensions remain, the fate of the refugees looks bleak.

"However cynical it might look," noted a diplomatic observer sympathetic to the Thai concern for security, "refugees and Pol Pot's fighters remain the two main tools to badger the Vietnamese occupation force in Kampuchea."[50] However, although the Khmer Rouge fighters, adequately armed by China, can defend themselves and go behind the Vietnamese lines, the refugees huddled along the border remain a defenseless human factor.

Cambodian Representation Issue

Soviet-backed Vietnamese forces toppled the Pol Pot regime, and a puppet regime now controls the capital of Cambodia. However, Vietnam has not been able to gain control of the whole of Cambodia. In the countryside, the forces of the Pol Pot regime remain in control, and they still receive significant support from China. The present regime in Cambodia survives only because of the active support and presence of the Vietnamese troops. So the Cambodian situation is a perplexing one: The pro-Vietnamese regime cannot claim full control of the country, nor can the Chinese-backed Pol Pot forces overthrow the new regime. Many nations have condemned the excesses committed by the Pol Pot regime, yet few nations will accept the fact that an outside power — Vietnam — should invade and rule a sovereign state with a puppet regime, which survives only with the support of the conquering military forces.

At the 1978 UN General Assembly session, when the Pol Pot regime could not be unseated despite the combined efforts of Vietnam and the Soviet bloc, the Cambodian representation problem became a "hot issue." It was also "by far the most vexing issue facing the delegates" at the Sixth Nonaligned Summit Conference in September 1979.[51] At that conference, Castro's abuse of his office was most obvious in the matter of the Cambodian seat, and no satisfactory solution evolved. A lack of consensus led to a deadlock, and both the Pol Pot and Heng Samrin regimes remained unseated.

Soon after the Sixth Nonaligned Summit Conference in Havana, the Cambodian representation issue was again discussed at the Thirty-fourth Session of the General Assembly in September 1979. The issue was then sent to the 152-nation General Assembly plenary session, which voted a clear 2 to 1 victory for the Pol Pot regime. China, the ASEAN countries, the United States, and Yugoslavia joined in supporting the incumbent, and the Soviet Union, its bloc, Vietnam, and a handful of Third World Soviet friends or allies were the challengers. The sharp polemical exchanges between the Chinese and the Russian ambassadors during the debate reflected the growing rift between the two communist giants in Asia.

The question of Cambodia's representation was raised again at the 1980 session of the UN General Assembly. The ASEAN countries again took the lead in the campaign to shore up support for the Pol Pot regime's continued seat at the United Nations, notwithstanding their disgust for the atrocities of that regime. The United States endorsed the ASEAN move; India recognized the Vietnamese-backed Heng Samrin government in Cambodia; and Britain withdrew its recognition of the Pol Pot regime but did not recognize the Heng Samrin government. India's recognition could have made some nonaligned countries abstain when the issue came to a vote, but the ASEAN countries and their supporters were confident of success.[52] The voting took place on October 31, 1980, and the General Assembly rejected a move to oust the representative of the Pol Pot government. The combination of the Southeast Asian nations, China, and the United States won enough Third World votes to reject the combined efforts of Moscow and Hanoi to replace Cambodia's representative at the United Nations.[53] The issue was raised at the 1981 UN General Assembly session, and the result was the same.

Notes

1. For details see G. W. Choudhury, *India, Pakistan, Bangladesh, and the Major Powers: Politics of a Divided Subcontinent* (New York: Free Press, 1975).

2. See Prime Minister Nehru's speech delivered to Lok Sabha on September 30, 1954, in *Jawaharlal Nehru's Speeches,* Vol. 3, *1953–57* (New Delhi: Ministry of Information and Broadcasting, 1958), pp. 240–243.

3. *People's Daily* (Peking), June 26, 1970.

4. Ibid.

5. Referred to in *Scinteia* (Bucharest), October 26, 1971.

6. Based on the author's interviews and research in London.

7. See *Recognizing the People's Republic of China: The Experiences of Japan, Australia, France, and West Germany,* Report by the Foreign Affairs and National Defense Divsion, Congressional Research Service, Library of Congress (Washington, D.C.: Government Printing Office, 1979), p. 8.

8. Joseph Kraft, "Japan's Crucial Role in Sino-American Relations," *Washington Post,* December 17, 1975.

9. *Recognizing the People's Republic of China,* p. 11.

10. Tomas W. Robinson, "China's Asia Policy," *Current History* (September 1980), p. 1.

11. See Golam W. Choudhury, *Brezhnev's Collective Security Plan for Asia* (Washington, D.C.: Center for Strategic and International Studies, Georgetown University, 1976), p. 37.

12. Based on the author's research and interviews in London.

13. Japan, Ministry of Defense, *A Study of Japan's Defense Issues* (Tokyo, 1975), p. 16.

14. Based on the author's research and interviews in London.

15. *Washington Post,* December 8, 1979.

16. See Chapter 6 in this book.

17. See "From Foe to Friend," *Newsweek,* October 30, 1978.

18. *New York Times,* January 19, 1976.

19. *Peking Review,* July 30, 1976.

20. *New York Times,* June 20, 1978.

21. Ibid.

22. See Tracy Dahlby, "A Great Alliance as the Lion Awakes," *Far Eastern Economic Review,* November 3, 1978, pp. 10–12.

23. Ibid., p. 11.

24. *Dawn,* (Karachi), October 26, 1978.

25. Andrew H. Malcolm, "Japan and China Sign 8-Year Pact for $20 Billion Industrial Deals," *New York Times,* February 17, 1978.

26. Ibid.

27. *Washington Post,* December 8, 1979.

28. See William Chapman, "China Turns to Nemesis Japan as Economic Model," *Washington Post,* October 30, 1978.

29. *Washington Post,* December 8, 1979.

30. *People's Daily* (Peking), April 19, 1975.

31. Based on the author's research and talks with Chinese leaders in Beijing and Chinese ambassadors abroad.

32. Ibid.

33. Elmo Zumwalt and Worth H. Bagley, "Strategic Determination in the Pacific: The Dilemma for the U.S. and Japan," *Pacific Community* (Tokyo), (January 1978), pp. 115–129.

34. David Bonavia, "Security: The Soviet Way," *Far Eastern Economic Review,* May 20, 1977.

35. See Ron Richardson, "Pyongyang Begins to Realign Relationship," *Far Eastern Economic Review,* November 14, 1980, pp. 45–46.

36. Ibid.

37. See U.S., Congress, House of Representatives, Committee on International Relations, *Shifting Balance of Power in Asia: Implications for Future U.S. Policy,* Hearings before the Subcommittee on Future Foreign Policy Research and Development, 94th Cong. (Washington, D.C.: Government Printing Office, 1976), pp. 150–151.

38. Based on the author's research and talks with Chinese leaders in Beijing, July 1976.

39. U.S., Congress, *Shifting Balance of Power in Asia,* pp. 150–151.

40. See "China '77," *Far Eastern Economic Review,* October 7, 1977.

41. Based on the author's reading of a memo written by the Cambodian embassy in Beijing, May 12, 1978 (through the courtesy of the Bangladesh ambassador in Beijing).

42. *Washington Post,* January 4, 1978.
43. *U.S. News and World Report,* November 27, 1978, pp. 56–58.
44. Ibid.
45. *Washington Post,* February 10, 1979.
46. For the texts of the Chinese and Vietnamese statements, see *New York Times* and *Washington Post,* February 18, 1979.
47. *New York Times,* April 3, 1980.
48. See *Far Eastern Economic Review,* April 18, 1980, p. 8.
49. Ibid., August 1, 1980, pp. 21–22.
50. Ibid., July 25, 1980, pp. 9–11.
51. Ibid., September 21, 1979, pp. 12–13, and *Newsweek,* September 17, 1979.
52. Ibid., September 22, 1980, pp. 12–13.
53. *New York Times,* October 14, 1980.

9
China and Its Asian Neighbors: Southeast and South Asia

China's view of a world dominated by the rivalry of the two super-powers—the United States and the USSR—and its attempt to identify itself as belonging to the developing countries of the Third World have not prevented it from pursuing major foreign policy objectives in Southeast Asia. These objectives include China's being the center of influence in Southeast Asia—an area of close geographic proximity to China and of great strategic importance to its security—but the competition from the Soviet Union is a limiting factor in Beijing's bid to acquire influence and power in Southeast Asia, as in many other parts of the Third World.

Prediplomatic Relations Era (1970-1974)

As China emerged from its self-imposed diplomatic isolation after the Cultural Revolution of 1966–1969, and as the situation in Southeast Asia became more uncertain in the context of the proposed U.S. withdrawal from the area under the Nixon doctrine, China began to make an effort to cultivate better relations with its neighbors in Southeast Asia—such as Thailand, the Philippines, Malaysia, Indonesia, and Singapore. However, those countries were alienated from China because of its "revolutionary policy" toward the Asian countries, and by 1970, Beijing had "opted for a long-term, gradual political and economic strategy designed to reassure neighboring states suspicious of Chinese intentions."[1]

In the 1950s and 1960s, China sharply attacked the U.S. military presence in Southeast Asia, and SEATO and U.S. military bases in Southeast Asian countries like Thailand and the Philippines were the targets of severe condemnation. Pakistani Prime Minister Husain Shahid Suhrawardy, while justifying his country's participation in SEATO, told Chairman Mao in 1956 that the "Americans are not enemies of China but only afraid of China's designs in Asia." Mao's reply was: "If because the United States is afraid of us, they must control the Philippines, Thailand and Japan, then we can say that because we are afraid of the United

States, we must control Mexico, Nicaragua and even Pakistan."[2]

But the whole situation changed, almost dramatically, when, thanks to China's growing fear of a Soviet preemptive attack on its northern border in 1969–1970, China and the United States began to normalize relations, and China and Japan also established full diplomatic relations. China was no longer worried about either the U.S. military presence in Asia or Japan's alleged remilitarization. China then began an active policy of cultivating closer relations with its close neighbors in Southeast Asia and no longer denounced noncommunist Southeast Asian leaders as "stooges of American imperialism." The Chinese also reduced their practice of publicizing the alleged successes of Chinese-backed insurgent activities in Southeast Asian countries.[3] The United States was no longer regarded as China's number-one enemy; that status was given to the Soviet social imperialists, and as a result, China's policy toward its Southeast Asian neighbors, many of who were U.S. allies, changed profoundly. There were corresponding changes in the attitudes of the Southeast Asian countries. In the context of the new U.S. policy, as enunciated under the Nixon doctrine and by the normalization of relations with China, Southeast Asian countries also wanted to establish closer relations with Beijing, and were eager to participate in regional groups such as ASEAN.

On November 26–27, 1971, the foreign ministers of the ASEAN countries met in Malaysia to prepare a plan for a zone of peace, freedom, and neutrality for Southeast Asia, which would be guaranteed by the three major powers—the United States, the USSR, and the PRC. Initially, the Chinese attitude toward a neutral Southeast Asia was circumspect, but when the Soviet Union began to preach the virtues of its collective security plan for Asia, Beijing began to look upon the plan favorably. Kuala Lumpur Radio reported on May 18 and 19, 1972, that Premier Zhou Enlai had reacted favorably to the Malaysian proposal for a neutral Southeast Asia, though the Voice of the Malayan Revolution (VMR), a pseudoclandestine radio station broadcasting from South China, had said on April 17, 1972, that the "Razak clique was alarmed by the development of armed struggle throughout Southeast Asia: your [Razak's] so-called guarantee of neutrality in Southeast Asia by the big powers is, to put it bluntly, only a by-product of the Nixon Doctrine. Your policy of non-alignment is only a cover for your service to imperialism in opposing communism, the people and China."[4]

Hitherto and especially during the Cultural Revolution, China had made its presence felt in Southeast Asia mainly through its support of insurgent movements. Chinese backing of such movements subsequently declined, but the Southeast Asian countries were among the last to benefit from the change of atmosphere in Beijing. The improved Sino-American relations have affected the attitudes of both China and its neighbors, and Southeast Asia's ties with the West, which have in any case been loosened, are no longer looked upon with disfavor by the Chinese, who see them as a counterbalance to the Soviet Union's advances.

Yet until 1973, China had diplomatic relations with only three countries in the area—Burma, Laos, and North Vietnam—and two rebel regimes—the Vietcong Provisional Revolutionary Government (PRG) and Prince Sihanouk's Royal Government of National Union of Cambodia (RGNUC). Links had been established with Indonesia in 1950, but those had been suspended in 1967 because of a deterioration of relations in the wake of an attempted communist coup in that country two years before, and China had had only informal contacts with the five members of the Association of Southeast Asian Nations (ASEAN)—Indonesia, Malaysia, the Philippines, Singapore, and Thailand. Tentative moves toward trade with Thailand and the Philippines took on a new aspect in November 1973, when there were reports that China had offered to supply oil to those countries. Official talks about the establishment of diplomatic relations between China and Malaysia and other Southeast Asian countries began in June 1973, but they had little result until 1974–1975, though the Malaysian prime minister, Tun Abdul Razak, said at a press conference in Singapore on November 15, 1973, that it was only a question of time. Should obstacles be removed, the other ASEAN countries were expected to follow suit.[5]

The ASEAN nations put China on a par with the Soviet Union and the United States as a major power, according to a Jakarta Radio commentary of September 5, 1973, which cited China's membership in the nuclear club and its 1972 veto against Bangladesh in the UN Security Council as qualifying it for that status. The broadcast recalled that all three powers were supposed to guarantee the neutral zone in Southeast Asia, which had been proposed in the ASEAN states' Kuala Lumpur Declaration of November 1971. The Chinese had not publicly stated their attitude toward that proposal, though the Thai deputy foreign minister, Major-General Chartichai Chunhawan, had told a press conference in Bangkok on August 29, 1973, that the Chinese had recently expressed support for the ASEAN policy, and the leader of a Malaysian trade mission in May 1971 had reported that Zhou Enlai had reacted favorably to the Malaysian idea from which the Kuala Lumpur Declaration stemmed. But China's ambivalence was apparent when the neutralization proposal was attacked by two of the pseudoclandestine radio stations that broadcast from South China in support of communist insurgents—the Voice of the Malayan Revolution (VMR) and the Voice of the People of Burma (VPB).[6]

The continued existence of those two stations and of the Voice of the

People of Thailand (VPT) was one of the biggest obstacles to better relations between China and its Southeast Asian neighbors. Although the VPT and VMR date from 1962 and 1969, respectively, the inauguration of the VPB in 1971 showed that this kind of propaganda support was not simply a relic of a more militant phase of Chinese policy, but was a device to help insurgents while disclaiming official responsibility for doing so. China's own propaganda organs could thus reduce the amount of material likely to be offensive to the Southeast Asian governments. However, Beijing's approach was again revealed during the visit of a Chinese table tennis team to Thailand and Malaysia, when the VPT on June 17, 1973 (followed by the VMR on June 28, 1973), welcomed the "envoys of peace" while attacking the host government and suggesting that public opinion had forced the visit upon it.

The pseudoclandestine radios are only one aspect, though now possibly the most important one, of Chinese aid to communist insurgents. Beijing has the problem, long faced by Moscow, of trying to reconcile the state's need for normal intergovernmental relations with the party's ideological commitment to support foreign communists and revolutionaries. The Soviet answer has often been to abandon those revolutionaries, although in Southeast Asia (outside Indochina), the fact that the local communists were mainly pro-Chinese left Moscow little choice. To emulate Soviet policy in this respect would greatly damage Beijing's revolutionary image and entail the sacrifice of a weapon in the Sino-Soviet competition for influence. The local communists, like the radio stations, are also a useful means of bringing pressure to bear on governments. Beijing will therefore continue to try to have the best of both worlds, by gradually improving relations with its neighbors while continuing to give moral support to the insurgents in those countries.

The Chinese have told Southeast Asian visitors that Beijing is obliged to support the liberation movements, though they have said that they would not interfere in internal affairs and that revolution was not exportable. "The rider that ideas know no frontiers can presumably be used to justify the pseudo-clandestine broadcasts."[7] Although the late and disgraced Chinese leader, Lin Biao, gave specific support to Southeast Asian "armed struggles" in his report to the party's Ninth Congress in 1969, Zhou Enlai spoke at the Tenth Congress, in August 1973, in general terms of the "just struggles of the Third World," but only Vietnam, Laos, and Cambodia received particular mention.[8]

Zhou Enlai assured a secret Filipino emissary, Governor Romualdez, in February 1972 that elements associated with Lin Biao had been responsible for the training of insurgent rebels in the Philippines and other Southeast Asian countries and that this practice would not continue. President Ferdinand Marcos disclosed that assurance to a U.S.

visitor in 1973,[9] but Marcos also referred to China's support of the rebel groups in his country in his speech on the second anniversary of the imposition of martial law in the Philippines in September 1973, adding, however, that he would seek a normalization of relations with Beijing.

China's trade contacts with the countries of Southeast Asia began in 1964, even before the establishment of diplomatic relations with them. The Southeast Asian governments were also concerned about Beijing's influence among the large overseas Chinese communities, although visitors had been given explicit guarantees on that issue. China has reverted to the pre–Cultural Revolution policy of abandoning its traditional claims to the allegiance of the Chinese abroad and encouraging them to become citizens of the states in which they live – at the same time, China gives them special treatment when they visit the mother country. Zhou Enlai said on November 3, 1973 at a banquet in Beijing for the Australian prime minister, Edward Whitlam, that the Chinese government was glad that many Chinese had adopted Australian nationality and was willing to help them exchange visits with relatives or to have the latter unite with them. The Chinese foreign minister, Ji Pengfei, told his Indonesian counterpart, Adam Malik, while they were both attending the Vietnam peace conference in Paris in February 1973, that the Commission for Overseas Chinese Affairs (COCA) had been abolished. China's insistence on this point was intended to underline its change of policy, particularly since COCA, when controlled by the Cultural Revolution extremists, had incited overseas Chinese to take part in subversive activities.[10] In accordance with this policy, the PRC repatriated 100,000 Chinese from Indonesia in 1966 and has refrained from complaining about the anti-Chinese campaign in Malaysia since 1971.

Era of Diplomatic Relations with Southeast Asian Countries (1974–1980)

China's relations with its Southeast Asian neighbors, many of which had close ties with the United States, began to change profoundly as the Sino-American relations began to normalize after the 1972 Peking Summit. Just as the Sino-Japanese diplomatic relationship was established soon after that summit, China's diplomatic relations with Malaysia, Thailand, and the Philippines were established by 1974–1975. Burma, as stated earlier, has had diplomatic ties with Beijing since the 1950s. China's diplomatic relationship with Indonesia has been suspended since 1967, and Singapore, the other member of ASEAN, has not wanted to establish diplomatic ties with Beijing before the Indonesians resume theirs.

So China's post–Cultural Revolution policy, begun before the deaths of Mao and Zhou Enlai, has led to the establishment of formal diplomatic relations with many major Southeast Asian countries. It has also included, as mentioned earlier, a reversal in the PRC's attitude toward ASEAN. When that group was formed in 1967, Beijing denounced it as "a new anti-China, anti-communist alliance."[11] But on January 18, 1976, Peking Radio praised the ASEAN nations' efforts at economic cooperation in the context of successive victories in their common struggle against hegemonism—*hegemonism* being the Chinese term for Soviet expansionism. The Chinese also now fully endorse the ASEAN proposal to establish a zone of peace, freedom, and neutrality in Southeast Asia as reaffirmed in ASEAN's Bali Declaration of February 24, 1976.[12]

Dichotomy Between Beijing's Diplomatic Relationships and Its Support to Insurgents in Southeast Asia

China had established diplomatic relations with three of the ASEAN countries by 1975—Malaysia, Thailand, and the Philippines—and the diplomatic ties between China and Burma date back to the early 1950s. Yet the opening of diplomatic relations between China and its Southeast Asian neighbors did not put an end to Beijing's propaganda backing for the communist rebel movements in the region. Attacks on the Malaysian government, for instance, by a radio station calling itself the Voice of the Malayan Revolution, which was based in the South China Sea, continued despite the establishment of formal relations between Beijing and Kuala Lumpur, thus underlining the contrast between China's apparent efforts to improve its image abroad and its commitment to support communist insurgents.

During 1972–1975, when Chairman Mao was alive and the leftist group, popularly known as the Gang of Four, led by Mao's wife was still the ruling elite in China, Beijing was unwilling to give up its revolutionary role in Southeast Asia. During this period, the Chinese told Southeast Asian visitors that China was committed to support liberation movements. In the joint communiqué signed by the Chinese and Malaysian prime ministers when diplomatic relations were established in May 1974, it was agreed that all foreign interference, control, and subversion were impermissible. A Malaysian paper, *Straits Times,* reported on June 2, 1974, that Chairman Mao had told the Malaysian prime minister, Tun Razak, that Malaysian terrorists were an internal movement to be dealt with as Malaysia thought best. Yet the VMR, commenting on the diplomatic links between China and Malaysia said, "The Razak clique had no alternative but to follow its imperialist masters in making the so-called readjustment to its China policy." This dichotomy between China's desire to improve relations with the existing governments of Southeast

Asia and its propaganda through clandestine radio stations in Thailand, Burma, and Malaysia reflected the internal political division in China between radicals, led by the Gang of Four and moderates under Premier Zhou Enlai and his close follower Deng, who was ousted for the second time after Zhou's death in 1976.

A statement by the government of Singapore on June 21, 1974, referred to strong indications that Chinese-backed communists were rebuilding their organizations. On the other hand, Zhou Enlai, in welcoming Tun Razak in Beijing on May 28, 1974, said that the two countries wanted "traditional friendship," and the *People's Daily* on May 28, 1974, talked about "complete accord with aspirations and interests of the peoples of China and Malaysia for our two countries to establish and develop friendly relations."

The inconsistency between Beijing's diplomatic relations and China's support of insurgent groups in the region was illustrated on the front page of a Rangoon newspaper, *Working People's Daily*, on March 26, 1974. It reported both the opening of the Takraw bridge built over the Salween River with Chinese aid and the "foreign-assisted" border insurgents in Northeast Burma. It was not clear whether Burma was once again (as during the Cultural Revolution in 1966–1969) bearing the brunt of a tougher Chinese foreign policy resulting from an increased radical influence in Beijing on the eve of the deaths of Mao and Zhou Enlai.

The Voice of the People of Thailand, like the Voice of the People of Burma or the Voice of the Malayan Revolution, continued its propaganda against the Thai government in the early 1970s. Yet Beijing's support for the Thai communist insurgents did not prevent the growth of Beijing-Bangkok state to state relations. The Thai air chief, Marshal Dawee, went to Beijing in February 1974, and Zhou Enlai told him that China no longer supported the insurgents, but the Bangkok newspaper *Nation*, on February 28, 1974, questioned whether Zhou Enlai could really have meant what he said as the Voice of the People of Thailand had called upon the Thai people on April 10, 1973, to unite in the struggle to overthrow the Thai government. Zhou Enlai was perhaps sincere in his assurances, but China had, at that time, no unified government voice on foreign policy. The rift between the moderate and radical groups was perhaps responsible for China's inconsistency in its dealings with its Southeast Asian neighbors.

Post-Mao Era

After Mao's death in 1976, China did not revert to a self-imposed isolation as it had during the Cultural Revolution but was more engaged with internal problems and problems of stability in 1976–1977. China's first year without Mao and Zhou Enlai was devoted mainly to bringing about internal cohesion and stability rather than to taking an active role in world affairs or even in Asian affairs. But by early 1978, China had reemerged on the world scene and was paying greater attention to the Asian-Pacific region. The Hua and Deng trips to Iran, Japan, and Southeast Asia as well as to Europe, both Eastern and Western, signaled China's dynamic new foreign policy. The top Chinese leaders visited more than twenty-five countries in a period of three months— June–August 1978—and they began actively cultivating friendship on a global scale, giving priority to China's Asian neighbors. The new dynamic policy is similar to Zhou Enlai's active and outward-looking foreign policy that began at the Bandung Conference in 1955 and continued until the late 1950s. There is certainly an anti-Soviet theme in the new Chinese policy. The Chinese defense minister, Xu Xiangqian, said bluntly, "Wherever the Soviet Union stirs up trouble, we shall support the people there in waging a resolute fight against it and in destroying its tentacles."[13]

In the post-Mao era, China has persisted in its efforts to cultivate better relations with all the existing governments of Southeast Asia. For example, when the ASEAN foreign ministers met in a special session in Manila on February 24, 1977, the Beijing media reported the gathering without adverse comment.[14] Moreover, China welcomed the agreement signed in 1977 by Malaysia, Indonesia, and Singapore to increase the safety of navigation through the Strait of Malacca, and the Chinese called the conclusion of the agreement "a telling blow to Soviet maritime hegemony."[15]

For the ASEAN countries, also, China is no longer "an ominous cloud on the distant horizon."[16] China's main interest in Southeast Asia since 1976 has been to increase its influence with the existing governments of the region, rather than promoting insurgent movements or championing the causes of the overseas Chinese in those countries.

Beijing, Hanoi, and ASEAN

Asia's communist rivals, Vietnam and China, have each begun an intensified campaign to win friends among the ASEAN countries, and post-Mao China's strong man, Deng Xiaoping, and the Vietnamese prime minister, Pham Van Dong, both visited ASEAN countries in October–November 1978. The aim of each of the two Asian communist countries is to increase influence, at the other's cost, among the ASEAN countries. When visiting the ASEAN countries, the two communist leaders accused each other of dark motives. Beijing accuses Vietnam of seeking to bring Southeast Asia under its regional hegemony, with the backing and blessing of the global hegemonist power, the Soviet Union. Hanoi, the Chinese theme goes, "is Moscow's new Cuba.'[17] Vietnam, on the other hand, warns the ASEAN countries of China's expansionism, saying that the ASEAN countries should view their 14 million ethnic Chinese residents as "latent fifth columnists for Peking."[18]

The ASEAN countries were baffled by the communist rivalry in wooing them, and until the Vietnam invasion of Cambodia, they wanted to maintain good neighborly relations with both Hanoi and Beijing. China endorsed ASEAN's policy, including its political–even potential military–cooperation in the region, and China also supported the plan for a neutral Southeast Asia as formulated by ASEAN. In the meantime, Hanoi began to try to sell its proposal for a zone of peace, independence, and genuine neutrality. Some of the ASEAN countries, such as Singapore, Indonesia, and the Philippines, were suspicious of Hanoi's plan and wondered if the Vietnamese plan had been inspired by Moscow, which had been unable to make any headway with its Asian collective security plan. Singapore's foreign minister, Sinnathamby Rajaratnam, asked what Hanoi meant by "independence"–Which countries in the region did Vietnam feel were not independent? Was the term a veiled reference to the remaining U.S. military bases in the Philippines, for instance? Because of China's consistent theme, Vietnam began to be suspected of being a Soviet satellite even before the Moscow-Hanoi friendship treaty of November 1978.

Although China has begun to extend friendly gestures to ASEAN, by 1980 it still had not been able to establish full diplomatic relations with two major partners of the group, Indonesia and Singapore, but both Moscow and Hanoi have established diplomatic relations with all five members of ASEAN. China realizes that Indonesia is the key member of ASEAN because of its large population, territories, and economic potential. China has put out feelers to Jakarta for a resumption of diplomatic relations, but although the civilian elements of the Indonesian government might be responsive to China's gestures, the Indonesian generals, who constitute the real power base in the country, still remember the abortive communist coup in 1965. They suspect it was backed by China, and as a result, the Indonesian generals are not yet ready to allow the functioning of a Chinese embassy in Jakarta.

Singapore, with a population that is 75 percent Chinese, has declared that it will be the last ASEAN country to establish diplomatic relations with Beijing. However, Singapore's Foreign Minister Rajaratnam is also the most outspoken critic among the noncommunist Asian leaders of Moscow and Hanoi's expansionist designs in Southeast Asia, and he takes a flexible view on China's changed role in Asia. He has said: "The Chinese, after a long period of quiescence in foreign policy, have now adopted more of an upright posture. . . . Under Chairman Mao's global revolutionary policy, the Chinese thought of Latin America, Cuba, Africa

. . . the enemy was the United States. Southeast Asia was run through their proxies, communist parties. Now [the Chinese] have come to the conclusion that it is a waste of time and money."[19] The Singapore prime minister, Lee Kuan Yew, paid a visit to China in May 1976 and declared that China has become a major factor in Asia, with an "abiding interest in Southeast Asia."[20]

Lee Kuan Yew made a second visit to China on November 12, 1980, and reaffirmed Singapore's policy of not establishing full diplomatic relations with China until Indonesia resumes its diplomatic ties with Beijing. The Chinese leaders told Prime Minister Lee that China was willing to resume diplomatic ties with Indonesia without any preconditions, but Lee's advice was to leave the matter between Beijing and Jakarta. In an interview with David Bonavia, *Far Eastern Economic Review*'s China correspondent, Lee also indicated some differences between the ASEAN's and Beijing's perceptions of the Indochinese crisis as a result of Vietnam's military intervention in Kampuchea (Cambodia). Lee stated that the Southeast Asian countries had no interest in weakening the Vietnamese position to the point where China would assume new influence through the Khmer Rouge. In spite of recent joint moves by China and the ASEAN countries to censure the Vietnamese military occupation of Cambodia, to demand the withdrawal of Vietnamese troops from there, and to support the continued seating of the Pol Pot regime in the United Nations, there are still differences between China's and the ASEAN countries' objectives concerning a solution of the current crisis in Indochina. Lee told Bonavia, "We are looking at the same world scene through different lenses: a wide-angle, fish-eye lens for China, a zoom lens for Singapore."[21] According to Lee, China's approach to the Indochinese crisis is wider because of China's opposition to the Soviet Union's global policy while the ASEAN countries' interest lies in regional peace and stability. In the meantime, Moscow's attempt to have Hanoi attend a meeting of the Warsaw Pact foreign ministers in October 1980 raised further suspicions among the Southeast Asian countries about Vietnam's growing links with Moscow (the attempt failed because of Romania's opposition).

Chinese leaders paid return visits to Southeast Asian countries in 1978. Vice-Premier Li Xiannian paid a successful visit to the Philippines in March 1978, returning President Marcos's visit to China in June 1975 when the two countries established diplomatic relations. Relations between Beijing and Manila have grown stronger and closer since the diplomatic ties were established in 1975. There have been regular exchanges of trade and cultural missions, and China and the Philippines are also prepared to soft-pedal a territorial dispute over some remote islands in an oil-rich area of the South China Sea in the interests of overall friendship between the two countries. At the end of Li's visit, the Beijing government said: "China is willing to resume or establish relations with all the countries of the region. The government and the people of China support them in their efforts to strengthen economic cooperation and bring about neutralization of Southeast Asia."[22]

Senior Vice–Premier Deng Xiaoping paid an equally rewarding visit to Burma and Nepal in February 1978. Deng's visit was part of a well-calculated diplomatic move to further China's interests on its southern flanks, which are strategic passageways for India and China's Yunnan and Xinjiang provinces, and Beijing wanted to ensure that the strategic areas are not exposed to "intrigue from the Soviet Union or its proxies."[23] Burma wanted assurances from the Chinese leader that Beijing would control, if not totally stop, its support of the insurgent movement in that country, and Nepal wanted China's support for its zone of peace proposal. Deng gave the desired assurances to both Burma and Nepal as a good understanding between China and its close neighbors is mutually beneficial.

Deng also made an important tour of three ASEAN countries— Thailand, Malaysia, and Singapore—in November 1978. Although he got a warm welcome and support in Thailand, his receptions in Malaysia and Singapore were far more reserved. Summarizing the Malaysian reaction to Deng's visit, a Malaysian cabinet minister said: "He wants to give us the impression he is honest and has the authority to speak. His honesty is to the extent of China's interests."[24] This pragmatic appraisal of the Chinese visit—politeness without enthusiasm—distinguished the Malaysian reception from that of Thailand. In Bangkok, the Thai government pulled out all the stops of Thai hospitality and consistently muted its doubts about China's policy toward Southeast Asia, but the Malaysian government's welcome to the Chinese leader did not go beyond standard courtesies. The differences in the receptions reflect the way Thailand and Malaysia view Chinese policy in Asia, particularly Southeast Asia. Thailand, with its long border with Vietnam and Laos, is anxious to get full support from Beijing, but Malaysia, which has had bitter experiences because of communist insurgent movements and which has a large Chinese population, has some reservations about Beijing's policy of peaceful coexistence with China's next-door neighbors. During Deng's visit to Singapore, a similar fear of China's influence on the local population (mainly ethnic Chinese) was evident.

Although Deng did not visit Indonesia during his November 1978 Southeast Asian tour, his travels to the three Southeast Asian countries he did visit produced commentary that shed light on Jakarta's outlook concerning China. Prior to Deng's 1978 tour, China and Indonesia had appeared to be moving toward a resumption of diplomatic relations, but some of Deng's remarks during his tour prompted the Indonesian foreign minister, Mochtar Kusumaatmadja, to declare that "the issue of Indonesia-China relations has been put back to mothball."[25]

Yet the general trend in the area, even before the Vietnamese invasion of Cambodia in December 1978, was a tilt toward China. The ASEAN countries, with Indonesia the only possible exception, were already more favorably inclined toward China than toward Moscow or its client, Hanoi. The cold war polarities in Asia were being replaced by a "soft alignment" among the United States, Japan, China, ANZUS, and ASEAN, and the Sino-Soviet cold war appeared to be locked in a spiral of encirclement and counterencirclement. Just as the Chinese leader, Chairman Hua, penetrated into Balkans by visiting Romania and Yugoslavia, Moscow secured an even stronger foothold in the "Balkans" of Southeast Asia by drawing Vietnam into COMECON and then into a treaty of friendship in November 1978 on the eve of the communist wars in Indochina.[26]

Era of Closer Relations (1979–1980)

The Southeast Asian countries began developing their relations with Beijing after the thaw in the Sino-American relationship in 1971–1972, and particularly after the 1975 communist victory in Indochina, but the noncommunist countries of the region, particularly the ASEAN nations tried to maintain a policy of nonalignment in the Southeast Asian triangle of China, ASEAN countries, and Soviet-backed Vietnam. They were concerned about the growing entente between Moscow and Hanoi, but they were not prepared to side either with Beijing or with Hanoi over the "Reds versus Reds" struggle in Indochina or in Southeast Asia.[27]

But the situation changed in late 1978 when Vietnam's image as a neutral power in Southeast Asia was seriously damaged by its growing tie with Moscow. Hanoi was dragged into the Soviet orbit, first by becoming a mentor of the Soviet showpiece, COMECON, in June 1978 and then by entering into a de facto military alliance with Moscow in November 1978. Hanoi's talks about a neutral Southeast Asia could no longer make any headway with the noncommunist countries of the region because Vietnam had become a Soviet proxy. If Vietnam wanted to establish its credentials as a nonaligned, trusted friend of ASEAN, the 1978 friendship treaty between Moscow and Hanoi destroyed that goal. The treaty confirmed the ASEAN countries' suspicions that Vietnam considered China as its primary enemy and that the Soviet Union, aided by Vietnam, wanted to increase its power and influence, not only in Indochina, but in the whole of Southeast Asia. Article 6 of the Moscow-Hanoi treaty shows clearly that the alliance is aimed against Beijing, just as the

1971 Indo-Soviet friendship treaty had been aimed against China in the context of the tensions in the Indian subcontinent over the Bangladesh issue. It is obvious that Vietnam wants to ensure Moscow's support and backing in any armed confrontation with Beijing, just as India had wanted to ensure Soviet help against China in the 1971 Indo-Pakistani War.

China had been telling the ASEAN countries that Vietnam is merely a Soviet tool and that that country was moving quietly into a Cuban-style role in Southeast Asia,[28] and the prospects of a Soviet military base at Cam Ranh Bay in Vietnam alarmed the noncommunist Southeast Asian countries. They did not subscribe to Beijing's version of Moscow-Hanoi threats to the Southeast Asian countries, but the Vietnam invasion of Cambodia drew the ASEAN countries closer to the Chinese interpretation of Moscow and Hanoi's expansionist designs in the region.

The noncommunist countries in Southeast Asia were worried about Beijing's covert support of the communist insurgent activities against the governments of the ASEAN countries, and the communist parties of Southeast Asia were more pro-Beijing than pro-Moscow, so the noncommunist countries' apprehensions about the spread of communism were directed against China. That was one of the main reasons why China failed to establish diplomatic relations with its next-door neighbors in Southeast Asia until the 1970s and why it was not until the mid 1970s that Beijing could establish diplomatic ties with the majority of the noncommunist countries of the region. But Vietnam's invasion of Cambodia in 1978, backed by a de facto military alliance with Moscow, and the Soviet naval presence at Cam Ranh Bay in Vietnam caused worries among the Southeast Asian countries.

The Soviet Vice–Foreign Minister, Nikolai P. Firyubin, told the Japanese on May 14, 1979, that Russian warships were using Vietnam's huge military base at Cam Ranh Bay under the newly signed treaty between Moscow and Hanoi, and the Japanese deputy foreign minister, Masuo Takashima, told his Russian counterpart that the Soviet naval presence in Vietnam was causing apprehension among the countries of Southeast Asian nations and that it "runs counter to efforts for detente in Asia."[29] Beijing issued a warning to the leaders of the Southeast Asian countries: "The flames of war which Vietnam has kindled in Cambodia [Kampuchea] might spread to other Southeast Asian countries at any time."[30] After Vietnam's invasion of Cambodia in December 1978, the noncommunist countries in Southeast Asia wondered if they would become "dominoes" because of Moscow and Hanoi's expansionist designs in the region, and an emergency meeting of the ASEAN countries was held in Bangkok.

Only four months before Hanoi's blitzkrieg against Cambodia, the

Vietnamese prime minister, Van Dong, had visited Southeast Asian countries to win goodwill and to assure the ASEAN countries of Hanoi's peaceful intentions, but the Vietnamese invasion made the ASEAN countries realize the factualness of Beijing's earlier warnings about Moscow-backed Hanoi's regional hegemonist aspirations, not only in Indochina, but in Southeast Asia as a whole. The prospect of a Hanoi- and Moscow-dominated Indochinese federation consisting of Vietnam, Cambodia, and Laos was alarming to the ASEAN countries. As a senior Thai official put it: "We will have less flexibility now. There will be the five of us on one side and the three communist countries on the other. Their bargaining position is more powerful than it was."[31]

The ASEAN nations had to face the delicate choice of having closer links with Beijing, which alone could "teach a lesson" to Vietnam, or of adopting a policy of appeasement toward the Moscow-Hanoi entente. Thailand, Singapore, the Philippines, and Malaysia began moving in the direction of closer cooperation with China against the growing threats from Moscow and Hanoi's joint ventures; Indonesia still had some reservations about China.

But the course of developments in Indochina in 1979–1980 led to closer cooperation, not alliance, between Beijing and the ASEAN countries. They began to voice strong disapproval of Hanoi's military actions against Cambodia, and China and the ASEAN countries voted together at the United Nations against the Soviet-backed Hanoi action. China was obviously pleased with the new trends among the ASEAN countries' roles and policy, and the ANZUS countries and Japan also joined in condemning Hanoi's action. China's opportunities for closer collaboration with the ASEAN countries became brighter.

Then the Soviet invasion of Afghanistan in December 1979 — just one year after Vietnam's invasion of Cambodia — made the ASEAN nations really alarmed about Moscow and Hanoi's expansionist designs, about which Beijing had been preaching consistently and persistently. Condemnation of Soviet and Vietnamese military adventures in Indochina and Afghanistan became a common feature of the diplomatic efforts of both China and the ASEAN countries, and the condemnation became stronger when Vietnam crossed the Thai border in 1979, even though Bangkok was the headquarters of SEATO, the military alliance formed by the United States in 1954 against China.

Thailand had followed the U.S. policy of containment against the PRC in the 1950s and 1960s, but by 1980, Beijing and Washington had developed a common interest in safeguarding Thailand's territorial integrity and independence against the threats from Moscow's ally, Hanoi. Commenting on China's relations with Thailand, an American sinologist has pointed out:

Back in the days of the cold war, when lines were clearly drawn, Bangkok rightly feared Chinese support for the Thai communist party and for an uprising in the northeast. Every Thai government since the early 1950s has therefore looked to Washington to save itself from the Chinese. . . . for their part the Chinese merely reciprocated. . . . Peking did indeed supply the Thai communists with guns, training and propaganda . . . backed Thailand's regional foes, Vietnam and Cambodia. . . . But now look what has happened? The two capitals host each other's embassies, they trade a lot, the Thai communists have publicly been told to cool it, the bothersome radio station in Yunnan province has been shut down, Vice Premier Deng has visited Bangkok and Thailand has been advised to stick with the Americans even after their Vietnam defeat. The country is in effect under Sino-American protection. To be sure, much of this is due to Hanoi's pretentions of regional empire and Beijing's opposition to it.[32]

Beijing's subsequent punitive actions against Vietnam, though not disapproved of by the noncommunist countries of Southeast Asia, raised some concern about China's allegedly treating the region as "its own Balkan."[33] Some leaders in the region are worried that China might try to settle contentious issues, such as sovereignty over the South China Sea and its oil resources, by using military measures—as it did against Vietnam. They also seemed to be worried that China might try to protect the rights of overseas Chinese in other Southeast Asian countries since China took up the cause of the overseas Chinese in Vietnam.[34]

But on the whole, the 1978–1979 communist wars in Indochina and the subsequent Soviet invasion of Afghanistan have increased the chances of success of China's diplomatic goals in Southeast Asia, in spite of any dormant worries about China's future policy or actions in the region. The delicate balance of power in Southeast Asia following the 1975 communist victory in Indochina was disturbed by the new regional wars in 1978–1979, and the continued presence of Vietnamese armies in Cambodia and Soviet armies in Afghanistan has not improved the images of China's two communist rivals in Asia. Although China's security problems have become more serious because of Vietnam's actions on China's southern borders, Beijing's diplomatic endeavors in Southeast Asia have been enhanced by Moscow's and Hanoi's military actions against their weaker neighbors. China has become the champion of the victims of aggression in both Southeast and Southwest Asia.

Whatever reservations the ASEAN and other noncommunist countries might have about China's long-term goals in Asia, the immediate effect of the communist wars in Indochina and the Afghanistan crisis was that the noncommunist countries of the region have collaborated more closely with China, both in the United Nations and in other international forums. Their immediate concerns are about Moscow and its ally,

Vietnam. Beijing might be a threat, but not yet; that threat will arise only in the future. Obviously, present dangers must receive greater attention than future ones. So in the triangle of Beijing, the ASEAN countries, and Moscow, the developments in 1978–1979 favored China at the cost of its two powerful communist rivals, the Soviet Union and Vietnam.

China and Burma

Burma was the first noncommunist country to recognize the PRC. It has a long land frontier – 1,357 miles – with China, the Burmese Communist party has always been pro-Beijing, and any active support by Beijing of the Burmese Communist party can complicate Burma's internal security and political stability. So Burma has always sought to maintain correct and, if possible, cordial relations with the PRC.

There was a border agreement between the two countries in the 1960s, in which China showed flexibility, but Sino-Burmese relations were disrupted in 1967, during the Chinese Cultural Revolution, when Beijing's support of the Communist party of Burma became more overt. But by 1971, relations between the two countries had again improved. China, under its post–Cultural Revolution policy, began to develop friendly relations with Burma, and when Burma's President Ne Win visited Beijing in 1971, the economic and technical cooperation agreement, which dated from 1961 but had been suspended in 1967, was revived. There were also cultural exchanges in the 1970s.

Madame Deng Yingchao, widow of the late Chinese Premier Zhou Enlai, paid a seven-day goodwill visit to Burma in February 1977. The Burmese president, in welcoming Madame Deng, referred to the "traditionally close and friendly relations" between Burma and China, and Madame Deng referred to the "2,000 year old Paukpaw (kinsmen-like) friendship" between the two countries.[35] Vice-Premier Deng went to Burma in 1978, and in 1979, President Ne Win paid another goodwill visit to China and reaffirmed his country's continued friendship. Deng also assured Burma of his country's support concerning Burma's insurgent problems.

Most of the Communist parties of Southeast Asian countries are pro-Beijing, and in the 1950s and 1960s, China used its influence among the Southeast Asian Communist parties to put pressure on the governments of the region. At that time, China preferred to put priority on party to party relations over government to government relations, but thanks to the growing Sino-Soviet rivalry in Asia and China's new emphasis on its national needs for economic development under the four-modernization plans, Beijing's policy toward its Asian neighbors has changed. Beijing is now reversing that priority and giving more attention to government to government relations than to party to party relations.

China's recent attitude toward Burma, as toward other Southeast Asian countries, has been guided by a policy of maintaining friendly and closer relations with the Burmese government in Rangoon rather than of encouraging the insurgent communist movements in Burma, although the pseudoclandestine radio, Voice of the People of Burma, has not been closed. The stress, however, is now on trade and political and diplomatic relations between the two countries.

This analysis of the PRC's role in Southeast Asia may be concluded by referring to Ross Terrill's comments about China's aims in Southeast Asia. He says: "China does not need to seek dominance over Southeast Asia in the Western social science sense of dominance—even if it occurred to her to do so. It is not by the gun or by decree but by the shadow of her influence that China is powerful in Southeast Asia. . . . It will be very difficult for any power outside the region to counter China's influence in Southeast Asia."[36]

The developments in Southeast Asia in 1979–1980 seem to have substantiated Ross Terrill's forecasts. The countries of the region, whether they like it or not, have to look to Beijing for their economic, political, and security needs.

China and South Asia

China's policy toward South Asia has been noted for turbulent and unexpected developments, and China's relations with two major South Asian countries—India and Pakistan—have gone through almost revolutionary changes in the past two decades. When the PRC emerged in 1949, India, under Nehru, greeted the new regime in China with unqualified goodwill. In the initial years, 1949–1950, India was full of admiration and sympathy for the new China, and the Western concern about an international communist menace in Asia as a result of the emergence of the new regime in China had hardly any impact in India. Even in Muslim Pakistan, there was hardly any concern about the communist threat from China and no dearth of goodwill toward the regime, though in contrast to India, Pakistan displayed no romanticism about China either. Both countries were prompt in giving recognition to Communist China: India was the second of the noncommunist countries to recognize the People's Republic of China—Burma having been given the opportunity to be the first noncommunist country to recognize the new regime.

While announcing his country's recognition of the PRC on December 30, 1949, Nehru said: "It was not a question of approving or disapproving the changes that had taken place. It was a question of recognizing a major event in history and appreciating and dealing with it. The new government was a stable government and there is no force likely to supplant it or push it away."[37] According to Nehru, refusal to recognize the new China would lead to grave consequences for Asia, and he felt the world should recognize the freedom of every country "to develop according to its own way of thinking."[38] At the Colombo Conference of the British Commonwealth foreign ministers held in January 1950, Nehru urged the other members of the Commonwealth to recognize the new regime in China. In support of his argument, he told the conference that there had always been a crying need for change in China, and in recent years the Nationalist government had been unable to provide the basis of that change. He further commented that although he did not endorse the Chinese communists, they had at least given a promise of, and to that extent begun the fulfillment of, that long-needed change. They had also "in some ways, partially met the requirements of social justice, which was a crying need throughout Southeast Asia."[39]

Indian intellectuals and leaders were not even convinced that the new regime was a totally communist one, especially one of the Soviet type. Instead, they regarded it as a new form of Asian democracy in the context of the new Asian spirit and Asian awakening of which Nehru was a most brilliant spokesman.

India, under Nehru, became new China's chief supporter in the United Nations and at other international conferences. A study of the proceedings of the British Commonwealth prime ministers' conferences, such as the one I had the opportunity to make while working in the research division of Pakistan's Ministry of Foreign Affairs, would reveal that Nehru was an almost unqualified supporter of China on various issues involving international relations between 1950 and 1956.

China's policy toward the Indian subcontinent went through a number of phases. Initially, China subscribed to Mao's theory of two camps, so that Nehru's policy of nonalignment had no appeal in either Moscow or Beijing. But China was quicker in cultivating friendly relations with India soon after the Korean War, which culminated in the signing of the 1954 agreement on Tibet on the basis of Pancha Shila, or five principles of coexistence. However, the era of *Hindi-Chini bhai bhai* ("the Indians and Chinese are brothers") did not last very long, and by 1959, as a result of border disputes and armed clashes, the two largest Asian countries were drifting toward a war that finally broke out in late 1962.

The Sino-Indian border conflicts of 1962 had a profound impact on the South Asian triangle. It brought an end to the India-China friendship, and the era of Pancha Shila was replaced by an era of confrontation between the two Asian giants. India moved closer to Washington as a result of the United States' prompt response to India's request for military supplies, so the Indo-American relations, which had been bogged down by suspicion and misunderstanding since 1954 when U.S. arms aid had begun to flow to Pakistan, became warmer and closer. India's closer links with Washington caused some initial doubts in Moscow, but soon Moscow and Washington seemed to share the common objective of building up India against China. The containment of China in South and Southeast Asia seemed to have become a common objective of both the United States and the Soviet Union, and India fit into this global strategy of the two superpowers against China.

India began a huge military buildup with support and supplies from both Washington and Moscow, and that upset the balance of power in the area to the advantage of India and to the detriment of Pakistan. Pakistan – terribly upset by and bitter at its Western allies, particularly the United States – began a process of disengagement from military pacts like SEATO and CENTO and tried to improve its relations with its two big communist neighbors, China and the Soviet Union.

China moved very close to Pakistan, so a curious phenomenon developed in the South Asian triangle. There was an atmosphere of closest friendship between Pakistan and the People's Republic of China on the one hand, and on the other, the United States and Pakistan. That situation raised speculation and suspicion in many capitals. In New Delhi, it was regarded as a "Beijing-Rawalpindi axis" against India; in Moscow, it stimulated a new interest in Pakistan. The Soviet Union was not happy at China's extension of its influence in the subcontinent through Pakistan, and that unhappiness became a major factor in the Soviet Union's overtures to Rawalpindi in the period 1965 to 1970. In Washington, "Ayub's flirtation with Mao," as the new relationship was called, was a complicating factor in the relationship between the United States and Pakistan until it received the blessing of President Nixon during his twenty-two-hour visit to Pakistan in August 1969. Not only were Pakistan's links with Beijing approved of, but their potential to provide links between Washington and Beijing was fully examined during the dialogue between President Nixon and President Yahya Khan in August 1969, when the latter was asked to find out China's reaction to Nixon's new China policy.

China and the 1971 Bangladesh Movement

China was placed in a difficult position by the crisis in East Pakistan. True to its traditional sympathy for and support of the causes of national liberation, China was expected to extend support to the movement for Bangladesh, but the real question before the policymakers in Beijing was whether the movement in East Pakistan was a genuine national liberation movement or, according to Maoist interpretation, a bourgeois

movement supported and sustained by the reactionary Indian government and the socialist imperialist Soviet Union. China seems to have
come to the conclusion that the movement fell under the second descrip-
tion, but in fact, China never opposed the legitimate hopes and aspirations of the people of East Pakistan. When President Yahya visited Beijing in November 1970, Premier Zhou Enlai expressed deep concern
about the situation in East Pakistan and urged Yahya to find a rational
solution to the growing conflict between East and West Pakistan.[40] When
the elections in Pakistan were over in December, Zhou Enlai sent letters
to both Sheikh Mujibur Rahman (Mujib) and Zulfikar Ali Bhutto, the
leaders of East and West Pakistan, respectively, urging them to come to a
satisfactory settlement. But Mujib was not in a mood to listen to the
Chinese overtures or good wishes, and Bhutto was busy with his plan to
capture power at any cost; President Yahya himself was totally in-
capable of listening to any friendly advice or warning.

The civil war in Pakistan created difficult and embarrassing diplomatic
problems for China: "The crisis confronts China's leaders with a seem-
ingly irreconcilable conflict between practical and ideological goals."[41]
As an emerging major power, China could not watch with equanimity
the disintegration of Pakistan, its closest ally in South Asia, and the birth
of a new country that was destined to be friendly to New Delhi and
Moscow, both of whom China had unfriendly relations with.

When the trouble finally started in East Pakistan in March 1971,
neither the Chinese press nor the government made any hasty comment.
The first reaction was expressed in the *People's Daily* on April 11, 1971,
and it neither supported nor directly condemned Pakistan's military action in East Pakistan; similarly, it neither supported nor attacked the
Bengali movement there. Its main attack was against "open interference
in the internal matters of Pakistan" by the Indian government, and the
Soviet role was also criticized as an interference in Pakistan's internal
affairs.

The year 1971 was a successful year for Beijing's diplomacy elsewhere:
President Nixon's new China policy had enhanced China's prestige and
image among the countries of the Third World, many countries were
eager to open diplomatic relations with Beijing, and China's entry into
the United Nations was almost ensured—it finally came on the eve of the
war over Bangladesh. By contrast, South Asia was the sore point in
China's diplomacy in 1971, so the Pakistani crisis was a real source of
disappointment and embarrassment for Beijing.

Analyzing the Chinese attitude to the Bangladesh crisis, a British expert on Chinese policy took the view that the term *support* for China's attitude toward President Yahya was not correct; that China, in fact,
declared a "policy of strict non-intervention." Even Zhou Enlai's letter to

President Yahya of April 11, 1971, if one reads between the lines, can be construed "as a plea for negotiation instead of bloodshed." The expert also referred to a pamphlet, *The People's War,* written by the Maoist communist party of Bangladesh, in which it was claimed, perhaps rightly, "The Chinese have never opposed the right of the people of Bangladesh to self-determination."[42] The Maoist groups inside Bangladesh, led by Mohammed Toha, had joined the liberation movement, and Maulana Bhashani, the leader of the pro-Beijing group of the National Awami party (which worked in East Pakistan for the banned Communist party there), had appealed to Mao Zedong urging that Beijing should recognize Bangladesh.[43]

Notwithstanding all these charitable interpretations and benefits of doubt, China's support of the Yahya regime after it had unleashed its reign of terror in East Pakistan suffered from the wide gap between ideological and diplomatic considerations. It was unfortunate for China—as, indeed, it was for the suffering Bengalis. Mujib's constant antipathy to China's gestures of goodwill was perhaps the real reason for the dichotomy. Mujib relied exclusively on New Delhi for his potential showdown with West Pakistan, and his single-minded devotion to New Delhi blinded him to Beijing. China could not be expected to lend support to a regime so dependent on New Delhi and, through New Delhi, on Moscow.

Yet when Bhutto went to Beijing as President Yahya's special emissary in November 1971, on the eve of the war over Bangladesh, he had to return practically empty-handed. China publicly demanded that a rational solution should be found for East Pakistan, clearly indicating that China did not approve of the military atrocities there, and concerning China's help and cooperation in the case of a war between India and Pakistan, the Chinese left Bhutto with no doubt that Pakistan had better not expect the help that China had once promised—a serious factor in the outbreak of the Indo-Pakistani War in 1965. Pakistan got "a declaration of support" from Beijing, but China gave no specific commitment or assurance. The acting foreign minister, Ji Pengfei, while speaking at a banquet given in honor of the Pakistani delegation headed by Bhutto on November 7, 1971, gave vague support to Pakistan in the case of foreign aggression. The statement, however, did not go "beyond the ambiguously worded promise that Mr. Chou En-lai, the Chinese Prime Minister, made to President Yahya Khan in a letter on April 11."[44]

The vital assurance that the Pakistanis were seeking from Beijing in 1971 was whether, in the event of a war, China would hold down Indian divisions by diversionary action on India's northern frontier, as China had threatened to do in the Indo-Pakistani War of 1965. No such assurance was given this time. Indeed, it was reliably learned that the

Chinese had advised the Pakistani military regime to negotiate a political settlement of the crisis. China's cool response to Bhutto's mission in November was a direct response to the hawkish elements of the ruling junta in West Pakistan and a clear indication that China would not intervene militarily in a new Indo-Pakistani War.[45]

When the war finally broke out as the result of Indian military intervention to "liberate" Bangladesh, China supported Pakistan in the Security Council, but its support was confined to verbal support, and its real wrath was expressed against the Soviet Union rather than against Bangladesh. China's role during the war revealed the bitter rivalry between the two communist giants in South Asia. China was bitter at the success of Soviet diplomacy in the area, not at seeing the emergence of a new nation on the subcontinent. China's policy on Bangladesh was a source of disappointment and puzzlement to many people, particularly to those who saw China as a revolutionary power urging on revolutionary forces all over the Third World. But one must remember that in realpolitik, ideology is not the sole factor in guiding the foreign policy of a great power. China's policy on Bangladesh should be judged in the context of all the many factors that prevailed in the South Asian triangle in 1971.

The New Order in South Asia and China

The new order that emerged on the South Asian subcontinent after the Indo-Pakistani War over Bangladesh was a disappointing one for Beijing. China's South Asian ally, Pakistan, had been defeated, a new nation, Bangladesh, had been created out of the dismemberment of Pakistan. Beijing had supported Pakistan, and the Soviet Union and Moscow-backed India had given full support to the creation of Bangladesh. China could not or would not prevent the dismemberment of Pakistan, so the Soviet Union's image and influence were greatly enhanced in South Asia as a result of the 1971 events. Premier Zhou Enlai stated to the British author, Neville Maxwell, that the "fall of Dacca [the capital of Bangladesh] was the beginning of troubles in the sub-continent."[46] There have been political upheavals on the subcontinent since 1971, but nothing special as predicted by Zhou Enlai. China denounced the new government in Bangladesh as a puppet regime set up by India and backed by the Russians. China also exercised its first veto in the Security Council against Bangladesh's entry into the United Nations—China did it in deference to Pakistan's request.

There were hints that China and India might restore a full diplomatic relationship, which had been suspended after the 1965 Indo-Pakistani War. In November 1970, Zhou Enlai had told President Yahya that there might be an exchange of ambassadors between Beijing and New Delhi, but the 1971 Indo-Pakistani War dashed those hopes until April 1975, when the two countries resumed a full diplomatic relationship. During 1971–1974, the Sino-Indian relationship continued to remain frozen because of China's support of Pakistan during the 1971 war and because of China's continuing to send military supplies to Pakistan, which India still regarded as a hostile neighbor. China's continued friendship with Pakistan was dramatized in 1973 by Pakistani Army Chief of Staff Tikka Khan's trip to Beijing and the return visit of the Chinese deputy chief of staff, Zhang Caijian, to Pakistan. It was claimed that the friendly relations and cooperation between China and Pakistan in the economic, cultural, and military spheres were further increased, and on the Pakistani side, friendship and closer cooperation with the PRC continued to be major objectives of Pakistan's foreign policy.

During 1972–1975, China had no diplomatic ties with Bangladesh, and although India and China resumed full diplomatic relations in April 1975, there was no remarkable improvement in the Sino-Indian relationship. China's main link in South Asia was Pakistan. Then in August 1975, China and Bangladesh established diplomatic relations, and the countries' top leaders also exchanged visits in 1976–1977.

During the short tenure of Prime Minister Desai's rule in India (1977–1979), there was some speculation about an improvement in the Sino-Indian relationship, but no substantial development took place during that period. With the return of Mrs. Gandhi to power in 1980, there have been new attempts to improve the Sino-Indian relationship, and Beijing has been sending signals to Mrs. Gandhi that China wants to improve its relations with India. In early 1980, China made a proposal for a technical meeting to explore the possibility of a Sino-Indian air agreement,[47] and more significant was the Chinese foreign minister's attendance at the Indian National Day reception in Beijing on January 26, 1980, the first time in twenty years that the Chinese foreign minister had attended that celebration. China also sent a top-ranking ambassador to New Delhi soon after Mrs. Gandhi's return to power, without waiting for the Indian government to send a new ambassador to China. Mrs. Gandhi, on her part, declared that India would continue the process of normalizing relations with China – a process that she had begun in 1975 by sending an Indian ambassador to China.

The major hurdles in normalizing relations between the two largest Asian countries are the border issue, over which the two countries fought a war in 1962, and India's special relationship with the Soviet Union, which keeps a vigilant watch on any new developments in the Sino-Indian relationship. A third complicating factor is the Sino-Pakistani friendship, which is disliked by India.

India considers a settlement of the Sino-Indian border dispute a precondition for normal relations between the two countries. China, on the other hand, wants a step by step improvement to prepare a favorable climate for the solution of the border dispute. As there has not yet been any significant progress in the border issue, India seems to have accepted China's step by step approach, though India never misses any opportunity to stress the importance of the border issue. Trade between the two countries has been resumed after about two decades, China has invited Indian leaders to visit China, and the Chinese news media has stopped its anti-Indian propaganda. A relaxation of tensions between China and India is desirable for peace and stability in the South Asian subcontinent, but some mutually acceptable compromise has to be agreed upon concerning the border dispute before a relationship between the two largest Asian countries can be fully restored.

Sino-Indian Border Dispute

Differences over common borders are not unusual between countries, as is demonstrated by China's problems with Afghanistan, Burma, Mongolia, Nepal, Pakistan, and, of course, the Soviet Union. But China has peacefully concluded border agreements with every southern neighbor except India. "A survey of these other Chinese boundaries," wrote Alastair Lamb, "shows that China can make a peaceful boundary settlement with her neighbors and can, as in the Sino-Burmese negotiations culminating in the treaty of January 1960, surrender claim to extensive tracts of territory."[48] Why could there be no such peaceful agreement between China and India, which had maintained such close ties in the preceding seven years? Was China's attitude more aggressive toward India? Or did India have a special reason to quarrel with China?

The mountainous borders between China and its neighbors, including India, are a legacy of history; they are also a legacy of Western colonial rule in Asia. The Sino-Indian border is divided into three sectors. The western sector is the boundary between the Ladakh area of Indian-held Kashmir and China's provinces of Xinjiang and Xizang (Tibet). The middle sector, much shorter in length, touches three Indian states—East Punjab, Himachal Pradesh, and Uttar Pradesh, and the eastern sector separates Xizang from the Indian states of Assam and the newly formed Nagaland. In 1959, the Indians, adhering to the McMahon line, controlled the disputed areas in the eastern sector, and in the western sector, the Chinese were in possession of the strategically important disputed zone, Aksai Chin. In the middle sector, the total contested area was perhaps under 200 square miles.

It was over the eastern sector and Aksai Chin in the west that armed conflict flared in 1962. The dispute in the eastern sector was over the validity of the McMahon line, but the disagreement in the western sector touched upon strategic and security considerations: Through this largely wilderness area runs the only reliable road, built by the Chinese during 1954–1957 along an ancient caravan route, from Xinjiang to Xizang. Because it is difficult to bring historical evidence to bear in quarrels over sparsely populated areas, the honorable and peaceful course would have been to demarcate the frontiers by negotiation at the conference table. With the status quo established as the basis of negotiations, mutual adjustments could have been made, taking into account historical, geographic, and strategic factors and the interests of the parties concerned.

China denounced the McMahon line as a product of imperialism but apparently was inclined to accept it—China recognized the line in its boundary agreement with Burma—provided India accepted China's de facto possession of Aksai Chin. China was, in fact, asking for recognition of the status quo and wanted to compromise. Zhou reportedly told Pandit Sunder Lal, the founder/president of the India-China Friendship Association in New Delhi, "You keep what you hold, you take too, anything that is in dispute and occupied by neither and we keep what we hold,"[49] but Zhou's proposal was turned down by India. The result was the Sino-Indian border conflict in 1962 and two decades of frozen relations between Beijing and New Delhi.

Because of the great changes in Asian international relations in recent years, both China and India seem to be moving toward a rapprochement. China's new proposal for a border agreement was made by Vice-Premier Deng in an interview with the editor of *Vikrant,* a specialized Indian defense journal. Deng's proposal is based on Zhou Enlai's proposal made before the 1962 border war, and it suggests that the Chinese accept India's claim in the eastern sector of the Sino-Indian border in return for India's acceptance of China's de facto possession of Aksai Chin in the western sector. Deng made one major concession by declaring that the Indo-Pakistani dispute over Kashmir is a bilateral problem between India and Pakistan—until then, China had backed Pakistan's demand for self-determination in Kashmir.[50] That stand had been a major complicating factor in the Sino-Indian relationship in the 1960s, but on a later occasion, when Pakistan's Prime Minister Bhutto went to Beijing in May 1976, the Chinese premier, Hua, had departed from the Chinese stand on Kashmir to help Beijing's sorely strained relations with New Delhi by avoiding any reference to Kashmir in his welcoming speech for the Pakistani prime minister.[51]

Although Deng's proposal on the border issue is the same as the one Zhou Enlai made in 1962, there is now a precedent, set by India itself, for making a deal with Pakistan on the Kashmir issue. In the Simla agreement of 1972, neither India nor Pakistan formally gave up their claim to

Kashmir, yet the two countries agreed on a de facto division of the disputed territories there. So India may now accept China's actual possession of Aksai Chin without giving up its legal claim to it. There has not yet been any resumption of the border negotiations between China and India, but there is now a better chance for a settlement than in 1962.

The Soviet factor in the Sino-Indian relationship has already been discussed, but India seems to attach a greater importance and value to its long-standing friendship with Moscow than to uncertain and fragile ties with Beijing. Moreover, as long as China provides Pakistan with military supplies, India's misgivings about China are likely to continue. Moscow has recently begun a vigorous campaign against an alleged United States–China-Pakistan axis, which is supposed to be not only against the Soviet-backed puppet regime in Afghanistan, but also aimed at India. Although unhappy about the Afghan crisis and the continued presence of the Soviet army in Afghanistan, India can not entertain any idea of Pakistan's getting militarily stronger.

To maintain good relations with both India and Pakistan is as difficult for China as it is for a country like Japan to have simultaneous good relations with Moscow and Beijing, and Japan has had great difficulty in doing just that in recent years. India, however, realizes that there really is no "axis" between China, the United States, and Pakistan, and China has shown extreme caution in helping the Afghan "freedom fighters" oppose the Soviet occupation of their country. Similarly, Pakistan is not interested in any such axis because of its grave concern about the Soviet designs in Southwest Asia.

The current unrest and violence in the Indian state of Assam in the northeast part of the subcontinent is another compelling reason for an understanding between China and India, because China has not given any help to the rebel groups in Assam in the expectation of an overall improvement in the Sino-Indian relationship. Post-Mao China's interest in settling the Tibetan issue is yet another favorable reason for a rapprochement between China and India. So the Sino-Indian relationship has both positive and negative factors, and they will help determine whether there is any improvement in the relationship between those two important Asian neighbors.

Sino-Pakistani Relationship

China's special relationship with Pakistan—an Islamic country, a military dictatorship, and an ally of the United States in the heyday of the cold war—may be considered a contemporary miracle of diplomacy. The Sino-Pakistani friendship began soon after the 1962 Sino-Indian border conflict, and it has therefore been interpreted as based on the old adage, an enemy's enemy is a friend. China's objectives in developing good relations with Pakistan were alleged to include undoing CENTO and SEATO, gradually integrating Pakistan into a Chinese sphere of influence, further humiliating India, and obtaining access to the Muslim world. Whatever the interpretation of China's special link with a traditional Muslim country, Pakistan, it has grown both in depth and in warmth since it began in the mid 1960s. The special link has survived political upheavals in both countries, such as the 1971 civil war in Pakistan, the 1966–1969 Cultural Revolution in China, the 1976–1977 power struggle in China, and changes of government in both countries.

China's close and friendly relationship with Pakistan is an example of the consistency and reliability of Beijing's diplomacy. If a country can cultivate China's confidence and trust, it can be assured of China's consistent support and help. China wanted to intervene militarily when Pakistan was in real danger during the 1965 Indo-Pakistani War. After carefully studying the top-secret and unpublished records of the Sino-Pakistani discussions in 1965 dealing with China's plan to move militarily in favor of Pakistan, I published an account of China's role in the 1965 Indo-Pakistani War.[52] That account was challenged by many people on the grounds that China only talks but does not take action, but China's military intervention in favor of Cambodia in 1979 – in the presence of the grave risk of a direct confrontation with the Soviet Union – has proved that China not only talks but also takes action to help its real friends. China really meant business during the 1965 Indo-Pakistani War. China also continued to give support so Pakistan could maintain its territorial integrity during the 1971 Indo-Pakistani War at the cost of China's reputation that it upholds causes of national liberation movements.

China's special link with Pakistan is also an example of China's policy of peaceful coexistence with countries that have differing social and political systems. China has not intervened in Pakistan's internal affairs, nor has it exerted crude pressures to control Pakistan's external relations in return for Beijing's most valuable help – since Pakistan lost access to U.S. military supplies in 1965, China has been Pakistan's major supplier of military equipment. Any objective assessment of China's relations with Pakistan will prove Beijing's reliability, sincerity, and consistency in dealing with countries that are sincere friends of China.

In the 1970s, when China followed a dynamic policy and won many friends, entered the United Nations, and increased its image as an emerging major power in global politics, China's relations with Pakistan remained unscathed. At the beginning of the 1970s, Pakistan played its unique role in the secret Sino-American relationship, which culminated in Henry Kissinger's top-secret and first trip to Beijing in July 1971. Then came the tragic civil war in Pakistan. China was unhappy about Pakistan's handling of the Bangladesh issue, and particularly about the Pakistani army's atrocities against the people of Bangladesh, but when the war was over, China helped the "new" and truncated Pakistan rehabilitate its shattered economy and weakened defense apparatus. When India exploded its first nuclear device and Pakistan expressed fears of being blackmailed by India, China assured Pakistan it would be protected against any such blackmailing effort. The United States was Pakistan's most important supplier of military equipment and donor of economic assistance, but President Carter stopped all U.S. aid to Pakistan in the 1970s on the grounds that Pakistan had been secretly manufacturing an alleged "Islamic atom bomb." China has urged the United States not to penalize Pakistan for an alleged bomb, and during Vice-Premier Deng's discussions with President Carter in 1979, China made pleas on behalf of Pakistan—similar pleas have been made by China to top-ranking U.S. policymakers who have visited China in recent years.[53]

Because of the crisis in Southwest Asia that resulted from the Soviet Union's invasion of Afghanistan and from the continued presence of the Soviet armed forces in Afghanistan, Pakistan gravely fears a Soviet attack on its borders also, and again, China has assured Pakistan of its full support and assistance if Pakistan becomes a victim of the Soviet Union expansionist designs. The Chinese foreign minister, Huang Hua, went to Pakistan in January 1980 to make that assurance, and there has been some speculation that China and the United States might engage in some joint efforts to strengthen Pakistan's military capabilities. During a visit to Pakistan in February 1980, when Brzezinski also went to Pakistan with an offer of U.S. military help to Pakistan, I made inquiries about any such Sino-American joint ventures to help Pakistan against the Soviet Union, but according to Pakistan's President Zia and foreign minister, Aga Shahi, there was no basis for such speculation.

The Chinese foreign minister told Pakistan to make its own decisions in accordance with its interests and in the context of the geopolitics of the area. China was reported to be putting no pressure on Pakistan to follow any particular policy or actions.[54] After the failure of the U.S.-Pakistan talks on U.S. arms supplies to Pakistan under President Carter's Persian Gulf doctrine, President Zia went to Beijing in May 1980 for his most significant consultations with any foreign country since the Afghan crisis of December 1979. Zia told the press, after his extensive talks with Premier Hua and Senior Vice–Premier Deng, that Sino-Pakistani "ties are so deep and solid" that they "do not have to be qualified or need any further elaboration." He said, "China is the only country in Pakistan's experience which has stuck to its principles and whose policies are above any selfish interests."[55] One may make some alowances for rhetoric, yet there is no doubt that the Sino-Pakistani relationship during the past two decades has proved to be reliable and mutually beneficial to both countries.

China's recent bid to normalize its relations with India does not worry Pakistan as it feels confident that Beijing's friendship with New Delhi will not be at Pakistan's expense. Similarly, when Fidel Castro's foreign minister went to Pakistan in August 1979 and promised Cuba's support for Pakistan's membership in the nonaligned movement, there was some speculation in certain quarters that Pakistan might be endorsing Cuba's attempts to turn the nonaligned movement in Moscow's favor. When I raised that issue with the Chinese ambassador in Pakistan, Xu Yixin, in August 1979, he dismissed such speculations as fanciful. Such is the mutual confidence between the two countries bound together by an unwritten alliance since 1963. President Zia in a speech to the 1979 nonaligned summit meeting was forceful in defending China's role in helping the nonaligned countries.

Emerging Relations with the New Nation:
Beijing and Dacca

As already stated, there were no diplomatic relations between China and the new South Asian country, Bangladesh for several years (1971–1974), but since the establishment of diplomatic ties in 1975, the relations between China and Bangladesh have shown a steady development in all spheres. China contributed to Bangladesh's desperate needs for external economic aid, and China is also reported to have supplied Bangladesh with some military equipment. Bangladesh President Zia-Ur Rahman has paid two state visits to China and has met with top Chinese leaders on several other occasions in Third World countries, such as Korea. Chinese Vice-Premier Li and Foreign Minister Huang made a return visit to Bangladesh in March 1978. Both sides have expressed cordial feelings and support for each other, and China is happy to renew its friendship with the people of Bangladesh, formerly East Pakistan, which was suspended in 1972–1975. If the Sino-Bangladeshi relationship has not reached the same degree of warmth and confidence as the Sino-Pakistani one, it is because of Bangladesh's uncertainty and policy toward Beijing in the context of Dacca's dependency on India and, through India, on the Soviet Union. Bangladesh is cautious in its dealings with China, presumably for fear of offending New Delhi and Moscow, and Bangladesh's stands on the 1978–1979 wars in Indochina and Afghanistan reflect its uncertainty.

China and ANZUS

China's increasing relationship with its Asian neighbors, particularly the ASEAN countries and Japan, are interrelated with China's recent friendly ties with Australia and New Zealand. Before concluding this discussion on China and its Asian neighbors, I shall refer briefly to

Beijing's fast-growing ties with the two ANZUS countries, Australia and New Zealand—particularly the former as it has become an important aspect of China's role in the Asian-Pacific region. The new Sino-American relationship that emerged from the 1972 Peking Summit influenced China's relations with Australia and New Zealand, which were quick to establish diplomatic relations with Beijing soon after that summit meeting. There were frequent exchanges of visits and high-level contacts in the 1970s between China and those two ANZUS countries, and all three countries share a common concern about the growing Soviet influence and expansionist designs in the Asian-Pacific region.

Australian Prime Minister Malcolm Fraser, during a visit to China in June 1976, joined Chinese Premier Hua in praising the Sino-Australian interest in "maintaining stability and blocking suspected Soviet encroachments in the Asian/Pacific region."[56] Australian Foreign Minister Andrew Peacock, in an annual review of Australia's foreign relations in 1978, spoke warmly of growing ties between Beijing and Canberra and referred to significant progress and consolidations in the Sino-Australian relationship since 1973.[57] Australia's new relationship with China enjoys bipartisan support in Australia, and China supports Australia's policy toward the Soviet Union's expansionist designs. In an editorial on June 20, 1976, *People's Daily* praised Australia's repeated denunciation of Soviet maritime expansion in the Pacific and Indian oceans, its mistrust of detente, and its attempts to strengthen joint defense efforts with oceanic countries and to promote better relations with ASEAN nations.[58] Prime Minister Fraser, in an earlier foreign policy statement in Australia on June 1, 1976, had said: "Australia and China have a like interest in seeing that Soviet power in the Pacific and Southwest Asia is balanced by the power of other major states or by appropriate regional arrangements. We can therefore expect Chinese support of our views on the need for an effective American presence in the Pacific and Indian Oceans."[59]

As already mentioned, a stronger ANZUS, like a stronger NATO or a stronger ASEAN, is now regarded favorably by China because of its concern about the Soviet Union's global expansionist designs. Australia's condemnation of the Soviet-backed Vietnamese military occupation of Cambodia and the Soviet invasion of Afghanistan have received China's strong approval, and similarly, China's support of the U.S.-Japanese-Australian naval presence in the Pacific and Indian oceans has the approval of Australia. So China and Australia have developed certain common objectives in the Asian-Pacific region.

As a result of the political understanding between China and Australia, trade between the two countries has increased considerably in recent years. Apart from security and political considerations, China values its ties with Australia because of China's need for modern technology and technical assistance for its four-modernization plans. Cultural exchanges have also increased rapidly.

Like any other bilateral relationship, there are some points of difference between China and Australia. Australia, for instance, does not approve of China's nuclear tests in the South Pacific. When Chinese Vice-Premier Li Xiannian visited Australia and New Zealand in May 1980, China was about to fire a long-range missile into the South Pacific, and that fact caused some problems for the two host countries, each of which wished to extend a warm welcome to the top Chinese visitor since the establishment of diplomatic relations in 1973. Before Li's visit to Australia, the Australian Foreign Affairs officials stressed that China and Australia "share similar views over many issues, but an understanding of the differences still remains."[60] The incident served to highlight the ambiguities of a "transitional stage" in Sino-Australian relations.[61]

Like Australia, New Zealand was told by Chinese Premier Hua, during New Zealand's Deputy Prime Minister Brian Talboys's visit to Beijing in June 1979, that China is supportive of New Zealand's continued membership in ANZUS, which, like SEATO, was a target of Chinese attacks on U.S. policy in the Asian-Pacific region in the 1950s and 1960s. China also supports New Zealand's joint effort with Australia to strengthen their defenses as a part of what Hua called "the struggle against the expansionist forces of the Soviet Union."[62] On the economic front, China is interested in acquiring a wide range of technology from New Zealand, particularly its advanced agricultural technology, and New Zealand wants Chinese chemicals, minerals, and textiles.

The increasing international tensions are likely to link China and the two ANZUS countries, Australia and New Zealand, in their common objective of maintaining peace and stability in the Asian-Pacific region. The trends begun in the 1970s are likely to continue in the 1980s.

Notes

1. *China and Asia: An Analysis of China's Recent Policy Toward Neighboring States,* Report by the Foreign Affairs and National Defense Division, Congressional Research Service, Library of Congress, March 1979 (Washington, D.C.: Government Printing Office, 1979), pp. 31–32.
2. Based on the author's reading of unpublished documents and papers of the government of Pakistan, 1947–1971.
3. *China and Asia,* p. 32.
4. Based on the author's research and discussions in London.
5. Ibid.
6. Ibid.
7. Ibid.

8. Ibid.

9. Ibid.

10. Ibid.

11. New China News Agency, August 9, 1967.

12. *Times* (London), February 25, 1976.

13. See G. W. Choudhury, "China's Dynamic Foreign Policy," *Asia-Pacific Community* (Winter 1978-1979), p. 54.

14. New China News Agency, February 25, 1977.

15. *Peking Review*, March 25, 1978, p. 18.

16. See *Far Eastern Economic Review*, February 18, 1977, pp. 8-10.

17. Rodney Tasker, "Rivals for ASEAN's Hands," *Far Eastern Economic Review*, September 15, 1978, pp. 19-20.

18. Ibid., p. 19.

19. See Rodney Tasker, "Behind the Friendly Shadow," *Far Eastern Economic Review*, September 15, 1978, pp. 20-21.

20. Harvey Stockwin, "Lee: Pathfinding in the Forbidden City," *Far Eastern Economic Review*, May 14, 1976.

21. David Bonavia, "Interview: Lee Kuan Yew," *Far Eastern Economic Review*, November 21, 1980, p. 20.

22. New China News Agency, March 13, 1978.

23. K. M. Singh and others, "Teng's Triumps on the Frontiers," *Far Eastern Economic Review*, February 17, 1978, p. 10.

24. *New York Times*, November 13, 1978.

25. R. Tasker, "Old Fears Delay Friendship," *Far Eastern Economic Review*, December 15, 1978, p. 32.

26. See *Far Eastern Economic Review*, November 10, 1978, p. 21.

27. Don Oberdorfer, "Reds vs Reds in Indo-China: A New, Confusing Kind of War," *Washington Post*, April 1, 1979.

28. N. Chanda, "A Bear Hug from Moscow," *Far Eastern Economic Review*, November 17, 1978.

29. *Washington Post*, May 15, 1979.

30. Quoted in *Financial Times* (London), March 19, 1979.

31. *Newsweek*, January 22, 1979, p. 35.

32. Thomas W. Robinson, "China's Asia Policy," *Current History* (September 1980), p. 3.

33. David Bonavia, "Changing the Course of History—Gunboat Diplomacy, Marxist Style," *Far Eastern Economic Review*, March 2, 1979, pp. 8-9.

34. See *China and Asia*, p. 35.

35. M. C. Tum, "Those Bipedal Links," *Far Eastern Economic Review*, October 7, 1977.

36. See Ian Wilson, ed., *China and the World Community* (Sydney: Angers and Robertson, 1972), p. 219.

37. *Statesman* (New Delhi), December 31, 1949.

38. Ibid.

39. Based on the author's reading of unpublished documents and papers of the government of Pakistan, 1947-1971.

40. Ibid; the author was a member of President Yahya's entourage to China in November 1970.

41. *International Herald Tribune* (Paris), April 13, 1971.

42. J. Gittings, "How Many Wreaths For Bangladesh?" *Guardian* (London), June 18, 1971.

43. Ibid.

44. *Times* (London), November 8, 1971.

45. *Financial Times* (London), December 6, 1971.

46. *Times* (London), December 19, 1971.

47. M. Ram, "India: New Moves on the Chinese Dialogue," *Far Eastern Economic Review,* April 13, 1980.

48. Alastair Lamb, *The China-India Border* (London: Oxford University Press for the Royal Institute of International Affairs, 1964), p. 5.

49. For details, see G. W. Choudhury, *India, Pakistan, Bangladesh, and the Major Powers: Politics of a Divided Subcontinent* (New York: Free Press, 1975), pp. 170–175.

50. Arul B. Louis, "A Thaw in the Himalayas," *Far Eastern Economic* July 6, 1980.

51. *New York Times,* May 28, 1976.

52. See Choudhury, *India, Pakistan, Bangladesh, and the Major Powers.*

53. The author was told of China's pleas on behalf of Pakistan to the United States both by Chinese leaders in Beijing and by Pakistani President Zia in July 1979.

54. Based on the author's interviews with the Pakistani president and foreign minister in February 1980.

55. Della Denman, "Pakistan's Best Friend," *Far Eastern Economic Review,* May 16, 1980, p. 23.

56. *Recognizing the P.R.C.: The Experience of Japan, Australia, and West Germany,* Report prepared by the Foreign Affairs and National Defense Division, Congressional Research Service, Library of Congress, May 1979 (Washington, D.C.: Government Printing Office, 1979), p. 18.

57. See "Australia and Oceania '78," *Far Eastern Economic Review,* June 9, 1978.

58. Reprinted in *Recognizing the P.R.C.,* p. 18.

59. Ibid.

60. Helen Ester, "A Testing Time in Australia," *Far Eastern Economic Review,* May 16, 1980, p. 24.

61. Ibid.

62. *Far Eastern Economic Review,* June 8, 1979, p. 60.

10

China and the Third World

The foreign policy of the PRC since its founding in 1949 has largely been preoccupied with its security problems vis-à-vis the two super- powers, the United States and the USSR. As already pointed out, China and the United States were engaged in a limited war in Korea in 1950, which resulted in an era of hostile relations; since the 1960s, Beijing's worries have been aggravated as a result of the great Sino-Soviet rift.

Notwithstanding its problems with the two superpowers, the PRC has sought to play a significant role in world affairs and has paid particular attention to the Third World. China is an old country with an ancient civilization and centuries of checkered history, yet China is a new nation in world politics. China's role in world affairs is comparatively new and, until recently, limited. Judged by any criteria of military strength or economic growth, China is not yet a major power, let alone a super- power. Yet China is a vast country with one-fourth the world's popula- tion, and the PRC is also a growing member of the nuclear club, possess- ing a significant nuclear deterrent force with great potential.

Since its entry into the United Nations in 1971 and its recognition by an overwhelming majority of the countries of the world, China has become a central force in world politics. Its role in world affairs is developing fast and can no longer be ignored. As Doak Barnett points out, "China's increasing involvement in world affairs is significant and its international influence will certainly continue to grow."[1] The Chinese leaders have been actively cultivating friendship on a global scale since the early 1970s, a process that began under Mao and Zhou Enlai and is being vigorously continued by the post-Mao Chinese leaders. Through this fast-growing emergence on the world stage, China is turning global politics into a new ball game.[2]

The Chinese have emerged from seclusion and isolation. By mid 1975, Beijing had established formal ties with more than a hundred na- tions—more than double the number in 1968—and diplomatic ties and economic relations with the outside world are increasing rapidly. The post-Mao Chinese leaders have made grand tours to various parts of the world, including Eastern Europe, the Soviet Union's sphere of influence, and they have paid special attention to winning friends and allies among the countries of the Third World in Asia, Africa, and Latin America. The two previous chapters discussed China's growing relations with Asian countries and its increasing involvement in Asian-Pacific affairs, promoted by a fear of and hostility toward the Soviet Union. Some reference has also been made to China's relations with African countries in the review of the growth of Chinese foreign policy from 1949–1969 and also in the discussion on the growing Sino-Soviet rivalry in Africa. In this chapter, I wish to further elaborate on China's growing ties with African countries as well as with Latin American countries, another part of the so-called Third World. I shall also make reference to China's role in the volatile Middle Eastern countries.

China never tires of speaking about its close ties with, if not belonging to, the Third World: "We uphold the Three World Theory advanced by Chairman Mao," said China's present-day strong man, Deng Xiaoping, who added, "China will always remain a member of the 'Third World.' "[3] At a special session of the UN General Assembly in April 1974, Deng tried to play the role of spokesman for the Third World. He spoke against what he called the exploitation and plundering of the Third World by the two superpowers, especially the superpower "which styles itself a socialist country" (i.e., the Soviet Union). Then he championed vigorously the causes of the Third World countries by stating: "As we all know, in the last few centuries, colonialism and imperialism surreptitiously enslaved and plundered the people of Asia, Africa and Latin America. . . . The Third World countries strongly demanded that the present extremely unequal international economic relations be changed and they have made many rational proposals of reform. The Chinese government and people warmly endorse and firmly support just propositions made by the Third World countries."[4] Deng's speech, as Doak Barnett has pointed out, "reveals a very important facet of Chinese Communist thinking today that clearly has a major influence on Peking's foreign policy. . . . Peking has become the mecca for these nations" (Third World countries).[5]

There is a constant flow of visitors, including heads of state or of government, from the Third World countries to China. Although the PRC is a communist country and the Third World countries are mostly noncommunist national states, there is some sense of affinity between China and those newly independent countries. Both China and the Third World countries suffered under some form of colonialism; both the PRC and these new nations are also confronted with big challeneges in solving their gigantic socioeconomic problems. Initially, the PRC was thinking in terms of "exporting" revolution to the Third World countries, which created some Third World suspicions of and reservations about the PRC. But in recent years, China seems to have put the concept of world revolution into cold storage and more and more is stressing government to government relations as opposed to party to party relations. That change has facilitated contacts and closer ties between the PRC and Third World countries, and it has also enhanced China's role in world affairs.

China's ability to help the Third World countries is, however, limited. Its economic aid to developing nations is limited because of China's own underdeveloped economy; similarly, China is no match for either Washington or Moscow in providing military supplies or assistance to Third World countries. So, although there are some favorable psychological, cultural, and historical reasons for China's role concerning Third World countries, there are also great limiting factors. Yet the PRC, by a combination of constructive diplomacy and selective aid programs, has enhanced its role in Third World countries in recent years.

China and Africa in the 1970s

A clear component of China's more outward-looking policy in the 1970s is its renewed effort to assume the leadership of the liberation struggle in Africa, displacing the Soviet Union's predominating influence in the principal freedom movements. One obvious dilemma of this aspect of China's widening strategy is the degree of support China will give to dissident groups inside countries with which China is pursuing normal diplomatic relations. There are already signs of an increasing Chinese caution in dealing with such groups, and the Chinese are likely to concentrate on liberation movements that operate in areas where they have no diplomatic or economic relations to compromise. In announcing on June 11, 1971, that his government had recognized China, Libya's President Muammar al-Quadhafi pointed to China's growing importance as a world power – and at the same time, emphasized that Libya's decision was a realistic and political one that owed nothing to Beijing's ideological claims. He said that as a country on which atheism had been imposed, China was a stranger, and Chinese influence would never be allowed to spread in Libya.

Quadhafi's view is shared by many Middle Eastern and African leaders who are prepared to recognize China (in part to balance Soviet overtures) and to trade with that country, but they would resist any attempts on the part of China to influence their social and political systems. The Chinese leaders are now taking more notice of that way of thinking than they did in the early 1960s, when Zhou Enlai proclaimed that Africa was ripe for revolution, and at present, China's increased activity in Africa is mainly concentrated in the diplomatic and economic spheres. Relations have been established with Nigeria, Cameroon, Equatorial Guinea, Ethiopia, and Kuwait, and through economic, technical, and medical cooperation, Beijing is trying to show that China understands the needs of the developing world better than the Soviet Union does.

China's aid to Africa (but not the Middle East) now exceeds Moscow's, and China's agreeing to help build the Tanzania-Zambia railway was proof of its eagerness to extend its presence in the area. Personnel from the Chinese army first went to Tanzania in 1964, initially for a six-month stay, to assist in training police, army, and navy cadets, but they subsequently became involved in training exiled Congolese and other rebel guerrillas. The Chinese have become the sole instructors of the Tanzanian armed forces—a logical development, according to President Julius Nyerere, as that army uses mainly Chinese weapons.

China's other major recipient of military aid in Africa is Zaire, though recent visits by Chinese military delegations to Guinea and Mali may indicate attempts to secure an important role in those armies too. China's aid program has an outstanding reputation for rapid implementation, good terms, and lack of political strings, but it is still too small to make a major impact. Much goodwill was won by the completion of the 1,250-mile, $303-million Tanzania-Zambia railway ahead of schedule, but such massive undertakings are by no means typical.

Focus on Portuguese Colonies

The Chinese diplomatic effort in Africa in the early 1970s was concentrated on the Portuguese territories, and the Chinese were particularly interested in Mozambique, which they clearly regarded as an important element in the struggle for southern Africa. Chinese influence in the Mozambique Liberation Front (FRELIMO), the only Mozambique party to be recognized by the Organization of African Unity (OAU), was at a low ebb for a short time following the 1970 expulsion from leadership of the pro-Chinese Uria Simango, after a prolonged period of rivalry between pro-Chinese and pro-Soviet factions. But the turning point came in August 1971, when a FRELIMO delegation, led by the movement's president, Samora Machel, spent six weeks touring China, North Korea, and North Vietnam.

As well as challenging the Soviet grip on FRELIMO, the Chinese cultivated a number of Mozambican breakaway minority groups. Much of their support was given to the Mozambique Revolutionary Committee (COREMO), which was formed by dissidents from FRELIMO and led by Paulo Gumane. COREMO received financial aid from the Chinese, who also agreed to supply arms provided they were sent through channels other than those of the OAU Liberation Committee. (The committee had previously confiscated arms intended for COREMO, which it does not recognize.) The Chinese also offered guerrilla training, and by the end of 1971, a group including three members of the COREMO Central Committee had returned from a three-month course in China. A split in COREMO itself led to the formation of another splinter group, ULIPAMO, which also received Chinese assistance. Another small group, PAPOMO, was known to have been given funds by the Chinese in an attempt to build up a Mozambique Communist party, the nucleus of which had previously existed secretly.

In spite of their involvement in the smaller movements, the Chinese continued to give substantial military aid to FRELIMO. The movement was believed to be mainly equipped by the Chinese, who provided modern weapons (such as assault guns, antitank launchers, and projectiles), which were unloaded from Chinese ships at Dar es Salaam and Mtwara in Tanzania.[6]

Chinese military experts were also reported to be fighting alongside guerrillas in both Mozambique and Angola. In Angola, the Chinese stepped up attempts to influence the Popular Movement for the Liberation of Angola (MPLA), a traditionally Soviet-sponsored movement in which efforts to set up a pro-Chinese faction had failed in the past. As in the case of FRELIMO, new Chinese initiatives toward the MPLA can be traced back to mid 1971. In August of that year, an MPLA delegation, led by its president, Agostinho Neto, visited Beijing at the invitation of the Chinese-African Friendship Association.

China warmly greeted the emergence of Mozambique as an independent country on June 25, 1975, and *Peking Review* stated: "The Mozambian people have triumphed. Their great victory in gaining independence through armed struggle has set an example for the peoples fighting for national independence."[7] Although the Chinese were among the first to offer Mozambique economic assistance in the form of a loan worth $56 million in 1975, they have since played a much smaller role there than have the Russians, whom the Chinese accuse of political and military aggression in Africa.

In Angola, China miscalculated badly by throwing its weight behind the pro-Western National Union for the Total Independence of Angola (UNITA) in the civil war in 1974–1975 as UNITA was defeated by the MPLA after Moscow sent in a Cuban expeditionary force and armed it with powerful Soviet weapons. When Angola received independence in 1975, China did not recognize the MPLA government, but talks for a normalization of relations with Angola have begun.[8]

China accused the Soviet Union in the Security Council on March 18, 1976, of hatching new schemes in Africa and blamed the Russians bitterly for their armed intervention in Angola. China's chief delegate,

Huang Hua, listed the "crimes" that the Soviet Union was alleged to have committed in Angola to further its design of colonial expansion in Africa. The Soviet delegate, in his reply, stated that China had become a friend of the imperialist circles that had wanted to block the struggle for independence in Angola. The Chinese continued to condemn the Soviet-Cuban military presence in Angola and the Horn of Africa. As in Southeast and Southwest Asia, Beijing shares a common concern with Washington about the Soviet-Cuban military adventures in Africa, especially in Angola and the Horn of Africa. On July 2, 1976, *Peking Review* stated, "The Soviet 'foreign legion' to wit the Cuban troops, is nothing but a tool of the Kremlin for world hegemony."

Southern Africa

China has consistently and persistently supported the national aspirations of the black majorities in Rhodesia (Zimbabwe), Namibia, and South Africa. During his third state visit to China in April 1980, President Kenneth Kaunda of Zambia paid tribute to China's support of the black peoples in southern Africa, saying in Beijing, "China has always supported the struggles of the oppressed people of Southern Africa."[9] China has not only increased the level of assistance in southern Africa, but also extended assistance to parties previously connected mainly with the Russians, including smaller movements such as the South-West Africa People's Organization (SWAPO) and the Liberation Committee of São Tomé and Príncipe (CLSTP). In redesigning its aid program, China appears to be concentrating on those areas where the freedom fighters have a better chance of success.

China's permanent representative at the United Nations, Chen Chu, spoke forcefully at a meeting of the UN Security Council on December 12, 1979, on behalf of the Zimbabwean people and promised China's full support for the independence of Zimbabwe (Rhodesia). China was delighted when the British government reached an agreement in 1979 with the white minority government of Rhodesia, which ultimately led to the creation of the African nation, Zimbabwe, because China did not relish the idea of an armed conflict in Rhodesia after its unhappy experiences in Angola. In a major armed conflict, China can not afford to supply the more sophisticated weapons, and the Russians can. China could give the African freedom fighters only small arms, ammunition, and light vehicles; the Russians, on the other hand, not only could provide sophisticated weapons, they could also send Cuban troops to help the Africans. So the Chinese were genuinely happy about the London accord on Rhodesia, which led to the birth of the new African nation through negotiation rather than through bullets.

The Chinese Foreign Minister, Huang Hua, went to Salisbury to attend the independence celebration of Zimbabwe, and the country's prime minister, Robert Mugabe, has followed a tilt-toward-Beijing policy since his country gained independence. In Angola, China suffered diplomatic setbacks; in Zimbabwe, the Russians suffered similar setbacks. Beijing is moving quickly to consolidate its links with Zimbabwe while the Russians have not yet opened an embassy in Salisbury, and there has already been an exchange of visits by the leaders of China and Zimbabwe. The deputy prime minister of the new nation went to China in June 1980, and the Chinese vice-minister for economic relations with foreign countries, Li Ke, returned the visit in September 1980. The question of economic aid and technical assistance from China was discussed, and the Chinese promised full cooperation and support for the new African nation. A five-year interest-free Chinese loan of $26.6 million was announced during the vice-minister's visit in September 1980. Prime Minister Mugabe paid a highly successful and friendly visit to China in October 1980, and the Chinese leaders lavished high tributes on Mugabe for piloting his country to independence and for his postindependence policies.

The Chinese are anxious to ensure the success of Zimbabwe so that its example may be followed in South Africa and Namibia.[10] Although the PRC never tires of proclaiming its all-out support for the suffering black people in Namibia and South Africa, Beijing would like to see a peaceful settlement in both of those countries because the PRC does not want to have to compete with the Russians in providing arms to the Africans in any major armed conflicts. China, the ardent revolutionary country of the 1950s and the 1960s, now prefers the ballot rather than bullets as a solution to the political issues in southern Africa. Once again, both the Western powers, led by the United States, and China want a peaceful settlement through negotiation; the Russians, on the other hand, would not mind political upheavals and chaos in southern Africa at the expense of the Western powers as well as of China. Reviewing the African situation in 1979–1980, *Beijing Review* stated:

No large-scale wars through Africa in 1979 . . . but the continent was menaced by external threats and the dangers of war. Overt and covert superpower contention could be seen everywhere on the continent from the Horn of Africa in the northeast to West Sahara in northwest and from the heartland to Southern Africa.

The Soviet Union stepped up its drive for hegemony in Africa. More than 40,000 Soviet and Cuban military personnel continued to be stationed in Angola and Ethiopia and Moscow and Havana have attempted to expand their forces into surrounding areas. . . . The Soviet objectives in Africa, according to the Chinese assessment, is "to cut-off the U.S. and Western Europe's oil route."[11]

The Chinese assessment of the Soviet objectives in Africa, in particular, in areas like the Horn of Africa and Red Sea region, is shared by many Western experts on the African situation: "The Soviets," according to one American assessment, "have singled out Africa as a particularly promising spearhead against Western economic interests."[12]

In Africa, once a focus of China's revolutionary ardor (to the point where Beijing tried to subvert the governments of some newly independent African states), the Chinese now seem content to play a moderate role.[13] China has developed extensive relations with a wide range of African states and has diplomatic links with all but five black African states – Angola being the most notable exception. As in Southeast Asia, China now also favors regional cooperation and groups in Africa and welcomes the Economic Community of West African States (ECOWAS), just as it supports ASEAN's role in Southeast Asia. The Chinese point out with appreciation that ECOWAS, consisting of sixteen West African countries and embracing one-fifth of the African continent and one-third of its population, is the largest regional organization of economic cooperation in Africa. Initially, it was concerned solely with economic cooperation, but in recent years, ECOWAS, like ASEAN, has come to advocate regional, political, and military cooperation. The Chinese endorse its wider role "as there are grave outside threats to the independence and security of these countries."[14]

China and the Middle East

China's relations with the Arab world, unlike those of the Soviet Union, have not been hampered by diplomatic ties with Israel, although Israel recognized China in 1949 – and was the first Middle East country to do so. (The Soviet Union did not break off diplomatic relations with Israel until after the Middle East war in June 1967.) China's relative freedom from involvement with established Israeli governments, plus its nonmembership in the United Nations until 1971, has allowed it to adopt a flexible Mideast policy.

The undermining of Western influence was a primary aim of China's activity in the Middle East in the 1950s, but the escalation of the Sino-Soviet dispute has forced China to give increasing priority to attacking the Soviet Union's influence and role in the Middle East.

China has made use of its greater freedom of action chiefly through its support of the Palestine liberation organizations, contrasting a "people's war" interpretation of the Arab-Israeli dispute with the Soviet Union's search for a political solution. During a Middle East visit in 1963–1964, Zhou Enlai pointed out that China had "supported the people of Palestine in their struggle for national sovereignty and regaining their lost homeland" since the 1955 Bandung Conference.[15] At Bandung, Zhou had made the first clear statement of what is still China's interpretation of the creation of Israel: that it was the result of a U.S. imperialist intervention and that it is a tool of U.S. imperialism.[16]

The Chinese stand on the Arab cause in the Middle East was repeatedly expressed in the 1950s and 1960s by the Chinese leaders and by the Chinese press. Whether the question concerned the Suez Canal, Syria's fight for safeguarding national independence, or any other struggle of the Arab people against colonialism, China has consistently stood on the side of the Arab people. Concerning the Suez crisis, Mao said: "We firmly support the entirely lawful action of the Government of Egypt in taking back the Suez Canal Company and resolutely oppose any attempt to encroach on the sovereignty of Egypt and start armed intervention against that country. We must completely frustrate the schemes of imperialism to create tension and prepare for war."[17]

After the promising beginning for China's relations with the United Arab Republic, China's extremism and increased Soviet economic aid placed President Nasser effectively on the Soviet side in the Sino-Soviet dispute. After the 1967 war, China made an attempt to exploit Egypt's disillusion with the Soviet Union by offering the United Arab Republic wheat and money, but the offer was withdrawn after the Khartoum Conference made it clear that Egypt could not be won over to China's stand on Israel.

The internal difficulties of the Cultural Revolution prevented China from fully exploiting the Arab disillusion with the Soviet Union after the 1967 war and from developing relations with countries such as Syria, Algeria, and Iraq, which agree with China about leaving the Arab-Israeli dispute to the Palestinian guerrillas. At the same time, the role of some Chinese radicals in Arab countries during the Cultural Revolution led to difficulties with some countries, for example, Morocco, and to a break in diplomatic relations with Tunisia.

Thus, although China maintains diplomatic relations with countries in the Middle East, China's greatest impact has been as a result of its influence on such movements as the Dhofar Liberation Front (DLF) and, above all, the Palestinian guerrilla organizations. The Palestine Liberation Organization (PLO) was set up after a January 1964 Arab summit, and a PLO office was opened in Beijing after a visit to China in March 1965 by the PLO General Secretary Ahmed Shuqairy. The PLO lost influence after June 1967, and nothing was heard about the Beijing office after Shuqairy's dismissal in December of that year until it was announced, in July 1969, that a new head had been appointed to run the office. However, China has also continued to give training and some arms to other movements, such as al-Fatah, and China's ideological influence on the more extreme groups, most notably the Popular Democratic Front for the Liberation of Palestine (PDFLP), has been considerable.

China gave enthusiastic support to the PLO after its founding in the 1960s, but in 1979, there was some cooling off in Beijing's relations with the PLO. When China took military steps to penalize Vietnam in early 1979 following Hanoi's invasion of Cambodia, the PLO leaders were critical of China's punitive action against Vietnam. Vietnam has been a vociferous backer of the PLO, so the China-Vietnam war of 1979 caused strains and stresses in Beijing's long-standing, friendly relations with the PLO. Before the end of 1979, however, there was a reconciliation between the PRC and the PLO. The Chinese chairman, Hua Guofeng, received a high-powered PLO delegation in Beijing in November 1979, and Hua assured the leader of the delegation, Khaled Fahum, of China's "firm support for the Palestinians exercising self-determination in founding a Palestinian state."[18] This reconciliation may represent a new thrust and direction in China's Middle East policies.

There are, however, more weighty reasons for a lessening of Beijing's early enthusiasm for Arab revolutionary organizations like the PLO and the Dhofar Liberation Front. China has begun to realize, as it realized in Africa, that if it confines its support to revolutionary groups, its image with the established governments of the Middle East will be adversely affected. Further, the revolutionary groups rely heavily on Soviet support, including military support, and they are also extremely anti-American because of the United States' support of Israel. Also, the conservative and rich Middle Eastern states cannot trust China fully if it maintains too close a relationship with the revolutionary groups. Therefore, China has begun to make changes in its tactics in the Middle East, although Beijing continues to vociferously support the Arab causes both inside and outside the United Nations.

Every year the chief of the PRC's delegation to the UN General Assembly expresses China's unqualified and vigorous support of the Arab causes, including the rights of the people of Palestine, and also speaks against the two superpowers, in particular the Soviet Union.[19] But China's objectives in the Middle East, as in many other parts of the Third World, include the containment of Soviet influence and power in the region, and the Western powers, as well as the oil-producing countries of the region, are equally concerned about the Soviet Union's penetration in the Middle East. In recent years, China has sought to develop closer ties with countries like Djibouti, Jordan, and Oman. The establishment of diplomatic ties with Oman in 1978 was considered to be Beijing's Arab coup, because in the 1960s, China had agreed to give support to the Dhofar Liberation Front in its fight against the sultan of Oman. (The DLF is a Marxist-Leninist group that operates in Oman's mountainous province of Dhofar, and their activities against the ruler of Oman used to also be carried on in South Yemen, which has become a Soviet satellite in the Middle East and threatens the neighboring Arab states.)

In the changed circumstances, China is no longer interested in destabilizing the present regime in Oman, which shares China's concern about Soviet designs in the Middle East and the Persian Gulf. Oman is so strategically located that its control by the Soviet Union might cut off the oil supplies from the oil-producing Arab states to the Western countries and Japan. China would not like to see the Soviet Union acquire such a dominating position in the Persian Gulf area, so strategic considerations get preference over the revolutionary ideology in China's present-day Middle East policy.[20]

Sino-Egyptian Relations

President Anwar Sadat's abrogation of Egypt's friendship treaty with Russia on March 15, 1976, gave Beijing an excellent opportunity to enter into Middle Eastern affairs through an influential Arab country. Sadat spoke against the Soviet Union's crude diplomacy in dealings with smaller nations,[21] and he had approached both India and China with requests for military spare parts in October 1975 after the Soviet Union had refused to supply the much-needed parts—both India and China manufacture Soviet-style equipment. India turned down the Egyptian request because of a Soviet veto, but China gave Egypt thirty engines for MiG-17 and MiG-21 fighter/bombers as "gifts," which led to an immediate warm-up of the relationship between Beijing and Cairo. The then vice-president of Egypt, Hosni Mubarak, paid a visit to Beijing on April 20, 1976, and a Chinese-Egyptian military protocol agreement was signed the next day, April 21.[22] The signing of the pact marked a series of 1976 successes for Beijing in its diplomatic rivalry with Moscow.

During a three-day stay in Cairo in July 1976 en route to Beijing, I had lengthy talks with the Chinese ambassador in Cairo, an old friend, and with some senior Egyptian Foreign Ministry officials. Both sides seemed to be eager to develop closer and friendly relations. Beijing has always been unhappy about Moscow's growing influence in the Middle East since the mid 1950s, so Beijing is happy to develop friendly relations with the Middle Eastern countries. The Soviet Union, on the other hand, has stepped up its propaganda against China's claims of friendship for and support of Arab peoples; China's reply is to point to its record of unqualified support for the Arabs in the United Nations and other international forums.

Since Anwar Sadat signed the Camp David accord with Israel, the Arab countries have become critical of Egypt's policy. Egypt has been expelled from the Arab League and from the Islamic countries' grouping, and Sadat was accused of selling "Arab interests" under pressure from the United States. China realizes the Arab opposition to the Camp David accord, but it also appreciates the fact that the accord was a big diplomatic setback for the Soviet Union in the Middle East and a major gain for the United States. Although the PRC and the United States do not have identical views on the Middle East, both share a concern about Soviet designs in the region. So Beijing is facing the dilemma of all major powers in the Middle East: It cannot ignore the popular feelings among the Arabs, but the realpolitik in the Middle East dictates that China must develop closer links with countries that are thoroughly anti-Soviet, such as Egypt. For instance, China got some useful information and data about the Soviet Union's most sophisticated and modern weapons, which the Russians gave to Egypt before Sadat broke away from Moscow.[23] So China does not wish to break off or cool off its relations with Egypt. The then vice-president, Mubarak, paid his second visit to China in January 1980, and at the end of his visit, it was stated that China and Egypt "have many common or similar points of view on international affairs. China and Egypt need to carry out extensive cooperation in opposing hegemonism and safeguarding world peace."[24] President Sadat was also expected to visit China in 1979, but the visit did not materialize. China and Egypt's closer relations are based on the common objective of containment of Soviet involvement in the Middle East, and the military ties between the two countries since 1976 are also mutually beneficial to both countries.

China's current policy in the Middle East, as in Africa, is to put priority on government to government relations and to develop a common front with the United States and NATO countries to contain Soviet influence, but China also maintains its old links with revolutionary organizations such as the PLO. China is disillusioned because of the slow progress toward implementation of the Camp David accord, but Beijing, unlike the PLO and the radical Arab countries, has not denounced the accord outright.

"Ideology has been the first casualty of China's drive toward a more dynamic and effective policy" toward the Middle East in the 1970s,[25] and that situation is likely to be continued in the 1980s. A survey of the Middle East situation appeared in *Beijing Review* in January 1980, and it reflects the dichotomies in China's current policy toward the Middle East. The *Review* gave cautious approval to the Camp David accord and to Egypt's policy of negotiation with Israel without, however, offending the Arabs opposed to the accord: "The old pattern in the area, marked by confrontation between the Arab camp and Israel has radically changed since last [1979] March when Egypt and Israel concluded a peace treaty through the mediation of the United States. . . . The treaty put an end to a state of war between Egypt and Israel. . . . Egypt recovered part of the Sinai Peninsula."[26] *People's Daily* also indicated that China felt that the solution to the Arab-Israeli conflict lay in the course charted by Egyptian President Anwar Sadat—through reconciliation with Israel and through the Camp David accord.[27]

But Beijing is also fully aware of the Arab opposition to the Camp David agreement. The *Beijing Review* article therefore, added: "Most Arab countries boycott the peace treaty and call for a comprehensive set-tlement of the Middle East question"; then it again supported Egypt's policy by stating: "Egypt has time and again declared that the signing of the Egyptian-Israel treaty is only an initial step toward peace . . . a com-prehensive Middle East settlement, the key of which is the solution of the legitimate rights of the Palestinian people."

The *Beijing Review* also made some favorable comments on U.S. policy toward the Arab countries while it condemned the Soviet policy: "Since the end of the 1973 October war in the Middle East, the United States has been working for the improvement of its relations with the Arab coun-tries while continuing to support Israel. . . . To offset American efforts for peace and negotiations, the Soviet Union has been cultivating in-stability and division. Making capital of some Arab countries' discontent with the treaty, Moscow has been trying to sow discord in the Arab world in order to fan opposition to Egypt and to prevent other Arab countries from joining the peace process." The *Beijing Review* article con-cluded by stating that Moscow's opposition to the Camp David accord is not because of its genuine concern for the Arab cause, but is aimed at strengthening Moscow's Middle East position as a challenge to the United States.[28]

The foreign minister of Oman, Al Zawawi, stated the moderate Arab states' current attitude toward the PRC: "China has changed its attitude to the developing countries. Although China is dedicated to communism, it is also committed to the concept of peaceful co-existence with nations with different social systems."[29] The moderate Arab states and the Arab kings are no longer worried about threats resulting from the PRC's revolutionary zeal; they now regard the Soviet Union's designs as a greater threat to their existence. The conservative Arab states also recognize the potential role of China in the containment of Soviet expan-sionist designs. So there are some common, though not identical, in-terests between the PRC and the conservative Arab states, and there is a growing sense of confidence and closer links between the PRC and the conservative Arab countries, which feel threatened by the Soviet Union's designs in the region.

Saudi Arabia, the richest oil-producing state, a friend of the United States, and terribly upset by the recent Soviet moves, has not yet recognized "the godless" state, the PRC, but the day may not be far off when Beijing and Mecca may have diplomatic links, and Pakistan, a friend of both countries, may play a constructive role in developing diplomatic links between the PRC and Saudi Arabia. Most of the recent developments in the Indian Ocean–Persian Gulf area may bring the PRC closer to the conservative forces in the Arab world, but the PRC will still not abandon its links with the popular and revolutionary groups. China never misses an opportunity to express its support of the causes of the people of Palestine or of the role of the PLO, but the revolutionary zeal of the PRC is now adjusted to the realities in the Middle East, and when there is any conflict between vital national interests and ideology, the former gets preference.

China and Latin America

China's persistent and consistent support to the causes of the Third World countries—Asian, African, and Latin American—is as old as the PRC itself, and China not only champions those causes, but it considers itself as belonging to the Third World. Since its entry into the United Nations in 1971, which was largely supported by the Third World countries, China has aspired to being the self-appointed spokesman of the Third World.

According to the Chinese concept of the Third World, Latin America is an integral part of it, and under its forward-looking foreign policy since 1970, China has stepped up its activities in those countries. China is targeting some of its diplomatic efforts toward Latin America to complete its network of Third World supporters, stymie a successful rival effort from the Soviets, and further isolate Taiwan.[30] In a survey of China's role in Latin America an American scholar has written, "The leaders of communist China have manifested, both in word and deed, a deep abiding interest in Latin America."[31] He lists both favorable and limiting factors for China in its effort to develop relations with Latin American countries, and among the favorable factors for the Chinese involvement in Latin America are first, the prevalence of anti-imperialist sentiments in Latin America, feelings based on the experiences of Latin American countries in their dealings with the United States and Western European countries. Second, there is what he calls a "respectability of Marxist concepts" among Latin American intellectuals. And third, the political culture of the Latins leads them to settle political issues by the bullet rather than by the ballot, which is similar to Mao's theory that political power grows out of the barrel of a gun.

There are, of course, serious limiting factors to China's role in Latin America. First is the geographical distance coupled with the fact that the

United States controls the sea. During the era of the U.S. policy of containment of the PRC, Beijing could do little to overcome the United States' determination not to allow China to penetrate into Latin America. Second, the military regimes in many Latin American countries are strongly anticommunist and, as such, anti-China also. Third, China is not in a position to provide large-scale economic aid to developing Latin American countries; similarly, China's ability to provide arms supplies is limited and not comparable to that of its rival, the Soviet Union.[32] Yet China's diplomatic efforts in Latin America in recent years have proved fairly successful, particularly in view of the limiting factors.

China's early diplomatic and other initiatives toward Latin America were directed against U.S. imperialism, but by the beginning of the 1970s, the Soviet Union had been upgraded to the position of China's primary enemy, and Cuba, the only communist country in Latin America, had turned out to be a Soviet satellite. So China's new policy and tactics in Latin America are directed mainly against those two communist countries.

Pre-1970 Relations

Before its entry into the United Nations in 1971 and the Sino-American rapprochement in 1971–1972, China had trade and cultural contacts with several countries, but the only important relationship was with Castro's Cuba, the emergence of which was warmly welcomed by China both for anti-American reasons and because China imagined that the Cuban revolution would serve as a model for other Latin American countries. But Sino-Cuban relations have become uneasy, partially because of the Sino-Soviet dispute, in which Castro has repeatedly stressed he has no desire to become embroiled. China's inability to replace the Soviet Union as a source of military and economic aid, on which Cuba is dependent, has become the major factor in the relations between China and Cuba. Cuba's estrangement from China was also partly the fault of the Chinese themselves, who used the Soviet Union's failure to give Cuba full support during the missile crisis for propaganda purposes. Later attempts to subvert Cuban soldiers and officials, and the Chinese treatment of Cuban requests for rice, have contributed to the deterioration in Sino-Cuban relations.

In the Communist parties of Latin America generally, the growth of the Sino-Soviet dispute has encouraged the formation of small splinter groups. But the subsequent divergence of Cuban and Soviet policies toward Latin America, and the failure of the pro-Chinese groups to practice, as well as preach, "armed struggle," have led to the majority of the left-wing extremist groups being pro-Castro.

Chinese journalists and trade officials seem to have played a particularly active role in Latin America, where China's only full diplomatic mission has been in Cuba. By 1960, the NCNA had offices in eight Latin American countries, but the activities of that agency's correspondents resulted in the office in Ecuador being closed in 1963 and the Venezuelan representative's being arrested in the same year. After nine Chinese—two of them NCNA correspondents and three of them members of the permanent trade office—had been arrested in Brazil in 1964, they were found to possess a list of Brazilian generals to be assassinated, literature on guerrilla warfare, and information about a training camp for guerrillas about fifty miles from the capital. At the end of 1966, the Mexican authorities arrested some members of a pro-Chinese Marxist-Leninist movement that had been receiving funds through the NCNA office.[33]

By 1970, only two of the five Beijing-staffed NCNA bureaus in Latin America—those in Cuba and Chile—were still functioning, and after the death of Ché Guevara and some guerrilla setbacks, China seemed to give up its more ambitious plans to weaken the United States through the promotion of "people's wars." But China had not abandoned all such plans, as was underlined by a *People's Daily* commentary on November 20, 1970, which claimed that the "anti-American struggle" in Latin America would contribute to a decline in the United States' position as "overlord" of the continent. Another sign of Beijing's continuing interest was its decision in 1970 to double the number of broadcasts to Panama, Colombia, and Cuba (from seven to fourteen hours a week) and to increase the number of broadcasts to Peru, Ecuador, and the Dominican Republic. Yet, it seems that China has provided only minimal material or financial support to the Maoist groups in Latin America, and an article in the pro-Chinese Brazilian Communist party's organ, *Liberacion,* stressed that the party must rely on its own efforts in the liberation struggle.[34]

Chinese propaganda has continued to report the activities of the few remaining pro-Chinese parties and Maoist splinter groups and to highlight all anti-American actions, particularly those involving students and peasants. In 1970–1971, publicity was given to the Brazilian peasants' struggle, to the farce of the Brazilian parliamentary elections, and, for the first time in a year, to the operations of the Maoist Ejercito popular de liberacion (EPT) in Colombia.[35]

Following an improvement in relations with Cuba and Chile in 1970, China preferred to concentrate on developing ties through official and semiofficial channels. An exchange of greetings and diplomatic courtesies for Cuba's National Day in July and a visit to China by a Cuban friendship delegation were followed by the establishment of an office of the Cuban news agency, Prensa Latina, in Beijing in November. Shortly afterward, a Chinese ambassador was appointed to Havana (after a four-year gap).

Although Beijing reacted cautiously at first to the election of the Marxist Salvador Allende as president of Chile in September 1970, it eventually approved of his program as being anti-imperialist, and Zhou Enlai, in a congratulatory telegram, spoke of the Chilean people's "just struggle against imperialist aggression . . . for the defense of national independence."[36] The Chilean foreign minister announced on January 5, 1971, that his government had decided to recognize China and that an agreement had been reached to exchange ambassadors as soon as possible. Other likely targets for Chinese diplomatic and other overtures are Peru, Ecuador, and Bolivia.

New Era of Chinese Diplomacy in Latin America (1970–1980)

Beijing started the decade of the 1980s by establishing diplomatic relations with Ecuador, and the *People's Daily* predicted that the 1980s would witness a greater development of our relations with Latin America.[37] The example of Ecuador was followed by Colombia, Bolivia, the Dominican Republic, and later, Uruguay.

The large diplomatic thrust that began after China's entry into the United Nations and its normalization of relations with Washington has been supplemented by China's growing economic relations with Latin American countries. Those countries supply some of the commodities that are vital for China's four-modernization plans – such as grain, copper, and high-grade iron ore – and they buy China's prime exports – oil, textiles, and high-industrial products.[38]

China has been extremely cautious in its newly established relations with Latin American countries. Beijing no longer talks in terms of people's wars in Latin America to overthrow the military dictatorial regimes, and China now prefers to deal with the established governments rather than with Marxist-Leninist revolutionary groups. Although China has not abandoned its moral support of the national liberation movements in the Third World, China now puts a much higher priority on government to government relations than on promoting people's wars.

In Latin America, China is no longer interested in undermining the U.S. position; China's main target in Latin America today is Cuba. Cuba's "sinister hand" is seen everywhere in Latin America, and Cuba is depicted as having regional hegemonic designs in the region backed by the world hegemonic power, the Soviet Union, just as Vietnam is called Russia's "Asian Cuba" with regional hegemonic aspirations in Southeast Asia.

China's efforts to cultivate better relations with Spain seem to be geared toward China's role in Latin America because Spain still has a great deal of influence in that region. China's relations with the military juntas in Chile and Argentina are the subject of critical comments in certain quarters, just as Beijing's growing links with conservative Arab states such as Oman or with moderate ones such as Egypt are regarded as compromising Beijing's earlier zeal for revolution and people's wars. Since the 1973 army coup in Chile, China and Romania are the only two countries that have not broken diplomatic ties with the new regime. Similarly, Beijing's "flirting" with Argentina is also criticized on the basis that China is sacrificing its ideology in favor of national interests.

China's world role, whether in Africa, Asia, or Latin America, needed redefinition after its emergence from isolation and the xenophobia of the Cultural Revolution. Its role, both in the United Nations and outside the United Nations, dispelled early fears in many countries that extreme political attitudes would make the PRC a difficult country to deal with. In reality, the post-Mao Chinese leaders have displayed extreme caution and have adjusted China's earlier revolutionary ideology to promote China's new role in world affairs. The Latin American countries, like the Afro-Asian nations, have been pleasantly surprised by China's moderate and conciliatory tones and postures. The military adventures by the Soviet Union and its client-states, such as Cuba and Vietnam, have caused new fears about the Soviet Union's global role, and China's consistent and vigorous opposition to the Soviet expansionist designs has helped its role in the Third World, including Latin America.

Notes

1. A. Doak Barnett, *China and the Major Powers in East Asia* (Washington, D.C.: Brookings Institution, 1977), p. 5.

2. *Washington Post*, August 21, 1978.

3. See *Beijing Review*, April 21, 1980, p. 3.

4. See the text of the speech of the chairman of the PRC delegation, Deng Xiaoping, at the Special Session of the UN General Assembly, April 10, 1974, issued by the Foreign Languages Press, 1974, pp. 9 and 17.

5. Barnett, *China and the Major Powers in East Asia*, p. 14.

6. Based on the author's resarch and talks in London (British Ministry of Foreign Affairs), 1977–1978.

7. *Peking Review*, July 4, 1975, pp. 24–25.

8. R. Breeze, "China's African Connection," *Far Eastern Economic Review*, November 28, 1980.

9. *Beijing Review*, April 21, 1980, p. 3.

10. Breeze, "China's African Connection."

11. *Beijing Review*, January 14, 1980, p. 13.

12. Walter F. Hahn and Alvin J. Cohrell, *Soviet Shadow over Africa*, Monograph in International Affairs, Center for Advanced International Studies, University of Miami (Coral Gables, Fla.: University of Miami, 1976), p. 10.

13. Based on the author's research and discussion in London (British foreign officials), 1979–1980.

14. See *Beijing Review*, June 29, 1981, p. 11.

15. Based on the author's research in London.

16. Ibid.

17. See the text of Chairman Mao's speech at the Eighth National Congress of the Chinese Communist Party, September 15, 1956, in *China Supports the Arab Peoples' Struggle For National Independence* (Beijing: Foreign Languages Press), 1958, p. 5.

18. See Richard Breeze, "China Woos the Arabs," *Far Eastern Economic Review,* December 7, 1979, pp. 36–37.

19. For details, see G. W. Choudhury, *Chinese Perception of the World* (Washington, D.C.: University Press of America, 1977), pp. 64–67.

20. See Denzil Peinis, "Peking's Arab Coup," *Far Eastern Economic Review,* June 23, 1978.

21. *Washington Post,* September 10, 1976.

22. *New York Times,* April 23, 1976.

23. Based on the author's interviews and talks in Cairo in July 1976.

24. *Beijing Review,* January 21, 1981, p. 7.

25. David Bonavia, "China on the World Stage," *Far Eastern Economic Review,* July 28, 1978, pp. 22–23.

26. *Beijing Review,* January 28, 1980.

27. Quoted in Breeze, "China Woos the Arabs."

28. *Beijing Review,* January 28, 1980.

29. See Peinis, "Peking's Arab Coup," pp. 12–13.

30. Richard Breeze, "Peking's Sombrero Diplomacy," *Far Eastern Economic Review,* August 29, 1980.

31. Cecil Johnson, *Communist China and Latin America* (New York: Columbia University Press, 1970), p. 1.

32. Based on the author's research and discussions in London (British foreign officials), 1975–1978.

33. Ibid.

34. Ibid.

35. Ibid.

36. Ibid.

37. Quoted in Breeze, "Peking's Sombrero Diplomacy."

38. See ibid.

Selected Bibliography

GENERAL WORKS

Armstrong, J. D. *Revolutionary Diplomacy: Chinese Foreign Policy and the United Front Doctrine.* Berkeley: University of California Press, 1977.

Bachrack, Stanley D. *The Committee of One Million—"China Lobby" Politics, 1953-1971.* New York: Columbia University Press, 1976.

Barnds, William J., ed. *China and America: The Search for a New Relationship.* Council on Foreign Relations Book. New York: New York University Press, 1977.

Barnett, A. Doak. *Communist China and Asia: A Challenge to American Policy.* New York: Harper & Brothers for the Council on Foreign Relations, 1960.

_____ . *Communist China in Perspective.* New York: Frederick A. Praeger, 1962.

_____ . *A New U.S. Policy Toward China.* Washington, D.C.: Brookings Institution, 1971.

_____ . *China and the Major Powers in East Asia.* Washington, D.C.: Brookings Institution, 1977.

_____ . *China Policy: Old Problems and New Challenges.* Washington, D.C.; Brookings Institution, 1977.

_____ . *Uncertain Passage: China's Transition to the Post-Mao Era.* Washington, D.C.: Brookings Institution, 1979.

Barnett, A. Doak, and Reishauer, Edwin O., eds. *The United States and China: The Next Decade.* New York: Praeger Publishers for the National Committee on United States–China Relations, 1970.

Baum, Richard, ed. *China's Four Modernizations.* Boulder, Colo.: Westview Press, 1980.

Brown, Harrison. *China Among the Nations of the Pacific.* Boulder, Colo.: Westview Press, 1981.

Brzezinski, Zbigniew K. *The Soviet Bloc: Unity and Conflict.* Cambridge, Mass.: Harvard University Press, 1960.

_____ . *Between Two Ages: America's Role in the Technetronic Era.* New York: Viking Press, 1970.

Bueler, William M. *U.S. and China Policy and the Problem of Taiwan.* Boulder, Colo.: Associated University Press, 1971.

Choudhury, G. W. *India, Pakistan, Bangladesh, and the Major Powers.* New York: Free Press for the Foreign Policy Research Institute, 1975.

_____ . *Brezhnev's Collective Security Plan For Asia.* Washington, D.C.: Center for Strategic and International Studies, Georgetown University, 1976.

———. *Chinese Perception of the World.* Washington, D.C.: University Press of America, 1977.

Choudhury, G. W., ed. *Sino-American Relations in the Post-Mao Era.* Washington, D.C.: University Press of America, 1977.

Clubb, O. Edmund. *China and Russia: The Great Game.* New York: Columbia University Press, 1971.

Cohen, Jerome A., ed. *China's Practice of International Law: Some Case Studies.* Cambridge, Mass.: Harvard University Press, 1972.

Dentscher, Isaac. *Russia, China, and the West, 1953–1966.* Baltimore, Md.: Penguin Books, 1970.

Domes, Jurgen. *China After the Cultural Revolution.* Berkeley: University of California Press, 1977.

Doolin, Dennis J. *Territorial Claims in the Sino-Soviet Conflict: Documents and Analysis.* Stanford, Calif.: Hoover Institution on War, Revolution, and Peace, 1965.

Dutt, V. P. *China and the World: An Analysis of Communist China's Foreign Policy.* New York: Praeger, 1966.

Eckstein, Alexander. *Communist China's Economic Growth and Foreign Trade.* New York: McGraw-Hill Book Company for the Council on Foreign Relations, 1966.

Endicott, John E., and Heaton, William R. *The Politics of East Asia: China, Japan, Korea.* Boulder, Colo.: Westview Press, 1978.

Fairbank, John K. *Chinese-American Interactions.* New Brunswick, N.J.: Rutgers University Press, 1975.

———. *China Perceived: Images and Policies in China-America Relations.* New York: Alfred A. Knopf, 1976.

Fairbank, John K., ed. *The Chinese World Order: Traditional China's Foreign Relations.* Harvard University Press, 1968.

Fairbank, John K., and Reischauer, Edwin O. *East-Asia: The Great Tradition.* New York: Houghton, Mifflin, 1960.

Fingar, Thomas, ed. *China's Quest for Independence: Policy Evolution in the 1970s.* Boulder, Colo.: Westview Press, 1979.

Fitzgerald, C. P. *The Chinese View of Their Place in the World.* London: Oxford University Press for the Royal Institute of International Affairs, 1964.

Gelber, Harry G. *Technology, Defense, and External Relations in China 1975–1978.* Boulder, Colo.: Westview Press, 1979.

Gittings, John. *Survey of the Sino-Soviet Dispute 1963–1967.* London: Oxford University Press, 1968.

———. *A Chinese View of China.* New York: Pantheon Books, 1973.

———. *The World and China.* New York: Harper & Row, 1974.

Godwin, Paul. *PLA-Military Forces of the PRC.* Boulder, Colo.: Westview Press, 1981.

Griffin, William E. *The Sino-Soviet Rift.* Cambridge, Mass.: MIT Press, 1967.

———. *Peking, Moscow, and Beyond.* Washington Papers no. 6. Washington, D.C.: Center for Strategic and International Studies, Georgetown University, 1973.

Gurtov, Melvin. *China and Southeast Asia, the Politics of Survival: A Study of Foreign Policy Interactions.* Baltimore, Md.: John Hopkins University Press, 1971.

Halpern, A. M., ed. *Policies Toward China: Views from Six Continents.* New York: McGraw-Hill, 1965.

Harrison, Selig S. *China, Oil, and Asia: Conflict Ahead?* New York: Columbia University Press, 1977.

Hellmann, Donald C. *Japan and East Asia: The New International Order.* New York: Praeger, 1970.

Hinton, Harold C. *Communist China in World Politics.* New York: Macmillan, 1966.

_____ . *China's Turbulent Quest: An Analysis of China's Foreign Policy Since 1949.* Enlarged ed. New York: Macmillan, 1972.

_____ . *Peking-Washington: Chinese Foreign Policy and the United States.* Washington Papers no. 34. Beverly Hills, Calif.: Sage Publications for the Center for Strategic and International Studies, Georgetown University, 1976.

Hinton, Harold C., ed. *The People's Republic of China: A Handbook.* Boulder, Colo.: Westview Press, 1979.

Hsiao, Genet. *The Foreign Trade of China.* Berkeley: University of California Press, 1971.

Jain, J. P. *China, Pakistan, and Bangladesh.* New Delhi: Radiant Publishers, 1974.

Johnson, Cecil. *Communist China and Latin America.* New York: Columbia University Press, 1970.

Kalicki, J. H. *The Pattern of Sino-American Crises: Political-Military Interactions in the 1950s.* London: Cambridge University Press, 1975.

Karnow, Stanley. *Mao and China: From Revolution to Revolution.* London: Macmillan, 1973.

Kim, Samuel S. *China, the United Nations, and World Order.* Princeton, N.J.: Princeton University Press, 1979.

Kintner, William R. *The Impact of President Nixon's Visit to Peking on International Politics.* Research Monograph Series no. 13. Philadelphia: Foreign Policy Research Institute, 1972.

Kroff, Justus M. Van. *Communism in Southeast Asia.* Berkeley: University of California Press, 1975.

Lamb, Alastair. *The China-India Border.* London: Oxford University Press for the Royal Institute of International Affairs, 1964.

Larkin, Bruce D. *China and Africa 1949–1970.* Berkeley: University of California Press, 1973.

Lee, Hong Yung. *The Politics of the Chinese Cultural Revolution.* Berkeley: University of California Press, 1978.

Levine, Lawrence W. *U.S.-China Relations.* New York: Robert Speller & Sons, 1972.

Lindbeck, John M. H. *Understanding China: An Assessment of American Scholarly Resources.* New York: Praeger, 1971.

Mah Feng-Hwa. *The Foreign Trade of Mainland China.* Edinburgh: Edinburgh University Press, 1972.

Mao Zedong. *Selected Works of Mao Tse-Tung.* 5 vols. Beijing: Foreign Languages Press, 1967–1977.

Martin, Edwin W. *Southeast Asia and China: The End of Containment*. Boulder, Colo.: Westview Press, 1977.

Marwah, Onkar, and Pollack, Jonathan D., eds. *Military Power and Policy in Asian States: China, India, Japan*. Boulder, Colo.: Westview Press, 1979.

Maxwell, Neville. *India's China War*. London: Jonathan Cape, 1970.

Nail, J. A. *India, Russia, China, and Bangladesh*. New Delhi: S. Chad & Co., 1972.

O'Neil, Robert. *Peking-Hanoi Relations in 1970*. Canberra: Australian National University Press, 1971.

Nelson, Harvey W. *The Chinese Military System: An Organizational Study of the Chinese People's Liberation Army*. 2d ed rev. Boulder, Colo.: Westview Press, 1981.

Ness, Peter Van. *Revolution and Chinese Foreign Policy: Peking's Support for Wars of National Liberation*. Berkeley: University of California Press, 1971.

Ogunsanwo, Alaba. *China's Policy in Africa, 1958–1971*. New York: Cambridge University Press, 1979.

Oksenberg, Michel, and Oxnam, Robert B., eds. *Dragon and Eagle: United States–China Relations: Past and Future*. New York: Basic Books, 1978.

Oxnam, Robert B., and Bush, Richard C., eds. *China Briefing, 1980*. Boulder, Colo.: Westview Press, 1980.

Petrov, Vladimir. *U.S.-Soviet Detente: Past and Future*. Washington, D.C.: American Enterprise Institute for Public Policy Research, 1975.

Rhode, Grant F., and Reid, E. Whitlock. *Treaties of the People's Republic of China, 1949–1978: An Annotated Compilation*. Boulder, Colo.: Westview Press, 1980.

Rice, Edward. *Mao's Way*. Berkeley: University of California Press, 1972.

Robinson, Thomas W. *Peking's Revolutionary Strategy in the Developing World: The Failures of Success*. Santa Monica, Calif.: Rand Corp., August 1969.

Rubinstein, Alvin, ed. *Soviet and Chinese Influence in the Third World*. New York: Praeger, 1975.

Scalapino, Robert A. *Asia and the Road Ahead*. Berkeley: University of California Press, 1975.

Sen Gupta, Bhabani. *Fulcrum of Asia: Relations Among China, India, Pakistan, and the USSR*. New York: Pegasus, 1970.

Service, John S. *The American Papers: Some Problems in the History of U.S.-China Relations*. Berkeley: University of California Press, 1971.

Simmonds, J. D. *China's World: The Foreign Policy of a Developing State*. New York: Columbia University Press, 1970.

Snow, Edgar. *Red China Today*. New York: Random House, Vintage Books, 1971.

Stuart, Douglas T., and Tow, William T. *China, the Soviet Union, and the West: Strategic and Political Dimensions for the 1980s*. Boulder, Colo.: Westview Press, 1981.

Sutter, Robert G. *China Water: Toward Sino-American Reconciliation*. Baltimore, Md.: Johns Hopkins University Press, 1978.

———. *Chinese Foreign Policy After the Cultural Revolution, 1966–1973*. Boulder, Colo.: Westview Press, 1978.

Syed, Anwar H. *China and Pakistan: Diplomacy of an Entente Cordiale*. Amherst: University of Massachusetts Press, 1974.

Taylor, Jay. *China and Southeast Asia: Peking's Relations with Revolutionary Movements.* New York: Praeger, 1974.

Terrill, Ross. *800,000,000: The Real China.* Boston: Little, Brown, 1973.

——— . *Mao Zedong: A Biography.* New York: Harper & Row, 1981.

Thornton, Richard C. *China: A Political History, 1917–1980.* Boulder, Colo.: Westview Press, 1981.

Welfield, John. *Japan and Nuclear China.* Canberra: Australian National University Press, 1970.

Whiting, Allen S. *The Chinese Calculus of Deterrence: India and Indo-China.* Ann Arbor: University of Michigan Press, 1975.

Zagoria, Donald S. *The Sino-Soviet Conflict, 1956–61.* Princeton, N.J.: Princeton University Press, 1962.

DOCUMENTS

For further understanding of China's external relations, the following may be recommended.

U.S. Documents

1. *Sino-Soviet Conflict.* Report on the Sino-Soviet conflict and its implications by the Subcommittee on the Far East and the Pacific of the Committee on Foreign Affairs, House of Representatives, May 4, 1965. Washington, D.C.: Government Printing Office, 1965.
2. *United States Policy Toward Asia.* Report of the Subcommittee of the Far East and the Pacific of the Committee on Foreign Affairs, House of Representatives, May 19, 1966. Washington, D.C.: Government Printing Office, 1966.
3. *United States–China Relations: A Strategy For the Future.* Hearings before the Subcommittee on Asian and Pacific Affairs of the Committee on Foreign Affairs, House of Representatives, October 1970. Washington, D.C.: Government Printing Office, 1970.
4. *New China Policy: Its Impact on the United States and Asia.* Report of the Committee on Asian and Pacific Affairs of the Committee on Foreign Affairs, House of Representatives. Washington, D.C.: Government Printing Office, 1972.
5. *China Enters the Post-Mao Era.* Report by Senator Mike Mansfield to the Committee on Foreign Relations, U.S. Senate, report no. 3. Washington, D.C.: Government Printing Office, November 1976.
6. *Shifting Balance of Power in Asia: Implications for Future U.S. Policy.* Hearings before the Subcommittee on Future Foreign Policy Research and Development of the Committee on International Relations, House of Representatives, 94th Cong., November 18 and December 10, 1975; January 28, March 8, April 7, and May 18, 1976. Washington, D.C.: Government Printing Office, 1976.
7. *The United States and China.* Report by Senator Hugh Scott to the Committee on Foreign Relations, U.S. Senate, September 1976. Washington, D.C.: Government Printing Office, 1976.

8. *United States–Soviet Union–China: The Great Power Triangle.* Hearings before the Subcommittee on Future Foreign Policy and Development of the Committee on International Relations, House of Representatives, 94th Cong., parts 1 and 2. Washington, D.C.: Government Printing Office, 1976.

9. *Normalization of Relations with the People's Republic of China: Practical Implications.* Hearings before the Subcommittee on Asian and Pacific Affairs of the Committee on International Relations, 95th Cong., 1st sess., September 20, 21, 28, 29; October 11 and 13, 1977. Washington, D.C.: Government Printing Office, 1977.

10. *United States–Soviet Union–China: The Great Power Triangle.* Summary of hearings conducted by the Subcommittee on Future Foreign Policy Research and Development of the Committee on International Relations, October–December 1975; March–June 1976. Washington, D.C. Government Printing Office, August 1, 1977.

11. *A New Realism: Factfinding Mission to the People's Republic of China, July 3–13, 1978.* Report by the Subcommittee on Asian and Pacific Affairs to the Committee on International Relations, House of Representatives. Washington, D.C.: Government Printing Office, December 1978.

12. *China and Asia: An Analysis of China's Recent Policy Toward Neighboring States.* Report by the Foreign Affairs and National Defense Division, Congressional Research Service, Library of Congress, preceded by a State Department report on normalization negotiations with China. Prepared for the Subcommittee on Asian and Pacific Affairs of the Committee on Foreign Affairs, House of Representatives. Washington, D.C.: Government Printing Office, 1979.

13. *Playing the China Card: Implications for United States-Soviet-Chinese Relations.* Report prepared for the Subcommittee on Asian and Pacific Affairs of the Committee on Foreign Affairs, House of Representatives, by the Foreign Affairs and National Defense Division, Congressional Research Service, Library of Congress. Washington, D.C.: Government Printing Office, October 1979.

14. *Recognizing the People's Republic of China: The Experience of Japan, Australia, France, and West Germany.* Report prepared for the Subcommittee on Asian and Pacific Affairs of the Committee on Foreign Affairs, House of Representatives, by the Foreign Affairs and National Defense Division, Congressional Research Service, Library of Congress. Washington, D.C.: Government Printing Office, May 1979.

15. *The United States, China, and Japan.* Report to the Committee on Foreign Relations, U.S. Senate. Washington, D.C.: Government Printing Office, September 1979.

Chinese Documents

1. Documents of various sessions of the National Congress of the Communist Party of China. Beijing: Foreign Languages Press, 1966–1981.

2. Speeches of the Chinese foreign minister at the United Nations, 1971–1981. Beijing: Foreign Languages Press, 1971–1981.

JOURNALS, NEWSPAPERS, WEEKLIES, NEWS AGENCIES

A. Journals

Peking (Beijing) Review
China Quarterly (London)
International Affairs (London)
Economist (London)
Asian Survey (Berkeley, Calif.)
Foreign Affairs (New York)
Foreign Policy (New York)
Orbis (Philadelphia)
Pacific Affairs (Vancouver)
Asia-Pacific Community (Tokyo)
Far Eastern Economic Review (Hong Kong)
International Affairs (Moscow)
International Studies (New Delhi)

B. Newspapers, Weeklies, News Agencies

People's Daily (Beijing)
New China News Agency (Xinhua)
Foreign Broadcast Information Service (Hong Kong)
Pravda (Moscow)
Izvestia (Moscow)
Tass (Soviet News Agency, Moscow)
Reprints from the Soviet Press (Compass Publications, New York)
New York Times (New York)
Washington Post (Washington, D.C.)
Times (London)
Guardian (London)
Daily Telegraph (London)
Observer (London)

Index

Acheson, Dean, 14–15, 16, 19, 20
Aden, Gulf of, 151
Afghanistan, 126, 145, 194, 227. *See also* Soviet Union, and Afghanistan
Africa, 3, 11, 28, 63, 83, 132, 149, 157–159, 165, 167, 227, 270, 271–276. *See also* National liberation movements, African; People's Republic of China, and Third World; *individual countries*
Africa Institute (Moscow), 157
Afro-Asian Nations Conference
1955 (Bandung), 2, 25–26, 27–28, 207, 242, 277
1964 preparatory meeting, 27
1965 (Algeria) cancelled, 27, 29
Aigun treaty, 134
Aksai Chin zone, 258, 259, 260
Aleksandrov, I., 62
Algeria, 27, 29. *See also* People's Republic of China, and Algeria
Ali, Mohammed, 26
Alsop, Joseph, 86
Amin, Hafizullah, 151
Andropov, Yuri, 182
Angola. *See* People's Republic of China, and Angola; Soviet Union, and Angola
ANZUS mutual security pact, 6, 83, 165, 174, 200, 246, 248, 264, 265. *See also* People's Republic of China, and Australia; People's Republic of China, and New Zealand
Arab League, 280
Arbatov, Georgi A., 182, 198
"Arc of instability," 145, 146
Argentina. *See* People's Republic of China, and Argentina
ASEAN. *See* Association of Southeast Asian Nations

Asia, 3, 5, 6, 7, 9, 22–23, 28, 69, 90, 91, 125–126, 132, 139–146, 270
nonalignment, 11–12, 14, 25, 46, 143, 146, 246, 252
See also National liberation movements, Asian; People's Republic of China, and Third World; Soviet Union, collective security system; *individual countries*
Asian countries conference (1955), 25
Asian-Pacific region, 90, 91, 103, 105, 110, 120, 128, 165, 167, 192, 219, 220, 226, 242, 264–265. *See also* People's Republic of China, and Asian-Pacific region; *individual countries*
Asian table tennis championships (1974), 214
Assam (India), 258, 260
Association of Southeast Asian Nations (ASEAN) (1967), 6, 45, 75, 83, 117, 122, 126, 140, 142, 147, 150, 154, 170, 199–202, 208, 224, 225, 226, 227, 228, 229, 230, 231, 240
emergency meeting (Bangkok), 247
foreign ministers meeting (1971), 242
and new triangular relationship, 174, 179
1971 meeting, 236
and People's Republic of China, 242–251, 264. *See also* People's Republic of China, *and individual ASEAN countries*
and Soviet Union, 243. *See also* Soviet Union, *and individual ASEAN countries*
See also Bali Declaration; Kuala Lumpur Declaration; *individual countries*